Henry Morley, Ben Jonson

Plays and Poems

Henry Morley, Ben Jonson

Plays and Poems

ISBN/EAN: 9783744714396

Printed in Europe, USA, Canada, Australia, Japan

Cover: Foto ©Thomas Meinert / pixelio.de

More available books at **www.hansebooks.com**

PLAYS AND POEMS

BY

BEN JONSON

WITH AN INTRODUCTION BY HENRY MORLEY
LL.D., PROFESSOR OF ENGLISH LITERATURE AT
UNIVERSITY COLLEGE, LONDON

LONDON
GEORGE ROUTLEDGE AND SONS
BROADWAY, LUDGATE HILL
NEW YORK: 9 LAFAYETTE PLACE
1885

MORLEY'S UNIVERSAL LIBRARY.

VOLUMES ALREADY PUBLISHED.

SHERIDAN'S PLAYS.
PLAYS FROM MOLIÈRE. By English Dramatists.
MARLOWE'S FAUSTUS & GOETHE'S FAUST.
CHRONICLE OF THE CID.
RABELAIS' GARGANTUA and the HEROIC DEEDS OF PANTAGRUEL.
THE PRINCE. By MACHIAVELLI.
BACON'S ESSAYS.
DEFOE'S JOURNAL OF THE PLAGUE YEAR.
LOCKE ON CIVIL GOVERNMENT & FILMER'S "PATRIARCHA."
SCOTT'S DEMONOLOGY and WITCHCRAFT.
DRYDEN'S VIRGIL.
BUTLER'S ANALOGY OF RELIGION.
HERRICK'S HESPERIDES.
COLERIDGE'S TABLE-TALK.
BOCCACCIO'S DECAMERON.
STERNE'S TRISTRAM SHANDY.
CHAPMAN'S HOMER'S ILIAD.
MEDIÆVAL TALES.
VOLTAIRE'S CANDIDE & JOHNSON'S RASSELAS.
PLAYS and POEMS by BEN JONSON.

INTRODUCTION.

BEN JONSON'S "Alchemist" has been paired with Fielding's "Tom Jones" as one of the best examples of a well-constructed plot; and Coleridge, who justly gave Ben Jonson the place next to Shakespeare in dramatic literature, was inclined to think "The Fox" the greatest of his works. These plays, and "The Silent Woman," which stood in the first rank among Ben Jonson's plays, are here joined to some of the best of his minor poems.

Ben Jonson was the son of a gentleman who ruined himself by zeal for religion, and died a month before his son was born. The poet's mother came south, was poor, took a master bricklayer for her second husband, lived in Hartshorn Lane, near Charing Cross, and sent her boy to the parish school of St. Martin's. Through William Camden, the historian, who was then one of its masters, Ben Jonson obtained an admission to Westminster school. There he laid the foundations of the learning which became afterwards closely associated with the free and individual expression of his genius. His gratitude to William Camden was expressed in a poem, which will be found on page 314 of this volume. Ben Jonson, like Shakespeare, had not the benefit of university education, but by his own study he made himself one of the most scholarly of English poets. In his youth he followed for a little while the trade of his stepfather, then went to fight in the Low Countries, and then followed the bent of his genius by joining the players.

In 1596 Ben Jonson's first comedy, "Every Man in his Humour," was produced, with Italian characters. He had recast it, and changed the scene from Florence to London, when it was acted, in 1598, by the company to which Shakespeare belonged. This was a true comedy, with carefully constructed plot, and the action within limit of a single day. The three

plays that followed in the successive years 1599, 1600, 1601—
"Every Man out of his Humour," "Cynthia's Revels," and
"The Poetaster"—were exuberant in wit, and satirized the
affectations of the day in the city, at Court, and among writers
who used their skill upon low themes, and ran a broken pace for
common hire when they should seek rather

>   the high raptures of a happy muse
> Borne on the wings of her immortal thought.

He would have all solemn triflers understand

>   How far beneath the dignity of man
>   Their serious and most practised actions are,

and laboured to advance the time when

>   these vain joys, in which their wills consume
>   Such powers of wit and soul as are of force
>   To raise their beings to eternity,
>   May be converted on work, fitting men:
>   And, for the practice of a forcéd look,
>   An antic gesture, or a fustian phrase,
>   Study the native frame of a true heart,
>   An inward comeliness of bounty, knowledge,
>   And spirit that may conform them actually
>   To God's high figures, which they have in power.

Out of this sense of life Ben Jonson speaks with all his joviality. At his merriest he spurns low thought, and in his cups he seeks true poets and true scholars for his comrades. This worthiness of aim made him in after years of age and infirmity the Master around whom the best poets of the younger generation gathered with trust and affection, each happy if their chief once called him Son, and by so doing sealed him of the tribe of Ben.

Misunderstood in these his younger days by fellow-poets, who saw personality where the whole aim was to lift the public sense of what true literature means, Ben Jonson found himself put on the stage in a piece called "Satiromastix" by his friends Dekker and Marston. They paid him back in what they took to be his own coin, and set one of his own characters, Captain Tucca, to bully him; but in the characters through which they themselves spoke they clearly expressed their own friendship and admiration for him, which asked only that he should put away what they regarded as his fault. Says one of them:

> Where one true
> And wholly virtuous spirit for thy best part
> Loves thee, I wish one ten with all my heart.
> I make account, I put up as deep share
> In every good man's love which thy worth earns
> As thou thyself. We envy not to see
> Thy friends with bays to crown thy poesie.
> No, here the gall lies, we that know what stuff
> Thy very heart is made of, know the stalk
> On which thy learning grows, and can give life
> To thy, once dying, baseness, yet must we
> Dance antics on your paper.

"Faustus!" he interrupts; and his friend adds,

> "This makes us angry, but not envious.
> No, were thy warpt soul put in a new mould,
> I'd wear thee as a jewel set in gold.

This was but a wrestle among friends. Marston almost immediately afterwards was dedicating to Ben Jonson his best play, and in another play they were joint writers with the scholarly George Chapman. True men can differ vigorously and be friends.

Ben Jonson turned for a while from his misapprehended comedies, or, rather, from his dramatic satires; for the three pieces that followed "Every Man in his Humour" were rich in detail, but, as plays, weak in construction. He produced a tragedy, "Sejanus," in 1603, and then, in the first years of the reign of James I., gathered his strength and produced the three comedies given in this volume: "Volpone" in 1605, "The Silent Woman" in 1609, and "The Alchemist" in 1610. His other tragedy, "Catiline," followed in 1611. The ingenuity of sudden and frequent turns in the plot of "The Alchemist" is hardly less marked in "The Fox," and the three comedies contain a little crowd of distinct characters, with vigour of wit and worthy thought in every line that helps to give them being. Is there a book in the world that breathes nobler scorn of the worship of Mammon than Ben Jonson's play of "Volpone"? It opens with Volpone prostrate in soul before the idol figured in a heap of gold and silver plate, and then shows how, in low minds, all ties of love and honour snap when they restrain the grasp at gold. Corbaccio, tottering upon the verge of his own grave, casts off a worthy son, and the most jealous husband is ready to give his wife to shame, for lust of gold.

A spirit like this was in the club at the Mermaid—founded, it is said, by Sir Walter Raleigh—in which Shakespeare and Beaumont and Fletcher were among Ben Jonson's companions. Beaumont, in lines to Ben Jonson, recalled

> what things we have seen
> Done at the Mermaid ! Heard words that have been
> So nimble and so full of subtle flame,
> As if that every one from whom they came
> Had meant to put his whole wit in a jest,
> And had resolved to live a fool the rest
> Of his dull life.

Ben Jonson worked on under James I., but became weary of the audiences who sought plays of animal love, and so helped to quicken the departure of the earnest men whose presence had given strength to the best efforts of the players. The theatre declined in worth. Ben Jonson left it, and wrote Masques for the Court, but fell out with Inigo Jones, who provided the machinery for his Masques, lost favour at Court, and had a stroke of palsy added to his troubles just before Charles I. became King. Compelled to write again for the playgoers whom he openly despised, he gave them an opportunity for retort after their own kind, and wrote the indignant ode, "Come, Leave the Loathed Stage," which will be found at page 313 of this volume. The grace of his last years is in the fragment of "The Sad Shepherd." He died in August 1637. The University of Oxford had, in 1619, paid honour to his learning by conferring on him the degree of Master of Arts. Like Milton, Ben Jonson had a mind so highly cultivated that turns of thought or expression give evidence of his scholarship in every page he writes. Horace especially, Martial, Juvenal, Terence, Plautus, Lucian, Apollonius peep out from many a line of sound English. Even St. Chrysostom's Ω κακὸν κακῶν κάκιστον underlies the comic exclamation in the close of "The Silent Woman:" "This is worst of all worst worsts !" The spark of scholarship so flashed into the native humour of the poet is anything but pedantry. It is a finer light in light, wit within wit. But it did, in his own time, greatly exercise the minds of feeble critics, who, if they ventured to strike at a phrase of Ben Jonson's, trembled as they did so, lest perchance they might hit Horace unawares.

H. M.

December 1884.

The Alchemist.

TO THE READER.

If thou beest more, thou art an understander, and then I trust thee. If thou art one that takest up, and but a pretender, beware of what hands thou receivest thy commodity; for thou wert never more fair in the way to be cozened than in this age, in poetry, especially in plays: wherein now the concupiscence of dances and of antics so reigneth, as to run away from Nature and be afraid of her is the only point of Art that tickles the spectators. But how out of purpose and place do I name Art? When the professors are grown so obstinate contemners of it, and presumers on their own naturals, as they are deriders of all diligence that way, and, by simple mocking at the terms, when they understand not the things, think to get off wittily with their ignorance. Nay, they are esteemed the more learned and sufficient for this, by the many, through their excellent vice of judgment. For they commend writers as they do fencers and wrestlers; who, if they come in robustuously, and put for it with a great deal of violence, are received for the braver fellows: when many times their own rudeness is the cause of their disgrace, and a little touch of their adversary gives all that boisterous force the foil. I deny not but that these men, who always seek to do more than enough, may sometime happen on something that is good and great; but very seldom: and when it comes it doth not recompense the rest of their ill. It sticks out, perhaps, and is more eminent, because all is sordid and vile about it; as lights are more discerned in a thick darkness than a faint shadow. I speak not this out of a hope to do good to any man against his will; for I know, if it were put to the question of theirs and mine, the worse would find more suffrages: because the most favour common errors. But I give thee this warning, that there is a great difference between those that, to gain the opinion of copy, utter all they can, however unfitly; and those that use election and a mean. For it is only the disease of the unskilful to think rude things greater than polished, or scattered more numerous than composed.

THE PERSONS OF THE PLAY.

SUBTLE, *the Alchemist.*
FACE, *the Housekeeper.*
DOL COMMON, *their Colleague.*
DAPPER, *a Clerk.*
DRUGGER, *a Tobacco Man.*
LOVEWIT, *Master of the House.*
EPICURE MAMMON, *a Knight.*
PERTINAX SURLY, *a Gamester.*

TRIBULATION WHOLESOME, *a Pastor of Amsterdam.*
ANANIAS, *a Deacon there.*
KASTRIL, *the angry Boy.*
DAME PLIANT, *his Sister, a Widow.*
Neighbours, Officers, Mutes.

SCENE—LONDON.

ARGUMENT.

T HE sickness hot, a master quit, for fear,
H is house in town, and left one servant there.
E ase him corrupted, and gave means to know

A cheater and his punk; who now brought low,
L eaving their narrow practice, were become
C ozeners at large; and only wanting some
H ouse to set up, with him they here contract,
E ach for a share, and all begin to act.
M uch company they draw, and much abuse,
I n casting figures, telling fortunes, news,
S elling of flies, false putting of the stone,
T ill it, and they, and all in fume are gone.

PROLOGUE.

FORTUNE, that favours fools, these two short hours
  We wish away, both for your sakes and ours,
Judging Spectators; and desire, in place,
  To the author justice, to ourselves but grace.
Our scene is London, 'cause we would make known
  No country's mirth is better than our own:
No clime breeds better matter, for your bore,
  Shark, squire, impostor, many persons more,
Whose manners, now called humours, feed the stage;
  And which have still been subject for the rage
Or spleen of comic writers. Though this pen
  Did never aim to grieve, but better, men;
Howe'er the age he lives in doth endure
  The vices that she breeds, above their cure.
But when the wholesome remedies are sweet,
  And in their working gain and profit meet,
He hopes to find no spirit so much diseased
  But will with such fair correctives be pleased:
For here he doth not fear who can apply.
  If there be any that will sit so nigh
Unto the stream, to look what it doth run,
  They shall find things they'd think or wish were done;
They are so natural follies, but so shown
  As even the doers may see, and yet not own.

ACT I.

SCENE. I.—*A Room in* LOVEWIT'S *House.*

Enter FACE, *in a captain's uniform, with his sword drawn, and* SUBTLE *with a vial, quarrelling, and followed by* DOL COMMON.

  Face. Believe 't, I will.
  Sub. Thy worst. I spit at thee.
  Dol. Have you your wits? Why, gentlemen, for love——

Face. Sirrah, I'll strip you——
Sub. What to do?   Lick figs
Out at my——
Face. Rogue, rogue!—out of all your sleights.
Dol. Nay, look ye, sovereign, general, are you madmen?
Sub. Oh, let the wild sheep loose.   I'll gum your silks
With good strong water, an you come.
Dol. Will you have
The neighbours hear you? will you betray all?
Hark! I hear somebody.
Face. Sirrah——
Sub. I shall mar
All that the tailor has made, if you approach.
Face. You most notorious whelp, you insolent slave,
Dare you do this?
Sub. Yes, faith; yes, faith.
Fac. Why, who
Am I, my mongrel?   Who am I?
Sub. I'll tell you,
Since you know not yourself.
Face. Speak lower, rogue.
Sub. Yes, you were once (time's not long past) the good,
Honest, plain, livery three pound thrum that kept
Your master's worship's house here in the Friars,
For the vacations——
Face. Will you be so loud?
Sub. Since, by my means, translated suburb-captain.
Face. By your means, doctor dog!
Sub. Within man's memory,
All this I speak of.
Face. Why, I pray you, have I
Been countenanced by you, or you by me?
Do but collect, sir, where I met you first.
Sub. I do not hear well.
Face. Not of this, I think it.
But I shall put you in mind, sir;—at Pie-corner,
Taking your meal of steam in from cooks' stalls,
Where, like the father of hunger, you did walk
Piteously costive, with your pinch'd horn-nose,
And your complexion of the Roman wash,
Stuck full of black and melancholic worms,
Like powder corns shot at the artillery yard.
Sub. I wish you could advance your voice a little.
Face. When you went pinn'd up in the several rags
You had raked and pick'd from dunghills, before day;
Your feet in mouldy slippers, for your kibes;
A felt of rug, and a thin threaden cloak,
That scarce would cover your no buttocks——

Sub. So, sir!
Face. When all your alchemy and your algebra,
Your minerals, vegetals, and animals,
Your conjuring, cozening, and your dozen of trades,
Could not relieve your corps with so much linen
Would make you tinder, but to see a fire,
I gave you countenance, credit for your coals,
Your stills, your glasses, your materials;
Built you a furnace, drew you customers,
Advanced all your black arts; lent you, beside,
A house to practise in——
   Sub. Your master's house!
   Face. Where you have studied the more thriving skill
Of cozening since.
   Sub. Yes, in your master's house.
You and the rats here kept possession.
Make it not strange. I know you were one could keep
The buttery-hatch still lock'd, and save the chippings,
Sell the dole beer to aquavitæ men,
The which, together with your Christmas vails
At post-and-pair, your letting out of counters,
Made you a pretty stock, some twenty marks,
And gave you credit to converse with cobwebs,
Here, since your mistress' death 'hath broke up house.
   Face. You might talk softlier, rascal.
   Sub. No, you scarab,
I'll thuuder you in pieces: I will teach you
How to beware to tempt a Fury again,
That carries tempest in his hand and voice.
   Face. The place has made you valiant.
   Sub. No, your clothes.—
Thou vermin, have I ta'en thee out of dung,
So poor, so wretched, when no living thing
Would keep thee company, but a spider, or worse?
Rais'd thee from brooms, and dust, and watering-pots,
Sublimed thee, and exalted thee, and fix'd thee
In the third region, call'd our state of grace?
Wrought thee to spirit, to quintessence, with pains
Would twice have won me the Philosopher's work!
Put thee in words and fashion, made thee fit
For more than ordinary fellowships?
Giv'n thee thy oaths, thy quarrelling dimensions,
Thy rules to cheat at horse-race, cockpit, cards, dice,
Or whatever gallant tincture else?
Made thee a second in mine own great art?
And have I this for thanks! Do you rebel,
Do you fly out in the projection?
Would you be gone now?

Dol. Gentlemen, what mean you?
Will you mar all?
   Sub. Slave, thou hadst had no name——
   Dol. Will you undo yourselves with civil war?
   Sub. Never been known, past *equi clibanum*,
The heat of horse-dung, under ground, in cellars,
Or an ale-house darker than deaf John's; been lost
To all mankind but laundresses and tapsters,
Had not I been.
   Dol. Do you know who hears you, sovereign?
   Face. Sirrah——
   Dol. Nay, general, I thought you were civil.
   Face. I shall turn desperate if you grow thus loud.
   Sub. And hang thyself, I care not.
   Face. Hang thee, collier,
And all thy pots and pans, in picture, I will,
Since thou hast moved me——
   Dol. Oh, this will o'erthrow all.
   Face. Write thee up bawd in Paul's, have all thy tricks
Of cozening with a hollow coal, dust, scrapings,
Searching for things lost, with a sieve and shears,
Erecting figures in your rows of houses,
And taking in of shadows with a glass,
Told in red letters; and a face cut for thee
Worse than Gamaliel Ratsey's.
   Dol. Are you sound?
Have you your senses, masters?
   Face. I will have
A book, but barely reckoning thy impostures,
Shall prove a true philosopher's stone to printers.
   Sub. Away, you trencher-rascal!
   Face. Out, you log-leech!
The vomit of all prisons——
   Dol. Will you be
Your own destructions, gentlemen?
   Face. Still spewed out
For lying too heavy on the basket.
   Sub. Cheater!
   Face. Bawd!
   Sub. Cowherd!
   Face. Conjurer!
   Sub. Cut-purse!
   Face. Witch!
   Dol. O me!
We are ruin'd, lost! Have you no more regard
To your reputations? Where's your judgment? 'Slight
Have yet some care of me, of your republic——
   Face. Away this brach! I'll bring thee, rogue, within

The statute of sorcery, tricesimo tertio
Of Harry the Eighth : ay, and perhaps thy neck
Within a noose, for laundring gold and barbing it.
    Dol. [*Snatches* FACE'S *sword.*] You'll bring your head within
        a cockscomb, will you ?
And you, sir, with your menstrue. [*Dashes* SUBTLE'S *vial out
      of his hand.*] Gather it up.—
'Sdeath, you abominable pair of stinkards,
Leave off your barking, and grow one again,
Or, by the light that shines, I'll cut your throats.
I'll not be made a prey unto the marshal
For ne'er a snarling dog-bolt of you both.
Have you together cozen'd all this while,
And all the world, and shall it now be said
You've made most courteous shift to cozen yourselves ?
You will accuse him ! you will *bring him in*   [*To* FACE.
Within the statute ? Who shall take your word ?
A rascal, upstart, apocryphal captain,
Whom not a Puritan in Blackfriars will trust
So much as for a feather : and you, too,   [*To* SUBTLE.
Will give the cause, forsooth ! you will insult,
And claim a primacy in the divisions !
You must be chief ! as if you only had
The powder to project with, and the work
Were not begun out of equality ?
The venture tripartite ? all things in common ?
Without priority ? 'Sdeath ! you perpetual curs,
Fall to your couples again, and cozen kindly,
And heartily, and lovingly, as you should,
And lose not the beginning of a term,
Or, by this hand, I shall grow factious too,
And take my part, and quit you.
    Face. 'Tis his fault ;
He ever murmurs, and objects his pains,
And says, the weight of all lies upon him.
    Sub. Why, so it does.
    Dol. How does it ? Do not we
Sustain our parts ?
    Sub. Yes, but they are not equal.
    Dol. Why, if your part exceed to-day, I hope
Ours may to-morrow match it.
    Sub. Ay, they *may.*
    Dol. May, murmuring mastiff ! Ay, and do. Death on me !
Help me to throttle him.   [*Seizes* SUB. *by the throat.*
    Sub. Dorothy ! Mistress Dorothy !
'Ods precious, I'll do anything. What do you mean ?
    Dol. Because o' your fermentation and cibation ?
    Sub. Not I, by heaven——

Dol. Your Sol and Luna—— Help me. [*To* FACE.
Sub. Would I were hang'd then! I'll conform myself.
Dol. Will you, sir? Do so then, and quickly: swear.
Sub. What should I swear?
Dol. To leave your faction, sir,
And labour kindly in the common work.
Sub. Let me not breathe if I meant aught beside.
I only used those speeches as a spur
To him.
Dol. I hope we need no spurs, sir. Do we?
Face. 'Slid, prove to-day who shall shark best.
Sub. Agreed.
Dol. Yes, and work close and friendly.
Sub. 'Slight, the knot
Shall grow the stronger for this breach, with me.
[*They shake hands.*
Dol. Why, so, my good baboons! Shall we go make
A sort of sober, scurvy, precise neighbours,
That scarce have smiled twice since the king came in,
A feast of laughter at our follies? Rascals
Would run themselves from breath to see me ride,
Or you t' have but a hole to thrust your heads in,
For which you should pay ear-rent? No, agree.
And may don Provost ride a feasting long
In his old velvet jerkin and stain'd scarfs,
My noble sovereign and worthy general,
Ere we contribute a new crewel garter
To his most worsted worship.
Sub. Royal Dol!
Spoken like Claridiana, and thyself.
Face. For which at supper thou shalt sit in triumph,
And not be styled Dol Common, but Dol Proper,
Dol Singular: the longest cut at night
Shall draw thee for his Doll Particular. [*Bell rings without.*
Sub. Who's that? One rings. To the window, Dol. [*Exit* DOL.] Pray heaven
The master do not trouble us this quarter.
Face. Oh, fear not him. While there dies one a week
O' the plague, he's safe from thinking toward London:
Beside, he's busy at his hop-yards now;
I had a letter from him. If he do,
He'll send such word for airing of the house
As you shall have sufficient time to quit it:
Though we break up a fortnight, 'tis no matter.

Re-enter DOL.

Sub. Who is it Dol?
Dol. A fine young quodling.

    Face. Oh,
My lawyer's clerk I lighted on last night
In Holborn, at the Dagger. He would have
(I told you of him) a familiar,
To rifle with at horses, and win cups.
    Dol. Oh, let him in.
    Sub. Stay. Who shall do't?
    Face. Get you
Your robes on : I will meet him as going out.
    Dol. And what shall I do?
    Face. Not be seen ; away!   [*Exit* DOL.
Seem you very reserv'd.
    Sub. Enough.   [*Exit.*
    Face. [*Aloud and retiring.*] God be wi' you, sir,
I pray you, let him know that I was here :
His name is Dapper. I would gladly have staid, but——
    Dap. [*Within.*] Captain, I am here.
    Face. Who's that?—He's come, I think, doctor.

                    Enter DAPPER.

Good faith, sir, I was going away.
    Dap. In truth,
I am very sorry, captain.
    Face. But I thought
Sure I should meet you.
    Dap. Ay, I am very glad.
I had a scurvy writ or two to make,
And I had lent my watch last night to one
That dines to-day at the sheriff's, and so was robb'd
Of my pastime.

      Re-enter SUBTLE, *in his velvet cap and gown.*

Is this the cunnning-man?
    Face. This is his worship.
    Dap. Is he a doctor?
    Face. Yes.
    Dap. And you have broke with him, captain?
    Face. Ay.
    Dap. And how?
    Face. Faith, he does make the matter, sir, so dainty
I know not what to say.
    Dap. Not so, good captain.
    Face. Would I were fairly rid of it, believe me.
    Dap. Nay, now you grieve me, sir. Why should you wish so?
I dare assure you, I'll not be ungrateful.
    Face. I cannot think you will, sir. But the law
Is such a thing—and then he says, Read's matter
Falling so lately—

Dap. Read! he was an ass,
And dealt, sir, with a fool.
  Face. It was a clerk, sir.
  Dap. A clerk!
  Face. Nay, hear me, sir, you know the law
Better, I think——
  Dap. I should, sir, and the danger:
You know, I showed the statute to you.
  Face. You did so.
  Dap. And will I tell then! By this hand of flesh,
Would it might never write good court-hand more,
If I discover. What do you think of me,
That I am a Chiause?
  Face. What's that?
  Dap. The Turk was here.
As one would say, do you think I am a Turk?
  Face. I'll tell the doctor so.
  Dap. Do, good sweet captain.
  Face. Come, noble doctor, pray thee, let's prevail;
This is the gentleman, and he is no chiause.
  Sub. Captain, I have return'd you all my answer.
I would do much, sir, for your love; but this
I neither may nor can.
  Face. Tut, do not say so.
You deal now with a noble fellow, doctor,
One that will thank you richly, and he is no chiause.
Let that, sir, move you.
  Sub. Pray you, forbear——
  Face. He has
Four angels here.
  Sub. You do me wrong, good sir.
  Face. Doctor, wherein? to tempt you with these spirits?
  Sub. To tempt my art and love, sir, to my peril.
'Fore heaven, I scarce can think you are my friend,
That so would draw me to apparent danger.
  Face. I draw you! A horse draw you, and a halter,
You, and your flies together——
  Dap. Nay, good captain.
  Face. That know no difference of men.
  Sub. Good words, sir.
  Face. Good deeds, sir, Doctor Dogs-meat. 'Slight, I bring you
No cheating Clim of the Cloughs, or Claribels,
That look as big as five-and-fifty, and flush;
And spit out secrets like hot custard——
  Dap. Captain!
  Face. Nor any melancholic under-scribe,
Shall tell the vicar, but a special gentle,
That is the heir to forty marks a year,

Consorts with the small poets of the time,
Is the sole hope of his old grandmother;
That knows the law, and writes you six fair hands,
Is a fine clerk, and has his cyphering perfect,
Will take his oath o' the Greek Testament,
If need be, in his pocket; and can court
His mistress out of Ovid.
   Dap. Nay, dear captain——
   Face. Did you not tell me so?
   Dap. Yes; but I'd have you
Use Master Doctor with some more respect.
   Face. Hang him, proud stag, with his broad velvet head!—
But for your sake, I'd choke ere I would change
An article of breath with such a puckfist:
Come, let's be gone.   [*Going.*
   Sub. Pray you, let me speak with you.
   Dap. His worship calls you, captain.
   Face. I am sorry
I e'er embark'd myself in such a business.
   Dap. Nay, good sir; he did call you.
   Face. Will he take then?
   Sub. First, hear me——
   Face. Not a syllable, 'less you take.
   Sub. Pray you, sir——
   Face. Upon no terms, but an *assumpsit*.
   Sub. Your humour must be law.   [*He takes the four angels.*
   Face. Why, now, sir, talk.
Now I dare hear you with mine honour. Speak.
So may this gentleman too.
   Sub. Why, sir——   [*Offering to whisper* FACE.
   Face. No whispering.
   Sub. 'Fore heaven, you do not apprehend the loss
You do yourself in this.
   Face. Wherein? for what?
   Sub. Marry, to be so importunate for one
That, when he has it, will undo you all;
He'll win up all the money in the town.
   Face. How!
   Sub. Yes, and blow up gamester after gamester,
As they do crackers in a puppet play.
If I do give him a familiar,
Give you him all you play for; never set him:
For he will have it.
   Face. You are mistaken, doctor.
Why he does ask one but for cups and horses
A rifling fly; none of your great familiars.
   Dap. Yes, captain, I would have it for all games.
   Sub. I told you so.

Face. [*Taking* DAP. *aside.*] 'Slight, that is a new business!
I understood you, a tame bird, to fly
Twice in a term, or so, on Friday nights,
When you had left the office, for a nag
Of forty or fifty shillings.
   Dap. Ay, 'tis true, sir;
But I do think now I shall leave the law,
And therefore——
   Face. Why, this changes quite the case.
Do you think that I dare move him?
   Dap. If you please, sir;
All's one to him, I see.
   Face. What! for that money?
I cannot with my conscience; nor should you
Make the request, methinks.
   Dap. No, sir; I mean
To add consideration.
   Face. Why, then, sir,
I'll try. [*Goes to* SUBTLE.] Say that it were for all games, doctor?
   Sub. I say then, not a mouth shall eat for him
At any ordinary, but on the score,
That is a gaming mouth, conceive me.
   Face. Indeed!
   Sub. He'll draw you all the treasure of the realm,
If it be set him.
   Face. Speak you this from art?
   Sub. Ay, sir, and reason too, the ground of art.
He is of the only best complexion
The Queen of Fairy loves.
   Face. What! Is he?
   Sub. Peace.
He'll overhear you. Sir, should she but see him——
   Face. What?
   Sub. Do not you tell him.
   Face. Will he win at cards too?
   Sub. The spirits of dead Holland, living Isaac,
You'd swear were in him; such a vigorous luck
As cannot be resisted. 'Slight, he'll put
Six of your gallants to a cloke, indeed.
   Face. A strange success, that some man shall be born
   Sub. He hears you, man——
   Dap. Sir, I'll not be ungrateful.
   Face. Faith, I have confidence in his good nature:
You hear, he says he will not be ungrateful.
   Sub. Why, as you please; my venture follows yours.
   Face. Troth, do it, doctor; think him trusty, and make him.
He may make us both happy in an hour;
Win some five thousand pounds, and send us two on't.

Dap. Believe it, and I will, sir.
Face. And you shall, sir. [*Takes him aside.*
You have heard all?
Dap. No, what was't? Nothing, I, sir.
Face. Nothing!
Dap. A little, sir.
Face. Well, a rare star
Reigned at your birth.
Dap. At mine, sir! No.
Face. The doctor
Swears that you are——
Sub. Nay, captain, you'll tell all now.
Face. Allied to the Queen of Fairy.
Dap. Who? that I am?
Believe it no such matter——
Face. Yes, and that
You were born with a caul on your head.
Dap. Who says so?
Face. Come,
You know it well enough, though you dissemble it.
Dap. I' fac, I do not: you are mistaken.
Face. How!
Swear by your fac? And in a thing so known
Unto the doctor? How shall we, sir, trust you
In the other matter? can we ever think,
When you have won five or six thousand pounds,
You'll send us shares in 't, by this rate?
Dap. By Jove, sir,
I'll win ten thousand pounds, and send you half.
I' fac 's no oath.
Sub. No, no; he did but jest.
Face. Go to. Go thank the doctor: he's your friend,
To take it so.
Dap. I thank his worship.
Face. So!
Another angel.
Dap. Must I?
Face. Must you! 'Slight,
What else is thanks? Will you be trivial?—Doctor,
[DAPPER *gives him the money.*
When must he come for his familiar?
Dap. Shall I not have it with me?
Sub. Oh, good sir!
There must a world of ceremonies pass;
You must be bath'd and fumigated first:
Besides, the Queen of Fairy does not rise
Till it be noon.
Face. Not, if she danced, to-night.

SCENE I.]   *THE ALCHEMIST.*   21

   Sub. And she must bless it.
   Face. Did you never see
Her royal grace yet?
   Dap. Whom?
   Face. Your aunt of Fairy?
   Sub. Not since she kissed him in the cradle, captain;
I can resolve you that.
   Face. Well, see her grace,
Whate'er it cost you, for a thing that I know.
It will be somewhat hard to compass; but
However, see her. You are made, believe it,
If you can see her. Her grace is a lone woman,
And very rich; and if she take a fancy,
She will do strange things. See her at any hand.
'Slid, she may hap to leave you all she has:
It is the doctor's fear.
   Dap. How will 't be done, then?
   Face. Let me alone, take you no thought. Do you
But say to me, Captain, I'll see her grace.
   Dap. Captain, I'll see her grace.
   Face. Enough.   [*Knocking within.*
   Sub. Who's there?
Anon.—Conduct him forth by the back way.   [*Aside to* FACE.
Sir, against one o'clock prepare yourself,
Till when you must be fasting; only take
Three drops of vinegar in at your nose,
Two at your mouth, and one at either ear;
Then bathe your fingers' end and wash your eyes,
To sharpen your five senses, and cry *hum*
Thrice, and then *buz* as often; and then come.   [*Exit.*
   Face. Can you remember this?
   Dap. I warrant you.
   Face. Well then, away. It is but your bestowing
Some twenty nobles 'mong her grace's servants,
And put on a clean shirt: you do not know
What grace her grace may do you in clean linen.
                         [*Exeunt* FACE *and* DAPPER.
   Sub. [*Within.*] Come in! Good wives, I pray you forbear me now;
Troth I can do you no good till afternoon.

          Re-enters, followed by DRUGGER.

What is your name, say you—Abel Drugger?
   Drug. Yes, sir.
   Sub. A seller of tobacco?
   Drug. Yes, sir.
   Sub. Umph!
Free of the grocers?

Drug. Ay, an 't please you.
Sub. Well ——
Your business, Abel?
  Drug. This, an 't please your worship;
I am a young beginner, and am building
Of a new shop, an 't like your worship, just
At corner of a street :—Here is the plot on 't—
And I would know by art, sir, of your worship,
Which way I should make my door, by necromancy,
And where my shelves : and which should be for boxes,
And which for pots. I would be glad to thrive, sir :
And I was wish'd to your worship by a gentleman,
One Captain Face, that says you know men's planets,
And their good angels, and their bad.
  Sub. I do,
If I do see them——

            Re-enter FACE.

  Face. What ! my honest Abel?
Thou art well met here.
  Drug. Troth, sir, I was speaking,
Just as your worship came here, of your worship :
I pray you, speak for me to Master Doctor.
  Face. He shall do anything.—Doctor, do you hear?
This is my friend, Abel, an honest fellow ;
He lets me have good tobacco, and he does not
Sophisticate it with sack-lees or oil,
Nor washes it in muscadel and grains,
Nor buries it in gravel underground,
Wrapp'd up in greasy leather or sour clouts ;
But keeps it in fine lily pots, that, open'd,
Smell like conserve of roses or French beans.
He has his maple block, his silver tongs,
Winchester pipes, and fire of Juniper :
A neat, spruce, honest fellow, and no goldsmith.
  Sub. He is a fortunate fellow, that I am sure on.
  Face. Already, sir, have you found it? Lo thee, Abel !
  Sub. And in right way toward riches——
  Face. Sir !
  Sub. This summer
He will be of the clothing of his company,
And next spring call'd to the scarlet ; spend what he can.
  Face. What, and so little beard?
  Sub. Sir, you must think
He may have a receipt to make hair come :
But he'll be wise, preserve his youth, and fine for 't ;
His fortune looks for him another way.
  Face. 'Slid, doctor, how canst thou know this so soon?
I am amused at that !

Sub. By a rule, captain,
In metoposcopy, which I do work by;
A certain star in the forehead, which you see not.
Your chestnut or your olive-colour'd face
Does never fail: and your long ear doth promise.
I knew 't by certain spots, too, in his teeth,
And on the nail of his mercurial finger.
  Face. Which finger's that?
  Sub. His little finger. Look.
You were born upon a Wednesday?
  Drug. Yes, indeed, sir.
  Sub. The thumb, in chiromancy, we give Venus;
The fore-finger to Jove; the midst to Saturn;
The ring to Sol; the least to Mercury,
Who was the lord, sir, of his horoscope,
His house of life being Libra; which fore-showed
He should be a merchant, and should trade with balance.
  Face. Why, this is strange! Is it not, honest Nab?
  Sub. There is a ship now coming from Ormus
That shall yield him such a commodity
Of drugs. This is the west, and this the south?
            [*Pointing to the plan.*
  Drug. Yes, sir.
  Sub. And those are your two sides?
  Drug. Ay, sir.
  Sub. Make me your door, then, south; your broadside, west:
And on the east side of your shop, aloft,
Write Mathlai, Tarmiel, and Baraborat;
Upon the north part, Rael, Velel, Thiel.
They are the names of those mercurial spirits
That do fright flies from boxes.
  Drug. Yes, sir.
  Sub. And
Beneath your threshold bury me a loadstone
To draw in gallants that wear spurs: the rest
They'll seem to follow.
  Face. That's a secret, Nab!
  Sub. And on your stall, a puppet, with a vice
And a court-fucus to call city-dames:
You shall deal much with minerals.
  Drug. Sir, I have
At home, already——
  Sub. Ay, I know you have arsenic,
Vitriol, sal-tartar, argaile, alkali,
Cinoper: I know all.—This fellow, captain,
Will come, in time, to be a great distiller,
And give assay—I will not say directly,
But very fair—at the philosopher's stone.

Face. Why, how now, Abel! is this true?
Drug. Good captain,
What must I give? [*Aside to* FACE.
Face. Nay, I'll not counsel thee.
Thou hear'st what wealth—(he says, spend what thou canst)—
Thou'rt like to come to.
Drug. I would gi' him a crown.
Face. A crown! and toward such a fortune? Heart,
Thou shalt rather gi' him thy shop. No gold about thee?
Drug. Yes, I have a portague I have kept this half-year.
Face. Out on thee, Nab! 'Slight, there was such an offer—
Shalt keep't no longer, I'll give't him for thee. Doctor,
Nab prays your worship to drink this, and swears
He will appear more grateful as your skill
Does raise him in the world.
Drug. I would entreat
Another favour of his worship.
Face. What is't, Nab?
Drug. But to look over, sir, my almanac,
And cross out my ill days, that I may neither
Bargain nor trust upon them.
Face. That he shall, Nab;
Leave it, it shall be done 'gainst afternoon.
Sub. And a direction for his shelves.
Face. Now, Nab,
Art thou well pleased, Nab?
Drug. Thank, sir, both your worships.
Face. Away.— [*Exit* DRUGGER.
Why, now, you smoky persecutor of nature!
Now do you see that something's to be done
Beside your beech-coal and your corsive waters,
Your crosslets, crucibles, and cucurbites?
You must have stuff brought home to you, to work on:
And yet you think I am at no expense
In searching out these veins, then following them,
Then trying them out. 'Fore God, my intelligence
Costs me more money than my share oft comes to,
In these rare works.
Sub. You are pleasant, sir.

Re-enter DOL.

How now!
What says my Dainty Dolkin?
Dol. Yonder fishwife
Will not away. And there's your giantess,
Come out of Lambeth.
Sub. Heart, I cannot speak with them.
Dol. Not afore night, I have told them in a voice,

Thorough the trunk, like one of your familiars.
But I have spied Sir Epicure Mammon——
  Sub. Where?
  Dol. Coming along, at far end of the lane,
Slow of his feet, but earnest of his tongue
To one that's with him.
  Sub. Face, go you, and shift.   [*Exit* FACE.
Dol, you must presently make ready too.
  Dol. Why, what's the matter?
  Sub. Oh, I did look for him
With the sun's rising: marvel he could sleep;
This is the day I am to perfect for him
The magisterium, our great work, the stone;
And yield it, made, into his hands; of which
He has this month talk'd as he were possess'd.
And now he's dealing pieces on 't away.—
Methinks I see him entering ordinaries,
Dispensing for the pox and plaguy houses,
Reaching his dose, walking Moorfields for lepers,
And offering citizens' wives pomander bracelets,
As his preservative, made of the elixir;
Searching the spital, to make old bones young;
And the highways for beggars to make rich:
I see no end of his labours. He will make
Nature asham'd of her long sleep: when art,
Who's but a step-dame, shall do more than she,
In her best love to mankind, ever could:
If his dream lasts, he'll turn the age to gold.   [*Exeunt.*

ACT II.

SCENE I.—*An Outer Room in* LOVEWIT'S *House.*

Enter SIR EPICURE MAMMON *and* SURLY.

  Mam. Come on, sir. Now, you set your foot on shore
In *Novo Orbe;* here's the rich Peru:
And there within, sir, are the golden mines,
Great Solomon's Ophir! he was sailing to 't,
Three years, but we have reach'd it in ten months.
This is the day wherein, to all my friends,
I will pronounce the happy word, BE RICH;
THIS DAY YOU SHALL BE SPECTATISSIMI.
You shall no more deal with the hollow dye
Or the frail card. No more be at charge of keeping

The house of call for the young heir.   No more
Shall thirst of satin, or the covetous hunger
Of velvet entrails for a rude-spun cloak,
To be display'd at Madam Augusta's, make
The sons of Sword and Hazard fall before
The golden calf, and on their knees, whole nights,
Commit idolatry with wine and trumpets:
Or go a feasting, after drum and ensign.
No more of this. . You shall start up young viceroys,
And have your punks and punketees, my Surly.
And unto thee. I speak it first, BE RICH.
Where is my Subtle, there?   Within, ho!
    Face. [*Within.*] Sir, he'll come to you by and by.
    Mam. That is his fire-drake,
His Lungs, his Zephyrus, he that puffs his coals,
Till he firk nature up, in her own centre.
You are not faithful, sir.   This night I'll change
All that is metal, in my house, to gold:
And early in the morning will I send
To all the plumbers and the pewterers,
And buy their tin and lead up; and to Lothbury
For all the copper.
    Sur. What, and turn that too?
    Mam. Yes, and I'll purchase Devonshire and Cornwall,
And make them perfect Indies!   You admire now?
    Sur. No, faith.
    Mam. But when you see th' effects of the Great Medicine,
Of which one part projected on a hundred
Of Mercury, or Venus, or the moon,
Shall turn it to as many of the sun;
Nay, to a thousand, so *ad infinitum*:
You will believe me.
    Sur. Yes, when I see 't I will.
But if my eyes do cozen me so, and I
Giving them no occasion, sure I'll have
A crow shall pluck them out next day.
    Mam. Ha! why?
Do you think I fable with you?   I assure you,
He that has once the flower of the sun,
The perfect ruby, which we call elixir,
Not only can do that, but by its virtue
Can confer honour, love, respect, long life;
Give safety, valour, yea, and victory,
To whom he will.   In eight and twenty days,
I'll make an old man of fourscore a child.
    Sur. No doubt; he's that already. *(already a fool)*
    Mam. Nay, I mean,
Restore his years, renew him, like an eagle,

To the fifth age ; make him get sons and daughters,
Young giants ; as our philosophers have done,
The ancient patriarchs, afore the flood,
But taking, once a week, on a knife's point,
The quantity of a grain of mustard of it ;
Become stout Marses, and beget young Cupids.

Sur. The decay'd vestals of Pict-hatch would thank you,
That keep the fire alive there.

Mam. 'Tis the secret
Of nature naturized 'gainst all infections,
Cures all diseases coming of all causes ;
A month's grief in a day, a year's in twelve ;
And of what age soever, in a month :
Past all the doses of your drugging doctors.
I'll undertake, withal, to fright the plague
Out of the kingdom in three months.

Sur. And I'll
Be bound the players shall sing your praises then
Without their poets.

Mam. Sir, I'll do 't. Meantime,
I'll give away so much unto my man
Shall serve the whole city with preservative
Weekly ; each house his dose, and at the rate——

Sur. As he that built the waterwork does with water?

Mam. You are incredulous.

Sur. Faith, I have a humour
I would not willingly be gull'd.   Your stone
Cannot transmute me.

Mam. Pertinax, Surly,
Will you believe antiquity ? records ?
I'll show you a book where Moses and his sister,
And Solomon have written of the art ;
Ay, and a treatise penn'd by Adam——

Sur. How !

Mam. Of the philosopher's stone, and in High Dutch.

Sur. Did Adam write, sir, in High Dutch ?

Mam. He did ;
Which proves it was the primitive tongue.

Sur. What paper?

Mam. On cedar board.

Sur. Oh, that indeed, they say
Will last 'gainst worms.

Mam. 'Tis like your Irish wood
'Gainst cobwebs. I have a piece of Jason's fleece too,
Which was no other than a book of alchemy,
Writ in large sheepskin, a good fat ram-vellum.
Such was Pythagoras' thigh, Pandora's tub,
And all that fable of Medea's charms,

The manner of our work ; the bulls, our furnace,
Still breathing fire ; our argent-vive, the dragon :
The dragon's teeth, mercury sublimate,
That keeps the whiteness, hardness, and the biting ;
And they are gather'd into Jason's helm,
The alembic, and then sow'd in Mars his field,
And thence sublimed so often, till they're fix'd.
Both this, the Hesperian garden, Cadmus' story,
Jove's shower, the boon of Midas, Argus' eyes,
Boccace his Demogorgon, thousands more,
All abstract riddles of our stone.—

Enter FACE *as a Servant.*

　　　　　　　　　　　　　　How now !
Do we succeed ? Is our day come ? and holds it ?
　Face. The evening will set red upon you, sir ;
You have colour for it, crimson : the red ferment
Has done his office ; three hours hence prepare you
To see projection.
　Mam. Pertinax, my Surly,
Again I say to thee aloud, Be rich.
This day thou shalt have ingots ; and to-morrow
Give lords th' affront.—Is it, my Zephyrus, right ?
Blushes the bolt's head?
　Face. Like a wench with child, sir,
That were but now discover'd to her master.
　Mam. Excellent witty Lungs !—my only care is,
Where to get stuff enough now to project on ;
This town will not half serve me.
　Face. No, sir ! Buy
The covering off o' churches.
　Mam. That's true.
　Face. Yes.
Let them stand bare, as do their auditory ;
Or cap them, new, with shingles.
　Mam. No, good thatch :
Thatch will lie light upon the rafters, Lungs.—
Lungs, I will manumit thee from the furnace ;
I will restore thee thy complexion, Puff,
Lost in the embers ; and repair this brain,
Hurt with the fume o' the metals.
　Face. I have blown, sir,
Hard for your worship ; thrown by many a coal,
When 'twas not beech ; weigh'd those I put in, just,
To keep your heat still even ; these bleared eyes
Have waked to read your several colours, sir,
Of the pale citron, the green lion, the crow,
The peacock's tail, the plumed swan.

Mam. And, lastly,
Thou hast descried the flower, the sanguis agni?
　Face. Yes, sir.
　Mam. Where's master?
　Face. At his prayers, sir, he;
Good man, he's doing his devotions
For the success.
　Mam. Lungs, I will set a period
To all thy labours; thou shalt be the master
Of my seraglio.
　Face. Good, sir.
　Mam. But, do you hear?
I'll geld you, Lungs.
　Face. Yes, sir.
　Mam. For I do mean
To have a list of wives and concubines
Equal with Solomon, who had the stone
Alike with me; and I will make me a back
With the elixir, tough as Hercules.
Thou art sure thou saw'st it blood?
　Face. Both blood and spirit, sir.
　Mam. I will have all my beds blown up, not stuft:
Down is too hard: and then, mine oval room
Fill'd with such pictures as Tiberius took
From Elephantis, and dull Aretine
But coldly imitated. Then, my glasses
Cut in more subtle angles, to disperse
And multiply the figures, as I walk
Naked between my succubæ. My mists
I'll have of perfume, vapoured 'bout the room,
To lose ourselves in; and my baths, like pits
To fall into; from whence we will come forth,
And roll us dry in gossamer and roses.—
Is it arrived at ruby?—Where I spy
A wealthy citizen, or rich lawyer,
Have a sublimed pure wife, unto that fellow
I'll send a thousand pounds to make her mine.
　Face. And I shall carry it?
　Mam. No. I'll have no aids,
But fathers and mothers; they will do it best,
Best of all others. And my flatterers
Shall be the pure and gravest of divines
That I can get for money. My mere fools,
Eloquent burgesses; and then my poets,
The same that writ so subtly of foul wind,
Whom I will entertain still for that subject.
The few that would give out themselves to be
Court and town rakes, and everywhere belie

Ladies who are known most innocent for them,
Those will I beg to make me eunuchs of;
And they shall fan me with ten ostrich tails
Apiece, made in a plume to gather wind.
We will be brave, Puff, now we have the med'cine.
My meat shall all come in in Indian shells,
Dishes of agate set in gold, and studded
With emeralds, sapphires, hyacinths and rubies.
The tongues of carps, dormice, and camels' heels,
Boiled in the spirit of Sol and dissolv'd pearl,
Apicius' diet, 'gainst the epilepsy:
And I will eat these broths with spoons of amber,
Headed with diamond and carbuncle.
My foot-boy shall eat pheasants, calvered salmons,
Knots, godwits, lampreys: I myself will have
The beards of barbels served instead of salads;
Oiled mushrooms, and the swelling unctuous paps
Of a fat pregnant sow, newly cut off,
Drest with an exquisite and poignant sauce;
For which I'll say unto my cook, *There's gold:
Go forth, and be a knight.*
    Face. Sir, I'll go look
A little how it heightens.   [*Exit.*
    Mam. Do.—My shirts
I'll have of taffeta-sarsnet, soft and light
As cobwebs; and for all my other raiment,
It shall be such as might provoke the Persian,
Were he to teach the world riot anew.
My gloves of fishes and birds' skins, perfumed
With gums of paradise and eastern air——
    Sur. And do you think to have the stone with this?
    Mam. No, I do think t' have all this with the stone.
    Sur. Why, I have heard he must be *homo frugi*,
A pious, holy, and religious man,
One free from mortal sin, a very virgin.
    Mam. That makes it, sir; he is so: but I buy it;
My venture brings it me. He, honest wretch,
A notable, superstitious, good soul,
Has worn his knees bare and his slippers bald
With prayer and fasting for it: and, sir, let him
Do it alone, for me, still. Here he comes.
Not a profane word afore him: 'tis poison.—

                Enter SUBTLE.

Good-morrow, father.
    Sub. Gentle son, good-morrow,
And to your friend there. What is he, is with you?

    Mam. An heretic, that I did bring along,
In hope, sir, to convert him.
    Sub. Son, I doubt
You are covetous, that thus you meet your time
In the just point: prevent your day at morning.
This argues something worthy of a fear
Of importune and carnal appetite.
Take heed you do not cause the blessing leave you,
With your ungovern'd haste. I should be sorry
To see my labours, not even at perfection,
Got by long watching and large patience, .
Not prosper where my love and zeal hath placed them.
Which (heaven I call to witness, with yourself,
To whom I have poured my thoughts) in all my ends
Have look'd no way but unto public good,
To pious uses, and dear charity,
Now grown a prodigy with men. Wherein
If you, my son, should now prevaricate,
And to your own particular lusts employ
So great and catholic a bliss, be sure
A curse will follow, yea, and overtake
Your subtle and most secret ways.
    Mam. I know, sir;
You shall not need to fear me: I but come
To have you confute this gentleman.
    Sur. Who is,
Indeed, sir, somewhat costive of belief
Toward your stone; would not be gulled.
    Sub. Well, son,
All that I can convince him in is this,
The WORK IS DONE, bright Sol is in his robe.
We have a medicine of the triple soul,
The glorified spirit. Thanks be to heaven,
And make us worthy of it!—𝔘𝔩𝔢𝔫 𝔖𝔭𝔦𝔢𝔤𝔢𝔩!
    Face. [*Within.*] Anon, sir.
    Sub. Look well to the register.
And let your heat still lessen by degrees,
To the aludels.
    Face. [*Within.*] Yes, sir.
    Sub. Did you look
O' the bolt's head yet?
    Face. [*Within.*] Which? On D, sir?
    Sub. Ay;
What's the complexion?
    Face. [*Within.*] Whitish.
    Sub. Infuse vinegar,
To draw his volatile substance and his tincture:
And let the water in glass E be filter'd,

And put into the gripe's egg. Lute him well,
And leave him closed in balneo.
 Face. [*Within.*] I will, sir.
 Sur. What a brave language here is! Next to canting.
 Sub. I have another work, you never saw, son,
That three days since passed the philosopher's wheel
In the lent heat of Athanor and 's become
Sulphur of Nature.
 Mam. But 'tis for me?
 Sub. What need you?
You have enough in that is perfect.
 Mam. Oh, but——
 Sub. Why, this is covetise!
 Mam. No, I assure you,
I shall employ it all in pious uses,
Founding of colleges and grammar schools,
Marrying young virgins, building hospitals,
And now and then a church.

    Re-enter FACE.

 Sub. How now!
 Face. Sir, please you,
Shall I not change the filter?
 Sub. Marry, yes;
And bring me the complexion of glass B. [*Exit* FACE.
 Mam. Have you another?
 Sub. Yes, son; were I assured
Your piety were firm, we would not want
The means to glorify it; but I hope the best.—
I mean to tinct C in sand-heat to-morrow,
And give him imbibition.
 Mam. Of white oil?
 Sub. No, sir, of red. F is come over the helm too,
I thank my maker, in St. Mary's bath,
And shows *lac virginis.* Blessed be heaven!
I sent you of his fæces there calcined:
Out of that calx I have won the salt of mercury.
 Mam. By pouring on your rectified water?
 Sub. Yes, and reveberating in Athanor.

    Re-enter FACE.

How now! what colour says it?
 Face. 'Tis ground black, sir.
 Mam. That's your crow's head?
 Sur. Your cock's comb's, is it not?
 Sub. No, 'tis not perfect. Would it were the crow!
That work wants something.
 Sur. Oh, I looked for this.
The hay's a pitching.

SCENE I.]　　*THE ALCHEMIST.*　　33

　　Sub. Are you sure you loosed them
In their own menstrue?
　　Face. Yes, sir, and then married them,
And put them in a bolt's-head nipp'd to digestion,
According as you bade me when I set
The liquor of Mars to circulation
In the same heat.
　　Sub. The process then was right.
　　Face. Yes, by the token, sir, the retort brake,
And what was saved was put into the pelican,
And signed with Hermes' seal.
　　Sub. I think 'twas so.
We should have a new amalgama.
　　Sur. Oh, this ferret
Is rank as any pole-cat.　　　　　　　　　　　　[*Aside.*
　　Sub. But I care not:
Let him e'en die; we have enough beside,
In embrion. H has his white shirt on.
　　Face. Yes, sir,
He's ripe for inceration, he stands warm
In his ash fire. I would not you should let
Any die now, if I might counsel, sir,
For luck's sake to the rest: it is not good.
　　Mam. He says right.
　　Sur. Ay, are you bolted?　　　　　　　　　　[*Aside.*
　　Face. Nay, I know 't, sir,
I have seen the ill fortune. What is some three ounces
Of fresh materials?
　　Mam. Is 't no more?
　　Face. No more, sir,
Of gold, t' amalgame with some six of mercury.
　　Mam. Away, here's money. What will serve?
　　Face. Ask him, sir.
　　Mam. How much?
　　Sub. Give him nine pounds—you may give him ten.
　　Sur. Yes, twenty, and be cozen'd—do.
　　Mam. There 'tis..　　　　[*Gives* FACE *the money.*
　　Sub. This needs not; but that you will have it so,
To see conclusions of all; for two
Of our inferior works are at fixation,
A third is in ascension. Go your ways.
Have you set the oil of luna in kemia?
　　Face. Yes, sir.
　　Sub. And the philosopher's vinegar?
　　Face. Ay.　　　　　　　　　　　　　　　　[*Exit.*
　　Sur. We shall have a salad!
　　Mam. When do you make projection?
　　Sub. Son, be not hasty, I exalt our med'cine,

　　　　　　　　　　　　　　B

By hanging him *in balneo vaporoso*,
And giving him solution; then congeal him;
And then dissolve him; then again congeal him:
For look, how oft I iterate the work
So many times I add unto his virtue.
As, if at first one ounce convert a hundred,
After his second loose, he'll turn a thousand;
His third solution, ten; his fourth, a hundred;
After his fifth, a thousand thousand ounces
Of any imperfect metal, into pure
Silver or gold, in all examinations,
As good as any of the natural mine.
Get you your stuff here against afternoon,
Your brass, your pewter, and your andirons.
   Mam. Not those of iron?
   Sub. Yes, you may bring them too:
We'll change all metals.
   Sur. I believe you in that.
   Mam. Then I may send my spits?
   Sub. Yes, and your racks.
   Sur. And dripping pans, and pot-hangers, and hooks,
Shall he not?
   Sub. If he please.
   Sur. —To be an ass.
   Sub. How, sir!
   Mam. This gentleman you must bear withal:
I told you he had no faith.
   Sur. And little hope, sir;
But much less charity, should I gull myself.
   Sub. Why, what have you observed, sir, in our art,
Seems so impossible?
   Sur. But your whole work, no more.
That you should hatch gold in a furnace, sir,
As they do eggs in Egypt!
   Sub. Sir, do you
Believe that eggs are hatched so?
   Sur. If I should?
   Sub. Why, I think that the greater miracle.
No eggs but differs from a chicken more
Than metals in themselves.
   Sur. That cannot be.
The egg's ordained by nature to that end,
And is a chicken *in potentia*.
   Sub. The same we say of lead and other metals,
Which would be gold if they had time.
   Mam. And that
Our art doth further.
   Sub. Ay, for 'twere absurd

To think that nature in the earth bred gold
Perfect in the instant; something went before.
There must be remote matter.
  Sur. Ay, what is that?
  Sub. Marry, we say——
  Mam. Ay, now it heats: stand, father,
Pound him to dust.
  Sub. It is, of the one part,
A humid exhalation, which we call
Materia liquida, or the unctuous water;
On the other part, a certain crass and vicious
Portion of earth; both which, concorporate,
Do make the elementary matter of gold;
Which is not yet *propria materia*,
But common to all metals and all stones;
For, where it is forsaken of that moisture,
And hath more dryness, it becomes a stone;
Where it retains more of the humid fatness,
It turns to sulphur or to quicksilver,
Who are the parents of all other metals.
Nor can this remote matter suddenly
Progress so from extreme unto extreme,
As to grow gold, and leap o'er all the means.
Nature doth first beget the imperfect, then
Proceeds she to the perfect. Of that airy
And oily water, mercury is engendered;
Sulphur of the fat and earthy part; the one,
Which is the last, supplying the place of male,
The other of the female, in all metals.
Some do believe hermaphrodeity,
That both do act and suffer. But these two
Make the rest ductile, malleable, extensive.
And even in gold they are; for we do find
Seeds of them, by our fire, and gold in them;
And can produce the species of each metal
More perfect thence, than Nature doth in earth.
Beside, who doth not see in daily practice
Art can beget bees, hornets, beetles, wasps,
Out of the carcases and dung of creatures;
Yea, scorpions of an herb, being rightly placed?
And these are living creatures, far more perfect
And excellent than metals.
  Mam. Well said, father!
Nay, if he take you in hand, sir, with an argument,
He'll bray you in a mortar.
  Sur. Pray you, sir, stay.
Rather than I'll be bray'd, sir, I'll believe
That Alchemy is a pretty kind of game,

Somewhat like tricks o' the cards, to cheat a man
With charming.
  Sub. Sir?
  Sur. What else are all your terms,
Whereon no one of your writers 'grees with other?
Of your elixir, your *lac virginis*,
Your stone, your med'cine, and your chrysosperme,
Your sal, your sulphur, and your mercury,
Your oil of height, your tree of life, your blood,
Your marchesite, your tutie, your magnesia,
Your toad, your crow, your dragon, and your panther;
Your sun, your moon, your firmament, your adrop,
Your lato, azoch, zernich, chibrit, heautarit,
And then your red man and your white woman,
With all your broths, your menstrues, and materials,
Of lye and egg-shells, women's terms, man's blood,
Hair o' the head, burnt clouts, chalk, merds, and clay,
Powder of bones, scalings of iron, glass,
And worlds of other strange ingredients,
Would burst a man to name?
  Sub. And all these named,
Intending but one thing; which art our writers
Used to obscure their art.
  Mam. Sir, so I told him—
Because the simple idiot should not learn it,
And make it vulgar.
  Sub. Was not all the knowledge
Of the Egyptians writ in mystic symbols?
Speak not the Scriptures oft in parables?
Are not the choicest fables of the poets,
That were the fountains and first springs of wisdom,
Wrapp'd in perplexed allegories?
  Mam. I urged that,
And cleared to him that Sysiphus was damned
To roll the ceaseless stone, only because
He would have made Ours common. [DOL *appears at the door.*
                              Who is this?
  Sub. 'Sprecious!—What do you mean? Go in, good lady,
Let me entreat you. [DOL *retires.*] Where's this varlet?

Re-enter FACE.

  Face. Sir.
  Sub. You very knave! do you use me thus?
  Face. Wherein, sir?
  Sub. Go in and see, you traitor. Go!   [*Exit* FACE.
  Mam. Who is it, sir?
  Sub. Nothing, sir; nothing.

Mam. What's the matter, good sir?
I have not seen you thus distemper'd: who is't?
  Sub. All arts have still had, sir, their adversaries,
But ours the most ignorant.

Re-enter FACE.

What now?
  Face. 'Twas not my fault, sir; she would speak with you.
  Sub. Would she, sir! Follow me.   [*Exit.*
  Mam. [*Stopping him.*] Stay, Lungs.
  Face. I dare not, sir.
  Mam. Stay, man; what is she?
  Face. A lord's sister, sir.
  Mam. How! pray thee, stay.
  Face. She's mad, sir, and sent hither—
He'll be mad too——
  Mam. I warrant thee.
Why sent hither?
  Face. Sir, to be cured.
  Sub. [*Within.*] Why, rascal!
  Face. Lo you!—Here, sir!   [*Exit.*
  Mam. 'Fore God, a Bradamante, a brave piece.
  Sur. Heart, this is an evil house! I will be burnt else.
  Mam. Oh, by this light, no; do not wrong him. He's
Too scrupulous that way: it is his vice.
No, he's a rare physician, do him right,
An excellent Paracelsian, and has done
Strange cures with mineral physic. He deals all
With spirits, he; he will not hear a word
Of Galen or his tedious recipes.

Re-enter FACE.

How now, Lungs!
  Face. Softly, sir; speak softly. I meant
To have told your worship all. This must not hear.
  Mam. No, he will not be "gull'd": let him alone.
  Face. You are very right, sir; she is a most rare scholar,
And is gone mad with studying Broughton's works.
If you but name a word touching the Hebrew
She falls into her fit, and will discourse
So learnedly of genealogies,
As you would run mad, too, to hear her, sir.
  Mam. How might one do t' have conference with her, Lungs?
  Face. Oh, divers have run mad upon the conference:
I do not know, sir. I am sent in haste
To fetch a vial.
  Sur. Be not gull'd, Sir Mammon.
  Mam. Wherein? Pray ye, be patient.

Sur. Yes, as you are,
And trust confederate knaves and sharks and bawds.
   Mam. You are too foul, believe it.—Come here, Ulen,
One word.
   Face. I dare not, in good faith.   [*Going.*
   Mam. Stay, knave.
   Face. He is extreme angry that you saw her, sir.
   Mam. Drink that. [*Gives him money.*] What is she when
     she's out of her fit?
   Face. Oh, the most affablest creature, sir! So merry!
So pleasant! She'll mount you up like quicksilver
Over the helm, and circulate like oil,
A very vegetal; discourse of state,
Of mathematics, frolic, anything——
   Mam. Is she no way accessible? no means,
No trick to give a man a taste of her—wit—
Or so?
   Sub. [*Within.*] Ulen!
   Face. I'll come to you again, sir,   [*Exit.*
   Mam. Surly, I did not think one of your breeding
Would traduce personages of worth.
   Sur. Sir Epicure,
Your friend to use; yet still loth to be gulled:
I do not like your philosophical bawds.
Their stone is lechery enough to pay for
Without this bait.
   Mam. 'Heart, you abuse yourself.
I know the lady, and her friends, and means,
The original of this disaster. Her brother
Has told me all.
   Sur. And yet you never saw her
Till now!
   Mam. Oh yes, but I forgot. I have, believe it,
One of the treacherousest memories, I do think,
Of all mankind.
   Sur. What call you her brother?
   Mam. My Lord——
He will not have his name known, now I think on it.
   Sur. A very treacherous memory!
   Mam. On my faith——
   Sur. Tut, if you have it not about you, pass it
Till we meet next.
   Mam. Nay, by this hand, 'tis true,
He's one I honour, and my noble friend;
And I respect his house.
   Sur. Heart! can it be
That a grave sir, a rich, that has no need,
A wise, sir, too, at other times, should thus,

With his own oaths and arguments, make hard means
To gull himself? An this be your elixir,
Your *lapis mineralis* and your lunary,
Give me your honest trick yet at primero,
Or gleek : and take your *lutum sapientis*,
Your *menstruum simplex!* I'll have gold before you,
And with less danger of the quicksilver
Or the hot sulphur.

Re-enter FACE.

 Face. Here's one from Captain Face, sir [*to* SURLY]
Desires you meet him in the Temple Church
Some half-hour hence, and upon earnest business.
Sir—[*whispers* MAMMON]—if you please to quit us now, and come
Again within two hours, you shall have
My master busy examining o' the works ;
And I will steal you in unto the party,
That you may see her converse. Sir, shall I say
You'll meet the captain's worship?
 Sur. Sir, I will.   [*Walks aside.*
But, by attorney and to a second purpose,
Now, I am sure I understand this house ;
I'll swear it, were the marshal here to thank me :
The naming this commander doth confirm it.
Don Face ! why he 's the most authentic dealer
In these commodities, the superintendent
To all the quainter traffickers in town !
He is the visitor, and does appoint
Who visits whom, and at what hour ; what price ;
Which gown, and in what smock ; what fall ; what tire.
Him will I prove, by a third person, to find
The subtleties of this dark labyrinth :
Which if I do discover, dear Sir Mammon,
You'll give your poor friend leave, though no philosopher,
To laugh : for you that are, 'tis thought, shall weep.
 Face. Sir, he does pray you'll not forget.
 Sur. I will not, sir.
Sir Epicure, I shall leave you.   [*Exit.*
 Mam. I follow you straight.
 Face. But do so, good sir, to avoid suspicion.
This gentleman has a parlous head.
 Mam. But wilt thou, Ulen,
Be constant to thy promise?
 Face. As my life, sir.
 Mam. And wilt thou insinuate what I am, and praise me,
And say I am a noble fellow ?
 Face. Oh, what else, sir ?

And that you'll make her royal with the stone,
An empress: and yourself, King of Bantam.
   Mam. Wilt thou do this?
   Face. Will I, sir!
   Mam. Lungs, my Lungs!
I love thee.
   Face. Send your stuff, sir, that my master
May busy himself about projection.
   Mam. Thou hast witch'd me, rogue: take, go.
                                     [Gives him money.
   Face. Your jack, and all, sir.
   Mam. Thou art a villain—I will send my jack,
And the weights too. Slave, I could bite thine ear.
Away, thou dost not care for me.
   Face. Not I, sir!
   Mam. Come, I was born to make thee, my good weasel,
Set thee on a bench, and have thee twirl a chain
With the best lord's vermin of 'em all.
   Face. Away, sir.
   Mam. A count, nay, a count palatine——
   Face. Good, sir, go.
   Mam. Shall not advance thee better: no, nor faster.   *[Exit.*

         Re-enter SUBTLE *and* DOL.

   Sub. Has he bit? has he bit?
   Face. And swallowed too, my Subtle.
I have given him line, and now he plays, i' faith.
   Sub. And shall we twitch him?
   Face. Thorough both the gills.
For here is a rare bait, with which a man
No sooner 's taken, but he straight runs mad.
   Sub. Dol, my Lord What's'hums sister, you must now
Bear yourself *statelich*.
   Dol. Oh, let me alone.
I'll not forget my race, I warrant you.
I'll keep my distance, laugh and talk aloud;
Have all the tricks of a proud scurvy lady,
And be as rude as her woman.
   Face. Well said, sanguine!
   Sub. But will he send his andirons?
   Face. His jack too,
And 's iron shoeing-horn; I have spoke to him. Well,
I must not lose my wary gamester yonder.
   Sub. Oh, Monsieur Caution, that *will not be gull'd.*
   Face. Ay,
If I can strike a fine hook into him, now!
The Temple Church, there I have cast mine angle.
Well, pray for me. I'll about it.   *[Knocking without.*

Sub. What, more gudgeons!
Dol, scout, scout! [DOL *goes to the window.*] Stay, Face, you
    must go to the door.
Pray God it be my anabaptist.—Who is 't, Dol?
  Dol. I know him not: he looks like a gold-endman.
  Sub. Ods so! 'tis he, he said he would send—what call you
    him?
The sanctified elder, that should deal,
For Mammon's jack and andirons. Let him in.
Stay, help me off, first, with my gown. [*Exit* FACE *with the
    gown.*] Away,
Madam, to your withdrawing chamber. [*Exit* DOL.] Now,
In a new tune, new gesture, but old language.—
This fellow is sent from one negotiates with me
About the stone too; for the holy brethren
Of Amsterdam, the exiled saints; that hope
To raise their discipline by it. I must use him
In some strange fashion, now, to make him admire me.—

Enter ANANIAS.

Where is my drudge?   [*Aloud.*

Re-enter FACE.

  Face. Sir!
  Sub. Take away the recipient,
And rectify your menstrue from the phlegma.
Then pour it on the Sol, in the cucurbite,
And let them macerate together.
  Face. Yes, sir.
And save the ground?
  Sub. No: *terra damnata*
Must not have entrance in the work.—Who are you?
  Ana. A faithful brother, if it please you.
  Sub. What's that?
A Lullianist? a Ripley! *Filius artis?*
Can you sublime and dulcify? calcine?
Know you the sapor pontic? sapor stiptic?
Or what is homogene, or heterogene?
  Ana. I understand no heathen language, truly.
  Sub. Heathen! you Knipper-doling? is Ars sacra
Or chrysopœia, or spagyrica,
Or the pamphysic, or panarchic knowledge,
A heathen language?
  Ana. Heathen Greek, I take it.
  Sub. How heathen Greek?
  Ana. All's heathen but the Hebrew.
  Sub. Sirrah, my varlet, stand you forth and speak to him
Like a philosopher: answer in the language,

Name the vexations, and the martyrizations
Of metals in the work.
 Face. Sir, putrefaction,
Solution, ablution, sublimation,
Cohobation, calcination, ceration, and
Fixation.
 Sub. This is heathen Greek to you, now !—
And when comes vivification ?
 Face. After mortification.
 Sub. What's cohobation ?
 Face. 'Tis the pouring on
Your aqua regis, and then drawing him off,
To the trine circle of the seven spheres.
 Sub. What's the proper passion of metals ?
 Face. Malleation.
 Sub. What's your *ultimum supplicium auri?*
 Face. Antimonium.
 Sub. This is heathen Greek to you?—And what's your
  mercury?
 Face. A very fugitive, he will be gone, sir.
 Sub. How know you him ?
 Face. By his viscosity,
His oleosity, and his suscitability.
 Sub. How do you sublime him?
 Face. With the calce of egg-shells,
White marble, talc.
 Sub. Your magisterium, now,
What's that ?
 Face. Shifting, sir, your elements,
Dry into cold, cold into moist, moist into hot,
Hot into dry.
 Sub. This is heathen Greek to you still !
Your *lapis philosophicus ?*
 Face. 'Tis a stone,
And not a stone ; a spirit, a soul, and a body :
Which if you do dissolve, it is dissolved ;
If you coagulate, it is coagulated ;
If you make it to fly, it flieth.
 Sub. Enough.   [*Exit* FACE.
This is heathen Greek to you ! What are you, sir ?
 Ana. Please you, a servant of the exiled brethren
That deal with widows and with orphans' goods :
And make a just account unto the saints :
A deacon.
 Sub. Oh, you are sent from Master Wholesome,
Your teacher ?
 Ana. From Tribulation Wholesome,
Our very zealous pastor.

Sub. Good! I have
Some orphans' goods to come here.
   Ana. Of what kind, sir.
   Sub. Pewter and brass, andirons and kitchenware,
Metals, that we must use our medicine on :
Wherein the brethren may have a penn'orth
For ready money.
   Ana. Were the orphans' parents
Sincere professors?
   Sub. Why do you ask?
   Ana. Because
We then are to deal justly, and give in truth
Their utmost value.
   Sub. 'Slid, you 'd cozen else,
And if their parents were not of the faithful!—
I will not trust you, now I think on it,
Till I have talked with your pastor. Have you brought money
To buy more coals?
   Ana. No, surely.
   Sub. No, how so?
   Ana. The brethren bid me say unto you, sir,
Surely they will not venture any more
Till they may see projection.
   Sub. How!
   Ana. You have had,
For the instruments, as bricks, and loam and glasses,
Already thirty pounds; and for materials,
They say, some ninety more: and they have heard since
That one at Heidelberg made it of an egg
And a small paper of pin-dust.
   Sub. What 's your name?
   Ana. My name is Ananias.
   Sub. Out, the varlet
That cozen'd the apostles! Hence, away
Flee, mischief! Had your holy consistory
No name to send me of another sound
Than wicked Ananias? send your elders
Hither to make atonement for you quickly,
And give me satisfaction; or out goes
The fire; and down th' alembics, and the furnace,
Piger Henricus, or what not. Thou wretch!
Both sericon and bufo shall be lost,
Tell them. All hope of rooting out the bishops,
Or the antichristian hierarchy, shall perish,
If they stay threescore minutes: the aqueity,
Terreity, and sulphureity
Shall run together again, and all be annulled,
Thou wicked Ananias! [*Exit* ANANIAS.] This will fetch 'em,

And make them haste towards their gulling more.
A man must deal like a rough nurse, and fright
Those that are froward to an appetite.

Re-enter FACE *in his uniform, followed by* DRUGGER.

Face. He is busy with his spirits, but we'll upon him.
Sub. How now! what mates, what Bayards have we here?
Face. I told you he would be furious.—Sir, here's Nab
Has brought you another piece of gold to look on .
—We must appease him. Give it me—and prays you,
You would devise—what is it, Nab?
Drug. A sign, sir.
Face. Ay, a good lucky one, a thriving sign, doctor?
Sub. I was devising now.
Face. 'Slight, do not say so,
He will repent he gave you any more—
What say you to his constellation, doctor?
The Balance?
Sub. No, that way is stale and common.
A townsman born in Taurus gives the bull,
Or the bull's-head: in Aries, the ram,
A poor device! No, I will have his name
Formed in some mystic character; whose radii,
Striking the senses of the passers-by,
Shall, by a virtual influence, breed affections
That may result upon the party owns it:
As thus——
Face. Nab!
Sub. He shall have *a bel*, that's *Abel*;
And by it standing one whose name is *Dee*,
In a *rug* gown, there's *D*, and *Rug*, that's *drug*:
And right anenst him a dog snarling *er;*
There's *Drugger*, Abel Drugger. That's his sign.
And here's now mystery and hieroglyphic!
Face. Abel, thou art made.
Drug. Sir, I do thank his worship.
Face. Six o' thy legs more will not do it, Nab.
He has brought you a pipe of tobacco, doctor.
Drug. Yes, sir:
I have another thing I would impart——
Face. Out with it, Nab.
Drug. Sir, there is lodged, hard by me,
A rich young widow——
Face. Good! a bona roba?
Drug. But nineteen at the most.
Face. Very good, Abel.
Drug. Marry, she's not in fashion yet; she wears
A hood, but it stands a cop.

Face. No matter, Abel.
Drug. And I do now and then give her a fucus—
Face. What! dost thou deal, Nab?
Sub. I did tell you, captain.
Drug. And physic, too, sometime, sir; for which she trusts me
With all her mind. She's come up here of purpose
To learn the fashion.
Face. Good (his match too!)—On, Nab.
Drug. And she does strangely long to know her fortune.
Face. Ods lid, Nab, send her to the doctor, hither.
Drug. Yes I have spoke to her of his worship already;
But she's afraid it will be blown abroad,
And hurt her marriage.
Face. Hurt it! 'tis the way
To heal it, if 'twere hurt; to make it more
Followed and sought; Nab, thou shalt tell her this.
She'll be more known, more talked of; and your widows
Are ne'er of any price till they be famous:
Their honour is their multitude of suitors:
Send her, it may be thy good fortune. What!
Thou dost not know.
Drug. No, sir, she'll never marry
Under a knight: her brother has made a vow.
Face. What! and dost thou despair, my little Nab,
Knowing what the doctor has set down for thee,
And seeing so many of the city dubbed?
One glass o' thy water, with a madam I know,
Will have it done, Nab; what's her brother—a knight?
Drug. No, sir, a gentleman newly warm in his land, sir,
Scarce cold in his one-and-twenty, that does govern
His sister here; and is a man himself
Of some three thousand a year, and is come up
To learn to quarrel, and to live by his wits,
And will go down again, and die in the country.
Face. How! to quarrel?
Drug. Yes, sir, to carry quarrels,
As gallants do; to manage them by line.
Face. 'Slid, Nab, the doctor is the only man
In Christendom for him. He has made a table,
With mathematical demonstrations,
Touching the art of quarrels: he will give him
An instrument to quarrel by. Go, bring them both,
Him and his sister. And, for thee, with her
The doctor haply may persuade. Go to:
Shalt give his worship a new damask suit
Upon the premises.
Sub. Oh, good captain!

Face. He shall ;
He is the honestest fellow, doctor.—Stay not,
No offers ; bring the damask, and the parties.
    Drug. I'll try my power, sir.
    Face. And thy will, too, Nab.
    Sub. 'Tis good tobacco, this ! What is 't an ounce?
    Face. He'll send you a pound, doctor.
    Sub. Oh, no.
    Face. He will do 't.
It is the goodest soul Abel !—Abel, about it.
Thou shalt know more anon. Away, begone.—   [*Exit* ABEL.
A miserable rogue, and lives with cheese,
And has the worms. That was the cause, indeed,
Why he came now : he dealt with me in private,
To get a med'cine for them.
    Sub. And shall, sir, This works.
    Face. A wife, a wife for one of us, my dear Subtle !
We'll e'en draw lots, and he that fails, shall have
The more in goods, the other has in tail.
    Sub. Rather the less: for she may be so light
She may want grains.
    Face. Ay, or be such a burden,
A man would scarce endure her for the whole.
    Sub. Faith, best let 's see her first, and then determine.
    Face. Content ; but Dol must have no breath on 't.
    Sub. Mum.
Away you, to your Surly yonder, catch him.
    Face. Pray God, I have not stayed too long.
    Sub. I fear it.   [*Exeunt.*

---------ACT III.---------

SCENE I.—*The Lane before* LOVEWIT'S *House.*

Enter TRIBULATION WHOLESOME *and* ANANIAS.

    Tri. These chastisements are common to the saints,
And such rebukes, we of the separation
Must bear with willing shoulders, as the trials
Sent forth to tempt our frailties.
    Ana. In pure zeal,
I do not like the man, he is a heathen,
And speaks the language of Canaan, truly.
    Tri. I think him a profane person indeed.
    Ana. He bears
The visible mark of the beast in his forehead.
And for his stone, it is a work of darkness,
And with philosophy blinds the eyes of man.

Tri. Good brother, we must bend unto all means
That may give furtherance to the holy cause.
  Ana. Which his cannot : the sanctified cause
Should have a sanctified course.
  Tri. Not always necessary :
The children of perdition are oftimes
Made instruments even of the greatest works :
Beside, we should give somewhat to man's nature,
The place he lives in, still about the fire,
And fume of metals, that intoxicate
The brain of man, and made him prone to passion.
Where have you greater atheists than your cooks ?
Or more profane, or choleric, than your glass-men ?
More antichristian than your bell-founders ?
What makes the devil so devilish, I would ask you,
Satan, our common enemy, but his being
Perpetually about the fire, and boiling
Brimstone and arsenic ? We must give, I say,
Unto the motives, and the stirrers-up
Of humours in the blood. It may be so,
Whenas the work is done, the stone is made,
This heat of his may turn into a zeal,
And stand up for the beauteous discipline,
Against the filthy cloth and rag of Rome.
We must await his calling, and the coming
Of the good spirit. You did fault t' upbraid him
With the brethren's blessing of Heidelberg, weighing
What need we have to hasten on the work
For the restoring of the silenced saints,
Which ne'er will be, but by the philosopher's stone.
And so a learned elder, one of Scotland,
Assured me; *aurum potabile* being
The only med'cine for the civil magistrate
T' incline him to a feeling of the cause,
And must be daily used in the disease.
  Ana. I have not edified more, truly, by man;
Not since the beautiful light first shone on me :
And I am sad my zeal hath so offended.
  Tri. Let us call on him then.
  Ana. The motion's good,
And of the spirit ; I will knock first. [*Knocks.*] Peace within !
        [*The door is opened, and they enter.*

SCENE II.—*A Room in* LOVEWIT'S *House.*

Enter SUBTLE, *followed by* TRIBULATION *and* ANANIAS.

  Sub. Oh, are you come ? 'Twas time. Your threescore minutes
Were at last thread, you see ; and down had gone

Furnus acediæ, turris circulatorius:
Lembec, bolt's-head, retort and pelican
Had all been cinders.—Wicked Ananias!
Art thou returned? Nay then, it goes down yet.
   Tri. Sir, be appeased; he is come to humble
Himself in spirit, and to ask your patience,
If too much zeal hath carried him aside
From the due path.
   Sub. Why, this doth qualify!
   Tri. The brethren had no purpose, verily,
To give you the least grievance: but are ready
To lend their willing hands to any project
The spirit and you direct.
   Sub. This qualifies more!
   Tri. And for the orphan's goods, let them be valued,
Or what is needful else to the holy work,
It shall be numbered; here, by me, the saints
Throw down their purse before you.
   Sub. This qualifies most!
Why, thus it should be, now you understand.
Have I discoursed so unto you of our stone,
And of the good that it shall bring your cause?
Showed you (beside the main of hiring forces
Abroad, drawing the Hollanders, your friends,
From the Indies, to serve you with all their fleet)
That even the med'cinal use shall make you a faction
And party in the realm? As, put the case,
That some great man in state, he have the gout,
Why, you but send three drops of your elixir,
You help him straight: there you have made a friend.
Another has the palsy or the dropsy,
He takes of your incombustible stuff,
He's young again: there you have made a friend.
A lady that is past the feat of body,
Though not of mind, and hath her face decayed
Beyond all cure of paintings, you restore
With the oil of talc: there you have made a friend,
And all her friends. A lord that is a leper,
A knight that has the bone-ache, or a squire
That hath both these, you make them smooth and sound
With a bare fricace of your med'cine: still
You increase your friends.
   Tri. Ay, it is very pregnant.
   Sub. And then the turning of this lawyer's pewter
to plate at Christmas——
   Ana. Christ-tide, I pray you.
   Sub. Yet, Ananias!
   Ana. I have done.

Sub. Or changing
His parcel gilt to massy gold. You cannot
But raise your friends. Withal to be of power
To pay an army in the field, to buy
The king of France out of his realms, or Spain
Out of his Indies. What can you not do
Against lords spiritual or temporal,
That shall oppone you?
   Tri. Verily, 'tis true.
We may be temporal lords ourselves, I take it.
   Sub. You may be anything, and leave off to make
Long-winded exercises; or suck up
Your *ha!* and *hum!* in a tune. I not deny
But such as are not graced in a state,
May, for their ends, be averse in religion,
And get a tune to call the flock together:
For, to say sooth, a tune does much with women
And other phlegmatic people; it is your bell.
   Ana. Bells are profane; a tune may be religious.
   Sub. No warning with you! then farewell my patience.
'Slight, it shall down: I will not be thus tortured.
   Tri. I pray you, sir.
   Sub. All shall perish. I have spoke it.
   Tri. Let me find grace, sir, in your eyes: the man
He stands corrected: neither did his zeal,
But as yourself, allow a tune somewhere.
Which now, being tow'rd the stone, we shall not need.
   Sub. No, nor your holy vizard, to win widows
To give you legacies; or make zealous wives
To rob their husbands for the common cause:
Nor take the start of bonds broke but one day,
And say they were forfeited by providence.
Nor shall you need o'ernight to eat huge meals,
To celebrate your next day's fast the better;
The whilst the brethren and the sisters humbled,
Abate the stiffness of the flesh. Nor cast
Before your hungry hearers scrupulous bones;
As whether a Christian may hawk or hunt,
Or whether matrons of the holy assembly
May lay their hair out, or wear doublets,
Or have that idol starch about their linen.
   Ana. It is indeed an idol.
   Tri. Mind him not, sir.
I do command thee, spirit of zeal, but trouble,
To peace with him! Pray you, sir, go on.
   Sub. Nor shall you need to libel 'gainst the prelates,
And shorten so your ears against the hearing
Of the next wire-drawn grace. Nor of necessity

Rail against plays, to please the alderman
Whose daily custard you devour : nor lie
With zealous rage till you are hoarse. Not one
Of these so singular arts. Nor call yourselves
By names of Tribulation, Persecution,
Restraint, Long-patience, and such like, affected
By the whole family or wood of you,
Only for glory, and to catch the ear
Of the disciple.
    Tri. Truly, sir, they are
Ways that the godly brethren have invented
For propagation of the glorious cause,
As very notable means, and whereby also
Themselves grow soon, and profitably, famous.
    Sub. Oh, but the stone, all 's idle to it ! Nothing !
The art of angels, nature's miracle,
The divine secret that doth fly in clouds
From east to west ; and whose tradition
Is not from men, but spirits.
    Ana. I hate traditions ;
I do not trust them.——
    Tri. Peace !
    Ana. They are popish all.
I will not peace : I will not——
    Tri. Ananias !
    Ana. Please the profane, to grieve the godly ; I may not.
    Sub. Well, Ananias, thou shalt overcome.
    Tri. It is an ignorant zeal that haunts him, sir,
But truly, else, a very faithful brother,
A botcher, and a man, by revelation,
That hath a competent knowledge of the truth.
    Sub. Has he a competent sum there in the bag
To buy the goods within ? I am made guardian,
And must, for charity, and conscience sake,
Now see the most be made for my poor orphan ;
Though I desire the brethren too good gainers ;
There they are within. When you have view'd, and bought
    'em,
And ta'en the inventory of what they are,
They are ready for projection ; there's no more
To do ; cast on the med'cine so much silver
As there is tin there, so much gold as brass,
I'll give it you in, by weight.
    Tri. But how long time,
Sir, must the saints expect yet ?
    Sub. Let me see.
How 's the moon now ? Eight, nine, ten days hence,
He will be silver potate ; then three days

Before he citronise : some fifteen days,
The magisterium will be perfected.
   Ana. About the second day of the third week,
In the ninth month ?
   Sub. Yes, my good Ananias.
   Tri. What will the orphans' goods arise to, think you ?
   Sub. Some hundred marks, as much as filled three cars,
Unladed now : you'll make six millions of them.
But I must have more coals laid in.
   Tri. How !
   Sub. Another load,
And then we have finished. We must now increase
Our fire to *ignis ardens*, we are past
Fimus equinus, balnei, cineris,
And all those lenter heats. If the holy purse
Should with this draught fall low, and that the saints
Do need a present sum, I have a trick
To melt the pewter, you shall buy now, instantly,
And with a tincture make you as good Dutch dollars
As any are in Holland.
   Tri. Can you so?
   Sub. Ay, and shall 'bide the third examination.
   Ana. It will be joyful tidings to the brethren.
   Sub. But you must carry it secret.
   Tri. Ay, but stay,
This act of coining, is it lawful ?
   Ana. Lawful !
We know no magistrate ; or, if we did,
This is foreign coin.
   Sub. It is no coining, sir,
It is but casting.
   Tri. Ha ! you distinguish well :
Casting of money may be lawful.
   Ana. 'Tis, sir.
   Tri. Truly, I take it so.
   Sub. There is no scruple,
Sir, to be made of it ; believe Ananias :
This case of conscience he is studied in.
   Tri. I'll make a question of it to the brethren,
   Ana. The brethren shall approve it lawful, doubt not.
Where shall it be done ?   [*Knocking without.*
   Sub. For that we'll talk anon.
There's some to speak with me. Go in, I pray you,
And view the parcels. That's the inventory.
I'll come to you straight.   [*Exeunt* TRIB. *and* ANA.
        Who is it ?—Face ! appear.

Enter FACE *in his uniform.*

How now! Good prize?
  Face. Good plague! Yond' costive cheater
Never came on.
  Sub. How then?
  Face. I have walked the round
Till now, and no such thing.
  Sub. And have you quit him?
  Face. Quit him! an hell would quit him too, he were
    happy.
'Slight! Would you have me stalk like a mill-jade,
All day, for one that will not yield us grains?
I know him of old.
  Sub. Oh, but to have gulled him
Had been a mastery.
  Face. Let him go, black boy!
And turn thee that some fresh news may possess thee.
A noble count, a don of Spain, my dear
Delicious compeer, and my party-bawd,
Who is come hither private for his conscience,
And brought munition with him, six great slops,
Bigger than three Dutch hoys, beside round trunks,
Furnished with pistolets, and pieces of eight,
Will straight be here, my rogue, to have thy bath
(That is the colour), and to make his battery
Upon our Dol, our castle, our cinque-port,
Our Dover pier, our what thou wilt. Where is she?
She must prepare perfumes, delicate linen,
The bath in chief, a banquet, and her wit.
Where is the doxy?
  Sub. I'll send her to thee:
And but dispatch my brace of little John Leydens,
And come again myself.
  Face. Are they within, then?
  Sub. Numbering the sum.
  Face. How much?
  Sub. A hundred marks, boy.   [*Exit.*
  Face. Why, this is a lucky day. Ten pounds of Mammon!
Three of my clerk! A portague of my grocer!
This of the brethren! beside reversions,
And states to come in the widow, and my count!
My share to-day will not be bought for forty——

Enter DOL.

  Dol. What?
  Face. Pounds, dainty Dorothy! Art thou so near?
  Dol. Yes; say, lord general, how fares our camp?

Face. As with the few that had entrenched themselves
Safe, by their discipline, against a world, Dol,
And laughed within those trenches, and grew fat
With thinking on the booties, Dol, brought in
Daily by their small parties.   This dear hour
A doughty don is taken with my Dol ;
And thou may'st make his ransom what thou wilt,
My Dousabel ; he shall be brought here fettered
With thy fair looks, before he sees thee ; and thrown
In a down-bed, as dark as any dungeon,
Where thou shalt keep him waking with thy drum ;
Thy drum, my Dol, thy drum ; till he be tame
As the poor blackbirds were in the great frost,
Or bees are with a bason ; and so hive him
In the swan-skin coverlid and cambric sheets,
Till he work honey and wax, my little God's-gift.
  Dol. What is he, general?
  Face. An adalantado,
A grandee, girl.   Was not my Dapper here yet?
  Dol. No.
  Face. Nor my Drugger?
  Dol. Neither.
  Face. A plague on 'em,
They are so long a-furnishing !   Such stinkards
Would not be seen upon these festival days.—

Re-enter SUBTLE.

How now ! have you done?
  Sub. Done.   They are gone : the sum
Is here in bank, my Face.   I would we knew
Another chapman now would buy 'em outright.
  Face. 'Slid, Nab shall do 't against he have the widow
To furnish household.
  Sub. Excellent, well thought on :
Pray God he come !
  Face. I pray he keep away
Till our new business be o'erpast.
  Sub. But, Face,
How cam'st thou by this secret don?
  Face. A spirit
Brought me th' intelligence in a paper here,
As I was conjuring yonder in my circle
For Surly ; I have my flies abroad.   Your bath
Is famous, Subtle, by my means.   Sweet Dol,
Tickle him with thy mother-tongue.   His great
Verdugoship has not a jot of language ;
So much the easier to be cozened, my Dolly.
He will come here in a hired coach, obscure,

And our own coachman, whom I have sent as guide,
No creature else. [*Knocking without.*] Who's that? [*Exit* DOL.
   Sub. It is not he?
   Face. O no, not yet this hour.

Re-enter DOL.

   Sub. Who is't?
   Dol. Dapper,
Your clerk.
   Face. God's will then, Queen of Fairy,
On with your tire;—[*Exit* DOL]—and doctor, with your robes.
Let's dispatch him, for God's sake.
   Sub. 'T will be long.
   Face. I warrant you, take but the cue I give you,
It shall be brief enough.—[*Goes to the window.*]—'Slight, here
     are more!
Abel, and I think the angry boy, the heir,
That fain would quarrel.
   Sub. And the widow?
   Face. No.
Not that I see. Away!   [*Exit* SUB.

Enter DAPPER.

                   Oh, sir, you are welcome.
The doctor is within a-moving for you;
I have had the most ado to win him to it!
He swears you'll be the darling of the dice:
He never heard her highness dote till now,
Your aunt has given you the most gracious words
That can be thought on.
   Dap. Shall I see her grace?
   Face. See her, and kiss her too.—

Enter ABEL, *followed by* KASTRIL.

                   What, honest Nab!
Hast brought the damask?
   Drug. No, sir; here's tobacco.
   Face. 'Tis well done, Nab: thou'lt bring the damask too?
   Drug. Yes: here's the gentleman, captain, Master Kastril,
I have brought to see the doctor.
   Face. Where's the widow?
   Drug. Sir, as he likes, his sister, he says, shall come.
   Face. Oh, is it so? Good time. Is your name Kastril, sir?
   Kas. Ay, and the best of the Kastrils, I'd be sorry else,
By fifteen hundred a-year. Where is the doctor?
My mad tobacco-boy, here, tells me of one
That can do things: has he any skill?

Face. Wherein, sir?
Kas. To carry a business, manage a quarrel fairly,
Upon fit terms.
   Face. It seems, sir, you are but young
About the town, that can make that a question.
   Kas. Sir, not so young but I have heard some speech
Of the angry boys, and seen them take tobacco,
And in his shop; and I can take it too.
And I would fain be one of 'em, and go down
And practise in the country.
   Face. Sir, for the duello,
The doctor, I assure you, shall inform you,
To the least shadow of a hair, and show you
An instrument he has of his own making,
Wherewith no sooner shall you make report
Of any quarrel, but he will take the height on 't
Most instantly, and tell in what degree
Of safety it lies in, or mortality.
And how it may be borne, whether in a right line,
Or a half-circle; or may else be cast
Into an angle blunt, if not acute:
All this he will demonstrate. And then, rules
To give and take the lie by.
   Kas. How! to take it?
   Face. Yes, in oblique he 'll show you, or in circle;
But never in diameter. The whole town
Study his theorems, and dispute them ordinarily
At the eating academies.
   Kas. But does he teach
Living by the wits too?
   Face. Anything whatever.
You cannot think that subtlety but he reads it.
He made me a captain. I was a stark pimp,
Just of your standing, 'fore I met with him;
It is not two months since. I 'll tell you his method:
First, he will enter you at some ordinary.
   Kas. No, I 'll not come there; you shall pardon me.
   Face. For why, sir?
   Kas. There's gaming there, and tricks.
   Face. Why, would you be
A gallant, and not game?
   Kas. Ay, 'twill spend a man.
   Face. Spend you! It will repair you when you are spent:
How do they live by their wits there, that have vented
Six times your fortunes?
   Kas. What, three thousand a-year!
   Face. Ay, forty thousand.
   Kas. Are there such?

Face. Ay, sir,
And gallants yet. Here's a young gentleman
Is born to nothing—[*Points to* DAPPER]—forty marks a-year,
Which I count nothing :—he is to be initiated,
And have a fly of the doctor. He will win you,
By irresistible luck, within this fortnight,
Enough to buy a barony. They will set him
Upmost, at the groom porters, all the Christmas :
And for the whole year through, at every place
Where there is play, present him with the chair ;
The best attendance, the best drink ; sometimes
Two glasses of canary, and pay nothing ;
The purest linen and the sharpest knife,
The partridge next his trencher ; and somewhere
The dainty nook in private with the dainty.
You shall have your ordinaries bid for him,
As playhouses for a poet ; and the master
Pray him aloud to name what dish he affects,
Which must be buttered shrimps ; and those that drink
To no mouth else, will drink to his, as being
The goodly president mouth of all the board.
  Kas. Do you not gull one ?
  Face. Ods, my life ! do you think it ?
You shall have a cast commander (can but get
In credit with a glover, or a spurrier,
For some two pair of either's ware aforehand),
Will by most swift posts, dealing with him,
Arrive at competent means to keep himself,
And be admired for 't.
  Kas. Will the doctor teach this ?
  Face. He will do more, sir : when your land is gone,
As men of spirit hate to keep earth long
In a vacation, when small money is stirring,
And ordinaries suspended till the term,
He'll show a perspective, where on one side
You shall behold the faces and the persons
Of all sufficient young heirs in town,
Whose bonds are current for commodity ;
On th' other side, the merchants' forms, and others,
That without help of any second broker,
Who would expect a share, will trust such parcels :
In the third square, the very street and sign
Where the commodity dwells, and does but wait
To be delivered, be it pepper, soap,
Hops, or tobacco, oatmeal, wood, or cheeses.
All which you may so handle, to enjoy
To your own use, and never stand obliged.
  Kas. I' faith ! is he such a fellow ?

Face. Why, Nab here knows him.
And then for making matches for rich widows,
Young gentlewomen, heirs, the fortunatest man!
He's sent to, far and near, all over England,
To have his counsel, and to know their fortunes.
　Kas. God's will, my suster shall see him.
　Face. I'll tell you, sir,
What he did tell me of Nab. It's a strange thing:—
By the way, you must eat no cheese, Nab, it breeds melancholy,
And that same melancholy breeds worms; but pass it:—
He told me honest Nab here was ne'er at tavern
But once in 's life.
　Drug. Truth, and no more I was not.
　Face. And then he was so sick——
　Drug. Could he tell you that too?
　Face How should I know it?
　Drug. In troth we had been a-shooting,
And had a piece of fat ram mutton to supper,
That lay so heavy o' my stomach——
　Face. And he has no head
To bear any wine; for what with the noise of the fiddlers
And care of his shop, for he dares keep no servants——
　Drug. My head did so ache——
　Face. As he was fain to be brought home,
The doctor told me: and then a good old woman ——
　Drug. Yes, faith—she dwells in Sea-coal Lane—did cure me,
With sodden ale and pellitory of the wall;
Cost me but twopence.—I had another sickness
Was worse than that.
　Face. Ay, that was with the grief
Thou took'st for being 'sessed at eighteen-pence
For the waterwork.
　Drug. In truth, and it was like
T' have cost me almost my life.
　Face. Thy hair went off?
　Drug. Yes, sir; 't was done for spite.
　Face. Nay, so says the doctor.
　Kas. Pray thee, tobacco boy, go fetch my suster;
I'll see this learned boy before I go,
And so shall she.
　Face. Sir, he is busy now;
But if you have a sister to fetch hither,
Perhaps your own pains may command her sooner,
And he by that time will be free.
　Kas. I go.   [*Exit.*
　Face. Drugger, she's thine: the damask!   [*Exit* ABEL.
　　　　　　　　　　　　　　　　Subtle and I
Must wrestle for her. [*Aside.*] Come on, Master Dapper,

To give your cause dispatch ; have you performed
The ceremonies were enjoined you?
   Dap. Yes, of the vinegar
And the clean shirt.
   Face. 'Tis well : that shirt may do you
More worship than you think. Your aunt's a-fire,
But that she will not show it, t' have a sight of you.
Have you provided for her grace's servants ?
   Dap. Yes, here are six score Edward shillings.
   Face. Good !
   Dap. And an old Harry sovereign.
   Face. Very good !
   Dap. And three James shillings, and an Elizabeth groat ;
Just twenty nobles.
   Face. Oh, you are too just.
I would you had had the other noble in Maries.
   Dap. I have some Philip and Maries.
   Face. Ay, those same
Are best of all : where are they ? Hark, the doctor.

Enter SUBTLE *disguised like a priest of Fairy, with a stripe of
cloth.*

   Sub. [*In a feigned voice.*] Is yet her grace's cousin come ?
   Face. He is come.
   Sub. And is he fasting ?
   Face. Yes.
   Sub. And hath cried *hum ?*
   Face. Thrice, you must answer.
   Dap. Thrice.
   Sub. And as oft *buz ?*
   Face. If you have, say.
   Dap. I have.
   Sub. Then, to her cuz,
Hoping that he hath vinegared his senses,
As he was bid, the Fairy Queen dispenses,
By me, this robe, the petticoat of fortune ;
Which that he straight put on, she doth importune.
And though to fortune near be her petticoat,
Yet nearer is her smock, the queen doth note :
And therefore, even of that a piece she hath sent,
Which, being a child, to wrap him in was rent ;
And prays him for a scarf he now will wear it,
With as much love as then her grace did tear it,
About his eyes—[*They blind him with the rag*]—to show he is
    fortunate.
And, trusting unto her to make his state,
He'll throw away all worldly pelf about him ;
Which that he will perform, she doth not doubt him.

Face. She need not doubt him, sir. Alas, he has nothing
But what he will part withal as willingly
Upon her grace's word—throw away your purse—
As she would ask it ;—handkerchiefs and all—
 [He throws away as they bid him.
She cannot bid that thing but he'll obey.—
If you have a ring about you, cast it off,
Or a silver seal at your wrist ; her grace will send
Her fairies here to search you, therefore deal
Directly with her highness : if they find
That you conceal a mite, you are undone.
 Dap. Truly, there's all.
 Face. All what ?
 Dap. My money : truly.
 Face. Keep nothing that is transitory about you.
Bid Dol play music.—[*Aside to* SUBTLE.]—Look, the elves are
 come [DOL *plays on the cittern within.*
To pinch you, if you tell not truth. Advise you.
 [They pinch him.
 Dap. Oh ! I have a paper with a spur-ryal in 't.
 Face. Ti, ti.
They knew 't, they say.
 Sub. Ti, ti, ti, ti. He has more yet.
 Face. Ti, ti-ti-ti. In the other pocket. [*Aside to* SUB.
 Sub. Titi, titi, titi, titi, titi.
They must pinch him or he will never confess, they say.
 [They pinch him again.
 Dap. Oh, oh !
 Face. Nay, pray you hold : he is her grace's nephew.
Ti, ti, ti ? What care you ? Good faith, you shall care.—
Deal plainly, sir, and shame the fairies. Show
You are innocent.
 Dap. By this good light, I have nothing.
 Sub. Ti, ti, ti, ti, to, ta. He does equivocate, she says :
Ti, ti, do ti, ti, ti, do, ti, da ; and swears by the *light* when he is
 blinded.
 Dap. By this good *dark*, I have nothing but a half-crown
Of gold about my wrist, that my love gave me ;
And a leaden heart I wore since she forsook me.
 Face. I thought 'twas something. And would you incur
Your aunt's displeasure for these trifles ? Come,
I had rather you had thrown away twenty half-crowns.
 [Takes it off.
You may wear your leaden heart still.—

Enter DOL *hastily.*
 How now !
 Sub. What news, Dol ?

Dol. Yonder's your knight, Sir Mammon.
Face. Ods lid, we never thought of him till now!
Where is he?
Dol. Here hard by: he is at the door.
Sub. And you are not ready, now! Dol, get his suit.
[*Exit* DOL.
He must not be sent back.
Face. Oh, by no means.
What shall we do with this same puffin here,
Now he's on the spit?
Sub. Why, lay him back awhile
With some device.

Re-enter DOL *with* FACE'S *clothes.*

—*Ti, ti, ti, ti, ti, ti.* Would her grace speak with me?
I come.—Help, Dol! [*Knocking without.*
Face. [*Speaks through the key-hole.*] Who's there? Sir Epicure,
My master's in the way. Please you to walk
Three or four turns, but till his back be turned,
And I am for you. Quickly, Dol!
Sub. Her grace
Commends her kindly to you, Master Dapper.
Dap. I long to see her grace.
Sub. She now is set
At dinner in her bed, and she has sent you
From her own private trencher a dead mouse,
And a piece of gingerbread, to be merry withal,
And stay your stomach, lest you faint with fasting.
Yet if you could hold out till she saw you, she says
It would be better for you.
Face. Sir, he shall
Hold out, an 'twere this two hours, for her highness;
I can assure you that. We will not lose
All we have done.
Sub. He must not see nor speak
To anybody till then.
Face. For that we'll put, sir,
A stay in 's mouth.
Sub. Of what?
Face. Of gingerbread.
Make you it fit. He that hath pleased her grace
Thus far, shall not now crinkle for a little.—
Gape, sir, and let him fit you.
[*They thrust a gag of gingerbread in his mouth.*
Sub. Where shall we now
Bestow him?
Dol. In the privy.

Sub. Come along, sir,
I now must show you Fortune's privy lodgings.
   Face. Are they perfumed, and his bath ready?
   Sub. All:
Only the fumigation's somewhat strong.
   Face. [*Speaking through the key-hole.*] Sir Epicure, I am
     yours, sir, by-and-by.   [*Exeunt with* DAPPER.

ACT IV.

SCENE I.—*A Room in* LOVEWIT'S *House.*

Enter FACE *and* MAMMON.

Face. Oh, sir, you are come in the only finest time.
Mam. Where's master?
Face. Now preparing for projection, sir.
Your stuff will be all changed shortly.
   Mam. Into gold?
   Face. To gold and silver, sir.
   Mam. Silver I care not for.
   Face. Yes, sir, a little to give beggars.
   Mam. Where's the lady?
   Face. At hand here. I have told her such brave things of you,
Touching your bounty and your noble spirit——
   Mam. Hast thou?
   Face As she is almost in her fit to see you.
But, good sir, no divinity in your conference,
For fear of putting her in rage.
   Mam. I warrant thee.
   Face. Six men will not hold her down; and then
If the old man should hear or see you——
   Mam. Fear not.
   Face. The very house, sir, would run mad. You know it,
How scrupulous he is, and violent,
'Gainst the least act of sin. Physic or mathematics,
Poetry, state, or frolic, as I told you,
She will endure, and never startle; but
No word of controversy.
   Mam. I am schooled, good Ulen.
   Face. And you must praise her house, remember that,
And her nobility.
   Mam. Let me alone:
No herald, no, nor antiquity, Lungs,
Shall do it better. Go.
   Face. Why, this is yet

A kind of modern happiness to have
Dol Common for a great lady.   [*Aside, and exit.*
   Mam. Now, Epicure,
Heighten thyself, talk to her all in gold ;
Rain her as many showers as Jove did drops
Unto his Danaë ; show the god a miser
Compared with Mammon. What ! The stone will do 't.
She shall feel gold, taste gold, hear gold, sleep gold ;
Nay, we will *concumbere* gold : I will be puissant
And mighty in my talk to her.

Re-enter FACE, *with* DOL *richly dressed.*

Here she comes.
   Face. To him, Dol, suckle him. This is the noble knight ;
I told your ladyship——
   Mam. Madam, with your pardon,
I kiss your vesture.
   Dol. Sir, I were uncivil
If I would suffer that; my lip to you, sir.
   Mam. I hope my lord, your brother, be in health, lady.
   Dol. My lord, my brother is, though I no lady, sir.
   Face. Well said my Guinea bird.   [*Aside.*
   Mam. Right noble madam——
   Face. Oh, we shall have most fierce idolatry,   [*Aside.*
   Mam. 'Tis your prerogative——
   Dol. Rather your courtesy.
   Mam. Were there nought else to enlarge your virtues to me,
These answers speak your breeding and your blood.
   Dol. Blood we boast none, sir, a poor baron's daughter.
   Mam. Poor! And gat you ? Profane not. Had your father
Slept all the happy remnant of his life
After that act, lien but there still and panted,
He had done enough to make himself, his issue,
And his posterity noble.
   Dol. Sir, although
We may be said to want the gilt and trappings,
The dress of honour, yet we strive to keep
The seeds and the materials.
   Mam. I do see
The old ingredient, virtue, was not lost,
Nor the drug money used to make your compound.
There is a strange nobility in your eye,
This lip, that chin ! Methinks you do resemble
One of the Austrian princes.
   Face. Very like!
Her father was an Irish costermonger.   [*Aside.*
   Mam. The House of Valois just had such a nose,

And such a forehead yet the Medici
Of Florence boast.
  Dol. Troth, and I have been likened
To all these princes.
  Face. I'll be sworn I heard it.
  Mam. I know not how! It is not any one,
But e'en the very choice of all their features.
  Face. I'll in, and laugh.   *[Aside, and exit.*
  Mam. A certain touch, or air,
That sparkles a divinity beyond
An earthly beauty!
  Dol. Oh, you play the courtier.
  Mam. Good lady, give me leave——
  Dol. In faith I may not,
To mock me, sir.
  Mam. To burn in this sweet flame;
The phœnix never knew a nobler death.
  Dol. Nay, now you court the courtier, and destroy
What you would build: this art, sir, in your words
Calls your whole faith in question.
  Mam. By my soul——
  Dol. Nay, oaths are made of the same air, sir.
  Mam. Nature
Never bestow'd upon mortality
A more unblamed, a more harmonious feature;
She played the step-dame in all faces else:
Sweet madam, let me be particular——
  Dol. Particular, sir! I pray you know your distance.
  Mam. In no ill sense, sweet lady; but to ask
How your fair graces pass the hours? I see
You are lodged here in the house of a rare man,
An excellent artist; but what's that to you?
  Dol. Yes, sir; I study here the mathematics
And distillation.
  Mam. Oh, I cry your pardon.
He's a divine instructor: can extract
The souls of all things by his art; call all
The virtues and the miracles of the sun
Into a temperate furnace; teach dull nature
What her own forces are. A man, the emperor
Has courted above Kelly; sent his medals
And chains to invite him.
  Dol. Ay, and for his physic, sir——
  Mam. Above the art of Æsculapius,
That drew the envy of the Thunderer!
I know all this, and more.
  Dol. Troth, I am taken, sir,
Whole with these studies, that contemplate nature.

Mam. It is a noble humour; but this form
Was not intended to so dark a use.
Had you been crooked, foul, of some coarse mould,
A cloister had done well; but such a feature
That might stand up the glory of a kingdom,
To live recluse, is a mere solecism,
Though in a nunnery. It must not be.
I muse, my lord your brother will permit it:
You should spend half my land first, were I he.
Does not this diamond better on my finger
Than in the quarry?
   Dol. Yes.
   Mam. Why, you are like it.
You were created, lady, for the light.
Here, you shall wear it; take it, the first pledge
Of what I speak, to bind you to believe me.
   Dol. In chains of adamant?
   Mam. Yes, the strongest bands.
And take a secret too—here, by your side,
Doth stand this hour the happiest man in Europe.
   Dol. You are contented, sir?
   Mam. Nay, in true being
The envy of princes and the fear of states.
   Dol. Say you so, Sir Epicure?
   Mam. Yes, and thou shalt prove it,
Daughter of honour. I have cast mine eye
Upon thy form, and I will rear this beauty
Above all styles.
   Dol. You mean no treason, sir?
   Mam. No, I will take away that jealousy.
I am the lord of the philosopher's stone,
And thou the lady.
   Dol. How sir! Have you that?
   Mam. I am the master of the mastery.
This day the good old wretch here o' the house
Has made it for us; now he's at projection.
Think therefore thy first wish now, let me hear it,
And it shall rain into thy lap, no shower,
But floods of gold, whole cataracts, a deluge,
To get a nation on thee.
   Dol. You are pleased, sir,
To work on the ambition of our sex.
   Mam. I am pleased the glory of her sex should know
This nook, here, of the Friars is no climate
For her to live obscurely in, to learn
Physic and surgery, for the constable's wife
Of some odd hundred in Essex; but come forth
And taste the air of palaces; eat, drink

The toils of empirics, and their boasted practice;
Tincture of pearl and coral, gold and amber;
Be seen at feasts and triumphs; have it asked,
What miracle she is; set all the eyes
Of court a-fire, like a burning glass,
And work them into cinders, when the jewels
Of twenty states adorn thee, and the light
Strikes out the stars! that when thy name is mentioned
Queens may look pale; and we but showing our love,
Nero's Poppæa may be lost in story!
Thus will we have it.
 Dol. I could well consent, sir.
But in a monarchy how will this be?
The prince will soon take notice, and both seize
You and your stone, it being a wealth unfit
For any private subject.
 Mam. If he knew it.
 Dol. Yourself do boast it, sir.
 Mam. To thee, my life.
 Dol. Oh, but beware, sir! you may come to end
The remnant of your days in a loathed prison,
By speaking of it.
 Mam. 'Tis no idle fear:
We'll therefore go withal, my girl, and live
In a free state, where we will eat our mullets
Soused in high-country wines, sup pheasants' eggs,
And have our cockles boiled in silver shells;
Our shrimps to swim again, as when they lived,
In a rare butter made of dolphins' milk,
Whose cream does look like opals: and with these
Delicate meats, set ourselves high for pleasure,
And take us down again, and then renew
Our youth and strength with drinking the elixir,
And so enjoy a perpetuity
Of life and lust! And thou shalt have thy wardrobe
Richer than nature's, still to change thyself,
And vary oftener, for thy pride, than she
Or art, her wise and almost equal servant.

Re-enter FACE.

 Face. Sir, you are too loud. I hear you every word
Into the laboratory. Some fitter place;
The garden, or great chamber above. How like you her?
 Mam. Excellent! Lungs. There's for thee.
[*Gives him money.*
 Face. But do you hear?
Good sir, beware, no mention of the rabbins.

Mam. We think not on 'em.   [*Exeunt* MAM. *and* DOL.
Face. Oh, it is well, sir.—Subtle!

Enter SUBTLE.

Dost thou not laugh?
Sub. Yes; are they gone?
Face. All's clear.
Sub. The widow is come.
Face. And your quarrelling disciple?
Sub. Ay.
Face. I must to my captainship again, then.
Sub. Stay, bring them in first.
Face. So I meant.   What is she?
A bonnibel?
Sub. I know not.
Face. We'll draw lots:
You'll stand to that?
Sub. What else?
Face. Oh, for a suit,
To fall now like a curtain, flap!
Sub. To the door, man.
Face. You'll have the first kiss, 'cause I am not ready. [*Exit.*
Sub. Yes, and perhaps hit you through both the nostrils.
Face. [*Within.*] Who would you speak with?
Kas. [*Within.*] Where's the captain?
Face. [*Within.*] Gone, sir,
About some business.
Kas. [*Within.*] Gone!
Face. [*Within.*] He'll return straight.
But Master Doctor, his lieutenant, is here.

Enter KASTRIL, *followed by* DAME PLIANT.

Sub. Come near, my worshipful boy, my *terræ fili*,
That is, my boy of land; make thy approaches:
Welcome; I know thy lusts and thy desires,
And I will serve and satisfy them.   Begin,
Charge me from thence, or thence, or in this line;
Here is my centre: ground thy quarrel.
Kas. You lie.
Sub. How, child of wrath and anger! the loud lie?
For what, my sudden boy?
Kas. Nay, that look you to,
I am aforehand.
Sub. Oh, this is no true grammar,
And as ill logic! You must render causes, child,
Your first and second intentions, know your canons
And your divisions, moods, degrees, and differences,
Your predicaments, substance, and accident,
Series, extern and intern, with their causes,

SCENE I.] *THE ALCHEMIST.* 67

Efficient, material, formal, final,
And have your elements perfect?
  Kas. What is this!
The angry tongue he talks in?   [*Aside.*
  Sub. That false precept
Of being aforehand has deceived a number,
And made them enter quarrels, oftentimes
Before they were aware ; and afterward
Against their wills.
  Kas. How must I do then, sir?
  Sub. I cry this lady mercy : she should first
Have been saluted. [*Kisses her.*] I do call you lady,
Because you are to be one ere 't be long,
My soft and buxom widow.
  Kas. Is she, i' faith?
  Sub. Yes, or my art is an egregious liar.
  Kas. How know you?
  Sub. By inspection on her forehead,
And subtlety of her lip, which must be tasted
Often, to make a judgment. [*Kisses her again.*]
                'Slight, she melts
Like a myrobolane:—here is yet a line,
In *rivo frontis*, tells me he is no knight.
  Dame P. What is he then, sir?
  Sub. Let me see your hand.
Oh, your *lina fortunæ* makes it plain ;
And stella here *in Monte Veneris*.
But, most of all, *junctura annularis*.
He is a soldier, or a man of art, lady,
But shall have some great honour shortly.
  Dame P. Brother,
He's a rare man, believe me!

       Re-enter FACE *in his uniform.*

  Kas. Hold your peace.
Here comes the t' other rare man.— Save you, captain.
  Face. Good Master Kastril! Is this your sister?
  Kas. Ay, sir.
Please you to kuss her, and be proud to know her.
  Face. I shall be proud to know you, lady.   [*Kisses her.*
  Dame P. Brother,
He calls me lady too.
  Kas. Ay, peace : I heard it.   [*Takes her aside.*
  Face. The count is come.
  Sub. Where is he?
  Face. At the door.
  Sub. Why, you must entertain him.

Face. What will you do
With these the while?
　Sub. Why, have them up, and show them
Some fustian book, or the dark glass.
　Face. 'Fore God,
She is a delicate dab-chick! I must have her.　　　　　*[Exit.*
　Sub. Must you! ay, if your fortune will, you must.—
Come sir, the captain will come to us presently:
I 'll have you to my chamber of demonstrations,
Where I will show you both the grammar and logic
And rhetoric of quarrelling; my whole method
Drawn out in tables; and my instrument,
That hath several scales upon 't, shall make you
Able to quarrel at a straw's breadth by moonlight.
And, lady, I 'll have you look in a glass,
Some half an hour, but to clear your eyesight,
Against you see your fortune; which is greater
Than I may judge upon the sudden, trust me.
　　　　　[Exit, followed by KAS. *and* Dame P.

　　　　　Re-enter FACE.

　Face. Where are you, doctor?
　Sub. [*Within.*] I 'll come to you presently.
　Face. I will have this same widow, now I have seen her,
On any composition.

　　　　　Re-enter SUBTLE.

　Sub. What do you say?
　Face. Have you disposed of them?
　Sub. I have sent them up.
　Face. Subtle, in troth, I needs must have this widow.
　Sub. Is that the matter?
　Face. Nay, but hear me.
　Sub. Go to,
If you rebel once, Dol shall know it all:
Therefore be quiet, and obey your chance.
　Face. Nay, thou art so violent now. Do but conceive
Thou art old and canst not serve——
　Sub. Who cannot? I?
'Slight, I will serve her with thee, for a——
　Face. Nay,
But understand: I 'll give you composition.
　Sub. I will not treat with thee; what! sell my fortune?
'Tis better than my birthright. Do not murmur:
Win her, and carry her. If you grumble, Dol
Knows it directly.
　Face. Well, sir, I am silent.
Will you go help to fetch in Don in state?　　　　　*[Exit.*

Sub. I follow you, sir: we must keep Face in awe,
Or he will overlook us like a tyrant.

Re-enter FACE, *introducing* SURLY *disguised as a Spaniard.*

Brain of a tailor! who comes here? Don John!
  Sur. Senores, beso las manos a vuestras mercedes.
  Sub. Would you had stooped a little, and kissed our *anos!*
  Face. Peace, Subtle.
  Sub. Stab me: I shall never hold, man.
He looks in that deep ruff like a head in a platter,
Served in by a short cloak upon two trestles.
  Face. Or, what do you say to a collar of brawn, cut down
Beneath the souse, and wriggled with a knife?
  Sub. 'Slud, he does look too fat to be a Spaniard.
  Face. Perhaps some Fleming or some Hollander got him
In D'Alva's time; Count Egmont's bastard.
  Sub. Don,
Your scurvy, yellow, Madrid face is welcome.
  Sur. Gratia.
  Sub. He speaks out of a fortification.
Pray God he have no squibs in those deep sets.
  Sur. Por dios, senores, muy linda casa!
  Sub. What says he?
  Face. Praises the house, I think;
I know no more but 's action.
  Yes, the *casa*,
My precious Diego, will prove fair enough
To cozen you in. Do you mark? You shall
Be cozened, Diego.
  Face. Cozened, do you see,
My worthy Donzel, cozened.
  Sur. Entiendo.
  Sub. Do you intend it? So do we, dear Don.
Have you brought pistolets or portagues,
My solemn Don?—Dost thou feel any?
  Face. [*Feels his pockets.*] Full.
  Sub. You shall be emptied, Don, pumped and drawn
Dry, as they say.
  Face. Milked, in troth, sweet Don.
  Sub. See all the monsters; the great lion of all, Don.
  Sur. Con licencia, se puede ver a esta senora?
  Sub. What talks he now?
  Face. Of the senora.
  Sub. Oh, Don,
That is the lioness, which you shall see
Also, my Don.
  Face. 'Slid, Subtle, how shall we do?
  Sub. For what?
  Face. Why Dol's employed, you know.

Sub. That's true,
'Fore heaven I know not: he must stay, that's all.
  Face. Stay! that he must not by no means.
  Sub. No! Why?
  Face. Unless you'll mar all. 'Slight, he will suspect it:
And then he will not pay, not half so well.
This is a travelled master, and does know
All the delays; a notable hot rascal,
And looks already rampant.
  Sub. 'Sdeath, and Mammon must not be troubled.
  Face. Mammon! in no case.
  Sub. What shall we do then?
  Face. Think: you must be sudden.
  Sur. Entiendo que la senora es tan hermosa, que codicio tan
    à verla, como la bien aventurança de mi vida.
  Face. Mi vida! 'Slid, Subtle, he puts me in mind o' the widow.
What dost thou say to draw her to it, ha!
And tell her 't is her fortune? All our venture
Now lies upon 't. It is but one man more,
Which of us chance to have her: and beside,—
What dost thou think on 't, Subtle?
  Sub. Who, I? Why——
  Face. The credit of our house too is engaged.
  Sub. You made me an offer for my share erewhile.
What wilt thou give me i' faith?
  Face. Oh, by that light
I'll not buy now: you know your doom to me.
E'en take your lot, obey your chance, sir; win her,
And wear her, sir, for me.
  Sub. 'Slight, I'll not have her then.
  Face. It is the common cause; therefore bethink you.
Dol else must know it as you said.
  Sub. I care not.
  Sur. Senores, porque se tarda tanta?
  Sub. Faith, I am not fit, I am old.
  Face. That's now no reason, sir.
  Sur. Puede ser, de hazer burla de mi amor?
  Face. You hear the Don too? by this air I call,
And loose the hinges: Dol!
  Sub. A plague of hell——
  Face. Will you then do?
  Sub. You are a terrible rogue!
I'll think of this: will you, sir, call the widow?
  Face. Yes, and I'll take her too with all her faults,
Now I do think on 't better.
  Sub. With all my heart, sir;
Am I discharged o' the lot?
  Face. As you please.

Sub. Hands. [*They take hands.*
Face. Remember now, that upon any change
You never claim her.
Sub. Much good joy and health to you, sir.
Marry her so! Fate, let me wed a witch first.
Sur. Por estas honradas barbas——
Sub. He swears by his beard.
Dispatch, and call the brother too. [*Exit* FACE.
Sur. Tiengo duda, senores,
Que no me hagan alguna traycion.
Sub. How, issue on? yes, præsto, senor. Please you
Enthratha the *chambratha*, worthy Don:
Where if you please the fates, in your *bathada*,
You shall be soaked, and stroked, and tubbed, and rubbed,
And scrubbed, and fubbed, dear Don, before you go.
You shall in faith, my scurvy baboon Don.
Be curried, clawed, and flawed, and tawed indeed.
I will the heartlier go about it now,
And make the widow yours so much the sooner,
To be revenged on this impetuous Face:
The quickly doing of it is the grace. [*Exeunt* SUB. *and* SURLY.

SCENE II.—*Another Room in the same.*

Enter FACE, KASTRIL, *and* Dame PLIANT.

Face. Come, lady: I knew the doctor would not leave
Till he had found the very nick of her fortune.
Kas. To be a countess, say you, a Spanish countess, sir?
Dame P. Why, is that better than an English countess?
Face. Better! 'Slight, make you that a question, lady?
Kas. Nay, she is a fool, captain, you must pardon her.
Face. Ask from your courtier, to your inns of court man,
To your mere milliner; they will tell you all,
Your Spanish gennet is the best horse; your Spanish
Stoup is the best garb: your Spanish beard
Is the best cut; your Spanish ruffs are the best
Wear; your Spanish pavin the best dance;
Your Spanish titillation in a glove
The best perfume: and for your Spanish pike
And Spanish blade, let your poor captain speak—
Here comes the doctor.

Enter SUBTLE, *with a paper.*

Sub. My most honoured lady,
For so I am now to style you, having found

By this my scheme you are to undergo
An honourable fortune very shortly,
What will you say now, if some——
   Face. I have told her all, sir ;
And her right worshipful brother here, that she shall be
A countess ; do not delay them, sir : a Spanish countess.
   Sub. Still, my scarce-worshipful captain, you can keep
No secret ! Well, since he has told you, madam,
Do you forgive him, and I do.
   Kas. She shall do that, sir ;
I 'll look to 't, 't is my charge.
   Sub. Well then ; nought rests
But that she fit her love now to her fortune.
   Dame P. Truly, I shall never brook a Spaniard.
   Sub. No !
   Dame P. Never since eighty-eight could I abide them,
And that was some three years afore I was born, in truth.
   Sub. Come, you must love him, or be miserable ;
Choose which you will.
   Face. By this good rush, persuade her,
She will cry strawberries else within this twelvemonth.
   Sub. Nay, shads and mackerel, which is worse.
   Face. Indeed, sir !
   Kas. Ods lid, you shall love him, or I 'll kick you
   Dame P. Why,
I 'll do as you will have me, brother.
   Kas. Do,
Or by this hand I 'll maul you.
   Face. Nay, good sir,
Be not so fierce.
   Sub. No, my enraged child ;
She will be ruled. What, when she comes to taste
The pleasures of a countess ! to be courted——
   Face. And kissed, and ruffled !
   Sub. Ay, behind the hangings.
   Face. And then come forth in pomp !
   Sub. And know her state !
   Face. Of keeping all the idolators of the chamber
Barer to her than at their prayers !
   Sub. Is served
Upon the knee !
   Face. And has her pages, ushers,
Footmen, and coaches——
   Sub. Her six mares——
   Face. Nay, eight !
   Sub. To hurry her through London, to the Exchange,
Bethlem, the china-houses——
   Face. Yes, and have

The citizens gape at her, and praise her tires,
And my lord's humble bands, that ride with her.
   Kas. Most brave! By this hand, you are not my suster
If you refuse.
   Dame P. I will not refuse, brother.

Enter SURLY.

   Sur. Que es esto, senores, que non se venga?
Esta tardanza me mata!
   Face. It is the Count come:
The doctor knew he would be here, by his art.
   Sub. En gallanta madama, Don! gallantissima!
   Sur. Por todos los dioses, la mas acabada
Hermosura, que hevisto en mi vida!
   Face. Is't not a gallant language that they speak?
   Kas. An admirable language! Is't not French?
   Face. No, Spanish, sir.
   Kas. It goes like law-French,
And that, they say, is the courtliest language.
   Face. List, sir.
   Sur. El sol ha perdido su lumbre, con el
Resplandor que traeesta dama! Valga me dios!
   Face. He admires your sister.
   Kas. Must not she make curtsey?
   Sub. Ods will, she must go to him, man, and kiss him!
It is the Spanish fashion for the women
To make first court.
   Face. 'Tis true he tells you, sir:
His art knows all.
   Sur. Porque no se acude?
   Kas. He speaks to her, I think.
   Face. That he does, sir.
   Sur. Por el amor de dios, que es esto, que se tarda?
   Kas. Nay, see: she will not understand him! Gull,
Noddy.
   Dame P. What say you, brother?
   Kas. Ass, my suster.
Go kuss him, as the cunning man would have you;
I'll thrust a pin in your back else.
   Face. Oh no, sir.
   Sur. Senora mia, mi persona esta muy indigna
De allegar atanta Hermosura.
   Face. Does he not use her bravely?
   Kas. Bravely, i' faith!
   Face. Nay, he will use her better.
   Kas. Do you think so?
   Sur. Senora si sera servida, entremus.
[Exit with DAME PLIANT.

Kas. Where does he carry her?
Face. Into the garden, sir;
Take you no thought: I must interpret for her.
　Sub. Give Dol the word.—[*Aside to* FACE, *who goes out.*]—
Come, my fierce child, advance,
We'll to our quarrelling lesson again.
　Kas. Agreed.
I love a Spanish boy with all my heart.
　Sub. Nay, and by this means, sir, you shall be brother
To a great count.
　Kas. Ay, I knew that at first.
This match will advance the house of the Kastrils.
　Sub. Pray God your sister prove but pliant!
　Kas. Why,
Her name is so, by her other husband.
　Sub. How?
　Kas. The Widow Pliant. Knew you not that?
　Sub. No, faith, sir;
Yet, by erection of her figure, I guessed it.
Come, let's go practise.
　Kas. Yes, but do you think, doctor,
I e'er shall quarrel well?
　Sub. I warrant you.　　　　　　　　　　　　　　[*Exeunt.*

SCENE III.—*Another Room in the same.*

Enter DOL *in her fit of raving, followed by* MAMMON.

　Dol. For after Alexander's death——
　Mam. Good lady——
　Dol. That Perdiccas and Antigonus were slain,
The two that stood, Seleuc', and Ptolemy——
　Man. Madam.
　Dol. Made up the two legs, and the fourth beast,
That was Gog-north and Egypt-south: which after
Was called Gog-iron-leg and South-iron-leg——
　Mam. Lady——
　Dol. And then Gog-horned. So was Egypt too:
Then Egypt-clay-leg and Gog-clay-leg——
　Mam. Sweet madam——
　Dol. And last Gog-dust and Egypt-dust, which fall
In the last link of the fourth chain. And these
Be stars in story, which none see or look at——
　Mam. What shall I do?
　Dol. For, as he says, except
We call the rabbins, and the heathen Greeks——
　Mam. Dear lady——

Dol. To come from Salem and from Athens,
And teach the people of Great Britain——

Enter FACE, *hastily, in his Servant's dress.*

Face. What's the matter, sir?
Dol. To speak the tongue of Eber and Javan——
Mam. Oh,
She's in her fit.
Dol. We shall know nothing——
Face. Death, sir,
We are undone!
Dol. Where then a learned linguist
Shall see the ancient used communion
Of vowels and consonants——
Face. My master will hear!
Dol. A wisdom which Pythagoras held most high——
Mam. Sweet honourable lady!
Dol. To comprise
All sounds of voices, in few marks of letters——
Face. Nay, you must never hope to lay her now.
                                         [*They all speak.*
Dol. And so we may arrive by Talmud skill
And profane Greek, to raise the building up
Of Helen's house against the Ishmaelite,
King of Thogarma, and his habergions
Brimstony, blue, and fiery; and the force
Of King Abaddon, and the beast of Cittim:
Which Rabbi David Kimchi, Onkelos,
And Aben Ezra do interpret Rome.
Face. How did you put her into 't?   [*Together with* DOL.
Mam. Alas! I talked
Of a fifth monarchy I would erect.
With the philosopher's stone, by chance, and she
Falls on the other four straight.
Face. Out of Broughton!
I told you so. 'Slid, stop her mouth.
Mam. Is 't best?
Face. She'll never leave else. If the old man hear her——
Sub. [*Within.*] What's to do there?
Face. Oh, we are lost! Now she hears him, she is quiet.

Enter SUBTLE; *they run different ways.*

Mam. Where shall I hide me!
Sub. How! what sight is here?
Close deeds of darkness, and that shun the light!
Bring him again. Who is he? What, my son!
Oh, I have lived too long.

Mam. Nay, good, dear father,
There was no evil purpose.
  Sub. Not! and flee me,
When I come in?
  Mam. That was my error.
  Sub. Error!
Guilt, guilt, my son: give it the right name. No marvel
If I found check in our great work within,
When such affairs as these were managing.
  Mam. Why, have you so?
  Sub. It has stood still this half-hour:
And all the rest of our less works gone back.
Where is the instrument of wickedness,
My lewd false drudge?
  Mam. Nay, good sir, blame not him;
Believe me, 't was against his will or knowledge:
I saw her by chance.
  Sub. Will you commit more sin,
To excuse a varlet?
  Mam. By my hope 't is true sir.
  Sub. Nay, then I wonder less, if you, for whom
The blessing was prepared, would so tempt heaven,
And lose your fortunes.
  Mam. Why, sir?
  Sub. This will retard
The work a month at least.
  Mam. Why, if it do,
What remedy? But think it not, good father:
Our purposes were honest.
  Sub. As they were,
So the reward will prove.— [*A loud explosion within.*
                   How now! Ah me!
God and all saints be good to us.

              Re-enter FACE.
                   What's that?
  Face. Oh, sir, we are defeated! All the works
Are flown *in fumo*, every glass is burst:
Furnace and all rent down; as if a bolt
Of thunder had been driven through the house.
Retorts, receivers, pelicans, bolt heads,
All struck in shivers!   [SUBTLE *falls down as in a swoon.*
         Help, good sir! Alas,
Coldness and death invades him. Nay, Sir Mammon,
Do the fair offices of a man! You stand
As you were readier to depart than he. [*Knocking within.*
Who's there? My lord her brother is come.
  Mam. Ha, Lungs!

Face. His coach is at the door. Avoid his sight,
For he's as furious as his sister's mad.
  Mam. Alas!
  Face. My brain is quite undone with the fume, sir,
I ne'er must hope to be mine own man again.
  Mam. Is all lost, Lungs? Will nothing be preserved
Of all our cost?
  Face. Faith, very little, sir;
A peck of coals or so, which is cold comfort, sir.
  Mam. Oh, my voluptuous mind! I am justly punished.
  Face. And so am I, sir.
  Mam. Cast forth from all my hopes——
  Face. Nay, certainties, sir.
  Mam. By mine own base affections.
  Sub. [*Seeming to come to himself.*] Oh, the curst fruits of vice
    and lust!
  Mam. Good father,
It was my sin. Forgive it.
  Sub. Hangs my roof
Over us still, and will not fall, O justice,
Upon us for this wicked man!
  Face. Nay, look, sir,
You grieve him now with staying in his sight;
Good, sir, the nobleman will come too, and take you,
And that may breed a tragedy.
  Mam. I'll go.
  Face. Ay, and repent at home, sir. It may be,
For some good penance you may have it yet;
A hundred pounds to the box at Bethlem——
  Mam. Yes.
  Face. For the restoring such as have their wits.
  Mam. I'll do't.
  Face. I'll send one to you to receive it.
  Mam. Do.
Is no projection left?
  Face. All flown, or stinks, sir.
  Mam. Will nought be saved that's good for med'cine,
    think'st thou?
  Face. I cannot tell, sir. There will be perhaps
Something about the scraping of the shards
Will cure the itch—though not your itch of mind, sir. [*Aside.*
It shall be saved for you, and sent home. Good, sir.
This way for fear the lord should meet you.
                                            [*Exit* MAMMON.
  Sub. [*Raising his head.*] Face!
  Face. Ay.
  Sub. Is he gone?
  Face. Yes, and as heavily

As all the gold he hoped for were in 's blood.
Let us be light, though.
   Sub. [*Leaping up.*] Ay, as balls, and bound
And hit our heads against the roof for joy:
There's so much of our care now cast away.
   Face. Now to our Don.
   Sub. Yes, your young widow by this time
Is made a countess, Face; she has been in travail
Of a young heir for you.
   Face. Good, sir.
   Sub. Off with your case,
And greet her kindly, as a bridegroom should,
After these common hazards.
   Face. Very well, sir,
Will you go fetch Don Diego off the while?
   Sub. And fetch him over too, if you'll be pleased, sir:
Would Dol were in her place, to pick his pockets now!
   Face. Why, you can do't as well, if you would set to't.
I pray you prove your virtue.
   Sub. For your sake, sir.   [*Exeunt.*

     Scene IV.—*Another Room in the same.*

     Enter Surly *and* Dame Pliant.

   Sur. Lady, you see into what hands you are fallen;
'Mongst what a nest of villains! and how near
Your honour was to have catched a certain flaw,
Through your credulity, had I but been
So punctually forward, as place, time,
And other circumstances would have made a man;
For you're a handsome woman: would you were wise too!
I am a gentleman come here disguised,
Only to find the knaveries of this citadel;
And where I might have wronged your honour, and have not,
I claim some interest in your love. You are,
They say, a widow, rich; and I'm a bachelor,
Worth nought: your fortunes may make me a man,
As mine have preserved you a woman. Think upon it,
And whether I have deserved you or no.
   Dame P. I will, sir.
   Sur. And for these household rogues, let me alone
To treat with them
             Enter Subtle.
   Sub. How doth my noble Diego,
And my dear Madam Countess? Hath the Count
Been courteous, lady? liberal and open?
Donzel, methinks you look melancholic
After your interview, and scurvy: truly

I do not like the dulness of your eye ;
It hath a heavy cast, 't is upsee Dutch,
And says you are a lumpish cavalier.
Be lighter, I will make your pockets so.
          [*Attempts to pick them.*
 Sur. [*Throws open his cloak.*] Will you, Don Bawd and pick-
   purse? [*Strikes him down.*] How now! Reel you?
Stand up, sir; you shall find, since I am so heavy,
I'll give you equal weight.
 Sub. Help! murder!
 Sur. No, sir,
There's no such thing intended : a good cart
And a clean whip shall ease you of that fear.
I am the Spanish Don *that should be cozen'd—
Do you see, cozen'd!* Where's your Captain Face,
That parcel broker, and whole-bawd, all rascal !

    Enter FACE *in his uniform.*

 Face. How, Surly !
 Sur. Oh, make your approach, good captain.
I have found from whence your copper rings and spoons
Come, now, wherewith you cheat abroad in taverns.
'Twas here you learned to anoint your boot with brimstone,
Then rub men's gold on 't for a kind of touch,
And say 'twas nought, when you had changed the colour,
That you might have it for nothing. And this doctor,
Your sooty, smoky-bearded compeer, he
Will close you so much gold, in a bolt's head,
And, on a turn, convey in the stead another
With sublimed mercury, that shall burst in the heat,
And fly out all *in fumo* ! Then weeps Mammon ;
Then swoons his worship. [FACE *slips out.*] Or, he is the
  Faustus
That casteth figures and can conjure, cures
Plagues, piles, and pox, by the ephemerides,
And holds intelligence while you send in—
Captain—what! is he gone?—damsels with child,
Wives that are barren, or the waiting-maid
With the green sickness. [*Seizes* SUBTLE *as he is retiring.*
     Nay, sir, you must tarry,
Though he be 'scaped, and answer by the ears, sir.

    Re-enter FACE *with* KASTRIL.

 Face. Why, now's the time, if ever you will quarrel
Well, as they say, and be a true-born child :
The doctor and your sister both are abused.
 Kas. Where is he? Which is he? He is a slave.

Whate'er he is, and he must answer me.—Are you
The man, sir, I would know?

Sur. I should be loth, sir,
To confess so much.

Kas. Then you lie in your throat.

Sur. How!

Face. [*To* KASTRIL.] A very errant rogue, sir, and a cheater,
Employed here by another conjurer,
That does not love the doctor, and would cross him
If he knew how.

Sur. Sir, you are abused.

Kas. You lie;
And 't is no matter.

Face. Well said, sir! He is
The impudentest rascal——

Sur. You are indeed: will you hear me, sir?

Face. By no means: bid him begone.

Kas. Begone, sir, quickly.

Sur. This is strange!—Lady, do you inform your brother.

Face. There is not such a foist in all the town,
The doctor had him presently; and finds yet
The Spanish Count will come here.—Bear up, Subtle. [*Aside.*

Sub. Yes, sir, he must appear within this hour.

Face. And yet this rogue would come in a disguise,
By the temptation of another spirit,
To trouble our art, though he could not hurt it!

Kas. Ay,
I know—Away—[*to his Sister*]—you talk like a foolish mauther.

Sur. Sir, all is truth she says.

Face. Do not believe him, sir.
He is the lyingest swabber! Come your ways, sir.

Sur. You are valiant out of company!

Kas. Yes; how then, sir?

Enter DRUGGER, *with a piece of damask.*

Face. Nay, here 's an honest fellow too, that knows him
And all his tricks. Make good what I say, Abel;
This cheater would have cozened thee o' the widow.
[*Aside to* DRUG.
He owes this honest Drugger here, seven pounds,
He has had on him, in twopen'orths of tobacco.

Drug. Yes, sir.
And he has damned himself three terms to pay me.

Face. And what does he owe for lotium?

Drug. Thirty shillings, sir;
And for six syringes.

Sur. Hydra of villainy!

Sur. Nay, sir; you must quarrel him out o' the house.

Kas. I will:
—Sir, if you get not out o' doors you lie?
And you are a pimp.
  Sur. Why, this is madness, sir,
Not valour in you; I must laugh at this.
  Kas. It is my humour: you are a pimp and a trig,
And an *Amadis de Gaul* or a Don Quixote.
  Drug. Or a knight o' the curious coxcomb, do you see?

Enter ANANIAS.

  Ana. Peace to the household!
  Kas. I'll keep peace for no man.
  Ana. Casting of dollars is concluded lawful.
  Kas. Is he the constable?
  Sub. Peace, Ananias.
  Face. No, sir.
  Kas. Then you are an otter, a shad, a whit, a very tim.
  Sur. You'll hear me, sir?
  Kas. I will not.
  Ana. What is the motive?
  Sub. Zeal in the young gentleman
Against his Spanish slops.
  Ana. They are profane,
Lewd, superstitious, and idolatrous breeches.
  Sur. New rascals!
  Kas. Will you begone, sir?
  Ana. Avoid, Satan!
Thou art not of the light: That ruff of pride
About thy neck betrays thee; and is the same
With that which the unclean birds, in seventy-seven,
Were seen to prank it with on divers coasts:
Thou look'st like Antichrist, in that lewd hat.
  Sur. I must give way.
  Kas. Begone, sir.
  Sur. But I'll take
A course with you——
  Ana. Depart, proud Spanish fiend!
  Sur. Captain and Doctor.
  Ana. Child of perdition!
  Kas. Hence, sir!   [*Exit* SURLY.
Did I not quarrel bravely?
  Face. Yes, indeed, sir.
  Kas. Nay, and I give my mind to't, I shall do't.
  Face. Oh, you must follow, sir, and threaten him tame:
He'll turn again else.
  Kas. I'll re-turn him then.   [*Exit.*
                    [SUBTLE *takes* ANANIAS *aside.*
  Face. Drugger, this rogue prevented us for thee:

We had determined that thou should'st have come
In a Spanish suit, and have carried her so ; and he,
A brokerly slave! goes, puts it on himself.
Hast brought the damask?
   Drug. Yes, sir.
   Face. Thou must borrow
A Spanish suit : hast thou no credit with the players?
   Drug. Yes, sir ; did you never see me play the fool?
   Face. I know not, Nab :—Thou shalt, if I can help it.—
                                                                      [*Aside.*
Hieronimo's old cloak, ruff, and hat will serve ;
I'll tell thee more when thou bring'st 'em.   [*Exit* DRUGGER.
   Ana. Sir, I know
The Spaniard hates the brethren, and hath spies
Upon their actions : and that this was one
I make no scruple.—But the holy synod
Have been in prayer and meditation for it ;
And 'tis revealed, no less to them than me,
That casting of money is most lawful.
   Sub. True,
But here I cannot do it ; if the house
Should chance to be suspected, all would out,
And we be locked up in the Tower for ever,
To make gold there for the state, never come out ;
And then are you defeated.
   Ana. I will tell
This to the elders and the weaker brethren,
That the whole company of the separation
May join in humble prayer again.
   Sub. And fasting.
   Ana. Yea, for some fitter place. The peace of mind
Rest with these walls!   [*Exit.*
   Sub. Thanks, courteous Ananias.
   Face. What did he come for?
   Sub. About casting dollars,
Presently out of hand. And so I told him
A Spanish minister came here to spy
Against the faithful——
   Face. I conceive. Come, Subtle,
Thou art so down upon the least disaster!
How wouldst thou ha' done, if I had not helped thee out?
   Sub. I thank thee, Face, for the angry boy, i' faith.
   Face. Who would have looked it should have been that rascal
Surly? he had dyed his beard and all. Well, sir,
Here's damask come to make you a suit.
   Sub. Where's Drugger?
   Face. He is gone to borrow me a Spanish habit ;
I'll be the count, now.

Sub. But where's the widow?
Face. Within, with my lord's sister; Madam Dol
Is entertaining her.
Sub. By your favour, Face,
Now she is honest, I will stand again.
Face. You will not offer it.
Sub. Why?
Face. Stand to your word,
Or—here comes Dol, she knows——
Sub. You are tyrannous still.

Enter DOL, *hastily.*

Face. Strict for my right.—How now, Dol! Hast told her,
The Spanish Count will come?
Dol. Yes; but another is come
You little looked for!
Face. Who is that?
Dol. Your master;
The master of the house.
Sub. How, Dol!
Face. She lies,
This is some trick. Come, leave your quiblins, Dorothy.
Dol. Look out and see. [FACE *goes to the window.*
Sub. Art thou in earnest?
Dol. 'Slight,
Forty o' the neighbours are about him, talking.
Face. 'Tis he, by this good day.
Dol. 'Twill prove ill day
For some on us.
Face. We are undone, and taken.
Dol. Lost, I'm afraid.
Sub. You said he would not come
While there died one a week within the liberties.
Face. No: 'twas within the walls.
Sub. Was't so! cry you mercy.
I thought the liberties. What shall we do now, Face?
Face. Be silent: not a word, if he call or knock,
I'll into mine own shape again and meet him,
Of Jeremy, the butler. In the meantime,
Do you two pack up all the goods and purchase
That we can carry in the two trunks. I'll keep him
Off for to-day, if I cannot longer: and then
At night I'll ship you both away to Ratcliff,
Where we will meet to-morrow, and there we'll share.
Let Mammon's brass and pewter keep the cellar;
We'll have another time for that. But, Dol,
Pr'ythee go heat a little water quickly;

Subtle must shave me: all my captain's beard
Must off, to make me appear smooth Jeremy.
You'll do it?
   Sub. Yes, I'll shave you, as well as I can.
   Face. And not cut my throat, but trim me?
   Sub. You shall see, sir.   [*Exeunt.*

ACT V.

SCENE I.—*Before* LOVEWIT'S *Door.*

Enter LOVEWIT, *with several of the* Neighbours.

   Love. Has there been such resort, say you?
   1*st Nei.* Daily, sir.
   2*nd Nei.* And nightly, too.
   3*rd Nei.* Ay, some as brave as lords.
   4*th Nei.* Ladies and gentlewomen.
   5*th Nei.* Citizens' wives.
   1*st Nei.* And knights.
   6*th Nei.* In coaches.
   2*nd Nei.* Yes, and oyster women.
   1*st Nei.* Beside other gallants.
   3*d Nei.* Sailors' wives.
   4*th Nei.* Tobacco men.
   5*th Nei.* Another Pimlico!
   Love. What should my knave advance,
To draw this company? He hung out no banners
Of a strange calf with five legs to be seen,
Or a huge lobster with six claws?
   6*th Nei.* No, sir.
   3*rd Nei.* We had gone in then, sir.
   Love. He has no gift
Of teaching in the nose that e'er I knew of.
You saw no bills set up that promised cure
Of agues, or the tooth-ache?
   2*nd Nei.* No such thing, sir.
   Love. Nor heard a drum struck for baboons or puppets?
   5*th Nei.* Neither, sir.
   Love. What device should he bring forth now?
I love a teeming wit as I love my nourishment;
'Pray God he have not kept such open house
That he hath sold my hangings and my bedding!
I left him nothing else. If he have eat them,
A plague o' the moth, say I! Sure he has got
Some tempting pictures to call all this ging!
The friar and the nun; or the new motion
Of the knight's courser and the parson's mare;

The boy of six year old who is a man;
Or 't may be he has the fleas that run at tilt
Upon a table, or some dog to dance.
When saw you him?
  1st Nei. Who, sir, Jeremy?
  2nd Nei. Jeremy Butler?
We saw him not this month.
  Love. How!
  4th Nei. Not these five weeks, sir.
  6th Nei. These six weeks at the least.
  Love. You amaze me, neighbours!
  5th Nei. Sure, if your worship know not where he is,
He's slipped away.
  6th Nei. Pray God, he be not made away.
  Love. Ha! it's no time to question, then.

                             [*Knocks at the Door.*

  6th Nei. About
Some three weeks since, I heard a doleful cry,
As I sat up a-mending my wife's stockings.
  Love. 'Tis strange that none will answer! Didst thou hear
A cry, say'st thou?
  6th Nei. Yes, sir, like unto a man
That had been strangled an hour, and could not speak.
  2nd Nei. I heard it too, just this day three weeks at two
      o'clock
Next morning.
  Love. These be miracles, or you make them so.
A man an hour strangled, and could not speak,
And both you heard him cry?
  3rd Nei. Yes, downward, sir.
  Love. Thou art a wise fellow. Give me thy hand, I pray thee,
What trade art thou on?
  3rd Nei. A smith, an 't please your worship.
  Love. A smith! then lend me thy help to get this door open.
  3rd Nei. That I will presently, sir, but fetch my tools.

                                          [*Exit.*

  1st Nei. Sir, best to knock again, afore you break it.
  Love. [*Knocks again.*] I will.

           Enter FACE, *in his butler's livery.*

  Face. What mean you, sir?
  1st, 2nd, 4th Nei. Oh, here's Jeremy!
  Face. Good sir, come from the door.
  Love. Why, what's the matter?
  Face. Yet farther, you are too near yet.
  Love. In the name of wonder,
What means the fellow!
  Face. The house, sir, has been visited.

Love. What, with the plague? stand thou then farther.
Face. No, sir,
I had it not.
Love. Who had it then? I left
None else but thee in the house.
Face. Yes, sir, my fellow,
The cat that kept the buttery, had it on her
A week before I spied it; but I got her
Conveyed away in the night: and so I shut
The house up for a month——
Love. How!
Face. Purposing then, sir,
To have burnt rose-vinegar, treacle, and tar,
And have made it sweet, that you should ne'er have known it;
Because I knew the news would but afflict you, sir.
Love. Breathe less, and farther off! Why this is stranger:
The neighbours tell me all here that the doors
Have still been open——
Face. How, sir!
Love. Gallants, men and women,
And of all sorts, tag-rag, been seen to flock here
In threaves, these ten weeks, as to a second Hogsden,
In days of Pimlico and Eyebright.
Face. Sir,
Their wisdoms will not say so.
Love. To-day they speak
Of coaches and gallants; one in a French hood
Went in, they tell me; and another was seen
In a velvet gown at the window: divers more
Pass in and out.
Face. They did pass through the doors then,
Or walls, I assure their eyesights, and their spectacles;
For here, sir, are the keys, and here have been,
In this my pocket, now above twenty days:
And for before, I kept the fort alone there.
But that 't is yet not deep in the afternoon,
I should believe my neighbours had seen double
Through the black pot, and made these apparitions!
For, on my faith to your worship, for these three weeks
And upwards the door has not been opened.
Love. Strange!
1st Nei. Good faith, I think I saw a coach.
2nd Nei. And I too,
I'd have been sworn.
Love. Do you but think it now?
And but one coach?
4th Nei. We cannot tell, sir: Jeremy
Is a very honest fellow.

Face. Did you see me at all?
1st Nei. No; that we are sure on.
2nd Nei. I'll be sworn o' that.
Love. Fine rogues to have your testimonies built on!

Re-enter THIRD NEIGHBOUR, *with his Tools.*

3rd Nei. Is Jeremy come?
1st Nei. Oh, yes; you may leave your tools.
We were deceived, he says.
2nd Nei. He has had the keys;
And the door has been shut these three weeks.
3rd Nei. Like enough.
Love. Peace and get hence, you changelings.

Enter SURLY *and* MAMMON.

Face. Surly come!
And Mammon made acquainted! They'll tell all.
How shall I beat them off? what shall I do?
Nothing's more wretched than a guilty conscience. [*Aside.*
Sur. No, sir, he was a great physician. This,
It was no evil house, but a mere chancel!
You knew the Lord and his sister.
Mam. Nay, good Surly——
Sur. The happy word, BE RICH——
Mam. Play not the tyrant——
Sur. Should be to-day pronounced to all your friends.
And where be your andirons now? and your brass pots,
That should have been golden flagons, and great wedges?
Mam. Let me but breathe. What, they have shut their doors,
Methinks!
Sur. Ay, now 'tis holiday with them. [*He and* SURLY *knock.*
Mam. Rogues,
Cozeners, rascals, cheats!
Face. What mean you, sir!
Mam. To enter if we can.
Face. Another man's house!
Here is the owner, sir; turn you to him,
And speak your business.
Mam. Are you, sir, the owner?
Love. Yes, sir.
Mam. And are those knaves within: your cheaters!
Love. What knaves, what cheaters?
Mam. Subtle and his Lungs.
Face. The gentleman is distracted, sir! No lungs,
Nor lights have been seen here these three weeks, sir,
Within these doors, upon my word.
Sur. Your word,
Groom, arrogant!

Face. Yes, sir, I am the housekeeper,
And know the keys have not been out of my hands.
  Sur. This is a new Face.
  Face.   You do mistake the house, sir:
What sign was 't at?
  Sur. You rascal! this is one
Of the confederacy.   Come, let 's get officers,
And force the door.
  Love. Pray you, stay, gentlemen.
  Sur. No, sir, we 'll come with warrant.
  Mam. Ay, and then
We shall have your doors open.   [*Exeunt* MAM. *and* SUR.
  Love. What means this?
  Face. I cannot tell, sir.
  1 *Nei.* These are two of the gallants
That we do think we saw.
  Face. Two of the fools!
You talk as idly as they.   Good faith, sir.
I think the moon has crazed 'em all.   Oh, me!

Enter KASTRIL.

The angry boy come too!   He 'll make a noise,
And ne'er away till he have betrayed us all.   [*Aside.*
  Kas. [*Knocking.*]   What rogues, cheats, slaves, you 'll open
      the door anon!
What, cockatrice, my suster!   By this light
I 'll fetch the marshal to you.   You are a toad
To keep your castle——
  Face. Who would you speak with, sir?
  Kas. The dirty doctor and the cozening captain,
And puss my suster.
  Love. This is something, sure.
  Face. Upon my trust, the doors were never open, sir.
  Kas. I have heard all their tricks told me twice over,
By the fat knight and the lean gentleman.
  Love. Here comes another.

Enter ANANIAS *and* TRIBULATION.

Face. Ananias too!
And his pastor!
  Tri. [*Beating at the door.*]   The doors are shut against us.
  Ana. Come forth, you seed of sulphur, sons of fire!
Your stench it is broke forth; abomination
Is in the house.
  Kas. Ay, my suster 's there.
  Ana. The place,
It is become a cage of unclean birds.
  Kas. Yes, I will fetch the scavenger and the constable.

SCENE I.]   *THE ALCHEMIST.*   89

Tri. You shall do well.
Ana. We'll join to weed them out.
Kas. You will not come, then, cockatrice, my suster!
Ana. Call her not sister; she's a harlot, verily.
Kas. I'll raise the street.
Love. Good gentleman, a word.
Ana. Satan avoid, and hinder not our zeal!
                    [*Exeunt* ANA. TRIB. *and* KAST.
Love. The world's turned Bethlem.
Face. These are all broke loose,
Out of St. Katherine's, where they used to keep
The better sort of mad-folks.
  1st Nei. All these persons
We saw go in and out here.
  2nd Nei. Yes, indeed, sir.
  3rd Nei. These were the parties.
  Face. Peace, you drunkards! Sir,
I wonder at it : please you to give me leave
To touch the door, I'll try an the lock be changed.
  Love. It amazes me!
  Face. [*Goes to the door.*] Good faith, sir, I believe
There's no such thing : 'tis all *deceptio visus*—
Would I could get him away.   [*Aside.*
  Dap. [*Within.*] Master Captain! Master Doctor!
  Love. Who's that?
  Face. Our clerk within, that I forgot! [*Aside.*] I know not,
    sir.
  Dap. [*Within.*] For God's sake, when will her grace be at
    leisure?
  Face. Ha!
Illusions, some spirit o' the air! His gag is melted,
And now he sets out the throat.   [*Aside.*
  Dap. [*Within.*] I am almost stifled——
  Face. Would you were altogether.   [*Aside.*
  Love. 'Tis in the house.
Ha! list.
  Face. Believe it, sir, in the air.
  Love. Peace, you.
  Dap. [*Within.*] Mine aunt's grace does not use me well.
  Sub. [*Within.*] You fool,
Peace, you'll mar all.
  Face. [*Speaks through the key-hole, while* LOVEWIT *advances
    to the door unobserved.*] Or you will else, you rogue.
  Love. Oh, is it so? Then you converse with spirits!
Come, sir. No more of your tricks, good Jeremy,
The truth, the shortest way.
  Face. Dismiss this rabble, sir—
What shall I do? I am catched.   [*Aside.*

Love. Good neighbours,
I thank you all. You may depart. [*Exeunt* Neighbours.] Come, sir,
You know that I am an indulgent master,
And therefore conceal nothing. What's your medicine,
To draw so many several sorts of wild-fowl?
   Face. Sir, you were wont to affect mirth and wit,
But here's no place to talk on't in the street.
Give me but leave to make the best of my fortune,
And only pardon me the abuse of your house:
It's all I beg. I'll help you to a widow,
In recompense, that you shall give me thanks for,
Will make you seven years younger, and a rich one.
'Tis but your putting on a Spanish cloak:
I have her within. You need not fear the house;
It was not visited.
   Love. But by me, who came
Sooner than you expected.
   Face. It is true, sir.
Pray you, forgive me.
   Love. Well: let's see your widow.   [*Exeunt*

SCENE II.—*A Room in the same.*

Enter SUBTLE, *leading in* DAPPER, *with his eyes bound as before*

   Sub. How! have you eaten your gag?
   Dap. Yes, faith, it crumbled
Away in my mouth.
   Sub. You have spoiled all, then.
   Dap. No!
I hope my aunt of Fairy will forgive me.
   Sub. Your aunt's a gracious lady; but in troth
You were to blame.
   Dap. The fume did overcome me,
And I did do't to stay my stomach. Pray you,
So satisfy her grace.

Enter FACE *in his uniform.*

Here comes the Captain,
   Face. How now! Is his mouth down?
   Sub. Ay, he has spoken!
   Face. A plague, I heard him, and you too. He's undone then.
I have been fain to say the house is haunted
With spirits, to keep churl back.
   Sub. And hast thou done it?
   Face. Sure, for this night.
   Sub. Why, then triumph and sing

Of Face so famous, the precious king
Of present wits.
   Face. Did you not hear the coil
About the door?
    Sub. Yes, and I dwindled with it.
   Face. Show him his aunt, and let him be despatched;
I'll send her to you.   [*Exit* FACE.
   Sub. Well, sir, your aunt her grace
Will give you audience presently, on my suit,
And the captain's word that you did not eat your gag
In any contempt of her highness.   [*Unbinds his eyes.*
   Dap. Not I, in troth, sir.

       Enter DOL *like the Queen of Fairy.*

   Sub. Here she is come. Down o' your knees and wriggle:
She has a stately presence. [DAPPER *kneels, and shuffles to-
    wards her.*] Good! Yet nearer,
And bid God save you!
   Dal. Madam!
   Sub. And your aunt.
   Dap. And my most gracious aunt, God save your grace.
   Dol. Nephew, we thought to have been angry with you;
But that sweet face of yours hath turned the tide,
And made it flow with joy, that ebb'd of love.
Arise, and touch our velvet gown.
   Sub. The skirts,
And kiss 'em. So!
   Dol. Let me now stroke that head.
Much, nephew, shalt thou win, much shalt thou spend,
Much shalt thou give away, much shalt thou lend.
   Sub. Ay, much indeed! [*Aside.*] Why do you not thank
    her grace?
   Dap. I cannot speak for joy.
   Sub. See the kind wretch!
Your grace's kinsman right.
   Dol. Give me the bird.
Here is your fly in a purse, about your neck, cousin;
Wear it, and feed it about this day seven-night,
On your right wrist——
   Sub. Open a vein with a pin,
And let it suck but once a week; till then
You must not look on 't.
   Dol. No: and, kinsman,
Bear yourself worthy of the blood you come on.
   Sub. Her grace would have you eat no more Woolsack pies,
Nor Dagger frumerty.
   Dol. Nor break his fast
In heaven and hell.

Sub. She's with you everywhere!
Nor play with costermongers at mum-chance, tray-trip.
God make you rich (when as your aunt has done it);
But keep
The gallant'st company and the best games——
　Dap. Yes, sir.
　Sub. Gleek and primero: and what you get, be true to us.
　Dap. By this hand, I will.
　Sub. You may bring's a thousand pounds
Before to-morrow night, if but three thousand
Be stirring, an you will.
　Dap. I swear I will, then.
　Sub. Your fly will learn you all games.
　Face. [*Within.*] Have you done there?
　Sub. Your grace will command him no more duties?
　Dol. No?
But come and see me often. I may chance
To leave him three or four hundred chests of treasure,
And some twelve thousand acres of Fairyland,
If he game well and comely with good gamesters.
　Sub. There's a kind aunt! Kiss her departing part.
But you must sell your forty marks a-year, now.
　Dap. Ay, sir, I mean.
　Sub. Or give't away; plague on't!
　Dap. I'll give't mine aunt: I'll go and fetch the writings.
　　　　　　　　　　　　　　　　　　　　　　[*Exit.*

Sub. 'Tis well—away!

　　　　　　　Re-enter FACE.

　Face. Where's Subtle?
　Sub. Here: what news?
　Face. Drugger is at the door; go take his suit,
And bid him fetch a parson. presently:
Say he shall marry the widow. Thou shalt spend
A hundred pounds by the service! [*Exit* SUBTLE.
　　　　Now, Queen Dol,
Have you packed up all?
　Dol. Yes.
　Face. And how do you like
The Lady Pliant?
　Dol. A good dull innocent.

　　　　　　　Re-enter SUBTLE.

　Sub. Here's your Hieronymus' cloak and hat.
　Face. Give me them.
　Sub. And the ruff too?
　Face. Yes; I'll come to you presently. [*Exit.*

Sub. Now he is gone about his project, Dol,
I told you of, for the widow.
  Dol. 'Tis direct
Against our articles.
  Sub. Well, we will fit him, wench.
Hast thou gulled her of her jewels or her bracelets?
  Dol. No; but I will do 't.
  Sub. Soon at night, my Dolly,
When we are shipped, and all our goods aboard,
Eastward for Ratcliff; we will turn our course
To Brainford, westward, if thou say'st the word,
And take our leaves of this o'er-weening rascal,
This peremptory Face.
  Dol. Content, I 'm weary of him.
  Sub. Thou 'st cause, when the slave will run a-wiving, Dol,
Against the instrument that was drawn between us.
  Dol. I 'll pluck his bird as bare as I can.
  Sub. Yes, tell her
She must by any means address some present
To the cunning man, make him amends for wronging
His art with her suspicion; send a ring
Or chain of pearl; she will be tortured else
Extremely in her sleep, say, and have strange things
Come to her. Wilt thou?
  Dol. Yes.
  Sub. My fine flitter-mouse,
My bird o' the night! we 'll tickle it at the Pigeons,
When we have all, and may unlock the trunks,
And say, this is mine, and thine; and thine, and mine.
                                                    [*They kiss.*

             Re-enter FACE.

  Face. What now! a-billing?
  Sub. Yes, a little exalted
In the good passage of our stock-affairs.
  Face. Drugger has brought his parson; take him in, Subtle,
And send Nab back again to wash his face.
  Sub. I will: and shave himself.   [*Exit.*
  Face. If you can get him.
  Dol. You are hot upon it, Face, whate'er it is!
  Face. A trick that Dol shall spend ten pounds a month by.

             Re-enter SUBTLE.

Is he gone?
  Sub. The chaplain waits you in the hall, sir.
  Face. I 'll go bestow him.   [*Exit.*
  Dol. He 'll now marry her, instantly.
  Sub. He cannot yet, he is not ready. Dear Dol,
Cozen her of all thou canst. To deceive him

Is no deceit, but justice, that would break
Such an inextricable tie as ours was.
   Dol. Let me alone to fit him.

Re-enter FACE.

   Face. Come, my venturers,
You have packed up all? Where be the trunks? Bring forth.
   Sub. Here.
   Face. Let us see them. Where's the money?
   Sub. Here,
In this.
   Face. Mammon's ten pounds; eight score before:
The brethren's money this. Drugger's and Dapper's.
What paper's that?
   Dol. The jewel of the waiting-maid's,
That stole it from her lady, to know certain——
   Face. If she should have precedence of her mistress?
   Dol. Yes.
   Face. What box is that?
   Sub. The fish-wives' rings, I think,
And the ale-wives' single money. Is't not Dol?
   Dol. Yes; and the whistle that the sailor's wife
Brought you to know an her husband were with Ward.
   Face. We'll wet it to-morrow; and our silver-beakers
And tavern cups. Where be the French petticoats,
And girdles and hangers?
   Sub. Here, in the trunk,
And the bolts of lawn.
   Face. Is Drugger's damask there,
And the tobacco?
   Sub. Yes.
   Face. Give me the keys.
   Dol. Why you the keys?
   Sub. No matter, Dol; because
We shall not open them before he comes.
   Face. 'Tis true, you shall not open them, indeed;
Nor have them forth, do you see? not forth, Dol.
   Dol. No!
   Face. No, my smock rampant. The right is, my master
Knows all, has pardoned me, and he will keep them;
Doctor, 'tis true—you look—for all your figures:
I sent for him indeed. Wherefore, good partners,
Both he and she be satisfied: for here
Determines the indenture tripartite
'Twixt Subtle, Dol, and Face. All I can do
Is to help you over the wall, o' the back-side,
Or lend you a sheet to save your velvet gown, Dol.
Here will be officers presently, bethink you

Of some course suddenly to escape the dock :
For thither you will come else.—[*Loud knocking.*]—Hark you,
    thunder.
  Sub. You are a precious fiend !
  Offi. [*Without.*] Open the door.
  Face. Dol, I am sorry for thee, i' faith ; but hear'st thou ?
It shall go hard but I will place thee somewhere :
Thou shalt have my letter to Mistress Amo——
  Dol. Hang you !
  Face. Or Madame Cæsarean.
  Dol. Out upon you, rogue !
Would I had but time to beat thee !
  Face. Subtle,
Let's know where you set up next ; I will send you
A customer now and then, for old acquaintance :
What new course have you ?
  Sub. Rogue, I'll hang myself,
That I may walk a greater devil than thou,
And haunt thee in the flock-bed and the buttery.   [*Exeunt.*

SCENE III.—*An outer Room in the same.*

Enter LOVEWIT *in the Spanish dress, with the* Parson.

[*Loud knocking at the door.*]

  Love. What do you mean, my masters ?
  Mam. [*Without.*] Open your door,
Cheaters, thieves, conjurors.
  Offi. [*Without.*] Or we will break it open.
  Love. What warrant have you ?
  Offi. [*Without.*] Warrant enough, sir, doubt not,
If you'll not open it.
  Love. Is there an officer, there ?
  Offi. [*Without.*] Yes, two or three for failing.
  Love. Have but patience,
And I will open it straight.

Enter FACE *as butler.*

  Face. Sir, have you done ?
Is it a marriage ? perfect ?
  Love. Yes, my brain.
  Face. Off with your ruff and cloak then ; be yourself, sir.
  Sur. [*Without.*] Down with the door.
  Kas. [*Without.*] 'Slight, ding it open.
  Love. [*Opening the door.*] Hold,
Hold, gentlemen, what means this violence ?

MAMMON, SURLY, KASTRIL, ANANIAS, TRIBULATION, *and* Officers *rush in.*

Mam. Where is this collier?
Sur. And my Captain Face?
Mam. These day owls.
Sur. That are birding in men's purses.
Mam. Madam Suppository.
Kas. Doxy, my suster.
Ana. Locusts
Of the foul pit.
Tri. Profane as Bel and the Dragon.
Ana. Worse than the grasshoppers or the lice of Egypt.
Love. Good gentlemen, hear me. Are you officers,
And cannot stay this violence?
1st Offi. Keep the peace.
Love. Gentlemen, what is the matter? Whom do you seek?
Mam. The chemical cozener.
Sur. And the captain pander.
Kas. The nun my suster.
Mam. Madam Rabbi
Ana. Scorpions
And caterpillars.
Love. Fewer at once, I pray you.
2nd. Offi. One after another, gentlemen, I charge you,
By virtue of my staff.
Ana. They are the vessels
Of pride, lust, and the cart.
Love. Good zeal, lie still
A little while.
Tri. Peace, Deacon Ananias.
Love. The house is mine here, and the doors are open:
If there be any such persons as you seek for,
Use your authority, search on, o' God's name.
I am but newly come to town, and finding
This tumult 'bout my door, to tell you true,
It somewhat 'mazed me; till my man here, fearing
My more displeasure, told me he had done
Somewhat an insolent part, let out my house
(Belike, presuming on my known aversion
From any air o' the town while there was sickness)
To a doctor and a captain: who, what are they,
Or where they be, he knows not.
Mam. Are they gone?
Love. You may go in and search, sir. [MAMMON, ANA. *and* TRIB. *go in.*] Here, I find
The empty walls worse than I left them, smoked,
A few cracked pots and glasses, and a furnace:

The ceiling filled with poesies of the candle,
And madam with a dildo writ o' the walls :
Only one gentlewoman, I met here,
That is within, that said she was a widow ——
 Kas. Ay, that's my suster ; I'll go thump her. Where is she?
               [*Goes in.*
 Love. And should have married a Spanish Count, but he,
When he came to 't, neglected her so grossly,
That I, a widower, am gone through with her.
 Sur. How! have I lost her then?
 Love. Were you the don, sir!
Good faith, now, she does blame you extremely, and says
You swore, and told her you had taken the pains
To dye your beard, and umbre o'er your face,
Borrowed a suit, and ruff, all for her love ;
And then did nothing. What an oversight,
And want of putting forward, sir, was this!
Well fare an old harquebuzier, yet,
Could prime his powder, and give fire, and hit,
All in a twinkling!

     Re-enter MAMMON.

 Mam. The whole nest are fled!
 Love. What sort of birds were they?
 Mam. A kind of choughs,
Or thievish daws, sir, that have pick'd my purse
Of eight score and ten pounds within these five weeks,
Beside my first materials ; and my goods,
That lie in the cellar, which I am glad they have left,
I may have home yet.
 Love. Think you so, sir?
 Mam. Ay.
 Love. By order of law, sir, but not otherwise.
 Mam. Not mine own stuff!
 Love. Sir, I can take no knowledge
That they are yours, but by public means.
If you can bring certificate that you were gull'd of them.
Or any formal writ out of a court,
That you did cozen yourself, I will not hold them.
 Mam. I'll rather lose them.
 Love. That you shall not, sir,
By me, in troth : upon these terms, they are yours.
What! should they have been, sir, turn'd into gold, all?
 Mam. No,
I cannot tell—It may be they should—What then?
 Love. What a great loss in hope have you sustain'd!
 Mam. Not I, the common-wealth has.
 Face. Ay, he would have built

The city new; and made a ditch about it
Of silver, should have run with cream from Hogsden;
That, every Sunday, in Moor-fields, the younkers,
And tits and tom-boys should have fed on, gratis.

Mam. I will go mount a turnip-cart, and preach
The end of the world, within these two months. Surly,
What! in a dream?

Sur. Must I needs cheat myself,
With that same foolish vice of honesty!
Come, let us go and hearken out the rogues:
That Face I'll mark for mine, if e'er I meet him.

Face. If I can hear of him, sir, I'll bring you word,
Unto your lodging; for in troth, they were strangers
To me, I thought them honest as my self, sir.
[*Exeunt Mam. and Sur.*

Re-enter ANANIAS *and* TRIBULATION.

Tri. 'Tis well, the saints shall not lose all yet. Go,
And get some carts——

Love. For what, my zealous friends?

Ana. To bear away the portion of the righteous
Out of this den of thieves.

Love. What is that portion?

Ana. The goods sometimes the orphan's, that the brethren
Bought with their silver pence.

Love. What, those in the cellar,
The knight sir Mammon claims?

Ana. I do defy
The wicked Mammon, so do all the brethren,
Thou profane man! I ask thee with what conscience
Thou canst advance that idol against us,
That have the seal? were not the shillings number'd,
That made the pounds; were not the pounds told out,
Upon the second day of the fourth week,
In the eighth month, upon the table dormant,
The year of the last patience of the saints,
Six hundred and ten?

Love. Mine earnest vehement botcher,
And deacon also, I cannot dispute with you:
But if you get you not away the sooner,
I shall confute you with a cudgel,

Ana. Sir!

Tri. Be patient, Ananias.

Ana. I am strong,
And will stand up, well girt, against an host
That threaten Gad in exile.

Love. I shall send you
To Amsterdam, to your cellar.

Ana. I will pray there,
Against thy house : may dogs defile thy walls,
And wasps and hornets breed beneath thy roof,
This seat of falsehood, and this cave of cozenage !
[*Exeunt* ANA. *and* TRIB.

Enter DRUGGER.

Love. Another too ?
Drug. Not I, sir, I am no brother.
Love. [*beats him.*] Away, you Harry Nicholas ! do you talk?
[*Exit* DRUG.
Face. No, this was Abel Drugger. Good sir, go,
[*To the* PARSON.
And satisfy him ; tell him all is done :
He staid too long a washing of his face.
The doctor, he shall hear of him at West-chester;
And of the captain, tell him, at Yarmouth, or
Some good port-town else, lying for a wind. [*Exit* PARSON.
If you can get off the angry child, now, sir——

Enter KASTRIL, *dragging in his sister.*

Kas. Come on, you ewe, you have match'd most sweetly, have
you not?
Did I not say, I would never have you tupp'd
But by a dubb'd boy, to make you a lady-tom ?
'Slight, you are a mammet ! O, I could touse you, now.
Death, mun' you marry, with a plague !
Love. You lie, boy ;
As sound as you ; and I'm aforehand with you.
Kas. Anon !
Love. Come, will you quarrel ? I will feize you, sirrah ;
Why do you not buckle to your tools ?
Kas. Od's light,
This is a fine old boy as e'er I saw !
Love. What, do you change your copy now ? proceed,
Here stands my dove : stoop at her, if you dare.
Kas. 'Slight, I must love him ! I cannot choose, i' faith,
An I should be hang'd for't ! Suster, I protest,
I honour thee for this match.
Love. O, do you so, sir ?
Kas. Yes; and thou canst take tobacco and drink, old boy,
I'll give her five hundred pound more to her marriage,
Than her own state.
Love. Fill a pipe full, Jeremy.
Face. Yes ; but go in and take it, sir.
Love. We will—
I will be ruled by thee in anything, Jeremy.

Kas. 'Slight, thou art not hide-bound, thou art a jovy boy!
Come, let us in, I pray thee, and take our whiffs.
    Love. Whiff in with your sister, brother boy.
              [*Exeunt* KAS. *and* Dame P.] That master
That had received such happiness by a servant,
In such a widow, and with so much wealth,
Were very ungrateful, if he would not be
A little indulgent to that servant's wit,
And help his fortune, though with some small strain
Of his own candour. [*advancing.*]—Therefore, gentlemen,
And kind spectators, if I have outstript
An old man's gravity, or strict canon, think
What a young wife and a good brain may do;
Stretch age's truth sometimes, and crack it too.
Speak for thy self, knave.
    Face. So I will, sir. [*advancing to the front of the stage.*]
        Gentlemen,
My part a little fell in this last scene,
Yet 'twas decorum. And though I am clean
Got off from Subtle, Surly, Mammon, Dol,
Hot Ananias, Dapper, Drugger, all
With whom I traded: yet I put my self
On you that are my country: and this pelf,
Which I have got, if you do quit me, rests
To feast you often, and invite new guests. [*Exeunt.*

VOLPONE; OR, THE FOX.

TO THE MOST NOBLE AND MOST EQUAL SISTERS,

THE TWO FAMOUS UNIVERSITIES,

FOR THEIR LOVE AND ACCEPTANCE SHOWN TO HIS POEM IN THE PRESENTATION,

BEN JONSON,

THE GRATEFUL ACKNOWLEDGER,

DEDICATES BOTH IT AND HIMSELF.

NEVER, most equal Sisters, had any man a wit so presently excellent, as that it could raise itself; but there must come both matter, occasion, commenders, and favours to it. If this be true, and that the fortune of all writers doth daily prove it, it behoves the careful to provide well towards these accidents; and, having acquired them, to preserve that part of reputation most tenderly, wherein the benefit of a friend is also defended. Hence is it, that I now render myself grateful, and am studious to justify the bounty of your act; to which, though your mere authority were satisfying, yet it being an age wherein poetry and the professors of it hear so ill on all sides, there will a reason be looked for in the subject. It is certain, nor can it with any forehead be opposed, that the too much license of poetasters in this time, hath much deformed their mistress; that, every day, their manifold and manifest ignorance doth stick unnatural reproaches upon her: but for their petulancy, it were an act of the greatest injustice, either to let the learned suffer, or so divine a skill (which indeed should not be attempted with unclean hands) to fail under the least contempt. For, if men with impartiality, and not asquint, look toward the offices and functions of a poet, they will easily conclude to themselves the impossibility of any man's being the good poet, without first being a good man. He that is, said to be able to inform young men to all good disciplines, inflame grown men to all great virtues, keep old men in their best and supreme state, or, as they decline to childhood, recover them to their first strength; that comes forth the interpreter and arbiter of nature, a teacher of things divine no less than human, a master in manners; and can alone, or with a few, effect the business of mankind: this, I take him, is no subject for pride and ignorance to exercise their railing rhetoric upon. But it will here be hastily answered, that the writers of these days are other things: that not only their manners, but their natures, are inverted, and nothing remaining with them of the dignity of poet, but the abused name, which every scribe usurps; that now, especially in dramatic, or, as they term it, stage-poetry, nothing but ribaldry, profanation, blasphemy, all license of offence to God and man is practised.

I dare not deny a great part of this, and am sorry I dare not, because in some men's abortive features (and would they had never boasted the light) it is over true ; but that all are embarked in this bold adventure for hell, is a most uncharitable thought, and, uttered, a more malicious slander. For my particular, I can, and from a most clear conscience, affirm, that I have ever trembled to think towards the least profaneness ; have loathed the use of such foul and unwashed bawdry, as is now made the food of the scene ; and, howsoever I cannot escape from some, the imputation of sharpness, but that they will say, I have taken a pride, or lust, to be bitter, and not my youngest infant but hath come into the world with all his teeth ; I would ask of these supercilious politics, what nation, society, or general order or state, I have provoked ? What public person ? Whether I have not in all these preserved their dignity, as mine own person, safe ? My works are read, allowed, (I speak of those that are intirely mine,) look into them, what broad reproofs have I used ? where have I been particular ? where personal ? except to a mimic, cheater, bawd, or buffon, creatures for their insolencies, worthy to be taxed ? yet to which of these so pointingly, as he might not either ingenuously have confest, or wisely dissembled his disease ? But it is not rumour can make men guilty, much less entitle me to other men's crimes. I know, that nothing can be so innocently writ or carried, but may be made obnoxious to construction ; marry, whilst I bear mine innocence about me, I fear it not, Application is now grown a trade with many ; and there are that profess to have a key for the decyphering of every thing : but let wise and noble persons take heed how they be too credulous, or give leave to these invading interpreters to be over-familiar with their fames, who cunningly, and often, utter their own virulent malice, under other men's simplest meanings. As for those that will (by faults which charity hath raked up, or common honesty concealed) make themselves a name with the multitude, or, to draw their rude and beastly claps, care not whose living faces they intrench with their petulant styles, may they do it without a rival for me ! I choose rather to live graved in obscurity, than share with them in so preposterous a fame. Nor can I blame the wishes of those severe and wise patriots, who providing the hurts these licentious spirits may do in a state, desire rather to see fools and devils, and those antique relics of barbarism retrieved, with all other ridiculous and exploded follies, than behold the wounds of private men, of princes and nations ; for, as Horace makes Trebatius speak among these,

"Sibi quisque timet, quanquam est intactus, et odit."

And men may justly impute such rages, if continued, to the writer, as his sports. The increase of which lust in liberty, together with the present trade of the stage, in all their miscelline interludes, what learned or liberal soul doth not already abhor ? where nothing but the filth of the time is uttered, and with such impropriety of phrase, such plenty of solecisms, such dearth of sense, so bold prolepses, so racked metaphors, with brothelry, able to violate the ear of a pagan, and blasphemy, to turn the blood of a christian to water. I cannot but be serious in a cause of this nature, wherein my fame, and the reputation of divers honest and learned are the question ; when a name so full of authority, antiquity, and all great mark, is, through their insolence, become the lowest scorn of the age ; and those men subject to the petulancy of every vernaculous orator, that were wont to be the care of kings and happiest monarchs. This it is that hath not only rapt me to present indignation, but made me studious heretofore, and by all my actions, to stand off from them ; which may most appear in this my latest work, which you, most learned Arbitresses, have seen, judged, and to my crown, approved : wherein I have laboured for their instruction and amendment, to reduce not only the ancient forms, but manners of the scene, the easiness, the propriety, the innocence, and last, the doctrine, which is the principal end of poesie, to inform men in the best reason of living. And though my catastrophe may, in the strict rigour of comic law, meet with censure, as turning back to my promise; I desire the learned and charitable critic, to have so much faith in me, to think it was done of industry: for, with what ease I could have varied it nearer his scale (but that I fear to boast my own faculty) I could here insert. But my special aim being to put the snaffle in their mouths, that cry out. "We never punish vice in our interludes," &c., I took the more liberty; though not without some lines of example, drawn even in the ancients themselves, the goings out of whose comedies are not always joyful, but oft times the bawds, the servants, the rivals, yea, and the masters are mulcted; and fitly, it being the office of a comic poet to imitate justice, and instruct to life, as well as purity of language, or stir up gentle affections; to which I shall take the occasion elsewhere to speak.

For the present, most reverend Sisters, as I have cared to be thankful for your affections past, and here made the understanding acquainted with some ground of your favours; let me not despair their continuance, to the maturing of some worthier fruits; wherein, if my muses be true to me, I shall raise the despised head of poetry again, and stripping her out of those rotten and base rags wherewith the times have adulterated her form, restore her to her primitive habit, feature, and majesty, and render her worthy to be embraced and kist of all the great and master-spirits of our world. As for the vile and slothful, who never affected an act worthy of celebration, or are so inward with their own vicious natures, as they worthily fear her, and think it an high point of policy to keep her in contempt, with their declamatory and windy invectives; she shall out of just rage incite her servants (who are *genus irritabile*) to spout ink in their faces, that shall eat farther than their marrow into their fames; and not Cinnamus the barber, with his art, shall be able to take out the brands; but they shall live, and be read, till the wretches die, as things worst deserving of themselves in chief, and then of all mankind.

FROM MY HOUSE IN THE BLACK-FRIARS,
this 11th day of February, 1607.

THE PERSONS OF THE PLAY.

VOLPONE, *a Magnifico.*
MOSCA, *his Parasite.*
VOLTORE, *an Advocate.*
CORBACCIO, *an old Gentleman.*
CORVINO, *a Merchant.*
BONARIO, *son to Corbaccio.*
SIR POLITICK WOULD-BE, *a Knight.*
PEREGRINE, *a Gentleman Traveller.*
NANO, *a Dwarf.*
CASTRONE, *an Eunuch.*
ANDROGYNO, *an Hermaphrodite.*

GREGE (*or Mob.*)
Commandodori, *Officers of Justice.*
Mercatori, *three Merchants.*
Avocatori, *four Magistrates.*
Notario, *the Register.*
LADY WOULD-BE, *Sir Politick's Wife.*
CELIA, *Corvino's Wife.*

Servitori; Servants, *two* Waiting-women, &c.

SCENE—VENICE.

ARGUMENT.

V olpone, childless, rich, feigns sick, despairs,
O ffers his state to hopes of several heirs,
L ies languishing; his parasite receives
P resents of all, assures, deludes; then weaves
O ther cross plots, which ope themselves, are told.
N ew tricks for safety are sought; they thrive; when bold,
E ach tempts the other again, and all are sold.

PROLOGUE.

Now, luck yet send us, and a little wit
  Will serve to make our play hit ;
(According to the palates of the season.)
  Here is rhime, not empty of reason.
This we were bid to credit from our poet,
  Whose true scope, if you would know it,
In all his poems still hath been this measure,
  To mix profit with your pleasure ;
And not as some, whose throats their envy failing,
  Cry hoarsely, All he writes is railing :
And when his plays come forth, think they can flout them,
  With saying, he was a year about them.
To this there needs no lie, but this his creature,
  Which was two months since no feature ;
And though he dares give them five lives to mend it,
  'Tis known, five weeks fully penn'd it,
From his own hand, without a co-adjutor,
  Novice, journey-man, or tutor.
Yet thus much I can give you as a token
  Of his play's worth, no eggs are broken,
Nor quaking custards with fierce teeth affrighted.
  Wherewith your route are so delighted ;
Nor hales he in a gull old ends reciting,
  To stop gaps in his loose writing ;
With such a deal of monstrous and forced action,
  As might make Bethlem a faction :
Nor made he his play for jests stolen from each table,
  But makes jests to fit his fable ;
And so presents quick comedy refined,
  As best critics have designed ;
The laws of time, place, persons he observeth,
  From no needful rule he swerveth.
All gall and copperas from his ink he draineth,
  Only a little salt remaineth,
Wherewith he'll rub your cheeks, till red, with laughter,
  They shall look fresh a week after.

ACT I.

Scene I.—*A Room in* Volpone's *House.*

Enter Volpone *and* Mosca.

Volp. Good morning to the day ; and next, my gold !—
Open the shrine, that I may see my saint.
      [Mosca *withdraws the curtain, and discovers piles
        of gold, plate, jewels, &c.*
Hail the world's soul, and mine ! more glad than is
The teeming earth to see the longed-for sun
Peep through the horns of the celestial Ram,
Am I, to view thy splendour darkening his ;

That lying here, amongst my other hoards,
Showest like a flame by night, or like the day
Struck out of chaos, when all darkness fled
Unto the centre. O thou son of Sol,
But brighter than thy father, let me kiss,
With adoration, thee, and every relic
Of sacred treasure in this blessed room.
Well did wise poets, by thy glorious name,
Title that age which they would have the best;
Thou being the best of things, and far transcending
All style of joy, in children, parents, friends,
Or any other waking dream on earth :
Thy looks when they to Venus did ascribe,
They should have given her twenty thousand Cupids;
Such are thy beauties and our loves! Dear saint,
Riches, the dumb god, that givest all men tongues,
Thou canst do nought, and yet makest men do all things;
The price of souls ; even hell, with thee to boot,
Is made worth heaven. Thou art virtue, fame,
Honour, and all things else. Who can get thee,
He shall be noble, valiant, honest, wise——
  Mos. And what he will, sir. Riches are in fortune
A greater good than wisdom is in nature.
  Volp. True, my beloved Mosca. Yet I glory
More in the cunning purchase of my wealth,
Than in the glad possession, since I gain
No common way; I use no trade, no venture;
I wound no earth with plough-shares, fat no beasts,
To feed the shambles; have no mills for iron,
Oil, corn, or men, to grind them into powder :
I blow no subtle glass, expose no ships
To threatenings of the furrow-faced sea ;
I turn no monies in the public bank,
Nor usure private.
  Mos. No, sir, nor devour
Soft prodigals. You shall have some will swallow
A melting heir as glibly as your Dutch
Will pills of butter, and ne'er purge for it ;
Tear forth the fathers of poor families
Out of their beds, and coffin them alive
In some kind clasping prison, where their bones
May be forthcoming, when the flesh is rotten :
But your sweet nature doth abhor these courses ;
You loathe the widow's or the orphan's tears
Should wash your pavements, or their piteous cries
Ring in your roofs, and beat the air for vengeance.
  Volp. Right, Mosca; I do loathe it.
  Mos. And besides, sir,

You are not like the thresher that doth stand
With a huge flail, watching a heap of corn,
And, hungry, dares not taste the smallest grain,
But feeds on mallows, and such bitter herbs;
Nor like the merchant, who hath filled his vaults
With Romagnia, and rich Candian wines,
Yet drinks the lees of Lombard's vinegar;
You will lie not in straw, whilst moths and worms
Feed on your sumptuous hangings and soft beds;
You know the use of riches, and dare give now
From that bright heap, to me, your poor observer,
Or to your dwarf, or your hermaphrodite,
Your eunuch, or what other household trifle
Your pleasure allows maintenance——

   Volp. Hold thee, Mosca,   [*Gives him money.*
Take of my hand; thou strik'st on truth in all,
And they are envious term thee parasite.
Call forth my dwarf, my eunuch, and my fool,
And let them make me sport. [*Exit* Mos.] What should I do,
But cocker up my genius, and live free
To all delights my fortune calls me to?
I have no wife, no parent, child, ally,
To give my substance to; but whom I make
Must be my heir: and this makes men observe me:
This draws new clients daily to my house,
Women and men of every sex and age,
That bring me presents, send me plate, coin, jewels,
With hope that when I die (which they expect
Each greedy minute) it shall then return
Tenfold upon them; whilst some, covetous
Above the rest, seek to engross me whole,
And counter-work the one unto the other,
Contend in gifts, as they would seem in love:
All which I suffer, playing with their hopes,
And am content to coin them into profit,
And look upon their kindness, and take more,
And look on that; still bearing them in hand,
Letting the cherry knock against their lips,
And draw it by their mouths, and back again,—
How now!

   Re-enter MOSCA *with* NANO, ANDROGYNO, *and* CASTRONE.

   Nan. Now, room for fresh gamesters, who do will you to know,
     They do bring you neither play nor university show;
   And therefore do intreat you, that whatsoever they rehearse,
     May not fare a whit the worse, for the false pace of the verse.
If you wonder at this, you will wonder more ere we pass,
   For know, here is inclosed the soul of Pythagoras,

That juggler divine, as hereafter shall follow;
  Which soul, fast and loose, sir, came first from Apollo,
And was breath'd into Æthalides, Mercurius his son,
  Where it had the gift to remember all that ever was done.
From thence it fled forth, and made quick transmigration
  To godly-lock'd Euphorbus, who was killed in good fashion,
At the siege of old Troy, by Menelaus of Sparta.
  Hermotimus was next (I find it in my charta)
To whom it did pass, where no sooner it was missing
  But with one Pyrrhus of Delos it learn'd to go a fishing;
And thence did it enter the sophist of Greece.
  From Pythagore, she went into a beautiful piece,
Hight Aspasia, the meretrix; and the next toss of her
  Was again of a witch, she became a philosopher,
Crates the cynic, as itself doth relate it:
  Since kings, knights, and beggars, knaves, lords, and fools
    gat it,
Besides ox and ass, camel, mule, goat, and brock,
  In all which it hath spoke, as in the cobler's cock.
But I come not here to discourse of that matter,
  Or his one, two, or three, or his great oath, BY QUATER!
His musics, his trigon, his golden thigh,
  Or his telling how elements shift, but I
Would ask, how of late thou hast suffered translation,
  And shifted thy coat in these days of reformation.
  And. Like one of the reformed, a fool, as you see,
    Counting all old doctrine heresie.
  Nan. But not on thine own forbid meats hast thou ventured?
  And. On fish, when first a Carthusian I enter'd.
  Nan. Why, then thy dogmatical silence hath left thee?
  And. Of that an obstreperous lawyer bereft me.
  Nan. O wonderful change, when sir lawyer forsook thee!
    For Pythagore's sake, what body then took thee?
  And. A good dull mule.
  Nan.   And how! by that means
    Thou wert brought to allow of the eating of beans?
  And. Yes.
  Nan.   But from the mule into whom didst thou pass?
  And. Into a very strange beast, by some writers call'd an ass;
    By others a precise pure, illuminate brother,
    Of those devour flesh, and sometimes one another;
And will drop you forth a libel, or a sanctified lie,
    Betwixt every spoonful of a nativity pie.
  Nan. Now quit thee, for heaven, of that profane nation,
    And gently report thy next transmigration.
  And. To the same that I am.
  Nan.   A creature of delight,
    And, what is more than a fool, an hermaphrodite!

And. No, 'tis your fool wherewith I am so taken,
The only one creature that I can call blessed;
For all other forms I have proved most distressed.
Nan. Spoke true, as thou wert in Pythagoras still.
This learned opinion we celebrate will,
Fellow eunuch, as behoves us, with all our wit and art,
To dignify that whereof ourselves are so great and special a part.
Volp. Now, very, very pretty. Mosca, this
Was thy invention?
Mos. If it please my patron,
Not else.
Volp. It doth, good Mosca.
Mos. Then it was, sir.

NANO *and* CASTRONE *sing.*

Fools, they are the only nation
Worth men's envy or admiration;
Free from care or sorrow-taking,
Selves and others merry making:
All they speak or do is sterling,
Your fool he is your great man's darling,
And your ladies' sport and pleasure;
Tongue and bauble are his treasure.
E'en his face begetteth laughter,
And he speaks truth free from slaughter;
He's the grace of every feast,
And sometimes the chiefest guest;
Hath his trencher and his stool,
When wit waits upon the fool.
O, who would not be
He, he, he?   [*Knocking without.*

Volp. Who's that? Away! [*Exeunt* NANO *and* CASTRONE.]
Look, Mosca. Fool. Begone!   [*Exit* ANDROGYNO.
Mos. 'Tis Signior Voltore, the advocate;
I know him by his knock.
Volp. Fetch me my gown,
My furs and nightcaps; say, my couch is changing,
And let him entertain himself awhile
Without i' the gallery. [*Exit* MOSCA.] Now, now, my clients
Begin their visitation! Vulture, kite,
Raven, and gorcrow, all my birds of prey,
That think me turning carcase, now they come;
I am not for them yet.

Re-enter MOSCA, *with the gown,* &c.

How now! The news?
Mos. A piece of plate, sir.
Volp. Of what bigness?
Mos. Huge,

Massy, and antique, with your name inscribed,
And arms engraven.
   Volp. Good! and not a fox
Stretched on the earth, with fine delusive sleights,
Mocking a gaping crow? Ha, Mosca!
   Mos. Sharp, sir.
   Volp. Give me my furs. [*Puts on his sick dress.*] Why dost
      thou laugh so, man?
   Mos. I cannot choose, sir, when I apprehend
What thoughts he has without now, as he walks:
That this might be the last gift he should give;
That this would fetch you; if you died to-day,
And gave him all, what he should be to-morrow;
What large return would come of all his ventures;
How he should worshipped be, and reverenced;
Ride with his furs, and foot-cloths; waited on
By herds of fools, and clients; have clear way
Made for his mule, as lettered as himself;
Be called the great and learned advocate:
And then concludes, there's nought impossible.
   Volp. Yes, to be learned, Mosca.
   Mos. O, no: rich
Implies it. Hood an ass with reverend purple,
So you can hide his two ambitious ears,
And he shall pass for a cathedral doctor.
   Volp. My caps, my caps, good Mosca. Fetch him in.
   Mos. Stay, sir; your ointment for your eyes.
   Volp. That's true;
Dispatch, dispatch: I long to have possession
Of my new present.
   Mos. That, and thousands more,
I hope to see you lord of.
   Volp. Thanks, kind Mosca.
   Mos. And that, when I am lost in blended dust,
And hundred such as I am, in succession——
   Volp. Nay, that were too much, Mosca.
   Mos. You shall live,
Still, to delude these harpies.
   Volp. Loving Mosca!
'Tis well: my pillow now, and let him enter.   [*Exit* MOSCA.
Now, my feigned cough, my phthisic, and my gout,
My apoplexy, palsy, and catarrhs,
Help, with your forced functions, this my posture,
Wherein, this three year, I have milked their hopes.
He comes; I hear him—Uh! [*coughing,*] uh! uh! uh! O——

   Re-enter MOSCA, *introducing* VOLTORE *with a piece of plate.*
   Mos. You still are what you were, sir. Only you,

Of all the rest, are he commands his love,
And you do wisely to preserve it thus,
With early visitation and kind notes
Of your good meaning to him; which, I know,
Cannot but come most grateful. Patron! sir!
Here's Signior Voltore is come——
    Volp. [*Faintly.*] What say you?
    Mos. Sir, Signior Voltore is come this morning
To visit you.
    Volp. I thank him.
    Mos. And hath brought
A piece of antique plate, bought of St. Mark,
With which he here presents you.
    Volp. He is welcome.
Pray him to come more often.
    Mos. Yes.
    Volt. What says he?
    Mos. He thanks you, and desires you see him often.
    Volp. Mosca.
    Mos. My patron!
    Volp. Bring him near, where is he?
I long to feel his hand.
    Mos. The plate is here, sir.
    Volt. How fare you, sir?
    Volp. I thank you, Signior Voltore;
Where is the plate? Mine eyes are bad.
    Volt. [*Putting it into his hands.*] I'm sorry
To see you still thus weak.
    Mos. That he's not weaker.   [*Aside.*
    Volp. You are too munificient.
    Volt. No, sir; would to heaven,
I could as well give health to you, as that plate!
    Volp. You give, sir, what you can: I thank you. Your love
Hath taste in this, and shall not be unanswered:
I pray you see me often.
    Volt. Yes, I shall, sir.
    Volp. Be not far from me.
    Mos. Do you observe that, sir?
    Volp. Harken unto me still; it will concern you.
    Mos. You are a happy man, sir; know your good.
    Volp. I cannot now last long——
    Mos. You are his heir, sir.
    Volt. Am I?
    Volp. I feel me going; Uh! uh! uh! uh!
I'm sailing to my port. Uh! uh! uh! uh!
And I am glad I am so near my haven.
    Mos. Alas, kind gentleman! Well, we must all go——
    Volt. But, Mosca——

Mos. Age will conquer.
Volt. 'Pray thee, hear me :
Am I inscribed his heir for certain?
　Mos. Are you!
I do beseech you, sir, you will vouchsafe
To write me in your family. All my hopes
Depend upon your worship : I am lost,
Except the rising sun do shine on me.
　Volt. It shall both shine and warm thee, Mosca.
　Mos. Sir,
I am a man that hath not done your love
All the worst offices? here I wear your keys,
See all your coffers and your caskets lock'd,
Keep the poor inventory of your jewels,
Your plate and monies ; am your steward, sir,
Husband your goods here.
　Volt. But am I sole heir?
　Mos. Without a partner, sir ; confirmed this morning :
The wax's warm yet, and the ink scarce dry
Upon the parchment.
　Volt. Happy, happy, me!
By what good chance, sweet Mosca?
　Mos. Your desert, sir ;
I know no second cause.
　Volt. Thy modesty
Is not to know it : well, we shall requite it.
　Mos. He ever liked your course, sir ; that first took him.
I oft have heard him say how he admired
Men of your large profession, that could speak
To every cause, and things mere contraries,
Till they were hoarse again, yet all be law ;
That, with most quick agility, could turn,
And turn and re-turn; make knots, and undo them ;
Give forkéd counsel ; take provoking gold
On either hand, and put it up ; these men,
He knew, would thrive with their humility.
And for his part he thought he should be blest
To have his heir of such a suffering spirit,
So wise, so grave, of so perplex'd a tongue,
And loud withal, that would not wag, nor scarce
Lie still, without a fee ; when every word
Your worship but let's fall, is a chequin!—
　　　　　　　　　　　　　　　　[*Knocking without.*
Who's that? one knocks ; I would not have you seen, sir.
And yet—pretend you came, and went in haste :
I'll fashion an excuse—and, gentle sir,
When you do come to swim in golden lard,
Up to the arms in honey, that your chin

Is borne up stiff with fatness of the flood,
Think on your vassal : but remember me :
I have not been your worst of clients.
    Volt. Mosca !——
    Mos. When will you have your inventory brought, sir?
Or see a copy of the will?——Anon !—
I'll bring them to you, sir. Away, be gone,
Put business in your face.   [*Exit* VOLTORE.
    Volp. [*springing up.*] Excellent Mosca !
Come hither, let me kiss thee.
    Mos. Keep you still, sir.
Here is Corbaccio.
    Volp. Set the plate away :
The vulture's gone, and the old raven's come !
    Mos. Betake you to your silence, and your sleep.
Stand there and multiply. [*Putting the plate to the rest.*] Now, shall we see
A wretch who is indeed more impotent
Than this can feign to be ; yet hopes to hop
Over his grave.

                Enter CORBACCIO.
                          Signior Corbaccio !
You're very welcome, sir.
    Corb. How does your patron ?
    Mos. Troth, as he did, sir ; no amends.
    Corb. What ! mends he ?
    Mos. No, sir : he's rather worse.
    Corb. That's well. Where is he ?
    Mos. Upon his couch, sir, newly fallen asleep.
    Corb. Does he sleep well ?
    Mos. No wink, sir, all this night.
Nor yesterday ; but slumbers.
    Corb. Good ! he should take
Some counsel of physicians : I have brought him
An opiate here, from mine own doctor.
    Mos. He will not hear of drugs.
    Carb. Why ? I myself
Stood by while it was made, saw all the ingredients :
And know it cannot but most gently work :
My life for his, 'tis but to make him sleep.
    Volp. Ay, his last sleep, if he would take it.   [*Aside.*
    Mos. Sir,
He has no faith in physic.
    Corb. Say you, say you ?
    Mos. He has no faith in physic : he does think
Most of your doctors are the greater danger,

And worse disease to escape. I often have
Heard him protest that your physician
Should never be his heir.
 Corb. Not I his heir!
 Mos. Not your physician, sir.
 Corb. O, no, no, no.
I do not mean it.
 Mos. No, sir, nor their fees
He cannot brook: he says they flay a man,
Before they kill him.
 Corb. Right, I do conceive you.
 Mos. And then they do it by experiment;
For which the law not only doth absolve them,
But gives them great reward: and he is loth
To hire his death so.
 Corb. It is true, they kill
With as much license as a judge.
 Mos. Nay, more:
For he but kills sir, where the law condemns,
And these can kill him too.
 Corb. Ay, or me;
Or any man. How does his apoplex?
Is that strong on him still?
 Mos. Most violent.
His speech is broken, and his eyes are set,
His face drawn longer than 'twas wont——
 Corb. How! how!
Stronger than he was wont?
 Mos. No, sir: his face
Drawn longer than 'twas wont.
 Corb. Oh, good!
 Mos. His mouth
Is ever gaping, and his eyelids hang.
 Corb. Good.
 Mos. A freezing numbness stiffens all his joints,
And makes the colour of his flesh like lead.
 Corb. 'Tis good.
 Mos. His pulse beats slow and dull.
 Corb. Good symptoms still.
 Mos. And from his brain——
 Corb. I conceive you; good.
 Mos. Flows a cold sweat, with a continual rheum,
Forth the resolved corners of his eyes.
 Corb. Is it possible? Yet I am better, ha!
How does he with the swimming of his head?
 Mos. Oh, sir, 'tis past the scotomy; he now
Hath lost his feeling, and hath left to snort!
You hardly can perceive him, that he breathes.

Corb. Excellent, excellent! Sure I shall outlast him:
This makes me young again, a score of years.
   Mos. I was a-coming for you, sir.
   Corb. Has he made his will?
What has he given me?
   Mos. No, sir.
   Corb. Nothing! ha?
   Mos. He has not made his will, sir.
   Corb. Oh, oh, oh!
What then did Voltore, the lawyer, here?
   Mos. He smelt a carcase, sir, when he but heard
My master was about his testament;
As I did urge him to it for your good——
   Corb. He came unto him, did he? I thought so.
   Mos. Yes, and presented him this piece of plate.
   Corb. To be his heir?
   Mos. I do not know, sir.
   Corb. True?
I know it too.
   Mos. By your own scale, sir.   [*Aside.*
   Corb. Well,
I shall prevent him yet. See, Mosca, look,
Here, I have brought a bag of bright chequines,
Will quite weigh down his plate.
   Mos. [*Taking the bag.*] Yea, marry, sir.
This is true physic. this your sacred medicine;
No talk of opiates, to this great elixir!
   Corb. 'Tis aurum palpabile, if not potabile.
   Mos. It shall be ministered to him, in his bowl,
   Corb. Ay, do, do, do!
   Mos. Most blessed cordial!
This will recover him.
   Corb. Yes, do, do, do!
   Mos. I think it were not best, sir.
   Corb. What?
   Mos. To recover him.
   Corb. Oh, no, no, no; by no means.
   Mos. Why, sir, this
Will work some strange effect, if he but feel it.
   Corb. 'Tis true, therefore forbear; I'll take my venture:
Give me it again.
   Mos. At no hand; pardon me:
You shall not do yourself that wrong, sir. I
Will so advise you, you shall have it all.
   Corb. How?
   Mos. All, sir; 'tis your right, your own: no man
Can claim a part: 'tis yours, without a rival,
Decreed by destiny.

Corb. How, how, good Mosca?
Mos. I'll tell you, sir: this fit he shall recover.
Corb. I do conceive you.
Mos. And, on first advantage
Of his gained sense, will I re-importune him
Unto the making of his testament:
And show him this.   [*Pointing to the money.*
Corb. Good, good.
Mos. 'Tis better yet,
If you will hear, sir.
Corb. Yes, with all my heart.
Mos. Now, would I counsel you, make home with speed;
There frame a will; whereto you shall inscribe
My master your sole heir.
Corb. And disinherit
My son!
Mos. Oh, sir, the better: for that colour
Shall make it much more taking.
Corb. Oh, but colour?
Mos. This will, sir, you shall send it unto me.
Now, when I come to enforce, as I will do,
Your cares, your watchings, and your many prayers,
Your more than many gifts, your this day's present,
And last, produce your will; where, without thought,
Or least regard, unto your proper issue,
A son so brave, and highly meriting
The stream of your diverted love hath thrown you
Upon my master, and made him your heir:
He cannot be so stupid, or stone-dead,
But out of conscience and mere gratitude——
Corb. He must pronounce me his?
Mos. 'Tis true.
Corb. This plot
Did I think on before.
Mos. I do believe it.
Corb. Do you not believe it?
Mos. Yes, sir.
Corb. Mine own project.
Mos. Which, when he hath done, sir——
Corb. Published me his heir?
Mos. And you so certain to survive him——
Corb. Ay.
Mos. Being so lusty a man——
Corb. 'Tis true.
Mos. Yes, sir——
Corb. I thought on that too. See how he should be
The very organ to express my thoughts.
Mos. You have not only done yourself a good——

Corb. But multiplied it on my son.
Mos. 'Tis right, sir.
Corb. Still, my invention.
Mos. 'Las, sir! heaven knows,
It hath been all my study, all my care,
(I e'en grow grey withal), how to work things——
Corb. I do conceive, sweet Mosca.
Mos. You are he
For whom I labour here.
Corb. Ay, do, do, do:
I'll straight about it.   [*Going.*
Mos. Rook go with you, raven!
Corb. I know thee honest.
Mos. You do lie, sir!   [*Aside.*
Corb. And——
Mos. Your knowledge is no better than your ears, sir.
Corb. I do not doubt to be a father to thee.
Mos. Nor I to gull my brother of his blessing.
Corb. I may have my youth restored to me, why not?
Mos. Your worship is a precious ass!
Corb. What sayest thou?
Mos. I do desire your worship to make haste, sir.
Corb. 'Tis done, 'tis done; I go.   [*Exit.*
Volp. [*Leaping from his couch.*] Oh, I shall burst!
Let out my sides, let out my sides—
Mos. Contain
Your flux of laughter, sir, you know this hope
Is such a bait, it covers any hook.
Volp. Oh, but thy working and thy placing it!
I cannot hold; good rascal let me kiss thee:
I never knew thee in so rare a humour.
Mos. Alas, sir, I but do as I am taught;
Follow your grave instructions; give them words;
Pour oil into their ears, and send them hence.
Volp. 'Tis true, 'tis true. What a rare punishment
Is avarice to itself!
Mos. Ay, with our help, sir.
Volp. So many cares, so many maladies,
So many fears attending on old age,
Yea, death so often called on, as no wish
Can be more frequent with them, their limbs faint,
Their senses dull, their seeing, hearing, going,
All dead before them; yea, their very teeth,
Their instruments of eating, failing them:
Yet this is reckoned life! Nay, here was one,
Is now gone home, that wishes to live longer!
Feels not his gout, nor palsy; feigns himself
Younger by scores of years, flatters his age

With confident belying it, hopes he may,
With charms, like Æson, have his youth restored :
And with these thoughts so battens, as if fate
Would be as easily cheated on, as he,
And all turns air !—[*Knocking within.*]—Who's that there,
    now? a third !
  Mos. Close, to your couch again ; I hear his voice :
It is Corvino, our spruce merchant.
  Volp. [*Lies down as before.*] Dead.
  Mos. Another bout, sir, with your eyes.—[*Anointing them.*]
    —Who's there?

Enter CORVINO.

Signor Corvino ! come, most wished for ! Oh,
How happy were you, if you knew it, now !
  Corv. Why? what? wherein?
  Mos. The tardy hour is come, sir.
  Corv. He is not dead?
  Mos. Not dead, sir, but as good ;
He knows no man.
  Corv. How shall I do then?
  Mos. Why, sir?
  Corv. I have brought him here a pearl.
  Mos. Perhaps he has
So much remembrance left as to know you, sir.
He still calls on you ; nothing but your name
Is in his mouth. Is your pearl orient, sir?
  Corv. Venice was never owner of the like.
  Volp. [*Faintly.*] Signor Corvino !
  Mos. Hark !
  Volp. Signor Corvino !
  Mos. He calls you ; step and give it him. He's here, sir,
And he has brought you a rich pearl.
  Corv. How do you, sir?
Tell him it doubles the twelfth carat.
  Mos. Sir,
He cannot understand, his hearing's gone ;
And yet it comforts him to see you——
  Corv. Say,
I have a diamond for him, too.
  Mos. Best show it, sir ;
Put it into his hand ; 'tis only there
He apprehends : he has his feeling yet.
See how he grasps it !
  Corv. 'Las, good gentleman !
How pitiful the sight is !
  Mos. Tut ! forget, sir,

The weeping of an heir should still be laughter
Under a visor.

    Corv. Why, am I his heir?

    Mos. Sir, I am sworn, I may not show the will
Till he be dead ; but here has been Corbaccio,
Here has been Voltore, here were others too,
I cannot number 'em, they were so many ;
All gaping here for legacies : but I,
Taking the 'vantage of his naming you,
Signor Corvino, Signor Corvino, took
Paper and pen, and ink, and there I asked him,
Whom he would have his heir ? Corvino. Who
Should be executor ? Corvino. And,
To any question he was silent to,
I 'still interpreted the nods he made,
Through weakness, for consent : and sent home the others,
Nothing bequeathed them, but to cry and curse.

    Corv. Oh, my dear Mosca !—[*They embrace.*]—Does he not perceive us ?

    Mos. No more than a blind harper. He knows no man,
No face of friend, nor name of any servant,
Who 'twas that fed him last, or gave him drink :
Not those he hath begotten, or brought up,
Can he remember.

    Corv. Has he children ?

    Mos. Bastards,
Some dozen, or more, that he begot on beggars,
Gipsies, and Jews, and blackmoors, when he was drunk.
Knew you not that, sir ? 'tis the common fable.
The dwarf, the fool, the eunuch, are all his ;
He 's the true father of his family,
In all, save me :—but he has given them nothing.

    Corv. That 's well, that 's well ! Art sure he does not hear us ?

    Mos. Sure, sir ! Why, look you, credit your own sense.

                              [*Shouts in* VOL.'S *ear.*
The pox approach, and add to your diseases,
If it would send you hence the sooner, sir,
For your incontinence, it hath deserved it
Thoroughly, and thoroughly, and the plague to boot !—
You may come near, sir. Would you would once close
Those filthy eyes of yours, that flow with slime,
Like two frog-pits ; and those same hanging cheeks,
Covered with hide instead of skin—Nay, help, sir—
That look like frozen dish-clouts set on end !

    Corv. [*Aloud.*] Or like an old smoked wall, on which the rain
Ran down in streaks !

    Mos. Excellent, sir ! Speak out :

You may be louder yet ; a culverin
Discharged in his ear would hardly bore it.
 Corv. His nose is like a common sewer, still running.
 Mos. 'Tis good ! And what his mouth ?
 Corv. A very draught.
 Mos. Oh, stop it up——
 Corv. By no means.
 Mos. 'Pray you, let me :
Faith I could stifle him rarely with a pillow,
As well as any woman that should keep him!
 Corv. Do as you will ; but I 'll begone.
 Mos. Be so :
It is your presence makes him last so long.
 Corv. I pray you, use no violence.
 Mos. No, sir ! Why ?
Why should you be thus scrupulous, pray you, sir ?
 Corv. Nay, at your discretion.
 Mos. Well, good sir, begone.
 Corv. I will not trouble him now, to take my pearl.
 Mos. Puh ! nor your diamond. What a needless care
Is this afflicts you ? Is not all here yours ?
Am not I here, whom you have made your creature ?
That owe my being to you ?
 Corv. Grateful Mosca !
Thou art my friend, my fellow, my companion,
My partner, and shalt share in all my fortunes.
 Mos. Excepting one.
 Corv. What 's that ?
 Mos. Your gallant wife, sir—.   [*Exit* CORV.
Now is he gone : we had no other means
To shoot him hence, but this.
 Volp. My divine Mosca !
Thou hast to-day outgone thyself. [*Knocking within.*]—Who 's
  there ?
I will be troubled with no more. Prepare
Me music, dances, banquet, all delights ;
The Turk is not more sensual in his pleasures,
Than will Volpone. [*Exit* MOS.] Let me see ; a pearl !
A diamond ! plate ! chequines ! Good morning's purchase
Why, this is better than rob churches, yet ;
Or fat, by eating, once a month, a man—

    Re-enter MOSCA.

Who is 't ?
 Mos. The beauteous Lady Would-be, sir,
Wife to the English knight, Sir Politick Would-be
(This is the style, sir, is directed me),

Hath sent to know how you have slept to-night,
And if you would be visited?
   Volp. Not now;
Some three hours hence—
   Mos. I told the squire so much.
   Volp. When I am high with mirth and wine; then, then:
'Fore heaven, I wonder at the desperate valour
Of the bold English, that they dare let loose
Their wives to all encounters!
   Mos. Sir, this knight
Had not his name for nothing, he is *politick*,
And knows, howe'er his wife affect strange airs,
She hath not set the face to be dishonest:
But had she Signor Corvino's wife's face—
   Volp. Has she so rare a face?
   Mos. Oh, sir, the wonder,
The blazing star of Italy! a wench
Of the first year! a beauty ripe as harvest!
Whose skin is whiter than a swan all over,
Than silver, snow, or lilies! a soft lip,
Would tempt you to eternity of kissing!
And flesh that melteth in the touch to blood!
Bright as your gold, and lovely as your gold.
   Volp. Why had not I known this before?
   Mos. Alas, sir,
Myself but yesterday discovered it.
   Volp. How might I see her?
   Mos. Oh, not possible;
She's kept as warily as is your gold;
Never does come abroad, never takes air
But at a window. All her looks are sweet
As the first grapes or cherries, and are watched
As near as they are.
   Volp. I must see her.
   Mos. Sir,
There is a guard of spies ten thick upon her,
All his whole household; each of which is set
Upon his fellow, and have all their charge
When he goes out, when he comes in, examined.
   Volp. I will go see her, though but at her window.
   Mos. In some disguise, then.
   Volp. That is true; I must
Maintain mine own shape still the same: we'll think. [*Exeunt.*

ACT II.

SCENE I.—ST. MARK'S PLACE; *a retired corner before* CORVINO'S *House.*

Enter Sir POLITICK WOULD-BE *and* PEREGRINE.

Sir P. Sir, to a wise man, all the world's his soil:
It is not Italy, nor France, nor Europe,
That must bound me, if my fates call me forth.
Yet, I protest, it is no salt desire
Of seeing countries, shifting a religion,
Nor any disaffection to the state
Where I was bred, and unto which I owe
My dearest plots, hath brought me out; much less,
That idle, antique, stale, grey-headed project
Of knowing men's minds and manners, with Ulysses!
But a peculiar humour of my wife's
Laid for this height of Venice, to observe,
To quote, to learn the language, and so forth—
I hope you travel, sir, with license?
  Per. Yes.
  Sir P. I dare the safelier converse. How long, sir,
Since you left England?
  Per. Seven weeks.
  Sir P. So lately!
You have not been with my Lord Ambassador?
  Per. Not yet, sir.
  Sir P. Pray you, what news, sir, vents our climate?
I heard last night a most strange thing reported
By some of my lord's followers, and I long
To hear how 'twill be seconded.
  Per. What was 't, sir?
  Sir P. Marry, sir, of a raven that should build
In a ship royal of the king's.
  Per. This fellow,
Does he gull me, trow? or is gulled? [*Aside.*] Your name, sir
  Sir P. My name is Politick Would-be.
  Per. Oh, that speaks him.—[*Aside.*]
A knight, sir!
  Sir P. A poor knight, sir.
  Per. Your lady
Lies here in Venice, for intelligence
Of tires, and fashions, and behaviour,
Among the courtezans? the fine Lady Would-be?
  Sir P. Yes, sir; the spider and the bee oftimes
Suck from one flower.
  Per. Good Sir Politick,

I cry you mercy; I have heard much of you:
'Tis true, sir, of your raven.

Sir P. On your knowledge?

Per. Yes, and your lion's whelping in the Tower.

Sir P. Another whelp!

Per. Another, sir.

Sir P. Now heaven!
What prodigies be these? The fires at Berwick!
And the new star! these things concurring, strange,
And full of omen! Saw you those meteors?

Per. I did, sir.

Sir P. Pray you, sir, confirm me,
Were there three porpoises seen above the bridge,
As they give out?

Per. Six, and a sturgeon, sir.

Sir P. I am astonished.

Per. Nay, sir, be not so;
I'll tell you a greater prodigy than these.

Sir P. What should these things portend?

Per. The very day
(Let me be sure) that I put forth from London,
There was a whale discover'd in the river,
As high as Woolwich, that had waited there,
Few know how many months, for the subversion
Of the Stode fleet.

Sir P. Is 't possible? believe it,
'Twas either sent from Spain, or the archdukes:
Spinola's whale, upon my life, my credit!
Will they not leave these projects? Worthy sir,
Some other news.

Per. Faith, Stone the fool is dead,
And they do lack a tavern fool extremely.

Sir P. Is Mass Stone dead?

Per. He's dead, sir; why, I hope
You thought him not immortal? O, this knight,
Were he well known, would be a precious thing
To fit our English stage: he that should write
But such a fellow, should be thought to feign
Extremely, if not maliciously.   [*Aside.*

Sir P. Stone dead!

Per. Dead. Lord! how deeply, sir, you apprehend it?
He was no kinsman to you?

Sir P. That I know of.
Well! that same fellow was an unknown fool.

Per. And yet you knew him, it seems?

Sir P. I did so. Sir,
I knew him one of the most dangerous heads
Living within the state, and so I held him.

Per. Indeed, sir?
Sir P. While he lived, in action.
He has received weekly intelligence,
Upon my knowledge, out of the Low Countries,
For all parts of the world, in cabbages;
And those dispensed again to ambassadors,
In oranges, musk melons, apricots,
Lemons, pome-citrons, and such like; sometimes
In Colchester oysters, and your Selsey cockles.
  Per. You make me wonder.
  Sir P. Sir, upon my knowledge,
Nay, I've observed him, at your public ordinary
Take his advertisement from a traveller,
A conceal'd statesman, in a trencher of meat;
And instantly, before the meal was done,
Convey an answer in a toothpick.
  Per. Strange!
How could this be, sir?
  Sir P. Why, the meat was cut
So like his character, and so laid, as he
Must easily read the cipher.
  Per. I have heard,
He could not read, sir.
  Sir P. So 'twas given out,
In policy, by those that did employ him:
But he could read, and had your languages,
And to 't, as sound a noddle——
  Per. I have heard, sir,
That your baboons were spies, and that they were
A kind of subtle nation near to China.
  Sir P. Ay, ay, your Mamaluchi. Faith, they had
Their hand in a French plot or two; but they
Were so extremely given to women, as
They made discovery of all: yet I
Had my advices here, on Wednesday last.
From one of their own coat, they were return'd,
Made their relations, as the fashion is,
And now stand fair for fresh employment.
  Per. Heart!
This Sir Pol will be ignorant of nothing.   [*Aside.*
It seems, sir, you know all.
  Sir P. Not all, sir, but
I have some general notions. I do love
To note and to observe: though I live out,
Free from the active torrent, yet I'd mark
The currents and the passages of things,
For mine own private use; and know the ebbs
And flows of state.

Per. Believe it, sir, I hold
Myself in no small tie unto my fortunes,
For casting me thus luckily upon you,
Whose knowledge, if your bounty equal it,
May do me great assistance, in instruction
For my behaviour, and my bearing, which
Is yet so rude and raw.
  Sir P. Why, came you forth
Empty of rules for travel?
  Per. Faith, I had
Some common ones, from out that vulgar grammar,
Which he that cried Italian to me, taught me.
  Sir P. Why this it is that spoils all our brave bloods,
Trusting our hopeful gentry unto pedants,
Fellows of outside, and mere bark. You seem
To be a gentleman, of ingenuous race :—
I not profess it, but my fate hath been
To be, where I have been consulted with,
In this high kind, touching some great men's sons,
Persons of blood and honour.——

Enter MOSCA *and* NANO *disguised, followed by persons with materials for erecting a Stage.*

  Per. Who be these, sir?
  Mos. Under that window, there 't must be. The same.
  Sir P. Fellows, to mount a bank. Did your instructor
In the dear tongues, never discourse to you
Of the Italian mountebanks?
  Per. Yes, sir.
  Sir P. Why,
Here you shall see one.
  Per. They are quacksalvers;
Fellows, that live by venting oils and drugs.
  Sir P. Was that the character he gave you of them?
  Per. As I remember.
  Sir P. Pity his ignorance.
They are the only knowing men of Europe!
Great general scholars, excellent physicians,
Most admired statesmen, professed favourites,
And cabinet counsellors to the greatest princes;
The only languaged men of all the world!
  Per. And, I have heard, they are most lewd impostors;
Made of all terms and shreds; no less beliers
Of great men's favours, than their own vile med'cines;
Which they will utter upon monstrous oaths:
Selling that drug for twopence, ere they part,
Which they have valued at twelve crowns before.

Sir P. Sir, calumnies are answered best with silence.
Yourself shall judge. Who is it mounts my friends?
 Mos. Scoto of Mantua, sir.
 Sir P. Is 't he? Nay, then
I'll proudly promise, sir, you shall behold
Another man that has been fant'sied to you.
I wonder yet, that he should mount his bank,
Here in this nook, that has been wont t' appear
In face of the Piazza!—Here he comes.

 Enter VOLPONE, *disguised as a mountebank Doctor, and followed by a crowd of people.*

 Volp. Mount, zany. [*To* NANO.]
 Mob. Follow, follow, follow, follow!
 Sir P. See how the people follow him! He's a man
May write ten thousand crowns in bank here. Note,
 [VOLPONE *mounts the stage.*
Mark but his gesture:—I do use to observe
The state he keeps in getting up.
 Per. 'Tis worth it, sir.
 Volp. Most noble gentlemen, and my worthy patrons! It may seem strange that I, your Scoto Mantuano, who was ever wont to fix my bank in face of the public Piazza, near the shelter of the Portico to the Procuratia, should now, after eight months' absence from this illustrious city of Venice, humbly retire myself into an obscure nook of the Piazza.
 Sir P. Did not I now object the same?
 Per. Peace, sir.
 Volp. Let me tell you: I am not, as your Lombard proverb saith, cold on my feet; or content to part with my commodities at a cheaper rate than I accustomed: look not for it. Nor that the calumnious reports of that impudent detractor and shame to our profession (Alessandro Buttone, I mean), who gave out in public I was condemned a sforzato to the galleys, for poisoning the Cardinal Bembo's —— cook, hath at all attached, much less dejected me. No, no, worthy gentlemen; to tell you true, I cannot endure to see the rabble of these ground ciarlitani, that spread their cloaks on the pavement, as if they meant to do feats of activity, and then come in lamely, with their mouldy tales out of Boccacio, like stale Tabarine, the fabulist: some of them discoursing their travels, and of their tedious captivity in the Turks galleys, when, indeed, were the truth known, they were the Christians galleys, where very temperately they ate bread and drunk water, as a wholesome penance, enjoined them by their confessors, for base pilferies.
 Sir P. Note but his bearing, and contempt of these.
 Volp. These dirty-facy-nasty-paty rogues, with one poor groat's-worth of unprepared antimony, finely wrapped up in

severals cartoccios, are able, very well, to kill their twenty a week, and play; yet these meagre, starved spirits, who have half stopped the organs of their minds with earthy oppilations, want not their favourers among your shrivelled salad-eating artisans, who are overjoyed that they may have their ha'porth of physic; though it purge them into another world, it makes no matter.

Sir P. Excellent! Have you heard better language, sir?

Volp. Well, let them go. And, gentlemen, honourable gentlemen, know that for this time our bank, being thus removed from the clamours of the canaglia, shall be the scene of pleasure and delight; for I have nothing to sell, little or nothing to sell.

Sir P. I told you, sir, his end.

Per. You did so, sir.

Volp. I protest, I and my six servants, are not able to make of this precious liquor, so fast as it is fetched away from my lodging by gentlemen of your city, strangers of the Terra-firma, worshipful merchants; ay, and senators too; who, ever since my arrival, have detained me to their uses, by their splendidous liberalities. And worthily, for what avails your rich man to have his magazines stuffed with moscadelli, or of the purest grape, when his physicians prescribe him, on pain of death, to drink nothing but water cocted with aniseeds? Oh, health, health! the blessing of the rich! the riches of the poor! who can buy thee at too dear a rate, since there is no enjoying this world without thee? Be not then so sparing of your purses, honourable gentlemen, as to abridge the natural course of life——

Per. You see his end.

Sir P. Ay, is't not good?

Volp. For when a humid flux or catarrh, by the mutability of air, falls from your head into an arm or shoulder, or any other part, take you a ducat, or your chequin of gold, and apply to the place affected: see what good effect it can work. No, no; 'tis this blessed unguenta, this rare extraction, that hath only power to disperse ull malignant humours, that procced either of hot cold, moist, or windy causes——

Per. I would he had put in dry too.

Sir P. 'Pray you, observe.

Volp. To fortify the most indigest and crude stomach, ay, were it of one that, through extreme weakness, vomited blood, applying only a warm napkin to the place, after the unction and fricace— for the vertegine in the head, putting but a drop into your nostrils, likewise behind the ears—a most sovereign and approved remedy: the mal caduco, cramps, convulsions, paralysies, epilepsies, tremor-cordia, retired nerves, ill vapours of the spleen, stopping of the liver, the stone, the strangury, hernia ventosa, iliaca passio; stops a dysenteria immediately; easeth the torsion of the small guts; and cures melancholia hypondriaca, being taken and applied according to my printed receipt. [*Pointing to his bill and his vial.*] For this is the physician, this the medicine; this counsels, this cures; this gives the direction, this works the effect; and, in sum, both together may be termed an abstract of the theorick and practick in the Æsculapian art. Twill cost you eight crowns. And—Zan Fritada, prithee sing a verse extempore in honour of it.

Sir P. How do you like him, sir?
Per. Most strangely, I!
Sir P. Is not his language rare?
Per. But alchemy,
I never heard the like; or Broughton's books.

NANO *sings*.

Had old Hippocrates, or Galen,
That to their books put med'cines all in,
But known this secret, they had never
(Of which they will be guilty ever)
Been murderers of so much paper,
Or wasted many a hurtless taper;
No Indian drug had e'er been famed,
Tobacco, sassafras not named;
Ne, yet, of guiacum one small stick, sir,
Nor Raymund Lully's great elixir.
Ne had been known the Danish Gonswort,
Or Paracelsus, with his long sword.

Per. All this, yet, will not do; eight crowns is high.
Volp. No more. Gentlemen, if I had but time to discourse to you the miraculous effects of this my oil, surnamed Oglio del Scoto; with the countless catalogue of those I have cured of the aforesaid and many more diseases: the patents and privileges of all the princes and commonwealths of Christendom; or but the depositions of those that appeared on my part before the signiary of the Sanita and most learned College of Physicians; where I was authorized, upon notice taken of the admirable virtues sf my medicaments, and mine own excellency in matter of rare and unknown secrets, not only to disperse them publicly in this famous city, but in all the territories, that happily joy under the government of the most pious and magnificent states of Italy. But may some other gallant fellow say, oh, there be divers that make profession to have as good and as experimented receipts as yours; indeed, very many have assayed, like apes, in imitation of that, which is really and essentially in me, to make of this oil; bestowed great cost in furnaces, stills, alembecks, continued fires, and preparation of the ingredients (as indeed there goes to it six hundred several simples, besides some quantity of human fat for the conglutination, which we buy of the anatomists), but when these practitioners come to the last decoction, blow, blow, puff, puff,

and all flies in fumo: ha, ha, ha! Poor wretches! I rather pity their folly and indiscretion, than their loss of time and money; for these may be recovered by industry: but to be a fool born is a disease incurable.

For myself, I always from my youth have endeavoured to get the rarest secrets, and book them either in exchange or for money? I spared not cost nor labour where anything was worthy to be learned. And, gentlemen, honourable gentlemen, I will undertake, by virtue of chemical art, out of the honourable hat that covers your head, to extract the four elements; that is to say, the fire, air, water and earth, and return you your felt without burn or stain. For, whilst others have been at the Balloo, I have been at my book; and am now past the craggy paths of study, and come to the flowery plains of honour and reputation.

Sir P. I do assure you, sir, that is his aim.

Volp. But to our price——

Per. And that withal, Sir Pol.

Volp. You all know, honourable gentlemen, I never valued this ampulla, or vial, at less than eight crowns; but for this time I am content to be deprived of it for six: six crowns is the price, and less in courtesy I know you cannot offer me; take it or leave it, howsoever, both it and I am at your service. I ask you not as the value of the thing, for then I should demand of you a thousand crowns, so the Cardinals Mentalto, Fernese, the great Duke of Tuscany, my gossip with divers other Princes have given me, but I despise money. Only to show my affection to you, honourable gentlemen, and your illustrious State here, I have neglected the messages of these Princes, mine own offices, framed my journey hither only to present you with the fruits of my travels.—Tune your voices once more to the touch of your instruments, and give the honourable assembly some delightful recreation.

Per. What monstrous and most painful circumstance
Is here, to get some three or four gazettes,
Some three-pence in the whole! for that 'twill come to.

NANO *sings*.

You that would last long, list to my song,
Make no more coil, but buy of this oil,
Would you be ever fair and young?
Stout of teeth, and strong of tongue?
Tart of palate? quick of ear?
Sharp of sight? of nostril clear?
Moist of hand? and light of foot?
Or, I will come nearer to 't,
Would you live free from all diseases?
Live the life that ever pleases,
Yet fright all aches from your bones?
Here's a med'cine for the nones.

Volp. Well, I am in a humour at this time to make a present of the small quantity my coffer contains, to the rich in courtesy, and to the poor for God's sake. Wherefore now mark: I asked you six crowns, and six crowns at other times you have paid me; you shall not give me six crowns, nor five, nor four, nor three, nor two, nor one, nor half a ducat; no, nor a moccinigo. Sixpence it will cost you, or six hundred pounds——expect no lower price, for, by the banner of my front, I will not bate a bagatine,— that I will have only a pledge of your loves, to carry something from amongst you, to show I am not condemned by you. Therefore now toss your handkerchiefs cheerfully, cheerfully, and be advertized that the first heroic spirit that deigns to grace me with an handkerchief, I will give it a little remembrance of something beside, shall please it better than if I had presented it with a double pistolet.

Per. Will you be that heroic spark, Sir Pol?

[CELIA, at a window above, throws down her handkerchief.]

Oh, see! the window has prevented you.

Volp. Lady, I kiss your bounty, and for this timely grace you have done your poor Scoto, of Mantua, I will return you, over and above my oil, a secret of that high and inestimable nature, shall make you for ever enamoured on that minute, wherein your eye first descended on so mean, yet not altogether to be despised, an object. Here is a powder concealed in this paper, of which, if I should speak to the worth, nine thousand volumes were but as one page, that page as a line, that line as a word; so short is this pilgrimage of man (which some call life) to the expression of it. Would I reflect on the price? Why the whole world is but as an empire, that empire as a province, that province as a bank, that bank as a private purse to the purchase of it. I will only tell you it is the powder that made Venus a goddess, (given her by Apollo,) that kept her perpetually young, cleared her wrinkles, firmed her gums, filled her skin, coloured her hair, from her derived to Helen, and at the sack of Troy unfortunately lost: till now, in this our age, it was as happily recovered, by a studious antiquary, out of some ruins of Asia, who sent a moiety of it to the Court of France (but much sophisticated), wherewith the ladies there now colour their hair. The rest, at this present, remains with me; extracted to a quintessence: so that, wherever it but touches in youth it perpetually preserves, in age restores the complexion; seats your teeth, did they dance like virginal jacks, firm as a wall; makes them white as ivory, that were black as——

Enter CORVINO.

Cor. Spight o' the devil, and my shame! come down here; Come down. No house but mine to make your scene? Signor Flaminio, will you down, sir? down?

What, is my wife your Franciscina, sir?
No windows on the whole piazza, here,
To make your properties but mine? but mine?
                    [*Beats away* VOLPONE, NANO, *&c.*
Heart! ere to-morrow I shall be new-christened,
And call'd the Pantalone di Besogniosi,
About the town.

  Per. What should this mean, Sir Pol?
  Sir P. Some trick of state, believe it; I will home.
  Per. It may be some design on you.
  Sir P. I know not;
I 'll stand upon my guard.
  Per. It is your best, sir.
  Sir P. This three weeks, all my advices, all my letters,
They have been intercepted.
  Per. Indeed, sir!
Best have a care.
  Sir P. Nay, so I will.
  Per. This knight,
I may not lose him, for my mirth, till night.   [*Exeunt.*

SCENE II.—*A Room in* VOLPONE'S *House.*

Enter VOLPONE *and* MOSCA.

  Volp. O, I am wounded!
  Mos. Where, sir?
  Volp. Not without;
Those blows were nothing: I could bear them ever.
But angry Cupid, bolting from her eyes,
Hath shot himself into me like a flame;
Where, now, he flings about his burning heat,
As in a furnace an ambitious fire,
Whose vent is stopt. The fight is all within me.
I cannot live, except thou help me, Mosca;
My liver melts, and I, without the hope
Of some soft air, from her refreshing breath,
Am but a heap of cinders.
  Mos. 'Las, good sir,
Would you had never seen her!
  Volp. Nay, would thou
Had'st never told me of her!
  Mos. Sir, 'tis true;
I do confess I was unfortunate,
And you unhappy: but I'm bound in conscience,
No less than duty, to effect my best
To your release of torment, and I will, sir.
  Volp. Dear Mosca, shall I hope?
  Mos. Sir, more than dear,

I will not bid you to despair of aught
Within a human compass.
 Volp. Oh, there spoke
My better angel. Mosca, take my keys,
Gold, plate, and jewels, all's at thy devotion;
Employ them how thou wilt; nay, coin me, too;
So thou, in this, but crown my longings, Mosca.
 Mos. Use but your patience.
 Volp. So I have.
 Mos. I doubt not
To bring success to your desires.
 Volp. Nay, then,
I not repent me of my late disguise.
 Mos. If you can horn him, sir, you need not.
 Volp. True:
Besides, I never meant him for my heir.
Is not the colour of my beard and eyebrows
To make me known?
 Mos. No jot.
 Volp. I did it well.
 Mos. So well, would I could follow you in mine,
With half the happiness!—and yet I would
Escape your epilogue.   [*Aside.*
 Volp. But were they gulled
With a belief that I was Scoto?
 Mos. Sir,
Scoto himself could hardly have distinguished!
I have not time to flatter you now; we'll part;
And as I prosper, so applaud my art.   [*Exeunt.*

   Scene III.—*A Room in* Corvino's *House.*

Enter Corvino, *with his sword in his hand, dragging in* Celia.

 Corv. Death of mine honour, with the city's fool!
A juggling, tooth-drawing, prating mountebank!
And at a public window! where, whilst he,
With his strained action, and his dole of faces,
To his drug-lecture draws your itching ears,
A crew of old, unmarried, noted letchers,
Stood leering up like satyrs; and you smile
Most graciously, and fan your favours forth,
To give your hot spectators satisfaction!
What, was your mountebank their call? Their whistle?
Or were you enamoured on his copper rings,
His saffron jewel, with the toad-stone in 't,
Or his embroidered suit, with the cope-stitch,
Made of a horse-cloth? Or his old tilt-feather?

Or his starched beard? Well, you shall have him, yes!
He shall come home to you. Or, let me see,
I think you'd rather mount; would you not mount?
Why, if you'll mount, you may; yes, truly you may!
And so you may be seen, down to the foot.
Get you a cittern, lady Vanity,
And be a dealer with the virtuous man;
Make one: I'll but protest myself a cuckold,
And save your dowry. I'm a Dutchman, I!
For, if you thought me an Italian,
You would be damned, ere you did this, you would!
Thou 'dst tremble to imagine, that the murder
Of a father, mother, brother, all thy race,
Should follow, as the subject of my justice.
   Cel. Good, sir, have patience.
   Corv. What couldst thou propose
Less to thyself, than in this heat of wrath,
And, stung with my dishonour, I should strike
This steel into thee, with as many stabs,
As thou wert gazed upon with goatish eyes?
   Cel. Alas, sir, be appeased! I could not think
My being at the window should more now
Move your impatience than at other times.
   Corv. No! not to seek and entertain a parley
With a known knave, before a multitude!
You were an actor with your handkerchief,
Which he most sweetly kissed in the receipt,
And might, no doubt, return it with a letter,
And point the place where you might meet; your sister's,
Your mother's, or your aunt's might serve the turn.
   Cel. Why, dear sir, when do I make these excuses,
Or ever stir abroad, but to the church?
And that so seldom——
   Corv. Well, it shall be less;
And thy restraint before was liberty
To what I now decree: and therefore mark me.
First, I will have this wicked light damned up;
And till 't be done, some two or three yards off
I'll chalk a line: o'er which if thou but chance
To set thy desperate foot, more hell, more horror,
More wild remorseless rage shall seize on thee,
Than on a conjurer that had heedless left
His circle's safety ere his devil was laid.
Then here's a lock which I will hang upon thee,
And, now I think on 't, I will keep thee backwards;
Thy lodging shall be backwards; thy walks backwards;
Thy prospect all be backwards; and no pleasure,
That thou shalt know but backwards; nay, since you force

SCENE III.]   *VOLPONE; OR, THE FOX.*   133

My honest nature, know it is your own,
Being too open makes me use you thus :
Since you will not contain your subtle nostrils
In a sweet room, but they must snuff the air
Of rank and sweaty passengers. [*Knocking within.*]—One
        knocks.
Away, and be not seen, pain of thy life;
Nor look toward the window : if thou dost——
Nay, stay, hear this—let me not prosper, woman,
But I will make thee an anatomy,
Dissect thee mine own self, and read a lecture
Upon thee to the city, and in public.
Away !—   [*Exit* CELIA.
            Enter SERVANT.
        Who's there?
    Serv. 'Tis Signor Mosca, sir.
    Corv. Let him come in. [*Exit* SERV.] His master's dead :
        there's yet
Some good to help the bad.—
            Enter MOSCA.
            My Mosca, welcome !
I guess your news.
    Mos. I fear you cannot, sir.
    Corv. Is 't not his death ?
    Mos. Rather the contrary.
    Corv. Not his recovery ?
    Mos. Yes, sir.
    Corv. I am cursed,
I an bewitched, my crosses meet to vex me.
How ? how ? how ? how ?
    Mos. Why, sir, with Scoto's oil ;
Corbaccio and Voltore brought of it,
Whilst I was busy in an inner room——
    Corv. Death ! that damned mountebank ; but for the law
Now, I could kill the rascal : it cannot be
His oils should have that virtue. Have not I
Known him a common rogue, come fidling in
To the osteria with a tumbling girl,
And, when he has done all his forced tricks, been glad
Of a poor spoonful of dead wine with flies in 't ?
It cannot be. All his ingredients
Are a sheep's gall, a roasted bitch's marrow,
Some few sod earwigs, pounded caterpillars,
A little capon's grease, and fasting spittle :
I know them to a dram.
    Mos. I know not, sir ;
But some on 't there, they poured into his ears,

Some in his nostrils, and recovered him;
Applying but the fricace.

   Corv. Plague o' that fricace!

   Mos. And since, to seem the more officious
And flattering of his health, there they have had
At extreme fees, the college of physicians
Consulting on him, how they might restore him;
Where one would have a cataplasm of spices,
Another a flayed ape clapped to his breast,
A third would have it a dog, a fourth an oil,
With wild cats' skins: at last they all resolved
That to preserve him was no other means
But some young woman must be straight sought out,
Lusty, and full of juice to sleep by him;
And to this service, most unhappily,
And most unwillingly am I now employed,
Which here I thought to pre-acquaint you with,
For your advice, since it concerns you most;
Because I would not do that thing might cross
Your ends, on whom I have my sole dependence, sir:
Yet, if I do it not, they may delate
My slackness to my patron, work me out
Of his opinion; and there all your hopes,
Ventures, or whatsoever, are all frustrate!
I do but tell you, sir. Besides, they are all
Now striving who shall first present him; therefore—
I could entreat you, briefly, conclude somewhat;
Prevent them if you can.

   Corv. Death to my hopes,
This is my villainous fortune! Best to hire
Some common courtezan.

   Mos. Ay, I thought on that, sir;
But they are all so subtle, full of art—
And age again doting and flexible,
So as—I cannot tell—we may, perchance,
Light on a quean may cheat us all.

   Corv. 'Tis true.

   Mos. No, no: it must be one that has no tricks, sir,
Some simple thing, a creature made unto it;
Some girl you may command. Have you no kinswoman?
Odso—Think, think, think, think, think, think, think, sir.
One o' the doctors offered there his daughter.

   Corv. How!

   Mos. Yes, Signor Lupo, the physician.

   Carv. His daughter!

   Mos. And a virgin, sir. Why, alas,
He knows the state of 's body, what it is;
That nought can warm his blood, sir, but a fever;

Nor any incantation raise his spirit;
A long forgetfulness hath seized that part.
Besides. sir, who shall know it? some one or two——
    Corv. I pray thee give me leave. [*Walks aside.*] If any man
But I had had this luck—The thing in 't self,
I know, is nothing—Wherefore should not I
As well command my blood and my affections
As this dull doctor? In the point of honour
The cases are all one of wife and daughter.
    Mos. I hear him coming.   [*Aside.*
    Corv. She shall do 't: 'tis done.
Slight! if this doctor, who is not engaged,
Unless 't be for his counsel, which is nothing,
Offer his daughter, what should I, that am
So deeply in? I will prevent him: Wretch!
Covetous wretch! Mosca, I have determined.
    Mos. How, sir?
    Corv. We 'll make all sure. The party you wot of
Shall be mine own wife, Mosca.
    Mos. Sir, the thing,
But that I would not seem to counsel you,
I should have motioned to you, at the first:
And make your count, you have cut all their throats,
Why, 'tis directly taking a possession!
And in his next fit we may let him go.
'Tis but to pull the pillow from his head,
And he is throttled: it had been done before,
But for your scrupulous doubts.
    Corv. Ay, a plague on't,
My conscience fools my wit! Well, I 'll be brief,
And so be thou, lest they should be before us:
Go home, prepare him, tell him with what zeal
And willingness I do it; swear it was
On the first hearing, as thou may'st do, truly,
Mine own free motion.
    Mos. Sir, I warrant you,
I 'll so possess him with it, that the rest
Of his starved clients shall be banished all;
And only you received. But come not, sir,
Until I send, for I have something else
To ripen for your good, you must not know 't.
    Corv. But do not you forget to send now.
    Mos. Fear not.   [*Exit.*
    Corv. Where are you, wife? My Celia! Wife!

Re-enter CELIA.

What! blubbering?
Come, dry those tears. I think thou thoughtst me in earnest

Ha! by this light I talked so but to try thee :
Methinks the lightness of the occasion
Should have confirmed thee.   Come, I am not jealous.
  Cel. No!
  Corv. Faith, I am not; I, nor never was;
It is a poor unprofitable humour.
Do not I know, if women have a will,
They'll do 'gainst all the watches of the world,
And that the fiercest spies are tamed with gold?
Tut, I am confident in thee, thou shalt see't;
And see, I'll give the cause, too, to believe it.
Come, kiss me.   Go, and make thee ready, straight,
In all thy best attire, thy choicest jewels,
Put them all on, and, with them, thy best looks:
We are invited to a solemn feast,
At old Volpone's, where it shall appear
How far I am free from jealousy or fear.   [*Exeunt.*

ACT III.

SCENE I.—*A Street.*

Enter MOSCA.

  Mos. I fear I shall begin to grow in love
With my dear self, and my most prosperous parts,
They do so spring and burgeon; I can feel
A whimsy in my blood: I know not how,
Success hath made me wanton.   I could skip
Out of my skin, now, like a subtle snake,
I am so limber.   Oh! your parasite
Is a most precious thing, dropt from above,
Not bred 'mongst clods and clodpoles, here on earth.
I muse, the mystery was not made a science,
It is so liberally professed!   Almost
All the wise world is little else, in nature,
But parasites or sub-parasites.   And yet,
I mean not those that have your bare town-art,
To know who's fit to feed them; have no house,
No family, no care, and therefore mould
Tales for men's ears, to bait that sense; or get
Kitchen-invention, and some stale receipts
To please the belly and the groin; nor those,
With their court dog-tricks, that can fawn and fleer,
Make their revenue out of legs and faces,
Echo my lord, and lick away a moth:
But your fine elegant rascal, that can rise,
And stoop, almost together, like an arrow;

Shoot through the air as nimbly as a star;
Turn short as doth a swallow; and be here,
And there, and here, and yonder, all at once;
Present to any humour, all occasion;
And change a visor, swifter than a thought!
This is the creature had the art born with him;
Toils not to learn it, but doth practice it
Out of most excellent nature: and such sparks
Are the true parasites others but their zanis.

Enter BONARIO.

Who's this? Bonario, old Corbaccio's son?
The person I was bound to seek.   Fair sir,
You are happily met.
  Bon. That cannot be by thee.
  Mos. Why, sir?
  Bon. Nay, pray thee, know thy way, and leave me:
I would be loth to interchange discourse
With such a mate as thou art.
  Mos. Courteous sir,
Scorn not my poverty.
  Bon. Not I, by heaven;
But thou shalt give me leave to hate thy baseness.
  Mos. Baseness!
  Bon. Ay; answer me, is not thy sloth
Sufficient argument? thy flattery?
Thy means of feeding?
  Mos. Heaven be good to me!
These imputations are too common, sir,
And easily stuck on virtue when she's poor.
You are unequal to me, and however
Your sentence may be righteous, yet you are not
That, ere you know me, thus proceed in censure:
St. Mark bear witness against you, 'tis inhuman.   [*Weeps.*
  Bon. What! does he weep? the sign is soft and good:
I do repent me that I was so harsh.   [*Aside.*
  Mos. 'Tis true, that, swayed by strong necessity,
I am enforced to eat my careful bread
With too much obsequy; 'tis true, beside,
That I am fain to spin mine own poor raiment
Out of my mere observance, being not born
To a free fortune: but that I have done
Base offices, in rending friends asunder,
Dividing families, betraying counsels,
Whispering false lies, or mining men with praises,
Trained their credulity with perjuries,
Corrupted chastity, or am in love
With mine own tender ease, but would not rather

Prove the most rugged and laborious course,
That might redeem my present estimation,
Let me here perish, in all hope of goodness.
　Bon. This cannot be a personated passion. 　　*[Aside.*
I was to blame, so to mistake thy nature;
Prithee, forgive me: and speak out thy business.
　Mos. Sir, it concerns you; and though I may seem,
At first to make a main offence in manners,
And in my gratitude unto my master;
Yet, for the pure love, which I bear all right,
And hatred of the wrong, I must reveal it.
This very hour your father is in purpose
To disinherit you——
　Bon. How!
　Mos. And thrust you forth,
As a mere stranger to his blood; 'tis true, sir,
The work no way engageth me, but, as
I claim an interest in the general state
Of goodness and true virtue, which I hear
To abound in you: and, for which mere respect
Without a second aim, sir, I have done it.
　Bon. This tale hath lost thee much of the late trust
Thou hadst with me; it is impossible;
I know not how to lend it any thought,
My father should be so unnatural.
　Mos. It is a confidence that well becomes,
Your piety; and form'd, no doubt, it is
From your own simple innocence: which makes
Your wrong monstrous and abhorr'd. But, sir,
I now will tell you more. This very minute,
It is, or will be doing; and, if you
Shall be but pleased to go with me, I'll bring you,
I dare not say where you shall see, but where
Your ear shall be a witness of the deed;
Hear yourself written bastard, and professed
The common issue of the earth.
　Bon. I am amazed!
　Mos. Sir, if I do it not, draw your just sword,
And score your vengeance on my front and face:
Mark me your villain: you have too much wrong,
And I do suffer for you, sir. My heart
Weeps blood in anguish——
　Bon. Lead; I follow thee. 　　　　　　　*[Exeunt.*

SCENE II.—*A Room in* VOLPONE'S *House.*

Enter VOLPONE.

Volp. Mosca stays long, methinks.—Bring forth your sports,
And help to make the wretched time more sweet.

Enter NANO, ANDROGYNO, *and* CASTRONE.

Nan. Dwarf, fool, and eunuch, well met here we be.
A question it were now, whether of us three,
Being all the known delicates of a rich man,
In pleasing him, claim the precedency can?
 Cas. I claim for myself.
 And. And so doth the fool.
 Nan. 'Tis foolish indeed: let me set you both to school.
First for your dwarf, he's little and witty,
And everything, as it is little, is pretty;
Else why do men say to a creature of my shape,
So soon as they see him, It's a pretty little ape?
And why a pretty ape, but for pleasing imitation
Of greater men's actions, in a ridiculous fashion?
Beside, this feat body of mine doth not crave
Half the meat, drink, and cloth, one of your bulks will have.
Admit your fool's face be the mother of laughter,
Yet, for his brain, it must always come after:
And though that do feed him, it's a pitiful case,
His body is beholding to such a bad face. [*Knocking within.*
 Volp. Who's there? my couch; away! look!
Nano, see. [*Exit* AND. *and* CAS.
Give me my caps, first.—Go, enquire.—[*Exit* NANO.]—Now,
 Cupid
Send it be Mosca, and with fair return!
 Nan. [*Within.*] It is the beauteous madam——
 Volp. Wouldbe——is it?
 Nan. The same.
 Volp. Now torment on me! Squire her in;
For she will enter, or dwell here for ever:
Nay, quickly.—[*Retires to his couch.*]—That my fit were past!
 I fear
A second hell, too, that my loathing this
Will quite expel my appetite to the other?
Would she were taking now her tedious leave.
Lord, how it threats me what I am to suffer!

Re-enter NANO *with* LADY POLITICK WOULD-BE.

 Lady P. I thank you, good sir. 'Pray you signify
Unto your patron, I am here.—This band
Shews not my neck enough.—I trouble you, sir;
Let me request you, bid one of my women

Come hither to me.—In good faith, I am drest
Most favourably to-day! It is no matter:
'Tis well enough.—

Enter First Waiting-woman.

Look, see, these petulant things.
How they have done this!
  Volp. I do feel the fever
Entering in at mine ears. Oh, for a charm,
To fright it hence!   [*Aside.*
  Lady P. Come nearer: is this curl
In his right place, or this? Why is this higher
Than all the rest? You have not washed your eyes, yet!
Or do they not stand even in your head?
Where is your fellow? Call her.   [*Exit First* Woman.
  Nan. Now, St Mark
Deliver us! anon, she'll beat her women,
Because her nose is red.

Re-enter First with Second Woman.

  Lady P. I pray you, view
This tire, forsooth: are all things apt, or no?
  First Wom. One hair a little, here, sticks out, forsooth.
  Lady P. Does't so, forsooth! and where was your dear sight,
When it did so, forsooth! What now! bird-eyed?
And you, too? 'Pray you, both approach and mend it.
Now, by that light, I muse you are not ashamed!
I, that have preach'd these things so oft unto you,
Read you the principles, argued all the grounds,
Disputed every fitness, every grace,
Call'd you to counsel of so frequent dressings—
  Nan. More carefully than of your fame or honour.   [*Aside.*
  Lady P. Made you acquainted, what an ample dowry
The knowledge of these things would be unto you,
Able, alone, to get you noble husbands
At your return: and you thus to neglect it!
Besides you seeing what a curious nation
The Italians are, what will they say of me?
The English lady cannot dress herself.
Here's a fine imputation to our country!
Well, go your ways, and stay in the next room.
This fucus was too coarse too; it's no matter.—
Good sir, you'll give them entertainment?
                    [*Exeunt* NANO *and* Waiting-women.
  Volp. The storm comes toward me.
  Lady P. [*Goes to the couch.*] How does my Volpone?
  Volp. Troubled with noise, I cannot sleep; I dreamt
That a strange fury entered, now, my house,

And, with the dreadful tempest of her breath,
Did cleave my roof asunder.
   Lady P. Believe me, and I
Had the most fearful dream, could I remember 't——
   Volp. Out on my fate! I have given her the occasion
How to torment me: she will tell me hers.   [*Aside.*
   Lady P. Methought, the golden mediocrity,
Polite and delicate——
   Volp. Oh, if you do love me,
No more: I sweat and suffer, at the mention
Of any dream; feel how I tremble yet.
   Lady P. Alas, good soul! the passion of the heart.
Seed-pearl were good now, boiled with syrup of apples,
Tincture of gold, and coral, citron-pills,
Your elicampane root, myrobalanes——
   Volp. Ah, me, I have taken a grasshopper by the wing!
                                                                             [*Aside.*
   Lady P. Burnt silk and amber: you have muscadel
Good in the house——
   Volp. You will not drink, and part?
   Lady P. No, fear not that. I doubt, we shall not get
Some English saffron, half a dram would serve;
Your sixteen cloves, a little musk, dried mints,
Bugloss, and barley-meal——
   Volp. She's in again!
Before I feigned diseases, now I have one.   [*Aside.*
   Lady P. And these applied with a right scarlet cloth.
   Volp. Another flood of words! a very torrent!   [*Aside.*
   Lady P. Shall I, sir, make you a poultice?
   Volp. No, no no,
I'm very well, you need prescribe no more.
   Lady P. I have a little studied physic; but now,
I'm all for music, save, in the forenoons,
An hour or two for painting. I would have
A lady, indeed, to have all, letters and arts,
Be able to discourse, to write, to paint,
But principal, as Plato holds, your music,
And so does wise Pythagoras, I take it,
Is your true rapture: when there is consent,
In face, in voice, and clothes: and is, indeed,
Our sex's chiefest ornament.
   Volp. The poet
As old in time as Plato, and as knowing,
Says, that your highest female grace is silence.
   Lady P. Which of your poets? Petrarch, or Tasso, or Dante?
Guarini? Ariosto? Aretine?
Cieco di Hadria? I have read them all.
   Volp. Is everything a cause to my destruction?   [*Aside.*

Lady P. I think I have two or three of them about me.
Volp. The sun, the sea, will sooner both stand still
Than her eternal tongue! nothing can escape it. [*Aside.*
Lady P. Here's Pastor Fido——
Volp. Profess obstinate silence;
That's now my safest. [*Aside.*
Lady P. All our English writers,
I mean such as are happy in the Italian,
Will deign to steal out of this author, mainly:
Almost as much as from Montagnié:
He has so modern and facile a vein,
Fitting the time and catching the court-ear!
Your Petrarch is more passionate, yet he,
In days of sonnetting, trusted them with much:
Dante is hard, and few can understand him.
But, for a desperate wit, there's Aretine;
Only his pictures are a little obscene—
You mark me not,
Volp. Alas, my mind's perturbed.
Lady P. Why, in such cases, we must cure ourselves,
Make use of our philosophy——
Volp. Oh me!
Lady P. And as we find our passions do rebel,
Encounter them with reason, or divert them,
By giving scope unto some other humour
Of lesser danger: as, in politic bodies,
There's nothing more doth overwhelm the judgment
And cloud the understanding than too much
Settling and fixing, and, as 'twere, subsiding
Upon one object. For the incorporating
Of these same outward things into that part
Which we call mental, leaves some certain fæces
That stop the organs, and, as Plato says,
Assassinate our knowledge.
Volp. Now, the spirit
Of patience help me! [*Aside.*
Lady P. Come, in faith, I must
Visit you more a days; and make you well:
Laugh and be lusty.
Volp. My good angel, save me! [*Aside.*
Lady P. There was but one sole man in all the world
With whom I e'er could sympathise; and he
Would lie you often three, four hours together
To hear me speak; and be sometime so wrapt
As he would answer me quite from the purpose,
Like you, and you are like him, just. I'll discourse,
An't be but only, sir, to bring you asleep,

How we did spend our time and loves together
For some six years.
   Volp. Oh, oh, oh, oh, oh, oh!
   Lady P. For we were coætanei, and brought up——
   Volp. Some power, some fate, some fortune, rescue me!

             Enter MOSCA.

   Mos. God save you, madam!
   Lady P. Good sir.
   Volp. Mosca! welcome,
Welcome to my redemption.
   Mos. Why, sir?
   Volp. Oh,
Rid me of this my torture, quickly, there;
My madam, with the everlasting voice:
The bells, in time of pestilence, ne'er made
Like noise, or were in that perpetual motion!
The Cock-pit comes not near it. All my house,
But now, steamed like a bath with her thick breath,
A lawyer could not have been heard; nor scarce
Another woman, such a hail of words
She has let fall. For hell's sake, rid her hence.
   Mos. Has she presented?
   Volp. Oh, I do not care;
I'll take her absence, upon any price,
With any loss.
   Mos. Madam——
   Lady P. I have brought your patron,
A toy, a cap here, of mine own work.
   Mos. 'Tis well.
I had forgot to tell you, I saw your knight,
Where you would little think it——
   Lady P. Where?
   Mos. Marry,
Where yet, if you make haste, you may apprehend
Rowing upon the water in a gondole
With the most cunning courtezan of Venice.
   Lady P. Is 't true?
   Mos. Pursue them, and believe your eyes:
Leave me to make your gift. [*Exit* Lady P. *hastily.*]—I knew
      'twould take:
For lightly, they that use themselves most license,
Are still most jealous.
   Volp. Mosca, hearty thanks,
For thy quick fiction, and delivery of me.
Now to my hopes, what sayest thou?

Re-enter LADY P. WOULD-BE.

Lady P. But do you hear, sir?——
Volp. Again! I fear a paroxysm.
Lady P. Which way
Rowed they together?
Mos. Toward the Rialto.
Lady P. I pray you lend me your dwarf.
Mos. I pray you take him.—   [*Exit* LADY P.
Your hopes, sir, are like happy blossoms, fair,
And promise timely fruit, if you will stay
But the maturing; keep you at your couch,
Corbaccio will arrive straight with the Will;
When he is gone I'll tell you more.   [*Exit.*
Volp. My blood,
My spirits are returned; I am alive:
And like your wanton gamester at primero,
Whose thought had whispered to him, not go less,
Methinks I lie and draw——for an encounter.
   [*The scene closes upon* VOLPONE.

SCENE II.—*The Passage leading to* VOLPONE'S *Chamber.*

Enter MOSCA *and* BONARIO.

Mos. Sir, here concealed [*shews him a closet,*] you may hear
   all. But, pray you.
Have patience, sir [*knocking within*]—the same's your father
   knocks:
I am compelled to leave you.   [*Exit.*
   Bon. Do so.—Yet
Cannot my thought imagine this a truth.   [*Goes into the closet.*

SCENE III.—*Another Part of the same.*

Enter MOSCA *and* CORVINO, CELIA *following.*

Mos. Death on me! your are come too soon, what meant you?
Did not I say I would send?
   Corv. Yes, but I feared
You might forget it, and then they prevent us.
   Mos. Prevent! Did e'er man haste so to his shame?
A courtier would not ply it so for a place.   [*Aside.*
Well, now there is no helping it, stay here;
I'll presently return.   [*Exit.*
   Corv. Where are you, Celia?
You know not wherefore I have brought you hither?
   Cel. Not well, except you told me.
   Corv. Now I will:
Hark hither.   (*Exeunt.*

SCENE IV.—*A Closet opening into a Gallery.*

Enter MOSCA *and* BONARIO.

Mos. Sir, your father hath sent word,
It will be half-an-hour ere he come;
And therefore, if you please to walk the while
Into that gallery—at the upper end,
There are some books to entertain the time:
And I'll take care no man shall come unto you, sir.
 Bon. Yes, I will stay there.—I do doubt this fellow.
 [*Aside and exit.*
 Mos. [*Looking after him.*] There, he is far enough, he can
  hear nothing:
And, for his father, I can keep him off. [*Exit.*

SCENE V. VOLPONE'S *Chamber.*—VOLPONE *on his Couch.*
MOSCA *sitting by him.*

Enter CORVINO, *forcing in* CELIA.

 Corv. Nay, now, there is no starting back, and therefore,
Resolve upon it: I have so decreed.
It must be done. Nor would I move it afore,
Because I would avoid all shifts and tricks,
That might deny me.
 Cel. Sir, let me beseech you,
Affect not these strange trials; if you doubt
My chastity, why, lock me up for ever;
Make me the heir of darkness. Let me live
Where I may please your fears, if not your trust.
 Corv. Believe it, I have no such humour, I.
All that I speak I mean; yet I'm not mad;
Nor horn-mad, see you? Go to show yourself
Obedient and a wife.
 Cel. O heaven!
 Corv. I say it,
Do so.
 Cel. Was this the train?
 Corv. I've told you reasons;
What the physicians have set down: how much
It may concern me; what my engagements are;
My means; and the necessity of those means,
For my recovery: wherefore, if you be
Loyal, and mine, be won, respect my venture.
 Cel. Before your honour?
 Corv. Honour! tut, a breath:
There's no such thing in nature: a mere term

Invented to awe fools. What is my gold
The worse for touching, clothes for being looked on?
Why this is no more. An old decrepit wretch,
That has no sense, no sinew; takes his meat
With others' fingers; only knows to gape
When you do scald his gums; a voice, a shadow;
And what can this man hurt you?

   Cel. Lord! what spirit
Is this hath entered him?   [*Aside.*
   Corv. And for your fame,
That's such a jig; as if I would go tell it,
Cry it on the Piazza! who shall know it,
But he that cannot speak it, and this fellow,
Whose lips are in my pocket? Save yourself
(If you'll proclaim it you may,) I know no other
Shall come to know it.

   Cel. Are heaven and saints then nothing?
Will they be blind or stupid?

   Corv. How!

   Cel. Good sir,
Be jealous still, emulate them; and think
What hate they burn with toward every sin.

   Corv. I grant you: if I thought it were a sin,
I would not urge you. Should I offer this
To some young Frenchman, or hot Tuscan blood
That had read Aretine, conned all his prints,
Knew every quirk within lust's labyrinth,
And were professed critic in lechery;
And I would look upon him, and applaud him,
This were a sin; but here, 'tis contrary,
A pious work, mere charity for physic,
And honest policy, to assure mine own.

   Cel. O heaven! canst thou suffer such a change?

   Volp. Thou art mine honour, Mosca, and my pride,
My joy, my tickling, my delight! Go, bring them.

   Mos. [*Advancing.*] Please, you draw near, sir.

   Corv. Come on, what——
You will not be rebellious? By that light——

   Mos. Sir,
Signor Corvino, here, is come to see you.

   Volp. Oh!

   Mos. And hearing of the consultation had,
So lately, for your health, is come to offer,
Or rather, sir, to prostitute——

   Corv. Thanks, sweet Mosca.

   Mos. Freely, unasked or unintreated——

   Corv. Well.

   Mos. As the true fervent instance of his love—

His own most fair and proper wife; the beauty
Only of price in Venice——
    Corv. 'Tis well urged.
    Mos. To be your comfortress, and to preserve you.
    Volp. Alas, I am past already! Pray you, thank him
For his good care and promptness; but for that,
'Tis a vain labour e'en to fight 'gainst heaven :
Applying fire to stone—uh, uh, uh, uh ! [*coughing*.]
Making a dead leaf grow again. I take
His wishes gently, though ; and you may tell him
What I have done for him : marry, my state is hopeless.
Will him to pray for me ; and to use his fortune
With reverence when he comes to it.
    Mos. Do you hear, sir?
Go to him with your wife.
    Corv. Heart of my father!
Wilt thou persist thus? Come, I pray thee, come.
Thou seest 'tis nothing, Celia. By this hand,
I shall grow violent. Come, do't, I say.
    Cel. Sir, kill me, rather. I will take down poison,
Eat burning coals, do anything——
    Corv. Be damned!
Heart, I will drag thee hence, home, by the hair ;
Cry thee a strumpet through the streets ; rip up
Thy mouth unto thine ears ; and slit thy nose
Like a raw rochet!—Do not tempt me ; come,
Yield, I am loth—Death ! I will buy some slave
Whom I will kill, and bind thee to him alive ;
And at my window hang you forth, devising
Some monstrous crime, which I, in capital letters,
Will eat into thy flesh with aquafortis,
And burning corrosives, on this stubborn breast,
Now, by the blood thou hast incensed, I'll do it !
    Cel. Sir, what you please, you may, I am your martyr.
    Cor. Be not thus obstinate, I have not deserved it :
Think who it is entreats you. Pr'thee, sweet ;—
Good faith, thou shalt have jewels, gowns, attires,
What thou wilt think, and ask. Do but go kiss him.
Or touch him, but. For my sake. At my suit.
This once. No! not! I shall remember this.
Will you digrace me thus? Do you thirst my undoing?
    Mos. Nay, gentle lady, be advised.
    Corv. No, no.
She has watched her time. Ods, precious, this is scurvy,
'Tis very scurvy ; and you are—
    Mos. Nay, good sir.
    Corv. An arrant locust, by heaven, a locust !

Slave, crocodile, that hast thy tears prepared,
Expecting how thou 'lt bid them flow——
   Mos. Nay, 'pray you, sir !
She will consider.
   Cel. Would my life would serve
To satisfy—
   Corv. 'Sdeath ! If she would but speak to him.
And save my reputation, it were somewhat;
But spitefully to affect my utter ruin !
   Mos. Ay, now you have put your fortune in her hands.
Why i' faith, it is her modesty, I must quit her.
If you were absent, she would be more coming ;
I know it : and dare undertake for her.
What woman can, before her husband ? 'pray you,
Let us depart, and leave her here.
   Corv. Sweet Celia,
Thou may'st redeem all, yet ; I 'll say no more :
If not, esteem yourself as lost. Nay, stay there.
                           [Shuts the door, and exit with MOSCA.
   Cel. Oh, God, and his good angels ! Whither, whither,
Is shame fled human breasts ! That with such ease,
Men dare put off your honours and their own ?
Is, that, which ever was a cause of life,
Now placed beneath the basest circumstance,
And modesty an exile made, for money ?
   Volp. Ay, in Corvino, and such earth-fed minds,
                                 [Leaping from his couch.
That never tasted the true heaven of love.
Assure thee, Celia, he that would sell thee,
Only for hope of gain, and that uncertain,
He would have sold his part of Paradise
For ready-money, had he met a cope-man.
Why art thou amazed to see me thus revived ?
Rather applaud thy beauty's miracle ;
'Tis thy great work : that hath, not now, alone,
But sundry times raised me, in several shapes,
And, but this morning, like a mountebank,
To see thee at thy window : ay, before
I would have left my practice for thy love,
In varying figures, I would have contended
With the blue Proteus, or the horned flood.
Now art thou welcome.
   Cel. Sir !
   Volp. Nay, fly me not.
Nor let thy false imagination
That I was bed-rid, make thee think I am so :
Thou shalt not find it. I am, now, as fresh,
As hot, as high, and in as jovial plight,

As when, in that so celebrated scene,
At recitation of our comedy,
For entertainment of the great Valois,
I acted young Antinous; and attracted
The eyes and ears of all the ladies present,
To admire each graceful gesture, note, and footing.   [*Sings.*

      Come, my Celia, let us prove,
      While we can, the sports of love,
      Time will not be ours for ever,
      He, at length, our good will sever;
      Spend not then his gifts in vain;
      Suns that set may rise again;
      But if once we lose this light,
      'Tis with us perpetual night.
      Why should we defer our joys?
      Fame and rumour are but toys.
      Cannot we delude the eyes
      Of a few poor household spies
      Or his easier ears beguile,
      Thus removéd by our wile?—
      'Tis no sin love's fruits to steal;
      But the sweet thefts to reveal;
      To be taken, to be seen,
      These have crimes accounted been.

  Cel. Some serene blast me, or dire lightning strike
This my offending face!
  Volp. Why droops my Celia?
Thou hast, in place of a base husband, found
A worthy lover: use thy fortune well,
With secresy and pleasure. See, behold,
What thou art queen of; not in expectation,
As I feed others; but possessed and crown'd.
See, here, a rope of pearl; and each more orient
Than that the brave Egyptian queen caroused:
Dissolve and drink them. See, a carbuncle,
May put out both the eyes of our St. Mark;
A diamond would have bought Lollia Paulina,
When she came in, like star-light, hid with jewels
That were the spoils of provinces; take these,
And wear, and lose them: yet remains an ear-ring
To purchase them again and this whole state.
A gem but worth a private patrimony
Is nothing: we will eat such at a meal.
The heads of parrots, tongues of nightingales,
The brains of peacocks and of ostriches,
Shall be our food; and could we get the phœnix,
Though nature lost her kind, she were our dish.
  Cel. Good sir, these things might move a mind affected
With such delights; but I, whose innocence
Is all I can think wealthy or worth th' enjoying,

And which, once lost, I have nought to lose beyond it,
Cannot be taken with these sensual baits:
If you have conscience——
  Volp. 'Tis the beggar's virtue;
If thou hast wisdom, hear me, Celia.
Thy baths shall be the juice of July-flowers,
Spirit of roses and of violets,
The milk of unicorns, and panthers' breath
Gather'd in bags and mixt with Cretan wines.
Our drink shall be preparéd gold and amber;
Which we will take until my roof whirl round
With the vertigo; and my dwarf shall dance,
My eunuch sing, my fool make up the antic,
Whilst we, in changéd shapes, act Ovid's tales;
Thou like Europa now, and I like Jove,
Then I like Mars, and thou like Erycine:
So of the rest, till we have quite run through
And wearied all the fables of the gods.
Then wlll I have thee in more modern forms,
Attiréd like some sprightly dame of France,
Brave Tuscan lady, or proud Spanish beauty;
Sometimes unto the Persian sophy's wife,
Or the grand signior's mistress; and, for change,
To one of our most artful courtezans,
Or some quick negro, or cold Russian;
And I will meet thee in as many shapes
Where we may so transfuse our wandering souls
Out at our lips, and score up sums of pleasures—   [*Sings.*

>   That the curious shall not know
>   How to tell them as they flow:
>   And the envious, when they find
>   What their number is, be pined.

  Cel. If you have ears that will be pierced— or eyes
That can be opened—a heart that may be touched—
Or any part that yet sounds man about you—
If you have touch of holy saints, or heaven—
Do me the grace to let me 'scape; if not,
Be bountiful, and kill me. You do know
I am a creature hither ill-betrayed
By one whose shame I would forget it were.
If you will deign me neither of these graces,
Yet feed your wrath, sir, rather than your lust
(It is a vice comes nearer manliness),
And punish that unhappy crime of Nature
Which you miscall my beauty: flay my face,
Or poison it with ointments, for seducing
Your blood to this rebellion. Rub these hands
With what may cause an eating leprosy

E'en to my bones and marrow; anything
That may disfavour me, save in my honour;
And I will kneel to you, pray for you, pay down
A thousand hourly vows, sir, for your health;
Report and think you virtuous——
   Volp. Think me cold,
Frozen, and impotent, and so report me;
That I had Nestor's hernia thou wouldst think.
I do degenerate and abuse my nation
To play with opportunity thus long;
I should have done the act, and then have parleyed.
Yield, or I'll force thee.   [*Seizes her.*
   Cel. Oh! just God!
   Volp. In vain——
   Bon. [*Rushing in.*] Forbear, foul ravisher, libidinous swine!
Free the forced lady, or thou diest, impostor.
But that I'm loth to snatch thy punishment
Out of the hand of justice, thou shouldst yet
Be made the timely sacrifice of vengeance
Before this altar and this dross, thy idol.——
Lady, let's quit the place; it is the den
Of villainy; fear nought, you have a guard;
And he, ere long, shall meet his just reward.
                                      [*Exeunt* BON. *and* CEL.
   Volp. Fall on me, roof, and bury me in ruin!
Become my grave that wert my shelter! Oh!
I am unmask'd, unspirited, undone,
Betrayed to beggary, to infamy——

                Enter MOSCA, *wounded and bleeding.*

   Mos. Where shall I run, most wretched shame of men,
To beat out my unlucky brains?
   Volp. Here, here.
What! dost thou bleed?
   Mos. Oh! that his well-driv'n sword
Had been so courteous to have cleft me down
Unto the navel ere I lived to see
My life, my hopes, my spirits, my patron, all
Thus desperately engaged by my error!
   Volp. Woe on thy fortune!
   Mos. And my follies, sir.
   Volp. Thou hast made me miserable.
   Mos. And myself, sir.
Who would have thought he would have hearkened so?
   Volp. What shall we do?
   Mos. I know not; if my heart
Could expiate the mischance, I'd pluck it out.
Will you be pleased to hang me, or cut my throat?

And I'll requite you, sir. Let's die like Romans,
Since we have lived like Grecians.   [*Knocking within.*

  Volp. Hark! Who's there?
I hear some footing; officers, the saffi,
Come to apprehend us! I do feel the brand
Hissing already at my forehead; now,
Mine ears are boring.

  Mos. To your couch, sir, you,
Make that place good; however. [VOLPONE *lies down as before.*]
        Guilty men
Suspect what they deserve still.

            Enter CORBACCIO.

Signor Corbaccio!
  Corb. Why, how now, Mosca?
  Mos. Oh, undone, amazed, sir.
Your son, I know not by what accident,
Acquainted with your purpose to my patron,
Touching your will, and making him your heir,
Entered our house with violence, his sword drawn,
Sought for you, called you wretch, unnatural,
Vowed he would kill you.
  Corb. Me?
  Mos. Yes, and my patron.
  Corb. This act shall disinherit him, indeed:
Here is the will.
  Mos. 'Tis well, sir.
  Corb. Right and well:
Be you as careful now for me.

            Enter VOLTORE, *behind*.

  Mos. My life, sir,
Is not more tendered; I am only yours.
  Corb. How does he? Will he die shortly, thinkest thou!
  Mos. I fear
He'll outlast May.
  Corb. To-day?
  Mos. No, last out May, sir.
  Corb. Couldst thou not give him a dram?
  Mos. Oh, by no means, sir.
  Corb. Nay, I'll not bid you.
  Volt. [*Coming forward.*] This is a knave, I see.
  Mos. [*Seeing* VOLTORE.] How! Signor Voltore!   Did he
    hear me?   [*Aside.*
  Volt. Parasite!
  Mos. Who's that? Oh, sir, most timely welcome——
  Volt. Scarce,
To the discovery of your tricks, I fear.
Your are his, *only?* and mine also, are you not?

Mos. Who? I, sir?
Volt. You, sir. What device is this
About a will?
Mos. A plot for you. sir,
Volt. Come,
Put not your foists upon me ; I shall scent them.
Mos. Did you not hear it?
Volt. Yes, I hear Corbaccio
Hath made your patron there his heir.
Mos. 'Tis true,
By my device, drawn to it by my plot,
With hope——
Volt. Your patron should reciprocate?
And you have promised?
Mos. For your good, I did, sir.
Nay, more, I told his son, brought, hid him here.
Where he might hear his father pass the deed :
Being persuaded to it by this thought, sir,
That the unnaturalness, first, of the act,
And then his father's oft disclaiming on him
(Which I did mean t' help on,) would sure enrage him
To do some violence upon his parent,
On which the law should take sufficient hold,
And you be stated in a double hope:
Truth be my comfort and my conscience,
My only aim was to dig you a fortune
Out of these two old rotten sepulchres—
Volt. I cry thee mercy, Mosca.
Mos. Worth your patience
And your great merit, sir. And see the change !
Volt. Why, what success?
Mos. Most hapless! you must help, sir.
Whilst we expected the old raven, in comes
Corvino's wife, sent hither by her husband—
Volt. What, with a present?
Mos. No, sir, on visitation ;
(I 'll tell you how anon ;) and staying long,
The youth he grows impatient, rushes forth,
Seizeth the lady, wounds me, makes her swear
(Or he would murder her, that was his vow)
To affirm my patron, to have done her rape :
Which how unlike it is, you see ! and hence,
With that pretext, he's gone to accuse his father,
Defame my patron, defeat you——
Volt. Where is her husband?
Let him be sent for, straight.
Mos. Sir, I 'll go fetch him.
Volt. Bring him to the Scrutineo.

Mos. Sir, I will.
Volt. This must be stopped.
Mos. Oh, you do nobly, sir.
Alas, 'twas laboured all, sir, for your good;
Nor was there want of counsel in the plot:
But fortune can, at any time, o'erthrow
The projects of a hundred learned clerks, sir.
   Corb. [*Listening.*] What's that?
   Volt. Will't please you, sir, to go along?
               [*Exit* CORBACCIO, *followed by* VOLTORE.
   Mos. Patron, go in, and pray for our success.
   Volp. [*Rising from his couch.*] Need makes devotion? heaven
     your labour bless!   [*Exeunt.*

ACT IV.

SCENE I.—*A Street.*

Enter Sir POLITICK WOULD-BE *and* PEREGRINE.

   Sir P. I told you, sir, it was a plot; you see
What observation is! You mentioned me
For some instructions: I will tell you, sir,
(Since we are met here in this height of Venice,)
Some few particulars I have set down,
Only for this meridian, fit to be known
Of your crude traveller; and they are these.
I will not touch, sir, at your phrase, or clothes,
For they are old.
   Per. Sir, I have better.
   Sir P. Pardon,
I meant, as they are themes.
   Per. Oh, sir, proceed:
I'll slander you no more of wit, good sir.
   Sir P. First, for your garb, it must be grave and serious,
Very reserved, and locked; not tell a secret
On any terms, not to your father; scarce
A fable, but with caution: make sure choice
Both of your company and discourse; beware
You never speak a truth——
   Per. How!
   Sir P. Not to strangers,
For those be they you must converse with most;
Others I would not know, sir, but at distance,
So as I still might be a saver in them;
You shall have tricks else passed upon you hourly.
And then, for your religion, profess none,

But wonder at the diversity of all :
And for your part, protest were there no other
But simply the laws o' th' land, you could content you,
Nic. Machiavel, and Monsieur Bodin, both
Were of his mind. Then must you learn the use
And handling of your silver fork at meals,
The metal of your glass ; (these are main matters
With your Italian ;) and to know the hour
When you must eat your melons and your figs.
 Per. Is that a point of state too ?
 Sir P. Here it is :
For your Venetian, if he see a man
Preposterous in the least, he has him straight ;
He has ; he strips him. I 'll acquaint you, sir,
I now have lived here, 'tis some fourteen months.
Within the first week of my landing here,
All took me for a citizen of Venice,
I knew the forms so well——
 Per. And nothing else.   [*Aside.*
 Sir P. I had read Contarene, took me a house,
Dealt with my Jews to furnish it with moveables—
Well, if I could but find one man, one man
To mine own heart, whom I durst trust, I would—
 Per. What, what, sir ?
 Sir P. Make him rich ; make him a fortune :
He should not think again. I would command it.
 Per. As how ?
 Sir P. With certain projects that I have ;
Which I may not discover.
 Per. If I had
But one to wager with, I would lay odds now,
He tells me instantly.   [*Aside.*
 Sir P. One is, and that
I care not greatly who knows, to serve the state
Of Venice with red herrings for three years,
And at a certain rate, from Rotterdam,
Where I have correspondence. There 's a letter,
Sent me from one o' the states, and to that purpose :
He cannot write his name, but that 's his mark.
 Per. He is a chandler ?
 Sir P. No, a cheesemonger.
There are some others, too, with whom I treat
About the same negociation ;
And I will undertake it : for, 'tis thus.
I 'll do 't with ease, I have cast it all : Your hoy
Carries but three men in her, and a boy ;
And she shall make me three returns a year :
So, if there come but one of three, I save ;

If two, I can default : but this is now,
If my main project fail.

   Per. Then you have others?

   Sir P. I should be loth to draw the subtle air
Of such a place, without my thousand aims.
I'll not dissemble, sir : where'er I come,
I love to be considerative ; and 'tis true,
I have at my free hours thought upon
Some certain goods unto the state of Venice,
Which I do call *my Cautions*; and, sir, which
I mean, in hope of pension, to propound
To the Great Council, then unto the Forty,
So to the Ten. My means are made already—

   Per. By whom?

   Sir P. Sir, one that, though his place be obscure,
Yet, he can sway, and they will hear him. He's
A commandador.

   Per. What ! A common sergeant?

   Sir P. Sir, such as they are put it in their mouths
What they should say, sometimes ; as well as greater :
I think I have my notes to show you. [*Searching his pockets.*

   Per. Good sir.

   Sir P. But you shall swear unto me, on your gentry,
Not to anticipate.

   Per. I, sir !

   Sir P. Nor reveal
A circumstance——My paper is not with me.

   Per. Oh, but you can remember, sir.

   Sir P. My first is
Concerning tinder-boxes. You must know,
No family is here without its box.
Now, sir, it being so portable a thing,
Put case, that you or I were ill-affected
Unto the state, sir ; with it in our pockets,
Might not I go into the Arsenal,
Or you, come out again, and none the wiser?

   Per. Except yourself, sir.

   Sir P. Go to; then. I therefore
Advertise to the state, how fit it were,
That none but such as were known patriots,
Sound lovers of their country, should be suffered
To enjoy them in their houses ; and even those
Sealed at some office, and at such a bigness
As might not lurk in pockets.

   Per. Admirable !

   Sir P. My next is, how to enquire, and be resolved,
By present demonstration, whether a ship,
Newly arrived from Soria, or from

Any suspected part of all the Levant,
Be guilty of the plague : and where they use
To lie out forty, fifty days, sometimes,
About the Lazaretto, for their trial ;
I'll save that charge and loss unto the merchant,
And in an hour clear the doubt.
    Per. Indeed, sir !
    Sir P. Or——I will lose my labour.
    Per. 'My faith, that's much.
    Sir P. Nay, sir conceive me. It will cost me in onions,
Some thirty livres——
    Per. Which is one pound sterling.
    Sir P. Beside my water-works: for this I do, sir.
First, I bring in your ship 'twixt two brick walls ;
But those the state shall venture : On the one
I strain me a fair tarpaulin, and in that
I stick my onions; cut in halves : the other
Is full of loop-holes, out at which I thrust
The noses of my bellows ; and those bellows
I keep, with water-works, in perpetual motion,
Which is the easiest matter of a hundred.
No, sir, your onion, which doth naturally
Attract the infection, and your bellows blowing
The air upon him, will show, instantly,
By this changed colour, if there be contagion ;
Or else remain as fair as at the first.
—Now it is known, 't is nothing.
    Per. You are right, sir.
    Sir P. I would I had my note.
    Per. Faith, so would I :
But you have done well for once, sir.
    Sir P. Were I false,
Or would be made so, I could show you reasons
How I could sell this state now to the Turk,
Spite of their gallies, or their——   [*Examining his papers.*
    Per. Pray you, Sir Pol.
    Sir P. I have them not about me.
    Per. That I feared :
They are there, sir.
    Sir P. No, this is my diary,
Wherein I note my actions of the day.
    Per. Pray you, let's see, sir. What is here ?   [*Reads.*
    Notandum,
A rat had gnawn my spur-leathers; notwithstanding,
I put on new, and did go forth; but first
I threw three beans over the threshold. Item,
I went and bought two toothpicks, whereof one
I burst immediately, in a discourse

With a Dutch merchant, 'bout religion del stato.
From him I went and paid a moccinigo
For piecing my silk stockings: by the way
I cheapened sprats; and at St. Mark's I urined.
'Faith, these are politic notes!
  Sir P. Sir, I do slip
No action of my life, but thus I quote it.
  Per. Believe me, it is wise!
  Sir P. Nay, sir, read forth.

Enter, at a distance, LADY POLITICK WOULD-BE, NANO, *and two* Waiting-women.

  Lady P. Where should this loose knight be, trow? sure, he's housed.
  Nan. Why, then he's fast.
  Lady P. Ay, he plays both with me.
I pray you stay. This heat will do more harm
To my complexion, than his heart is worth,
(I do not care to hinder, but to take him.)
How it comes off!   [*Rubbing her cheeks.*
  1st Wom. My master's yonder.
  Lady P, Where?
  2nd Wom. With a young gentleman.
  Lady P. That same's the party;
In man's apparel! 'Pray you, sir, jog my knight:
I will be tender to his reputation,
However he demerit.
  Sir P. [*Seeing her.*] My lady!
  Per. Where?
  Sir P. 'Tis she indeed, sir; you shall know her. She is,
Were she not mine, a lady of that merit,
For fashion and behaviour; and for beauty
I durst compare——
  Per. It seems you are not jealous,
That dare commend her.
  Sir P. Nay, and for discourse——
  Per. Being your wife, she cannot miss that.
  Sir P. [*introducing* PER.] Madam,
Here is a gentleman, pray you, use him fairly;
He seems a youth, but he is——
  Lady P. None.
  Sir P. Yes, one
Has put his face as soon into the world——
  Lady P. You mean, as early? but to-day?
  Sir P. How's this!
  Lady P. Why, in this habit, sir, you apprehend me:—
Well, Master Would-be, this doth not become you;

I had thought the odour, sir, of your good name
Had been more precious to you; that you would not
Have done this dire massacre on your honour;
One of your gravity and rank besides!
But knights, I see, care little for the oath
They make to ladies; chiefly their own ladies.
   Sir P. Now, by my spurs, the symbol of my knighthood.—
   Per. Lord, how his brain is humbled for an oath!   [*Aside.*
   Sir P. I reach you not.
   Lady P. Right, sir, your policy
May bear it through thus.—Sir, a word with you.   [*To* PER.
I would be loth to contest publicly
With any gentlewoman, or to seem
Froward or violent, as the courtier says;
It comes too near rusticity in a lady,
Which I would shun by all means: and however
I may deserve from master Would-be, yet
To have one fair gentlewoman thus be made
The unkind instrument to wrong another,
And one she knows not, ay, and to persevere;
In my poor judgment, is not warranted
From being a solecism in our sex,
If not in manners.
   Per. How is this!
   Sir P. Sweet madam,
Come nearer to your aim.
   Lady P. Marry and will, sir,
Since you provoke me with your impudence,
And laughter of your light land-syren here,
Your Sporus, your hermaphrodite——
   Per. What's here?
Poetic fury, and historic storms!
   Sir P. The gentleman, believe it, is of worth,
And of our nation.
   Lady P. Ay, your White-friars nation.
Come, I blush for you, master Would-be, I;
And am ashamed you should have no more forehead,
Than thus to be the patron, or St. George,
To a female devil, in a male outside.
   Sir P. Nay.
And you be such an one, I must bid adieu
To your delights. The case appears too liquid.   [*Exit.*
   Lady P. Hy, you may carry it clear with your state-face!—
But for your carnival concupiscence,
Who here is fled for liberty of conscience,
From furious persecution of the marshal,
Her will I disc'ple.
   Per. This is fine, i' faith!

And do you use this often? Is this part
Of your wit's exercise, 'gainst you have occasion?
Madam——
   Lady P. Go to, sir.
   Per. Do you hear me, lady!
Why, if your knight have set you to beg shirts,
Or to invite me home, you might have done it
A nearer way, by far.
   Lady P. This cannot work you
Out of my snare.
   Per. Why, am I in it, then?
Indeed your husband told me you were fair.
And so you are; only your nose inclines
That side that's next the sun, to the queen-apple.
   Lady P. This cannot be endured by any patience.

           Enter MOSCA.

   Mos. What is the matter, madam?
   Lady P. If the senate
Right not my quest in this, I will protest them
To all the world, no aristocracy.
   Mos. What is the injury, lady?
   Lady P. Why, the callet
You told me of, here I have ta'en disguised.
   Mos. Who? this! what means your ladyship? the creature
I mentioned to you is apprehended now,
Before the senate; you shall see her——
   Lady P. Where?
   Mos. I'll bring you to her. This young gentleman,
I saw him land this morning at the port.
   Lady P. Is't possible! how has my judgment wandered?
Sir, I must, blushing, say to you, I have erred;
And plead your pardon.
   Per. What, more changes yet!
   Lady P. I hope you have not the malice to remember
A gentlewoman's passion. If you stay
In Venice here, please you to use me, sir——
   Mos. Will you go, madam?
   Lady P. 'Pray you, sir, use me; in faith,
The more you see me, the more I shall conceive
You have forgot our quarrel.—[*Exeunt* Lady WOULD-BE, MOSCA,
      NANO, *and* Waiting-women.]
   Per. This is rare!
Sir Politick Would-be? no; sir Politick Gull,
To bring me thus acquainted with his wife!
Well, wise sir Pol, since you have practised thus
Upon my freshman-ship, I'll try your salt-head,
What proof it is against a counter-plot.   [*Exit.*

SCENE II.—*The Scrutineo or Senate-House.*

Enter VOLTORE, CORBACCIO, CORVINO, *and* MOSCA.

Volt. Well, now you know the carriage of the business,
Your constancy is all that is required
Unto the safety of it.
   Mos. Is the lie
Safely conveyed amongst us? is that sure?
Knows every man his burden?
   Corv. Yes.
   Mos Then shrink not.
   Corv. But knows the advocate the truth?
   Mos. Oh, sir,
By no means; I devised a formal tale,
That salved your reputation. But be valiant, sir.
   Corv. I fear no one but him, that this his pleading
Should make him stand for a co-heir——
   Mos. Co-halter!
Hang him; we will but use his tongue, his noise,
As we do croakers here.
   Corv. Ay, what shall he do?
   Mos. When we have done, you mean?
   Corv. Yes.
   Mos. Why, we'll think:
Sell him for mummia; he's half dust already.
Do you not smile—[*to* VOLTORE]—to see this buffalo,
How he doth sport it with his head?—I should,
If all were well and past.—[*Aside.*]—Sir—[*to* CORBOCCIO]—
    only you
Are he that shall enjoy the crop of all,
And these not know for whom they toil.
   Corb. Ay, peace,
   Mos. [*Turning to* CORVINO.—But you shall eat it. Much!—
   [*Aside.*]—Worshipful sir, [*to* VOLTORE.]
Mercury sit upon your thundering tongue,
Or the French Hercules, and make your language
As conquering as his club, to beat along,
As with a tempest, flat, our adversaries;
But much more yours, sir.
   Volt. Here they come, have done.
   Mos. I have another witness, if you need, sir,
I can produce.
   Volt. Who is it?
   Mos. Sir, I have her.

Enter Avocatori *and take their seats,* BONARIO, CELIA, Notario, Commandadori, Saffi, *and other* Officers *of justice.*

1st Avoc. The like of this the senate never heard of.
2nd Avoc. 'Twill come most strange to them when we report it.
4th. The gentlewoman has been ever held
Of unreprovéd name.
3rd Avoc. So has the youth.
4th Avoc. The more unnatural part that of his father.
2nd Avoc. More of the husband.
1st Avoc. I not know to give
His act a name, it is so monstrous!
4th Avoc. But the impostor, he's a thing created
To exceed example!
1st Avoc. And all after-times!
2nd Avoc. I never heard a true voluptuary
Described, but him.
3rd Avoc. Appear yet those were cited?
Not. All but the old magnifico, Volpone.
1st. Why is not he here?
Mos. Please your fatherhoods,
Here is his advocate: himself's so weak,
So feeble——
4th Avoc. What are you?
Bon. His parasite,
His knave, his pandar: I beseech the court,
He may be forced to come, that your grave eyes
May bear strong witness of his strange impostures.
Volt. Upon my faith and credit with your virtues,
He is not able to endure the air.
2nd Avoc. Bring him, however.
3rd Avoc. We will see him.
4th Avoc. Fetch him.
Volt. Your fatherhoods' fit pleasures be obeyed;
 [*Exeunt* Officers.
But sure, the sight will rather move your pities,
Than indignation. May it please the court,
In the meantime, he may be heard in me:
I know this place most void of prejudice,
And therefore crave it, since we have no reason
To fear our truth should hurt our cause.
3rd. Speak free.
Volt. Then know, most honoured fathers, I must now
Discover to your strangely abused ears,
The most prodigious and most frontless piece
Of solid impudence and treachery,
That ever vicious nature yet brought forth
To shame the State of Venice. This lewd woman,

That wants no official look or tears
To help the vizor she has now put on,
Hath long been known a close adulteress
To that lascivious youth there : not suspected,
I say, but known and taken in the act
With him ; and by this man, the easy husband,
Pardoned; whose timeless bounty makes him now
Stand here the most unhappy, innocent person,
That ever man's own goodness made accused.
For these not knowing how to owe a gift
Of that dear grace, but with their shame; being placed
So above all powers of their gratitude,
Began to hate the benefit ; and, in place
Of thanks, devise to extirpe the memory
Of such an act : wherein I pray your fatherhoods
To observe the malice, yea, the rage of creatures
Discovered in their evils ; and what heart
Such take, even from their crimes :—but that anon
Will more appear—This gentleman, the father,
Hearing of this foul fact, with many others,
Which daily struck at his too tender ears,
And grieved in nothing more than that he could not
Preserve himself a parent (his son's ills
Growing to that strange flood), at last decreed
To disinherit him.

   1st Avoc. These be strange turns!

  2nd Avoc. The young man's fame was ever fair and honest.

   Volt. So much more full of danger is his vice,
That can beguile so under shade of virtue.
But, as I said, my honoured sires, his father
Having this settled purpose, by what means
To him betrayed, we know not, and this day
Appointed for the deed ; that parricide,
I cannot style him better, by confederacy
Preparing this his paramour to be there,
Entered Volpone's house (who was the man,
Your fatherhoods must understand designed
For the inheritance), there sought his father :—
But with what purpose sought he him, my lords?
I tremble to pronounce it, that a son
Unto a father, and to such a father,
Should have so foul, felonious intent !
It was to murder him : when being prevented
By his more happy absence, what then did he ?
Not check his wicked thoughts ; no, now new deeds ;
(Mischief doth never end where it begins)
An act of horror, fathers ! he dragged forth
The aged gentleman that had there lain bed-rid

Three years and more, out of his innocent couch,
Naked upon the floor, there left him; wounded
His servant in the face: and, with this strumpet
The stale to his forged practice, who was glad
To be so active,—(I shall here desire
Your fatherhoods to note but my collections,
As most remarkable,—) thought at once to stop
His father's ends, discredit his free choice
In the old gentleman, redeem themselves,
By laying infamy upon this man,
To whom, with blushing, they should owe their lives.

 1st Avoc. What proofs have you of this?
 Bon. Most honoured fathers,
I humbly crave there be no credit given
To this man's mercenary tongue.
 2nd Avoc. Forbear.
 Bon. His soul moves in his fee.
 3rd Avoc. Oh, sir.
 Bon. This fellow,
For six sols more, would plead against his Maker.
 1st Avoc. You do forget yourself.
 Volt. Nay, nay, grave fathers,
Let him have scope: can any man imagine
That he will spare his accuser, that would not
Have spared his parent?
 1st Avoc. Well, produce your proofs.
 Cel. I would I could forget I were a creature.
 Volt. Signior Corbaccio.   [CORBACCIO *comes forward.*
 4th Avoc. What is he?
 Volt. Volt.
 2nd Avoc. Has he had an oath?
 Not. Yes.
 Corb. What must I do now?
 Not. Your testimony's craved.
 Corb. Speak to the knave?
I'll have my mouth first stopped with earth; my heart
Abhors his knowledge: I disclaim in him.
 1st Avoc. But for what cause?
 Corb. The mere portent of nature!
He is an utter stranger to my loins.
 Bon. Have they made you to this?
 Corb. I will not hear thee,
Monster of men, swine, goat, wolf, parricide!
Speak not, thou viper.
 Bon. Sir, I will sit down,
And rather wish my innocence should suffer,
Than I resist the authority of a father.
 Volt. Signor Corvino!   [CORVINO *comes forward.*

2nd Avoc. This is strange.
1st Avoc. Who's this?
Not. The husband.
4th Avoc. Is he sworn?
Not. He is.
3rd Avoc. Speak then.
Corv. This woman, please your fatherhoods, is a strumpet
Of most hot exercise, more than a partridge,
Upon record——
1st Avoc. No more.
Corv. Neighs like a jennet.
Not. Preserve the honour of the court.
Corv. I shall,
And modesty of your most reverend ears.
And yet I hope that I may say, these eyes
Have seen her glued into that piece of cedar,
That fine well-timbered gallant; and that here
The letters may be read through the horn,
That make the story perfect.
Mos. Excellent! sir.
Corv. There is no shame in this now, is there?
                                    [*Aside to* MOS.
Mos. None.
Corv. Or if I said I hoped that she were onward
To her damnation, if there be a hell
Greater than a foul woman; a good catholic
May make the doubt.
3rd Avoc. His grief hath made him frantic.
1st Avoc. Remove him hence.
2nd Avoc. Look to the woman.   [CELIA *swoons.*
Corv. Rare!
Prettily feigned, again!
4th Avoc. Stand from about her.
1st Avoc. Give her the air.
3rd Avoc. What can you say?   [*To* MOSCA.
Mos. My wound,
May it please your wisdoms, speaks for me, received
In aid of my good patron, when he missed
His sought-for father, when that well-taught dame
Had her cue given her to cry out A Rape!
Bon. Oh, most laid impudence! Fathers——
3rd Avoc. Sir, be silent;
You had your hearing free, so must they theirs.
2nd Avoc. I do begin to doubt the imposture here.
4th Avoc. This woman has too many moods.
Volt. Grave fathers,
She is a creature of a most profest
And prostituted lewdness.

Corv. Most impetuous,
Unsatisfied, grave fathers !
  Volt. May her feignings
Not take your wisdoms ; but this day she baited
A stranger, a grave knight, with her loose eyes
And more lascivious kisses. This man saw them
Together on the water, in a gondola.
  Mos. Here is the lady herself that saw them too,
Without. Who then had in the open streets
Pursued them, but for saving her knight's honour.
  1*st Avoc.* Produce that lady.
  2*nd Avoc.* Let her come. [*Exit* MOSCA.
  4*th Avoc.* These things,
They strike with wonder.
  3*rd Avoc.* I am turn'd a stone.

         Re-enter MOSCA *with* Lady WOULD-BE.

  Mos. Be resolute, madam.
  Lady P. Ay, this same is she. [*Pointing to* CELIA.
Out, thou camelion harlot ! Now thine eyes
Vie tears with the hyæna. Dar'st thou look
Upon my wrongéd face ? I cry your pardons ;
I fear I have forgettingly transgrest
Against the dignity of the court——
  2*nd Avoc.* No, madam.
  Lady P. And been exorbitant——
  2*nd Avoc.* You have not, lady.
  4*th Avoc.* These proofs are strong.
  Lady P. Surely, I had no purpose
To scandalize your honours or my sex's.
  3*rd Avoc.* We do believe it.
  Lady P. Surely, you may believe it.
  2*nd Avoc.* Madam, we do.
  Lady P. Indeed you may ; my breeding
Is not so coarse——
  4*th Avoc.* We know it.
  Lady P. To offend
With pertinacy——
  3*rd Avoc.* Lady——
  Lady P. Such a presence !
No surely.
  1*st Avoc.* We well think it.
  Lady P. You may think it.
  1*st Avoc.* Let her o'ercome. What witnesses have you
To make good your report ?
  Bon. Our consciences.
  Cel. And Heaven, that never fails the innocent.
  4*th Avoc.* These are no testimonies.

Bon. Not in your courts,
Where multitude and clamour overcomes.
  1st Avoc. Nay, then, you do wax insolent.

  Re-enter Officers, *bearing* VOLPONE *on a couch.*

Volt. Here, here,
The testimony comes that will convince,
And put to utter dumbness their bold tongues.
See here, grave fathers, here's the ravisher,
Insulter of men's wives, the great impostor,
The grand voluptuary! Do you not think
These limbs should affect venery? or these eyes
Covet a concubine? Pray you mark these hands;
Are they not fit to stroke a lady's face?
Perhaps he doth dissemble!
  Bon. So he does.
  Volt. Would you have him tortured?
  Bon. I would have him proved.
  Volt. Best try him with goads or burning irons;
Put him to the strappado; I have heard
The rack hath cured the gout; 'faith, give it him,
And help him of a malady! be courteous.
I'll undertake, before these honoured fathers,
He shall have yet as many left diseases
As she has known adulterers, or thou strumpets.
Oh, my most equal hearers, if these deeds,
Acts of this bold and most exorbitant strain,
May pass with sufferance, what one citizen
But owes the forfeit of his life, yea, fame,
To him that dares traduce him? Which of you
Are safe, my honour'd fathers? I would ask,
With leave of your grave fatherhoods, if their plot
Have any face or colour like to truth?
Or if unto the dullest nostril here
It smell not rank and most abhorred slander?
I crave your care of this good gentleman,
Whose life is much endangered by their fable;
And as for them, I will conclude with this:
That vicious persons, when they're hot and fleshed
In impious acts, their constancy abounds;
Damn'd deeds are done with greatest confidence.
  1st Avoc. Take them to custody, and sever them.
  2nd Avoc. 'Tis pity two such prodigies should live.
  1st Avoc. Let the old gentleman be returned with care.
            [*Exeunt* Officers *with* VOLPONE.
I'm sorry our credulity hath wronged him.
  4th Avoc. These are two creatures!
  3rd Avoc. I've an earthquake in me.

2nd Avoc. Their shame even in their cradles fled their faces.
4th Avoc. You have done a worthy service to the state, sir,
In their discovery. [*To* VOLT.
1st Avoc. You shall hear, ere night,
What punishment the court decrees upon them.
[*Exeunt* AVOCAT. NOT. *and* Officers *with* BONARIO *and* CELIA.
Volt. We thank your fatherhoods.—How like you it?
Mos. Rare.
I'd have your tongue, sir, tipt with gold for this;
I'd have you be the heir to the whole city;
The earth I'd have want men ere you want living;
They're bound to erect your statue in St. Marks.
Signior Corvino, I would have you go
And show yourself that you have conquer'd.
Corv. Yes.
Mos. It was much better that you should profess
Yourself a cuckold thus, than that the other
Should have been proved.
Corv. Nay, I considered that:
Now it is her fault.
Mos. Then it had been yours.
Corv. True: I do doubt this advocate still.
Mos. I' faith
You need not, I dare ease you of that care.
Corv. I trust thee, Mosca. [*Exit.*
Mos. As your own soul, sir.
Corb. Mosca!
Mos. Now for your business, sir.
Corb. How! have you business?
Mos. Yes, yours, sir.
Corb. Oh, none else?
Mos. None else, not I.
Corb. Be careful, then.
Mos. Rest you with both your eyes, sir.
Corb. Dispatch it.
Mos. Instantly.
Corb. And look that all,
Whatever, be put in, jewels, plate, moneys,
Household stuff, bedding, curtains.
Mos. Curtain-rings, sir:
Only the advocate's fee must be deducted.
Corb. I'll pay him now; you'll be too prodigal.
Mos. Sir, I must tender it.
Corb. Two chequines is well.
Mos. No, six, sir.
Corb. 'Tis too much.
Mos. He talked a great while;
You must consider that, sir.

Corb. Well, there's three——
Mos. I'll give it him.
Corb. Do so, and there's for thee. [*Exit.*
Mos. Bountiful bones! What horrid strange offence
Did he commit 'gainst nature, in his youth,
Worthy this age? [*Aside.*]—You see, sir, [*to* VOLT.] how I work
Unto your ends: take you no notice?
Volt. No,
I'll leave you. [*Exit.*
Mos. All is yours, the devil and all:
Good advocate!—Madam, I'll bring you home.
Lady P. No, I'll go see your patron.
Mos. That you shall not:
I'll tell you why. My purpose is to urge
My patron to reform his Will; and for
The zeal you have shown to-day, whereas before
You were but third or fourth, you shall be now
Put in the first; which would appear as begged
If you were present. Therefore——
Lady P. You shall sway me. [*Exeunt.*

——————————ACT V.——————————

SCENE I.—*A Room in* VOLPONE'S *House.*

Enter VOLPONE.

Volp. Well, I am here, and all this brunt is past.
I ne'er was in dislike with my disguise
Till this fled moment: here 'twas good in private;
But in your public,—*cave* whilst I breathe.
'Fore God, my left leg 'gan to have the cramp,
And I apprehended straight some power had struck me
With a dead palsy. Well, I must be merry,
And shake it off. A many of these fears
Would put me into some villainous disease,
Should they come thick upon me; I'll prevent 'em.
Give me a bowl of lusty wine, to fright
This humour from my heart. [*Drinks.*]—hum, hum, hum!
'Tis almost gone already; I shall conquer.
Any device, now, of rare ingenious knavery
That would possess me with a violent laughter,
Would make me up again. (*Drinks again.*)—So, so, so, so!
This heat is life; 't is blood by this time:—Mosca!

Enter MOSCA.

Mos. How now, sir! does the day look clear again?
Are we recover'd, and wrought out of error,

Into our way, to see our path before us?
Is our trade free once more?
  Volp. Exquisite Mosca!
  Mos. Was it not carried learnedly?
  Volp. And stoutly:
Good wits are greatest in extremities.
  Mos. It were a folly beyond thought, to trust
Any grand act unto a cowardly spirit:
You are not taken with it enough, methinks.
  Volp. Oh, more than if I had not been opposed:
The pleasure of all womankind's not like it.
  Mos. Why, now you speak, sir. We must here be fix'd;
Here we must rest; this is our masterpiece;
We cannot think to go beyond this.
  Volp. True,
Thou hast play'd thy prize, my precious Mosca.
  Mos. Nay, sir,
To gull the court——
  Volp. And quite divert the torrent
Upon the innocent.
  Mos. Yes, and to make
So rare a music out of discords——
  Volp. Right.
That yet to me's the strangest, how thou hast borne it!
That these, being so divided 'mongst themselves,
Should not scent somewhat, or in me or thee,
Or doubt their own side.
  Mos. True, they will not see 't.
Too much light blinds them, I think. Each of them
Is so possest and stuft with his own hopes,
That any thing unto the contrary,
Never so true, or never so apparent,
Never so palpable, they will resist it——
  Volp. Like a temptation of the devil.
  Mos. Right, sir.
Merchants may talk of trade, and your great signiors
Of land that yields well; but if Italy
Have any glebe more fruitful than these fellows,
I am deceiv'd. Did not your advocate rare?
  Volp. Oh—"My most honour'd fathers, my grave fathers,
Under correction of your fatherhoods,
What face of truth is here? If these strange deeds
May pass, most honour'd fathers"—I had much ado
To forbear laughing.
  Mos. It seem'd to me, you sweat, sir.
  Volp. In troth, I did a little.
  Mos. But confess, sir,
Were you not daunted?

Volp. In good faith, I was
A little in a mist, but not dejected;
Never, but still my self.
   Mos. I think it, sir.
Now, so truth help me, I must needs say this, sir,
And out of conscience for your advocate,
He has taken pains, in faith, sir, and deserv'd,
In my poor judgment, I speak it under favour,
Not to contrary you, sir, very richly—
Well—to be cozen'd.
   Volp. Troth, and I think so too,
By that I heard him, in the latter end.
   Mos. Oh, but before, sir: had you heard him first
Draw it to certain heads, then aggravate,
Then use his vehement figures—I look'd still
When he would shift a shirt: and, doing this
Out of pure love, no hope of gain——
   Volp. 'Tis right.
I cannot answer him, Mosca, as I would,
Not yet; but for thy sake, at thy entreaty,
I will begin, even now—to vex them all,
This very instant.
   Mos. Good sir.
   Volp. Call the dwarf
And eunuch forth.
   Mos. Castrone, Nano!

          Enter CASTRONE *and* NANO.

   Nano. Here.
   Volp. Shall we have a jig now?
   Mos. What you please, sir.
   Volp. Go,
Straight give out about the streets, you two,
That I am dead; do it with constancy,
Sadly, do you hear? Impute it to the grief
Of this late slander.   [*Exeunt* CAST. *and* NANO.
   Mos. What do you mean, sir?
   Volp. Oh,
I shall have instantly my Vulture, Crow,
Raven, come flying hither, on the news;
To peck for carrion, my she-wolf and all,
Greedy and full of expectation——
   Mos. And then to have it ravished from their mouths!
   Volp. 'Tis true. I will have thee put on a gown,
And take upon thee, as thou wert mine heir:
Show them a will: Open that chest, and reach
Forth one of those that has the blanks; I'll straight
Put in thy name.

Mos. It will be rare, sir. [*Gives him a paper.*
Volp. Ay,
When they e'en gape, and find themselves deluded——
Mos. Yes.
Volp. And then use them scurvily!
Dispatch, get on thy gown.
Mos. [*putting on a gown.*] But what, sir, if they ask
After the body?
Volp. Say, it was corrupted.
Mos. I'll say it stank, sir; and was fain to have it
Coffined up instantly, and sent away.
Volp. Anything; what thou wilt. Hold, here's my will.
Get thee a cap, a count-book, pen and ink,
Papers afore thee; sit as thou wert taking
An inventory of parcels: I'll get up
Behind the curtain, on a stool, and hearken;
Sometime peep over, see how they do look,
With what degrees their blood doth leave their faces,
O, 'twill afford me a rare meal of laughter!
Mos. [*putting on a cap, and setting out the table, &c.*] Your
  advocate will turn stark dull upon it.
Volp. It will take off his oratory's edge.
Mos. But your clarissimo, old round-back, he
Will crump you like a hog-louse, with the touch.
Volp. And what Corvino?
Mos. Oh, sir, look for him,
To-morrow morning, with a rope and dagger,
To visit all the streets; he must run mad.
My lady too, that came into the court
To bear false witness for your worship——
Volp. Yes,
And kiss'd me 'fore the fathers, when my face
Flowed all with oils.
Mos. And sweat, sir. Why, your gold
Is such another med'cine, it dries up
All those offensive savours: it transforms
The most deforméd, and restores them lovely,
As 'twere the strange poetical girdle. Jove
Could not invent t' himself a shroud more subtle
To pass Acrisius' guards. It is the thing
Makes all the world her grace, her youth, her beauty.
Volp. I think she loves me.
Mos. Who? the lady, sir?
She's jealous of you.
Volp. Dost thou say so? [*Knocking within.*
Mos. Hark,
There's some already.
Volp. Look.

SCENE I.] *VOLPONE; OR, THE FOX.*

Mos. It is the Vulture;
He has the quickest scent.
  Volp. I'll to my place,
Thou to thy posture.   [*Goes behind the curtain.*
  Mos. I am set.
  Volp. But, Mosca,
Play the artificer now, torture them rarely.

Enter VOLTORE.

  Volt. How now, my Mosca?
  Mos. [*writing.*] Turkey carpets, nine——
  Volt. Taking an inventory! that is well.
  Mos. Two suits of bedding, tissue——
  Volt. Where's the Will?
Let me read that the while.

Enter SERVANTS, *with* CORBACCIO *in a chair.*

  Corb. So, set me down,
And get you home.   [*Exeunt* SERVANTS.
  Volt. Is he come now, to trouble us?
  Mos. Of cloth of gold, two more——
  Corb. Is it done, Mosca?
  Mos. Of several velvets eight——
  Volt. I like his care.
  Corb. Dost thou not hear?

Enter CORVINO.

  Corb. Ha! is the hour come, Mosca?
  Volp. [*peeping over the curtain.*] Ay, now they muster.
  Corv. What does the advocate here,
Or this Corbaccio?
  Corb. What do these here?

Enter LADY POL. WOULD-BE.

  Lady P. Mosca!
Is his thread spun?
  Mos. Eight chests of linen——
  Volp. Oh,
My fine Dame Would-be, too!
  Corv. Mosca, the Will,
That I may show it these, and rid them hence.
  Mos. Six chests of diaper, four of damask.—There.
      [*Gives them the Will carelessly over his shoulder.*
  Corb. Is that the Will?
  Mos. Down-beds and bolsters——
  Volp. Rare!
Be busy still. Now they begin to flutter:
They never think of me. Look, see, see, see!
How their swift eyes run over the long deed

Unto the name, and to the legacies,
What is bequeathed them there——
   Mos. Ten suits of hangings——
   Volp. Ay, in their garters, Mosca. Now their hopes
Are at the gasp.
   Volt. Mosca the heir!
   Corb. What's that?
   Volp. My advocate is dumb; look to my merchant,
He has heard of some strange storm, a ship is lost,
He faints; my lady will swoon. Old glazen eyes,
He hath not reached his despair yet.
   Corb. All these
Are out of hope; I am, sure, the man.   [*Takes the Will.*
   Corv. But, Mosca——
   Mos. Two cabinets.
   Corv. Is this in earnest?
   Mos. One
Of ebony——
   Corv. Or do you but delude me?
   Mos. The other, mother of pearl—I am very busy.
Good faith, it is a fortune thrown upon me—
Item, one salt of agate—not my seeking.
   Lady P. Do you hear, sir?
   Mos. A perfumed box—'Pray you forbear,
You see I'm troubled—made of an onyx—
   Lady P. How!
   Mos. To-morrow or next day, I shall be at leisure
To talk with you all.
   Corv. Is this my large hope's issue?
   Lady P. Sir, I must have a fairer answer.
   Mos. Madam!
Marry, and shall: 'pray you, fairly quit my house.
Nay, raise no tempest with your looks; but hark you,
Remember what your ladyship offer'd me
To put you in an heir; go to, think on it:
And what you said e'en your best madams did
For maintenance; and why not you? Enough.
Go home, and use the poor Sir Pol, your knight, well,
For fear I tell some riddles; go, be melancholy.
                                 [*Exit* LADY WOULD-BE.
   Volp. Oh, my fine devil!
   Corv. Mosca, pray you a word.
   Mos. Lord! will you not take your despatch hence yet?
Methinks, of all, you should have been the example.
Why should you stay here? with what thought, what promise?
Hear you; do you not know, I know you an ass,
And that you would most fain have been a wittol,
If fortune would have let you? that you are

A declared cuckold, on good terms? This pearl,
You'll say, was yours? right: this diamond?
I'll not deny't, but thank you. Much here else?
It may be so. Why, think that these good works
May help to hide your bad. I'll not betray you;
Although you be but extraordinary,
And have it only in title, it sufficeth:
Go home, be melancholy too, or mad. [*Exit* CORVINO.
  Volp. Rare Mosca! how his villainy becomes him!
  Volt. Certain he doth delude all these for me.
  Corb. Mosca the heir!
  Volp. O, his four eyes have found it.
  Corb. I am cozen'd, cheated, by a parasite slave;
Harlot, thou hast gull'd me.
  Mos. Yes, sir. Stop your mouth,
Or I shall draw the only tooth is left.
Are not you he, that filthy covetous wretch,
With the three legs, that here, in hope of prey,
Have, any time this three years, snuff'd about,
With your most grovelling nose, and would have hired
Me to the poisoning of my patron, sir?
Are not you he that have to-day in court
Profess'd the disinheriting of your son?
Perjured yourself? Go home, and die, and stink;
If you but croak a syllable, all comes out:
Away, and call your porters!—[*Exit* CORBACCIO.]—Go, go,
    stink.
  Volp. Excellent varlet!
  Volt. Now, my faithful Mosca,
I find thy constancy.
  Mos. Sir!
  Volt. Sincere.
  Mos. [*writing.*] A table
Of porphyry—I marle you'll be thus troublesome.
  Volt. Nay, leave off now, they are gone.
  Mos. Why, who are you?
What! Who did send for you? Oh, cry you mercy,
Reverend sir! Good faith, I am grieved for you,
That any chance of mine should thus defeat
Your (I must needs say) most deserving travails:
But I protest, sir, it was cast upon me,
And I could almost wish to be without it,
But that the will o' the dead must be observed.
Marry, my joy is that you need it not;
You have a gift, sir, (thank your education,)
Will never let you want, while there are men,
And malice, to breed causes. Would I had
But half the like, for all my fortune, sir!

If I have any suits, as I do hope,
Things being so easy and direct, I shall not,
I will make bold with your obstreperous aid,
Conceive me, for your fee, sir. In the meantime,
You that have so much law, I know have the conscience
Not to be covetous of what is mine.
Good sir, I thank you for my plate ; 'twill help
To set up a young man. Good faith, you look
As you were costive; best go home and purge, sir.
[*Exit* VOLTORE.

Volp. [*Comes from behind the curtain.*] Bid him eat lettuce
    well. My witty mischief,
Let me embrace thee. Oh, that I could now
Transform thee to a Venus ! Mosca, go,
Straight take my habit of clarissimo,
And walk the streets ; be seen, torment them more :
We must pursue, as well as plot. Who would
Have lost this feast ?
    Mos. I doubt it will lose them.
    Volp. Oh, my recovery shall recover all.
That I could now but think on some disguise
To meet them in, and ask them questions :
How I would vex them still at every turn !
    Mos. Sir, I can fit you.
    Volp. Can'st thou ?
    Mos. Yes, I know
One o' the commandadori, sir, so like you ;
Him will I straight make drunk, and bring you his habit.
    Volp. A rare disguise, and answering thy brain !
Oh, I will be a sharp disease unto them.
    Mos. Sir, you must look for curses——
    Volp. Till they burst ;
The Fox fares ever best when he is curst. [*Exeunt.*

SCENE II.—*A hall in* SIR POLITICK'S *house.*

Enter PEREGRINE *disguised and three merchants.*

    Per. Am I enough disguised ?
    1*st Mer.* I warrant you.
    Per. All my ambition is to fright him only.
    2*nd Mer.* If you could ship him away, 'twere excellent.
    3*rd Mer.* To Zant, or to Aleppo ?
    Per. Yes, and have his
Adventures put i' the Book of Voyages,
And his gull'd story registered for truth.
Well, gentlemen, when I am in a while,
And that you think us warm in our discourse,
Know your approaches.

1st Mer. Trust it to our care. [*Exeunt* MERCHANTS.

Enter Waiting-woman.

Per. Save you, fair lady! Is Sir Pol within?
Wom. I do not know, sir.
Per. Pray you say unto him,
Here is a merchant upon earnest business
Desires to speak with him.
Wom. I will see, sir. [*Exit.*
Per. Pray you.——
I see the family is all female here.

Re-enter Waiting-woman.

Wom. He says, sir, he has weighty affairs of state,
That now require him whole; some other time
You may possess him.
Per. Pray you say again,
If those require him whole, these will exact him,
Whereof I bring him tidings. [*Exit* Woman.]—What might be
His grave affair of state now! how to make
Bolognian sausages here in Venice, sparing
One o' the ingredients?

Re-enter Waiting-woman.

Wom. Sir, he says he knows
By your word *tidings*, that you are no statesman,
And therefore wills you stay.
Per. Sweet, pray you return him;
I have not read so many proclamations,
And studied them for words, as he has done—
But—here he deigns to come. [*Exit* Woman.

Enter Sir POLITICK.

Sir P. Sir, I must crave
Your courteous pardon. There hath chanced to-day,
Unkind disaster 'twixt my lady and me;
And I was penning my apology,
To give her satisfaction, as you came now.
Per. Sir, I am grieved I bring you worse disaster:
The gentleman you met at the port to-day,
That told you, he was newly arrived——
Sir P. Ay, was
A fugitive punk?
Per. No, sir, a spy set on you;
And he has made relation to the Senate,
That you profest to him to have a plot
To sell the State of Venice to the Turk.
Sir P. Oh me!

Per. For which, warrants are signed by this time,
To apprehend you, and to search your study
For papers——
   Sir P. Alas, sir, I have none, but notes
Drawn out of play-books——
   Per. All the better, sir.
   Sir P. And some essays. What shall I do?
   Per. Sir, best
Convey yourself into a sugar-chest ;
Or, if you could lie round, a frail were rare,
And I could send you aboard.
   Sir P. Sir, I but talked so,
For discourse sake merely.   [*Knocking within.*
   Per. Hark! they are there.
   Sir P. I am a wretch, a wretch!
   Per. What will you do, sir?
Have you ne'er a currant-butt to leap into?
They'll put you to the rack ; you must be sudden.
   Sir P. Sir, I have an ingine——
   3*rd Mer.* [*within.*] Sir Politick Would-be!
   2*nd Mer.* [*within.*] Where is he?
   Sir P. That I have thought upon before time.
   Per. What is it?
   Sir P. I shall ne'er endure the torture.
Marry, it is, sir, of a tortoise-shell,
Fitted for these extremities : pray you, sir, help me.
Here I've a place, sir, to put back my legs,
Please you to lay it on, sir, [*Lies down while* PEREGRINE *places
      the shell upon him.*]—with this cap,
And my black gloves. I'll lie, sir, like a tortoise,
'Till they are gone.
   Per. And call you this an ingine?
   Sir P. Mine own device——Good sir, bid my wife's women
To burn my papers.   [*Exit* PEREGRINE

     The three Merchants *rush in.*

   1*st Mer.* Where is he hid?
   3*rd Mer.* We must
And will sure find him.
   2*nd Mer.* Which is his study?

     Re-enter PEREGRINE.

   1*st Mer.* What
Are you, sir?
   Per. I am a merchant, that came here
To look upon this tortoise.
   3*rd Mer.* How!
   1*st Mer.* St. Mark!
What beast is this!

Per. It is a fish.

2nd Mer. Come out here!

Per. Nay, you may strike him, sir, and tread upon him; He'll bear a cart.

1st Mer. What, to run over him?

Per. Yes, sir.

3rd Mer. Let's jump upon him.

2nd Mer. Can he not go?

Per. He creeps, sir.

1st Mer. Let's see him creep.

Per. No, good sir, you will hurt him.

2nd Mer. Heart, I will see him creep, or prick his guts.

3rd Mer. Come out here!

Per. Pray you, sir!—Creep a little. [*Aside to* SIR POLITICK.

1st Mer. Forth.

2nd Mer. Yet farther.

Per. Good sir!—Creep.

2nd Mer. We'll see his legs.

[*They pull off the shell and discover him.*

3rd Mer. 'Ods so, he has garters!

1st Mer. Ay, and gloves!

2nd Mer. Is this Your fearful tortoise?

Per. [*discovering himself.*] Now, Sir Pol, we are even; For your next project I shall be prepared: I am sorry for the funeral of your notes, sir.

1st Mer. 'Twere a rare motion to be seen in Fleet-street

2nd Mer. Ay, in the Term.

1st Mer. Or Smithfield, in the fair.

3rd Mer. Methinks 'tis but a melancholy sight.

Per. Farewell, most politic tortoise!

[*Exeunt* PER. *and* Merchants.

Re-enter Waiting-woman.

Sir P. Where's my lady? Knows she of this?

Wom. I know not, sir.

Sir P. Enquire—
Oh, I shall be the fable of all feasts,
The freight of the gazetti, ship-boy's tale;
And, which is worst, even talk for ordinaries.

Wom. My lady's come most melancholy home,
And says, sir, she will straight to sea for physic.

Sir P. And I to shun this place and clime forever,
Creeping with house on back, and think it well
To shrink my poor head in my politic shell. [*Exeunt.*

SCENE III.—*A room in* VOLPONE'S *house.*

Enter MOSCA *in the habit of a Clarissimo, and* VOLPONE *in that of a Commandadore.*

Volp. Am I then like him?
Mos. Oh, sir, you are he:
No man can sever you.
Volp. Good.
Mos. But what am I?
Volp. 'Fore heaven, a brave clarissimo; thou becom'st it!
Pity thou wert not born one.
Mos. If I hold
My made one, 'twill be well.   [*Aside.*
Volp. I'll go and see
What news first at the court.   [*Exit.*
Mos. Do so. My Fox
Is out of his hole, and ere he shall re-enter,
I'll make him languish in his borrowed case,
Except he come to composition with me.
Androgyno, Castrone, Nano!

Enter ANDROGYNO, CASTRONE *and* NANO.
All. Here.
Mos. Go, recreate yourselves abroad; go sport. [*Exeunt.*
So, now I have the keys, and am possest.
Since he will needs be dead afore his time,
I'll bury him, or gain by him: I am his heir,
And so will keep me, till he share at least.
To cozen him of all, were but a cheat
Well placed; no man would construe it a sin:
Let his sport pay for't. This is called the Fox-trap. [*Exit.*

SCENE IV.—*A street.*

Enter CORBACCIO *and* CORVINO.

Corb. They say, the Court is set.
Corv. We must maintain
Our first tale good, for both our reputations.
Corb. Why, mine's no tale: my son would there have killed me.
Corv. That's true, I had forgot: mine is, I'm sure. [*Aside.*
But for your Will, sir.
Corb. Ay, I'll come upon him
For that hereafter, now his patron's dead.

Enter VOLPONE.

Volp. Signior Corvino! and Corbaccio! Sir,
Much joy unto you.

Corv. Of what?
Volp. The sudden good
Dropt down upon you——
Corb. Where?
Volp. And none knows how,
From old Volpone, sir.
Corb. Out, arrant knave!
Volp. Let not your too much wealth, sir, make you furious.
Corb. Away, thou varlet!
Volp. Why, sir?
Corb. Dost thou mock me?
Volp. You mock the world, sir; did you not change Wills?
Corb. Out, harlot!
Volp. Oh! belike you are the man,
Signior Corvino? 'faith, you carry it well;
You grow not mad withal; I love your spirit:
You are not over-leavened with your fortune.
You should have some would swell now, like a wine-fat,
With such an autumn——Did he give you all, sir?
Corv. Avoid, you rascal!
Volp. Troth, your wife has shown
Herself a very woman; but you are well,
You need not care, you have a good estate,
To bear it out, sir, better by this chance:
Except Corbaccio have a share.
Corb. Hence, varlet.
Volp. You will not be acknown, sir; why, 't is wise.
Thus do all gamesters, at all games dissemble:
No man shall seem to win. (*Exeunt* CORVINO *and* CORBACCIO.)
      Here comes my vulture,
Heaving his beak up in the air, and snuffing.

Enter VOLTORE.

Volt. Outstripped thus by a parasite! a slave,
Would run on errands, and make legs for crumbs!
Well, what I 'll do——
Volp. The Court stays for your worship.
I e'en rejoice, sir, at your worship's happiness,
And that it fell into so learned hands,
That understand the fingering——
Volt. What do you mean?
Volp. I mean to be a suitor to your worship,
For the small tenement, out of reparations,
That at the end of your long row of houses,
By the Piscaria: it was, in Volpone's time,
Your predecessor, ere he grew diseased,
A handsome, pretty, customed house of call
As any was in Venice, none dispraised;

But fell with him: his body and that house
Decayed together.
   Volt. Come, sir, leave your prating.
   Volp. Why, if your worship give me but your hand,
That I may have the refusal, I have done.
'Tis a mere toy to you, sir; candle rents;
As your learned worship knows——
   Volt. What do I know?
   Volp. Marry, no end of your wealth, sir: God decrease it!
   Volt. Mistaking knave! what, mock'st thou my misfortune?
                                                [*Exit.*
   Volp. His blessing on your heart, sir; would 't were more!—
Now to my first again, at the next corner.   [*Exit.*

SCENE V.—*Another part of the Street.*

Enter CORBACCIO *and* CORVINO;—MOSCA *passes over the Stage, before them.*

   Corb. See, in our habit! see the impudent varlet!
   Corv. That I could shoot mine eyes at him like gun stones!

Enter VOLPONE.

   Volp. But is this true, sir, of the parasite?
   Corb. Again, to afflict us! monster!
   Volp. In good faith, sir,
I'm heartily grieved, a beard of your grave length
Should be so over-reached. I never brooked
That parasite's hair; methought his nose should cozen:
There still was somewhat in his look, did promise
The bane of a clarissimo.
   Corb. Knave——
   Volp. Methinks
Yet you, that are so traded in the world,
A witty merchant, the fine bird, Corvino,
That have such moral emblems on your name,
Should not have sung your shame, and dropt your cheese,
To let the Fox laugh at your emptiness.
   Corv. Sirrah, you think the privilege of the place,
And your red saucy cap, that seems to me
Nailed to your jolt-head with those two chequines,
Can warrant your abuses; come you hither:
You shall perceive, sir, I dare beat you; approach.
   Volp. No haste, sir, I do know your valour well,
Since you durst publish what you are, sir.
   Corv. Tarry,
I'd speak with you.
   Volp. Sir, sir, another time——

Corv. Nay, now.
Volp. Oh, lord, sir! I were a wise man,
Would stand the fury of a distracted husband.
                [*As he is running off, re-enter* MOSCA.
Corb. What, come again!
Volp. Upon 'em, Mosca; save me.
Corb. The air's infected where he breathes.
Corv. Let's fly him.   [*Exeunt* CORV. *and* CORB.
Volp. Excellent basilisk! turn upon the vulture.

            Enter VOLTORE.

Volt. Well, flesh-fly, it is summer with you now;
Your winter will come on.
Mos. Good advocate,
Prithee not rail, nor threaten out of place thus;
Thou 'lt make a solecism, as madam says.
Get you a biggin more, your brain breaks loose.   [*Exit*
Volt. Well, sir.
Volp. Would you have me beat the insolent slave,
Throw dirt upon his first good clothes?
Volt. This same
Is doubtless some familiar.
Volp. Sir, the Court,
In troth, stays for you. I am mad, a mule
That never read Justinian, should get up,
And ride an advocate. Had you no quirk
To avoid gullage, sir, by such a creature?
I hope you do but jest; he has not done it;
'Tis but confederacy, to blind the rest.
You are the heir.
Volt. A strange, officious,
Troublesome knave! thou dost torment me.
Volp. I know——
It cannot be, sir, that you should be cozened;
'Tis not within the wit of man to do it;
You are so wise, so prudent; and 'tis fit
That wealth and wisdom still should go together.   [*Exeunt.*

    SCENE VI.—*The Scrutineo or Senate-House.*

Enter Avocatori, Notario, BONARIO, CELIA, CORBACCIO, CORVINO, *Commandadori, Saffi, &c.*

1*st Avoc.* Are all the parties here?
Not. All but the advocate.
2*nd Avoc.* And here he comes.

        Enter VOLTORE *and* VOLPONE.

1*st Avoc.* Then bring them forth to sentence.

Volt. O my most honoured fathers, let your mercy
Once win upon your justice, to forgive—
I am distracted——
   Volp. What will he do now?   *[Aside.*
   Volt. Oh,
I know not which to address myself to first;
Whether your fatherhoods, or these innocents——
   Corv. Will he betray himself?   *[Aside.*
   Volt. Whom equally
I have abused, out of most covetous ends——
   Corv. The man is mad!
   Corb. What's that?
   Corv. He is possest.
   Volt. For which, now struck in conscience, here I prostrate
Myself at your offended feet, for pardon.
   1st, 2nd Avoc. Arise.
   Cel. O heaven, how just thou art!
   Volp. I am caught
In mine own noose——   *[Aside.*
   Corv. [*to* CORBACCIO.] Be constant, sir: nought now
Can help, but impudence.
   1st Avoc. Speak forward.
   Com. Silence!
   Volt. It is not passion in me, reverend fathers,
But only conscience, conscience, my good sires,
That makes me now tell truth. That parasite,
That knave, hath been the instrument of all.
   1st Avoc. Where is that knave? fetch him.
   Volp. I go.   *[Exit.*
   Corv. Grave fathers,
This man's distracted; he confest it now:
For, hoping to be old Volpone's heir,
Who now is dead——
   3rd Avoc. How!
   2nd Avoc. Is Volpone dead?
   Corv. Dead since, grave fathers.
   Bon. O sure vengeance!
   1st Avoc. Stay,
Then he was no deceiver.
   Volt. Oh, no, none:
The parasite, grave fathers.
   Corv. He does speak
Out of mere envy, 'cause the servant's made
The thing he gaped for: please your fatherhoods,
This is the truth, though I'll not justify
The other, but he may be some-deal faulty.
   Volt. Ay, to your hopes, as well as mine, Corvino:
But I'll use modesty. Pleaseth your wisdoms,

To view these certain notes, and but confer them;
As I hope favour, they shall speak clear truth.
  Corv. The devil has entered him!
  Bon. Or bides in you.
  4th Avoc. We have done ill, by a public officer
To send for him, if he be heir.
  2nd Avoc. For whom?
  4th Avoc. Him that they call the parasite.
  3rd Avoc. 'Tis true,
He is a man of great estate, now left.
  4th Avoc. Go you, and learn his name, and say, the Court
Entreats his presence here, but to the clearing
Of some few doubts.   [*Exit* Notary.
  2nd Avoc. This same's a labyrinth!
  1st Avoc. Stand you unto your first report?
  Corv. My state,
My life, my fame——
  Bon. Where is it?
  Corv. Are at the stake.
  1st Avoc. Is yours so too?
  Corb. The advocate's a knave,
And has a forked tongue——
  2nd Avoc. Speak to the point.
  Corb. So is the parasite too.
  1st Avoc. This is confusion.
  Volt. I do beseech your fatherhoods, read but those—
                           [*Giving them papers.*
  Corv. And credit nothing the false spirit hath writ:
It cannot be, but he's possest, grave fathers.   [*The scene closes.*

SCENE VII.—*A Street.*

Enter VOLPONE.

  Volp. To make a snare for mine own neck! and run
My head into it, wilfully! with laughter!
When I had newly 'scaped, was free, and clear,
Out of mere wantonness! Oh, the dull devil
Was in this brain of mine, when I devised it,
And Mosca gave it second; he must now
Help to sear up this vein, or we bleed dead.—

Enter NANO, ANDROGYNO, *and* CASTRONE.

How now! who let you loose? whither go you now?
What, to buy gingerbread, or to drown kitlings?
  Nan. Sir, Master Mosca called us out of doors,
And bid us all go play, and took the keys.
  And. Yes.
  Volp. Did Master Mosca take the keys? why so!

I'm farther in. These are my fine conceits!
I must be merry, with a mischief to me!
What a vile wretch was I, that could not bear
My fortune soberly? I must have my crotchets,
And my conundrums! Well, go you, and seek him:
His meaning may be truer than my fear.
Bid him he straight come to me to the court;
Thither will I, and, if't be possible,
Unscrew my advocate, upon new hopes:
When I provoked him, then I lost myself. [*Exeunt.*

SCENE VIII.—*The Scrutineo or Senate House.*

AVOCATORI, BONARIO, CELIA, CORBACCIO, CORVINO, Commandadori, Saffi, &c., *as before.*

1*st Avoc.* These things can ne'er be reconciled. He, here,
[*Shewing the papers.*
Professeth, that the gentleman was wronged,
And that the gentlewoman was brought thither,
Forced by her husband, and there left.
   Volt. Most true.
   Cel. How ready is Heaven to those that pray!
   1*st Avoc.* But that
Volpone would have ravished her, he holds
Utterly false, knowing his impotence.
   Corv. Grave fathers, he's possest; again, I say,
Possest: nay, if there be possession, and
Obsession, he has both.
   3*rd Avoc.* Here comes our officer.

Enter VOLPONE.

   Volp. The parasite will straight be here, grave fathers.
   4*th Avoc.* You might invent some other name, sir varlet.
   3*rd Avoc.* Did not the notary meet him?
   Volp. Not that I know.
   4*th Avoc.* His coming will clear all.
   2*nd Avoc.* Yet, it is misty.
   Volt. May't please your fatherhoods——
   Volp. [*whispers* VOLT.] Sir, the parasite
Will'd me to tell you, that his master lives;
That you are still the man; your hopes the same;
And this was only a jest——
   Volt. How?
   Volp. Sir, to try
If you were firm, and how you stood affected.
   Volt. Art sure he lives?
   Volp. Do I live, sir?

Volt. Oh me!
I was too violent.
   Volp. Sir, you may redeem it.
They said, you were possest; fall down, and seem so:
I 'll help to make it good. [VOLTORE *falls.*] God bless the
      man!——
Stop your wind hard, and swell—See, see, see, see!
He vomits crooked pins! His eyes are set,
Like a dead hare's hung in a poulter's shop!
His mouth's running away! Do you see, signior?
Now it is in his belly.
   Corv. Ay, the devil!
   Volp. Now in his throat.
   Corv. Ay, I perceive it plain.
   Volp. 'Twill out, 'twill out! Stand clear. See where it flies,
In shape of a blue toad, with a bat's wings!
Do you not see it, sir?
   Corb. What? I think I do.
   Corv. 'Tis too manifest.
   Volp. Look! he comes to himself!
   Volt. Where am I?
   Volp. Take good heart, the worst is past, sir.
You are dispossest.
   1st Avoc. What accident is this?
   2nd Avoc. Sudden, and full of wonder!
   3rd Avoc. If he were
Possest, as it appears, all this is nothing.
   Corv. He has been often subject to these fits.
   1st Avoc. Show him that writing:—Do you know it, sir?
   Volp. [*whispers* VOLT.] Deny it, sir, forswear it; know
      not.
   Volt. Yes, I do know it well, it is my hand;
But all that it contains is false.
   Bon. O practice!
   2nd Avoc. What maze is this!
   1st Avoc. Is he not guilty, then,
Whom you there name the parasite?
   Volt. Grave fathers,
No more than his good patron, old Volpone.
   4th Avoc. Why, he is dead.
   Volt. Oh, no, my honoured fathers,
He lives——
   1st Avoc. How! lives?
   Volt. Lives.
   2nd Avoc. This is subtler yet!
   3rd Avoc. You said he was dead.
   Volt. Never.
   3rd Avoc. You said so.

Corv. I heard so.

4th Avoc. Here comes the gentleman; make him way.

Enter MOSCA.

3rd Avoc. A stool.

4th Avoc. A proper man; and, were Volpone dead,
A fit match for my daughter. *[Aside.*

3rd Avoc. Give him way.

Volp. Mosca, I was almost lost; the advocate
Had betrayed all; but now it is recovered;
All's on the hinge again——Say, I am living. *[Aside to* Mos.

Mos. What busy knave is this! Most reverend fathers,
I sooner had attended your grave pleasures,
But that my order for the funeral
Of my dear patron did require me——

Volp. Mosca! *[Aside.*

Mos. Whom I intend to bury like a gentleman.

Volp. Ay, quick, and cozen me of all. *[Aside.*

2nd Avoc. Still stranger!
More intricate!

1st Avoc. And come about again!

4th Avoc. It is a match, my daughter is bestow'd. *[Aside.*

Mos. Will you give me half? *[Aside to* VOLP.

Volp. First, I'll be hanged.

Mos. I know
Your voice is good, cry not so loud.

1st Avoc. Demand
The advocate. Sir, did you not affirm
Volpone was alive?

Volp. Yes, and he is;
This gentleman told me so.—Thou shalt have half.
  [Aside to Mos.

Mos. Whose drunkard is this same! Speak, some that know him.
I never saw his face.—I cannot now
Afford it you so cheap. *[Aside to* VOLP.

Volp. No!

1st Avoc. What say you?

Volt. The officer told me.

Volp. I did, grave fathers,
And will maintain he lives with mine own life,
And that this creature [*points to* MOSCA] told me.—I was born
With all good stars my enemies. *[Aside.*

Mos. Most grave fathers,
If such an insolence as this must pass
Upon me, I am silent: 'twas not this
For which you sent, I hope.

2nd Avoc. Take him away.

Volp. Mosca!
3rd Avoc. Let him be whipt.
Volp. Wilt thou betray me? Cozen me?
3rd Avoc. And taught to bear himself
Toward a person of his rank.
    4th Avoc. Away.   [*The* Officers *seize* VOLPONE.
    Mos. I humbly thank your fatherhoods.
    Volp. Soft, soft. Whipt!
And lose all that I have! If I confess,
It cannot be much more.   [*Aside.*
    4th Avoc. Sir, are you married?
    Volp. They'll be allied anon; I must be resolute;
The fox shall here uncase.   [*Throws off his disguise.*
    Mos. Patron!
    Volp. Nay, now
My ruins shall not come alone: your match
I'll hinder sure: my substance shall not glue you,
Nor screw you into a family.
    Mos. Why, patron!
    Volp. I am Volpone, and this is my knave;
                                [*Pointing to* MOSCA.
This [*to* VOLT.] his own knave; this [*to* CORB.] avarice's fool;
This [*to* CORV.] a chimera of wittol, fool, and knave:
And, reverend fathers, since we all can hope
Nought but a sentence, let's not now despair it.
You hear me brief.
    Corv. May it please your fatherhoods——
    Com. Silence.
    1st Avoc. The knot is now undone by miracle.
    2nd Avoc. Nothing can be more clear.
    3rd Avoc. Or can more prove
These innocent.
    1st Avoc. Give them their liberty.
    Bon. Heaven could not long let such gross crimes be hid.
    2nd Avoc. If this be held the high-way to get riches,
May I be poor!
    3rd Avoc. This is not gain, but torment.
    1st Avoc. These possess wealth, as sick men possess fevers,
Which trulier may be said to possess them.
    2nd Avoc. Disrobe that parasite.
    Corv., Mos. Most honoured fathers!——
    1st Avoc. Can you plead aught to stay the course of justice?
If you can, speak.
    Corv., Volt. We beg favour.
    Cel. And mercy.
    1st Avoc. You hurt your innocence, suing for the guilty.
Stand forth; and first the parasite. You appear

T' have been the chiefest minister, if not plotter,
In all these lewd impostures; and now, lastly,
Have with your impudence abused the court
And habit of a gentleman of Venice,
Being a fellow of no birth or blood:
For which our sentence is, first, thou be whipt;
Then live perpetual prisoner in our gallies.
 Volp. I thank you for him.
 Mos. Bane to thy wolfish nature!
 1*st Avoc.* Deliver him to the saffi. [MOSCA *is carried out.*]
  Thou, Volpone,
By blood and rank a gentleman, canst not fall
Under like censure; but our judgment on thee
Is, that thy substance all be straight confiscate
To the hospital of the Incurabili:
And, since the most was gotten by imposture,
By feigning lame, gout, palsy, and such diseases,
Thou art to lie in prison, cramped with irons,
Till thou be'st sick and lame indeed. Remove him.
      [*He is taken from the Bar.*
 Volp. This is called mortifying of a Fox.
 1*st Avoc.* Thou, Voltore, to take away the scandal
Thou hast given all worthy men of thy profession,
Art banished from their fellowship, and our state.
Corbaccio!—bring him near. We here possess
Thy son of all thy state, and confine thee
To the monastery of San Spirito;
Where, since thou knewest not how to live well here,
Thou shalt be learned to die well.
 Corb. Ah! what said he?
 Com. You shall know anon, sir.
 1*st Avoc.* Thou, Corvino, shalt
Be straight embarked from thine own house, and rowed
Round about Venice, through the grand canale,
Wearing a cap, with fair long ass's ears,
Instead of horns; and so to mount, a paper
Pinned on thy breast, to the Berlina——
 Corv. Yes,
And have mine eyes beat out with stinking fish,
Bruised fruit, and rotten eggs——'Tis well. I am glad
I shall not see my shame yet.
 1*st Avoc.* And to expiate
Thy wrongs done to thy wife, thou art to send her
Home to her father, with her dowry trebled:
And these are all your judgments.
 All. Honoured fathers.—
 1*st Avoc.* Which may not be revoked. Now you begin,
When crimes are done and past, and to be punished,

To think what your crimes are: away with them.
Let all that see these vices thus rewarded,
Take heart and love to study 'em! Mischiefs feed
Like beasts, till they be fat, and then they bleed.   [*Exeunt.*

VOLPONE *comes forward.*

The seasoning of a play, is the applause.
Now, though the Fox be punished by the laws,
He yet doth hope there is no suffering due,
For any fact which he hath done 'gainst you;
If there be, censure him; here he doubtful stands:
If not, fare jovially and clap your hands.   [*Exit.*

Epicœne;

OR,

The Silent Woman.

THE PERSONS OF THE PLAY.

MOROSE, *a gentleman that loves no noise.*
SIR DAUPHINE EUGENIE, *a Knight, his Nephew.*
NED CLERIMONT, *a Gentleman, his Friend.*
TRUEWIT, *another Friend.*
SIR JOHN DAW, *a Knight.*
SIR AMOROUS LA-FOOLE, *a Knight also.*
THOMAS OTTER, *a Land and Sea Captain.*
CUTBEARD, *a Barber.*
MUTE, *one of* MOROSE'S *Servants.*

Parson.
Page *to* CLERIMONT.
EPICŒNE, *supposed the* Silent Woman.
LADY HAUGHTY, ⎫
LADY CENTAURE, ⎬ *Ladies*
MISTRESS DOL. ⎭ *Collegiates.*
MAVIS,
MISTRESS OTTER, ⎫
 The Captain's Wife. ⎬ *Preten-*
MISTRESS TRUSTY, Lady ⎭ *ders.*
 HAUGHTY'S *Woman.*

Pages, Servants, &c.

SCENE,—LONDON.

PROLOGUE.

Truth says, of old the art of making plays
Was to content the people; and their praise
Was to the poet money, wine, and bays.
But in this age, a sect of writers are,
That, only, for particular likings care,
And will taste nothing that is popular.
With such we mingle neither brains nor breasts;
Our wishes, like to those make public feasts,
Are not to please the cook's taste but the guests.
Yet, if those cunning palates hither come,
They shall find guests' entreaty, and good room;
And though all relish not, sure there will be some,
That, when they leave their seats, shall make them say,
Who wrote that piece, could so have wrote a play,
But that he knew this was the better way.

For, to present all custard, or all tart,
And have no other meats to bear a part,
Or to want bread and salt, were but coarse art.
The poet prays you then, with better thought
To sit ; and, when his cates are all inbrought,
Though there be none far-fet, there will dear-bought,
Be fit for ladies : some for lords, knights, 'squires ;
Some for your waiting-wench, and city-wires ;
Some for your men, and daughters of White-friars.
Nor is it, only, while you keep your seat
Here, that this feast will last ; but you shall eat
A week at ord'naries, on his broken meat :
    If his muse be true,
    Who commends her to you.

ANOTHER.

The ends of all, who for the scene do write,
Are, or should be, to profit and delight.
And still 't hath been the praise of all best times,
So persons were not touched, to tax the crimes.
Then, in this play, which we present to-night,
And make the object of your ear and sight,
On forfeit of yourselves, think nothing true :
Lest so you make the maker to judge you.
For he knows, poet never credit gained
By writing truths, but things, like truths, well feigned.
If any yet will, with particular sleight
Of application, wrest what he doth write ;
And that he meant, or him, or her, will say :
They make a libel, which he made a play.

ACT I.

SCENE I.—*A Room in* CLERIMONT'S *House.*

Enter CLERIMONT, *making himself ready, followed by his Page.*

Cler. Have you got the song yet perfect, I gave you, boy ?

Page. Yes, sir.

Cler. Let me hear it.

Page. You shall, sir ; but i'faith let nobody else.

Cler. Why, I pray ?

Page. It will get you the dangerous name of a poet in town, sir ; besides me a perfect deal of ill-will at the mansion you wot of, whose lady is the argument of it ; where now I am the welcomest thing under a man that comes there.

Cler. I think ; and above a man too, if the truth were rack'd out of you.

Page. No, faith, I'll confess before, sir. The gentlewomen play with me, and throw me on the ground, and carry me into my lady: and she kisses me with her oiled face, and puts a peruke on my head; and asks me an I will wear her gown? and I say no: and then she hits me a blow o' the ear, and calls me Innocent! and lets me go.

Cler. No marvel if the door be kept shut against your master, when the entrance is so easy to you——well, sir, you shall go there no more, lest I be fain to seek your voice in my lady's rushes, a fortnight hence. Sing, sir. [PAGE *sings.*

Still to be neat, still to be drest—

Enter TRUEWIT.

True. Why, here's the man that can melt away his time, and never feels it! What between his mistress abroad and his ingle at home, high fare, soft lodging, fine clothes, and his fiddle; he thinks the hours have no wings, or the day no post-horse. Well, sir gallant, were you struck with the plague this minute, or condemned to any capital punishment to-morrow, you would begin then to think, and value every article of your time, esteem it at the true rate, and give all for it.

Cler. Why, what should a man do?

True. Why, nothing; or that which, when 'tis done, is as idle. Hearken after the next horse-race, or hunting-match, lay wagers, praise Puppy, or Peppercorn, White-foot, Franklin; swear upon Whitemane's party; speak aloud, that my lords may hear you; visit my ladies at night, and be able to give them the character of every bowler or better on the green. These be the things wherein your fashionable men exercise themselves, and I for company.

Cler. Nay, if I have thy authority, I'll not leave yet. Come, the other are considerations, when we come to have grey heads and weak hams, moist eyes and shrunk limbs. We'll think on 'em then; then we'll pray and fast.

True. Ay, and destine only that time of age to goodness, which our want of ability will not let us employ in evil!

Cler. Why, then, 'tis time enough.

True. Yes; as if a man should sleep all the term, and think to effect his business the last day. O, Clerimont, this time, because it is an incorporeal thing, and not subject to sense, we mock ourselves the fineliest out of it, with vanity and misery indeed! not seeking an end of wretchedness, but only changing the matter still.

Cler. Nay, thou'lt not leave now—

True. See but our common disease! with what justice can we complain, that great men will not look upon us, nor be at leisure to give our affairs such dispatch as we expect, when we will never do it to ourselves? nor hear, nor regard ourselves?

Cler. Foh! thou hast read Plutarch's morals, now, or some such tedious fellow; and it shews so vilely with thee! 'fore God, 'twill spoil thy wit utterly. Talk to me of pins, and feathers, and ladies, and rushes, and such things: and leave this Stoicity alone till thou makest sermons.

True. Well, sir; if it will not take, I have learned to lose as little of my kindness as I can; I'll do good to no man against his will, certainly. When were you at the college?

Cler. What college?

True. As if you knew not!

Cler. No, faith, I came but from court yesterday.

True. Why, is it not arrived there yet, the news? A new foundation, sir, here in the town, of ladies, that call themselves the collegiates, an order between courtiers and country-madams, that live from their husbands; and give entertainment to all the wits and braveries of the time, as they call them: cry down, or up, what they like or dislike in a brain or a fashion, with most masculine, or rather hermaphroditical authority; and every day gain to their college some new probationer.

Cler. Who is the president?

True. The grave and youthful matron, the Lady Haughty.

Cler. A plague of her autumnal face, her pieced beauty! there's no man can be admitted till she be ready, now-a-days, till she has painted, and perfumed, and washed, and scoured, but the boy here; and him she wipes her oiled lips upon, like a sponge. I have made a song (I pray thee hear it) on the subject.

[PAGE *sings.*

> Still to be neat, still to be drest,
> As you were going to a feast;
> Still to be powdered, still perfumed:
> Lady, it is to be presumed,
> Though art's hid causes are not found,
> All is not sweet, all is not sound.
> Give me a look, give me a face;
> That makes simplicity a grace;
> Robes loosely flowing, hair as free:
> Such sweet neglect more taketh me,
> Than all the adulteries of art;
> They strike mine eyes, but not my heart.

True. And I am clearly on the other side: I love a good dressing before any beauty o' the world. Oh, a woman is then like a delicate garden; nor is there one kind of it; she may vary every hour; take often counsel of her glass, and choose the best. If she have good ears, shew them; good hair, lay it out; good legs, wear short clothes; a good hand, discover it often; practice any art to mend breath, cleanse teeth, repair eye-brows; paint, and profess it.

Cler. How! publicly?

True. The doing of it, not the manner: that must be private. Many things that seem foul in the doing, do please done. A lady should indeed study her face when we think she sleeps; nor, when the doors are shut, should men be inquiring; all is sacred within, then. Is it for us to see their perukes put on, their false teeth, their complexion, their eyebrows, their nails? You see gilders will not work, but inclosed. They must not discover how little serves, with the help of art, to adorn a great deal. How long did the canvas hang afore Aldgate? Were the people suffered to see the city's Love and Charity, while they were rude stone, before they were painted and burnished? No; no more should servants approach their mistresses, but when they are complete and finished.

Cler. Well said, my Truewit.

True. And a wise lady will keep a guard always upon the place, that she may do things securely. I once followed a rude fellow into a chamber, where the poor madam, for haste, and troubled, snatched at her peruke to cover her baldness; and put it on the wrong way.

Cler. O prodigy!

True. And the unconscionable knave held her in compliment an hour with that reversed face, when I still looked when she should talk from the t' other side.

Cler. Why, thou shouldst have relieved her.

True. No, faith, I let her alone, as we'll let this argument, if you please, and pass to another. When saw you Dauphine Eugenie?

Cler. Not these three days. Shall we go to him this morning? He is very melancholy, I hear.

True. Sick of the uncle, is he? I met that stiff piece of formality, his uncle, yesterday, with a huge turban of night-caps on his head, buckled over his ears.

Cler. Oh, that's his custom when he walks abroad. He can endure no noise, man.

True. So I have heard. But is the disease so ridiculous in him as it is made? They say he has been upon divers treaties with the fish-wives and orange-women; and articles propounded between them: marry, the chimney-sweepers will not be drawn in.

Cler. No, nor the broom-men: they stand out stiffly. He cannot endure a costard-monger, he swoons if he hear one.

True. Methinks a smith should be ominous.

Cler. Or any hammer-man. A brasier is not suffered to dwell in the parish, nor an armourer. He would have hanged a pewterer's prentice once upon a Shrove-Tuesday's riot, for being of that trade, when the rest were quit.

True. A trumpet should fright him terribly, or the hautboys.

Cler. Out of his senses. The waits of the city have a pension of him not to come near that ward. This youth practised on him one night like the bell-man, and never left till he had brought him down to the door with a long sword, and there left him flourishing with the air.

Page. Why, sir, he hath chosen a street to lie in so narrow at both ends, that it will receive no coaches, nor carts, nor any of these common noises: and therefore we that love him, devise to bring him in such as we may, now and then, for his exercise, to breathe him. He would grow resty else in his case: his virtue would rust without action. I entreated a bearward, one day, to come down with the dogs of some four parishes that way, and I thank him he did; and cried his games under Master Morose's window: till he was sent crying away, with his head made a most bleeding spectacle to the multitude. And, another time, a fencer marching to his prize, had his drum most tragically run through, for taking that street in his way at my request.

True. A good wag! how does he for the bells?

Cler. Oh, in the Queen's time, he was wont to go out of town every Saturday at ten o'clock, or on holy day eves. But now, by reason of the sickness, the perpetuity of ringing has made him devise a room, with double walls and treble ceilings; the windows close shut and caulk'd: and there he lives by candle-light. He turn'd away a man, last week, for having a pair of new shoes that creak'd. And this fellow waits on him now in tennis-court socks, or slippers soled with wool: and they talk each to other in a trunk. See, who comes here!

Enter SIR DAUPHINE EUGENIE.

Daup. How now! what ail you, sirs? dumb?

True. Struck into stone, almost, I am here, with tales o' thine uncle. There was never such a prodigy heard of.

Daup. I would you would once lose this subject, my masters, for my sake. They are such as you are, that have brought me into that predicament I am with him.

True. How is that?

Daup. Mary, that he will disinherit me; no more. He thinks, I and my company are authors of all the ridiculous Acts and Monuments are told of him.

True. 'Slid, I would be the author of more to vex him; that purpose deserves it: it gives thee law of plaguing him. I'll tell thee what I would do. I would make a false almanack, get it printed; and then have him drawn out on a coronation day to the Tower-wharf, and kill him with the noise of the ordnance. Disinherit thee! he cannot, man. Art not thou next of blood, his sister's son?

Daup. Ay, but he will thrust me out of it, he vows, and marry.

True. How! that's a more portent. Can he endure no noise, and will venture on a wife!

Cler. Yes: why thou art a stranger, it seems, to his best trick, yet. He has employed a fellow this half year all over England to hearken him out a dumb woman; be she of any form, or any quality, so she be able to bear children: her silence is dowry enough, he says.

True. But I trust to God he has found none.

Cler. No; but he has heard of one that's lodged in the next street to him, who is exceedingly soft-spoken; thrifty of her speech; that spends but six words a day. And her he's about now, and shall have her.

True. Is't possible! who is his agent in the business?

Cler. Marry, a barber, one Cutbeard; an honest fellow, one that tells Dauphine all here.

True. Why, you oppress me with wonder: a woman, and a barber, and love no noise!

Cler. Yes, faith. The fellow trims him silently, and has not the knack with his shears or his fingers, and that continence in a barber he thinks so eminent a virtue, as it has made him chief of his counsel.

True. Is the barber to be seen, or the wench?

Cler. Yes, that they are.

True. I prithee, Dauphine, let's go thither.

Daup. I have some business now: I cannot, i' faith.

True. You shall have no business shall make you neglect this, sir: we'll make her talk, believe it; or, if she will not, we can give out at least so much as shall interrupt the treaty; we will break it. Thou art bound in conscience, when he suspects thee without cause, to torment him.

Daup. Not I, by any means. I'll give no suffrage to 't. He shall never have that plea against me, that I opposed the least phant'sy of his. Let it lie upon my stars to be guilty, I'll be innocent.

True. Yes, and be poor, and beg; do, innocent: when some groom of his has got him an heir, or this barber, if he himself cannot. Innocent! I prithee, Ned, where lies she? let him be innocent still.

Cler. Why, right over against the barber's; in the house where Sir John Daw lies.

True. You do not mean to confound me!

Cler. Why?

True. Does he that would marry her know so much?

Cler. I cannot tell.

True. 'Twere enough of imputation to her with him.

Cler. Why?

True. The only talking sir in the town! Jack Daw! and he

teach her not to speak! God be wi' you. I have some business too.

Cler. Will you not go thither, then?

True. Not with the danger to meet Daw, for mine ears.

Cler. Why, I thought you two had been upon very good terms.

True. Yes, of keeping distance.

Cler. They say, he is a very good scholar.

True. Ay, and he says it first. A plague on him, a fellow that pretends only to learning, buys titles, and nothing else of books in him.

Cler. The world reports him to be very learned.

True. I am sorry the world should so conspire to belie him.

Cler. Good faith, I have heard very good things come from him.

True. You may; there's none so desperately ignorant to deny that: would they were his own! God be wi' you, gentlemen!

[*Exit hastily.*

Cler. This is very abrupt!

Daup. Come, you are a strange open man, to tell everything thus.

Cler. Why, believe it, Dauphine, Truewit's a very honest fellow.

Daup. I think no other: but this frank nature of his is not for secrets.

Cler. Nay, then, you are mistaken, Dauphine: I know where he has been well trusted, and discharged the trust very truly, and heartily.

Daup. I contend not, Ned; but with the fewer a business is carried, it is ever the safer. Now we are alone, if you'll go thither, I am for you.

Cler. When were you there?

Daup. Last night: and such a Decameron of sport fallen out! Boccace never thought of the like. Daw does nothing but court her; and the wrong way. He would have her, and praises her modesty; desires that she would talk and be free, and commends her silence in verses; which he reads, and swears are the best that ever man made. Then rails at his fortunes, stamps, and mutines, why he is not made a counsellor and called to affairs of state.

Cler. I pr'thee let's go. I would fain partake this.—Some water, boy. [*Exit* Page.

Daup. We are invited to dinner together, he and I, by one that came thither to him, Sir La-Foole.

Cler. Oh, that's a precious mannikin!

Daup. Do you know him?

Cler. Ay, and he will know you too, if e'er he saw you but once, though you should meet him at church in the midst of prayers. He is one of the braveries, though he be none of the wits. He will salute a judge upon the bench, and a bishop in the pulpit, a lawyer when he is pleading at the bar, and a lady when she is dancing in a masque, and put her out. He does give plays and suppers, and invites his guests to them, aloud, out of his window, as they ride by in coaches. He has a lodging in the Strand for the purpose : or to watch when ladies are gone to the china-houses or the Exchange, that he may meet them by chance, and give them presents—some two or three hundred pounds' worth of toys—to be laughed at. He is never without a spare banquet, or sweet-meats in his chamber, for their women to alight at, and come up to for a bait.

Daup. Excellent! He was a fine youth last night, but now he is much finer! What is his Christian name?—I have forgot.

Re-enter Page.

Cler. Sir Amorous La-Foole.
Page. The gentleman is here below that owns that name.
Cler. 'Heart, he's come to invite me to dinner, I hold my life.
Daup. Like enough : prithee, let's have him up.
Cler. Boy, marshal him.
Page. With a truncheon, sir?
Cler. Away, I beseech you. [*Exit* Page.] I'll make him tell us his pedigree now ; and what meat he has to dinner ; and who are his guests ; and the whole course of his fortunes, with a breath.

Enter SIR AMOROUS LA-FOOLE.

La-F. 'Save, dear Sir Dauphine! honoured Master Clerimont!
Cler. Sir Amorous! you have very much honested my lodging with your presence.
La-F. Good faith, it is a fine lodging : almost as delicate a lodging as mine.
Cler. Not so, sir.
La-F. Excuse me, sir, if it were. in the Strand, I assure you. I am come, Master Clerimont, to entreat you to wait upon two or three ladies, to dinner, to-day.
Cler. How, sir! wait upon them? Did you ever see me carry dishes?
La-F. No, sir, dispense with me ; I meant, to bear them company.
Cler. Oh, that I will, sir. The doubtfulness of your phrase, believe it, sir, would breed you a quarrel once an hour, with the terrible boys, if you should but keep them fellowship a day.
La-F. It should be extremely against my will, sir, if I contested with any man.

Cler. I believe it, sir. Where hold you your feast?

La-F. At Tom Otter's, sir.

Daup. Tom Otter! what's he?

La-F. Captain Otter, sir; he is a kind of gamester, but he has had command both by sea and by land.

Daup. Oh, then he is *animal amphibium?*

La-F. Ay, sir: his wife was the rich chinawoman, that the courtiers visited so often; that gave the rare entertainment. She commands all at home.

Cler. Then she is Captain Otter.

La-F. You say very well, sir; she is my kinswoman, a La-Foole by the mother-side, and will invite any great ladies for my sake.

Daup. Not of the La-Fooles of Essex?

La-F. No, sir, the La-Fooles of London.

Cler. Now he's in. [*Aside.*

La-F. They all come out of our house, the La-Fooles of the north, the La-Fooles of the west, the La-Fooles of the east and south—we are as ancient a family as any is in Europe—but I myself am descended lineally of the French La-Fooles—and, we do bear for our coat yellow, or *or*, checker'd *azure*, and *gules*, and some three or four colours more, which is a very noted coat, and has, sometimes, been solemnly worn by divers nobility of our house—but let that go, antiquity is not respected now.—I had a brace of fat does sent me, gentlemen, and half a dozen of pheasants, a dozen or two of god-wits, and some other fowl, which I would have eaten, while they are good, and in good company:—there will be a great lady or two, my Lady Haughty, my Lady Centaure, Mistress Dol Mavis—and they come o' purpose to see the silent gentlewoman, Mistress Epicœne, that honest Sir John Daw has promised to bring thither.—and then Mistress Trusty, my lady's woman, will be there too, and this honourable knight, sir Dauphine, with yourself, Master Clerimont—and we'll be very merry, and have fiddlers, and dance.—I have been a mad wag in my time, and have spent some crowns since I was a page in court, to my Lord Lofty, and after, my lady's gentleman-usher, who got me knighted in Ireland, since it pleased my elder brother to die.—I had as fair a gold jerkin on that day, as any worn in the island voyage, or at Cadiz, none dispraised; and I came over in it hither, showed myself to my friends in court, and after went down to my tenants in the country, and surveyed my lands, let new leases, took their money, spent it in the eye o' the land here, upon ladies: and now I can take up at my pleasure.

Daup. Can you take up ladies, sir?

Cler. Oh, let him breathe, he has not recovered.

Daup. Would I were your half in that commodity!

La-F. No, sir, excuse me: I meant money, which can take

up anything. I have another guest or two to invite, and say as much to, gentlemen. I'll take my leave abruptly, in hope you will not fail——Your servant. [*Exit.*

Daup. We will not fail you, sir precious La-Foole; but she shall, that your ladies come to see, if I have credit afore Sir Daw.

Cler. Did you ever hear such a wind-sucker, as this?

Daup. Or such a rook as the other, that will betray his mistress to be seen! Come, 'tis time we prevented it.

Cler. Go. [*Exeunt.*

———————ACT II.———————

SCENE I.—*A Room in* MOROSE'S *House.*

Enter MOROSE, *with a tube in his hand, followed by* MUTE.

Mor. Cannot I, yet, find out a more compendious method than by this trunk, to save my servants the labour of speech, and mine ears the discords of sounds? Let me see: all discourses but my own afflict me; they seem harsh, impertinent, and irksome. Is it not possible that thou shouldst answer me by signs, and I apprehend thee, fellow? Speak not, though I question you. You have taken the ring off from the street door, as I bade you? answer me not by speech, but by silence; unless it be otherwise [MUTE *makes a leg.*]—very good. And you have fastened on a thick quilt, or flock-bed on the outside of the door; that if they knock with their daggers, or with brick-bats, they can make no noise?—But with your leg, your answer, unless it be otherwise. [*makes a leg.*]—Very good. This is not only fit modesty in a servant, but good state and discretion in a master. And you have been with Cutbeard the barber, to have him come to me? (*makes a leg.*)—Good. And, he will come presently? Answer me not but with your leg, unless it be otherwise: if it be otherwise, shake your head or shrug. (*makes a leg.*)—So! Your Italian and Spaniard are wise in these: and it is a frugal and comely gravity. How long will it be ere Cutbeard come? Stay; if an hour, hold up your whole hand; if half an hour, two fingers; if a quarter, one; [*holds up a finger bent.*]—Good: half a quarter? 'tis well. And have you given him a key, to come in without knocking?—[*makes a leg*]—good. And, is the lock oiled, and the hinges, to-day?—[*makes a leg.*]—good. And the quilting of the stairs nowhere worn out and bare?—[*makes a leg.*]—Very good. I see, by much doctrine and impulsion, it may be effected; stand by. The Turk, in this divine discipline, is admirable, exceeding all the potentates of the earth; still waited on by mutes: and all his commands so executed; yea, even in the war, as I have heard, and in his marches, most of his charges and directions given by signs, and with silence: an exquisite art! and I am heartily ashamed, and angry oftentimes, that the princes of Christendom should suffer a barbarian to transcend them in so high a point of felicity. I will practise it hereafter.—[*A horn winded within.*]—How now? oh! oh! what villain, what prodigy of mankind is that? look.—[*Exit* MUTE.]—[*Horn again.*]—Oh! cut his throat, cut his throat! what murderer, hell-hound, devil can this be?

Re-enter MUTE.

Mute. It is a post from the court——
Mor. Out, rogue! and must thou blow thy horn too?
Mute. Alas, it is a post from the court, sir, that says, he must speak with you, pain of death——
Mor. Pain of thy life, be silent!

Enter TRUEWIT *with a post-horn, and a halter in his hand.*

True. By your leave, sir;—I am a stranger here:—Is your name Master Morose? is your name Master Morose? Fishes! Pythagoreans all! This is strange. What say you, sir? nothing! Has Harpocrates been here with his club, among you? Well, sir, I will believe you to be the man at this time: I will venture upon you, sir. Your friends at court commend them to you, sir——
Mor. Oh men! Oh manners! was there ever such an impudence?
True. And are extremely solicitous for you, sir.
Mor. Whose knave are you?
True. Mine own knave, and your compeer, sir.
Mor. Fetch me my sword——
True. You shall taste the one half of my dagger, if you do, groom; and you the other, if you stir, sir: Be patient, I charge you, in the king's name, and hear me without insurrection. They say, you are to marry; to marry! do you mark, sir?
Mor. How then, rude companion!
True. Marry, your friends do wonder, sir, the Thames being so near, wherein you may drown, so handsomely; or London-bridge at a low fall, with a fine leap, to hurry you down the stream; or, such a delicate steeple in the town, as Bow, to vault from; or, a braver height, as Paul's: Or, if you affected to do it nearer home, and a shorter way, an excellent garret-window into the street; or, a beam in the said garret, with this halter—[*shows him the halter*]—which they have sent, and desire, that you would sooner commit your grave head to this knot, than to the wedlock noose; or, take a little sublimate, and go out of the world like a rat; or, a fly, as one said, with a straw in your body:

anyway, rather than follow this goblin Matrimony. Alas, sir, do you ever think to find a chaste wife in these times? now? when there are so many masques, plays, Puritan preachings, mad folks, and other strange sights to be seen daily, private and public? If you had lived in king Etheldred's time, sir, or Edward the Confessor, you might, perhaps, have found one in some cold country hamlet, then, a dull frosty wench, would have been contented with one man : now, they will as soon be pleased with one leg, or one eye. I'll tell you, sir, the monstrous hazards you shall run with a wife.

Mor. Good sir, have I ever cozened any friends of yours of their land? bought their possessions? taken forfeit of their mortgage? begged a reversion from them? bastarded their issue? What have I done, that may deserve this?

True. Nothing, sir, that I know, but your itch of marriage.

Mor. Why, if I had made an assassinate upon your father, vitiated your mother, ravished your sisters——

True. I would kill you, sir, I would kill you, if you had.

Mor. Why, you do more in this, sir : it were a vengeance centuple, for all facinorous acts that could be named, to do that you do.

True. Alas, sir, I am but a messenger : I but tell you, what you must hear. It seems your friends are careful after your soul's health, sir, and would have you know the danger : (but you may do your pleasure for all them, I persuade not, sir.) If, after you are married, your wife do run away with a vaulter, or the Frenchman that walks upon ropes, or him that dances the jig, or a fencer for his skill at his weapon ; why it is not their fault, they have discharged their consciences ; when you know what may happen. Nay, suffer valiantly, sir, for I must tell you all the perils that you are obnoxious to. If she be fair, young and vegetous, no sweetmeats ever drew more flies; all the yellow doublets and great roses in the town will be there. If foul and crooked, she'll be with them, and buy those doublets and roses, sir. If rich, and that you marry her dowry, not her, she'll reign in your house as imperious as a widow. If noble, all her kindred will be your tyrants. If fruitful, as proud as May, and humorous as April; she must have her doctors, her midwives, her nurses, her longings every hour; though it be for the dearest morsel of man. If learned, there was never such a parrot; all your patrimony will be too little for the guests that must be invited to hear her speak Latin and Greek ; and you must lie with her in those languages too, if you will please her. If precise, you must feast all the silenced brethren, once in three days ; salute the sisters ; entertain the whole family or wood of them ; and hear long-winded exercises, singings, and catechisings, which you are not given to, and yet must give for; to please the zealous matron your wife, who for the holy cause, will cozen you over and above. You begin to sweat, sir! but this is not half, i' faith: you may do your pleasure, notwithstanding, as I said before: I come not to persuade you. (MUTE *is stealing away*.) —Upon my faith, master serving-man, if you do stir, I will beat you.

Mor. Oh, what is my sin! what is my sin!

True. Then, if you love your wife, or rather dote on her, sir; Oh, how she 'll torture you, and take pleasure in your torments! you shall lie with her but when she lists; she will not hurt her beauty, her complexion; or it must be for that jewel, or that pearl, when she does: every half hour's pleasure must be bought anew, and with the same pain and charge you wooed her at first. Then you must keep what servants she please; what company she will; that friend must not visit you without her licence; and him she loves most, she will seem to hate eagerliest, to decline your jealousy; or, feign to be jealous of you first; and for that cause go live with her she-friend, or cousin at the college, that can instruct her in all the mysteries of writing letters, corrupting servants, taming spies; where she must have that rich gown for such a great day; a new one for the next; a richer for the third; be served in silver; have the chamber filled with a succession of grooms, footmen, ushers, and other messengers; besides embroiderers, jewellers, tire-women, sempsters, feathermen, perfumers; whilst she feels not how the land drops away, nor the acres melt; nor foresees the change, when the mercer has your woods for her velvets; never weighs what her pride costs, sir; so she may kiss a page, or a smooth chin that has the despair of a beard: be a stateswoman, know all the news, what was done at Salisbury, what at the Bath, what at court, what in progress; or, so she may censure poets, and authors, and styles, and compare them; Daniel with Spenser, Jonson with the t' other youth, and so forth: or be thought cunning in controversies, or the very knots of divinity: and have often in her mouth the state of the question; and then skip to the mathematics, and demonstration: and answer in religion to one, in state to another, in folly to a third.

Mor. Oh, oh!

True. All this is very true, sir. And then her going in disguise to that conjurer, and this cunning woman: where the first question is, how soon you shall die? Next, if her present servant love her? Next, if she shall have a new servant? And how many? Which of the family would make the best go-between, male or female? What precedence she shall have by her next match? And sets down the answers, and believes them above the scriptures. Nay, perhaps she 'll study the art.

Mor. Gentle sir, have you done? Have you had your pleasure of me? I 'll think of these things.

True. Yes, sir : and then comes reeking home of vapour and sweat, with going a foot, and lies in a month of a new face, all oil and birdlime ; and rises in asses' milk, and is cleansed with a new fucus : God be wi' you, sir. One thing more, which I had almost forgot. This too, with whom you are to marry, may have made a conveyance of her virginity aforehand, as your wise widows do of their states, before they marry, in trust to some friend, sir : Who can tell ? Or if she have not done it yet, she may do, upon the wedding-day, or the night before, and antedate you. The like has been heard of in nature. 'Tis no devised, impossible thing, sir. God be wi' you : I 'll be bold to leave this rope with you, sir, for a remembrance.—Farewell, Mute ! [*Exit.*

Mor. Come, have me to my chamber : but first shut the door. [TRUEWIT *winds the horn without.*] Oh, shut the door, shut the door ! Is he come again ?

Enter CUTBEARD.

Cut. 'Tis I, sir, your barber.

Mor. Oh, Cutbeard, Cutbeard, Cutbeard ! here has been a cut-throat with me : help me into my bed, and give me physic with thy counsel. [*Exeunt.*

SCENE II.—*A Room in* SIR JOHN DAW'S *House.*

Enter DAW, CLERIMONT, DAUPHINE *and* EPICŒNE.

Daw. Nay, and she will, let her refuse at her own charges ; 'tis nothing to me, gentlemen : but she will not be invited to the like feasts or guests every day.

Cler. Oh, by no means, she may not refuse——to stay at home, if you love your reputation : 'Slight, you are invited thither o' the purpose to be seen, and laughed at by the lady of the college, and her shadows. This trumpeter hath proclaimed you. [*Aside to* EPI.

Daup. You shall not go ; let him be laughed at in your stead, for not bringing you : and put him to his extemporal faculty of fooling and talking loud, to satisfy the company. [*Aside to* EPI.

Cler. He will suspect us ; talk aloud. 'Pray mistress Epicœne, let's see your verses ; we have Sir John Daw's leave ; do not conceal your servant's merit, and your own glories.

Epi. They 'll prove my servant's glories, if you have his leave so soon.

Daup. His vain-glories, lady !

Daw. Show them, show them, mistress ; I dare own them.

Epi. Judge you, what glories.

Daw. Nay, I'll read them myself too : an author must recite his own works. It is a madrigal of Modesty.
   "Modest and fair, for fair and good are near
                     Neighbours, howe'er."—
Daup. Very good.
Cler. Ay, is't not?
Daw. "No noble virtue ever was alone,
                     But two in one."
Daup. Excellent!
Cler. That again, I pray, Sir John.
Daup. It has something in 't like rare wit and sense.
Cler. Peace.
Daw. "No noble virtue ever was alone,
                     But two in one,
   Then, when I praise sweet modesty, I praise
                     Bright beauty's rays:
   And having praised both beauty and modesty,
                     I have praised thee."
Daup. Admirable!
Cler. How it chimes, and cries tink in the close, divinely!
Daup. Ay, 'tis Seneca.
Cler. No, I think 'tis Plutarch.
Daw. The dor on Plutarch and Seneca! I hate it : they are mine own imaginations, by that light. I wonder those fellows have such credit with gentlemen.
Cler. They are very grave authors.
Daw. Grave asses! mere essayists : a few loose sentences, and that's all. A man would talk so, his whole age : I do utter as good things every hour, if they were collected and observed, as either of them.
Daup. Indeed, Sir John!
Cler. He must needs ; living among the wits and braveries too.
Daup. Ay, and being president of them, as he is.
Daw. There's Aristotle, a mere common-place fellow; Plato, a discourser ; Thucydides and Livy, tedious and dry ; Tacitus, an entire knot : sometimes worth the untying, very seldom.
Cler. What do you think of the poets, Sir John?
Daw. Not worthy to be named for authors. Homer, an old tedious, prolix ass, talks of curriers and chines of beef; Virgil, of dunging of land, and bees ; Horace, of I know not what.
Cler. I think so.
Daw. And so, Pindarus, Lycophron, Anacreon, Catullus, Seneca the tragedian, Lucan, Propertius, Tibullus, Martial, Juvenal, Ausonius, Statius, Politian, Valerius Flaccus, and the rest——

Cler. What a sack full of their names he has got!

Daup. And how he pours them out! Politian with Valerius Flaccus!

Cler. Was not the character right of him?

Daup. As could be made, i'faith.

Daw. And Persius, a crabbed coxcomb, not to be endured.

Daup. Why, whom do you account for authors, Sir John Daw?

Daw. Syntagma juris civilis; Corpus juris civilis; Corpus juris canonici; the King of Spain's bible——

Daup. Is the King of Spain's bible an author?

Cler. Yes, and Syntagma.

Daup. What was that Syntagma, sir?

Daw. A civil lawyer, a Spaniard.

Daup. Sure, Corpus was a Dutchman.

Cler. Ay, both the Corpuses, I knew 'em: they were very corpulent authors.

Daw. And then there's Vatablus, Pomponatius, Symancha: the other are not to be received, within the thought of a scholar.

Daup. 'Fore God, you have a simple learned servant, lady,—in titles. [*Aside.*

Cler. I wonder that he is not called to the helm, and made a counsellor.

Daup. He is one extraordinary.

Cler. Nay, but in ordinary: to say truth, the state wants such.

Daup. Why, that will follow.

Cler. I muse a mistress can be so silent to the dotes of such a servant.

Daw. 'Tis her virtue, sir. I have written somewhat of her silence too.

Daup. In verse, Sir John?

Cler. What else?

Daup. Why, how can you justify your own being of a poet, that so slight all the old poets?

Daw. Why, every man that writes in verse is not a poet; you have of the wits that write verses, and yet are no poets: they are poets that live by it, the poor fellows that live by it.

Daup. Why, would not you live by your verses, Sir John?

Cler. No, 'twere pity he should. A knight live by his verses! he did not make them to that end, I hope.

Daup. And yet the noble Sidney lives by his, and the noble family not ashamed.

Cler. Ay, he profest himself; but Sir John Daw has more caution: he'll not hinder his own rising in the state so much. Do you think he will? Your verses, good Sir John, and no poems.

Daw. "Silence in woman, is like speech in man;
  Deny 't who can."
Daup. Not I, believe it: your reason, sir.
Daw.   "Nor is 't a tale,
  That female vice should be a virtue male,
  Or masculine vice a female virtue be:
    You shall it see
    Proved with increase;
  I know to speak, and she to hold her peace."
Do you conceive me, gentlemen?
Daup. No, faith; how mean you with increase, Sir John?
Daw. Why, with increase is, when I court her for the common cause of mankind, and she says nothing, but *consentire videtur*; and in time is *gravida*.
Daup. Then this is a ballad of procreation?
Cler. A madrigal of procreation; you mistake.
Epi. 'Pray give me my verses again, servant.
Daw. If you'll ask them aloud, you shall.
  [*Walks aside with the papers.*

Enter TRUEWIT *with his horn.*

Cler. See, here's Truewit again!—Where hast thou been, in the name of madness, thus accoutred with thy horn?
True. Where the sound of it might have pierced your senses with gladness, had you been in ear-reach of it. Dauphine, fall down and worship me; I have forbid the banns, lad: I have been with thy virtuous uncle, and have broke the match.
Daup. You have not, I hope.
True. Yes, faith; an thou should'st hope otherwise, I should repent me: this horn got me entrance; kiss it. I had no other way to get in, but by feigning to be a post; but when I got in once, I proved none, but rather the contrary, turned him into a post, or a stone, or what is stiffer, with thundering into him the incommodities of a wife, and the miseries of marriage. If ever Gorgon were seen in the shape of a woman, he hath seen her in my description: I have put him off o' that scent for ever. Why do you not applaud and adore me, sirs? Why stand you mute? Are you stupid? You are not worthy of the benefit.
Daup. Did not I tell you? Mischief!
Cler. I would you had placed this benefit somewhere else.
True. Why so?
Cler. 'Slight, you have done the most inconsiderate, rash, weak thing, that ever man did to his friend.
Daup. Friend! If the most malicious enemy I have, had studied to inflict an injury upon me, it could not be a greater.
True. Wherein, for God's sake? Gentlemen, come to yourselves again.

Daup. But I presaged thus much afore to you.

Cler. Would my lips had been soldered when I spake on 't ! 'Slight, what moved you to be thus impertinent?

True. My masters, do not put on this strange face to pay my courtesy; off with this vizor. Have good turns done you, and thank 'em this way!

Daup. 'Fore heaven, you have undone me. That which I have plotted for, and been maturing now these four months, you have blasted in a minute: Now I am lost, I may speak. This gentlewoman was lodged here by me o' purpose, and, to be put upon my uncle, hath profest this obstinate silence for my sake; being my entire friend, and one that for the requital of such a fortune to marry him, would have made me very ample conditions; where now, all my hopes are utterly miscarried by this unlucky accident.

Cler. Thus 'tis when a man will be ignorantly officious, do services, and not know his why: I wonder what courteous itch possest you. You never did absurder part in your life, nor a greater trespass to friendship or humanity.

Daup. Faith, you may forgive it best; 'twas your cause principally.

Cler. I know it; would it had not.

Enter CUTBEARD.

Daup. How now, Cutbeard! what news?

Cut. The best, the happiest that ever was, sir. There has been a mad gentleman with your uncle this morning, [*seeing* TRUEWIT.]—I think this be the gentleman—that has almost talked him out of his wits, with threatening him from marriage—

Daup. On, I prithee.

Cut. And your uncle, sir, he thinks 'twas done by your procurement; therefore he will see the party you wot of presently; and if he like her, he says, and that she be so inclining to dumb as I have told him, he swears he will marry her to-day, instantly, and not defer it a minute longer.

Daup. Excellent! Beyond our expectation!

True. Beyond our expectation! By this light, I knew it would be thus.

Daup. Nay, sweet Truewit, forgive me.

True. No, I was *ignorantly officious, impertinent;* this was the *absurd, weak part.*

Cler. Wilt thou ascribe that to merit now, was mere fortune!

True. Fortune! mere providence. Fortune had not a finger in 't. I saw it must necessarily in nature fall out so: my genius is never false to me in these things. Show me how it could be otherwise.

Daup. Nay, gentlemen, contend not; 'tis well now.

True. Alas, I let him go on with *inconsiderate,* and *rash,* and what he pleased.

Cler. Away, thou strange justifier of thyself, to be wiser than thou wert, by the event!

True. Event! By this light, thou shalt never persuade me, but I foresaw it as well as the stars themselves.

Daup. Nay, gentlemen, 'tis well now. Do you two entertain Sir John Daw with discourse, while I send her away with instructions.

True. I'll be acquainted with her first, by your favour.

Cler. Master Truewit, lady, a friend of ours.

True. I am sorry I have not known you sooner, lady, to celebrate this rare virtue of your silence.

[*Exeunt* DAUP. EPI. *and* CUTBEARD.

Cler. Faith, an you had come sooner, you should have seen and heard her well-celebrated in Sir John Daw's madrigals.

True. [*advances to* DAW.] Jack Daw, God save you! when saw you La-Foole?

Daw. Not since last night, Master Truewit.

True. That's a miracle! I thought you two had been inseparable.

Daw. He's gone to invite his guests.

True. 'Odso! 'tis true! What a false memory have I towards that man! I am one: I met him even now, upon that he calls his delicate fine black horse, rid into foam, with posting from place to place, and person to person, to give them the cue——

Cler. Lest they should forget?

True. Yes, there was never poor captain took more pains at a muster to show men, than he, at this meal, to show friends.

Daw. It is his quarter-feast, sir.

Cler. What! do you say so, Sir John?

True. Nay, Jack Daw will not be out, at the best friends he has, to the talent of his wit. Where's his mistress to hear and applaud him? Is she gone?

Daw. Is Mistress Epicœne gone?

Cler. Gone afore, with Sir Dauphine, I warrant, to the place.

True. Gone afore! That were a manifest injury, a disgrace and a half; to refuse him at such a festival-time as this, being a bravery, and a wit too!

Cler. Tut, he'll swallow it like cream: he's better read in *jure civili* than to esteem anything a disgrace, is offered him from a mistress.

Daw. Nay, let her e'en go; she shall sit alone, and be dumb in her chamber a week together, for John Daw, I warrant her. Does she refuse me?

Cler. No, sir, do not take it so to heart; she does not refuse you, but a little neglects you. Good faith, Truewit, you were to blame, to put it into his head that she does refuse him.

True. Sir, she does refuse him palpably, however you mince it. An I were as he, I would swear to speak ne'er a word to her to-day for't.

Daw. By this light, no more I will not.

True. Nor to anybody else, sir.

Daw. Nay, I will not say so, gentlemen.

Cler. It had been an excellent happy condition for the company, if you could have drawn him to it. [*Aside.*

Daw. I'll be very melancholy, i'faith.

Cler. As a dog, if I were as you, Sir John.

True. Or a snail, or a hog-louse: I would roll myself up for this day; in troth, they should not unwind me.

Daw. By this pick-tooth, so I will.

Cler. 'Tis well done: he begins already to be angry with his teeth.

Daw. Will you go, gentlemen?

Cler. Nay, you must walk alone, if you be right melancholy, Sir John.

True. Yes, sir, we'll dog you, we'll follow you afar off.
[*Exit* DAW.

Cler. Was there ever such a two yards of knighthood measured out by time, to be sold to laughter?

True. A mere talking mole, hang him! no mushroom was ever so fresh. A fellow so utterly nothing, as he knows not what he would be.

Cler. Let's follow him: but first let's go to Dauphine, he's hovering about the house to hear what news.

True. Content. [*Exeunt.*

SCENE III.—*A Room in* MOROSE'S *House.*

Enter MOROSE *and* MUTE, *followed by* CUTBEARD *with* EPICŒNE.

Mor. Welcome, Cutbeard! draw near with your fair charge: and in her ear softly entreat her to unmask. [EPI. *takes off her mask.*]—So! Is the door shut? [MUTE *makes a leg.*]—Enough. Now, Cutbeard, with the same discipline I use to my family, I will question you. As I conceive, Cutbeard, this gentlewoman is she you have provided, and brought, in hope she will fit me in the place and person of a wife? Answer me not but with your leg, unless it be otherwise: [CUT. *makes a leg.*]—Very well done, Cutbeard. I conceive besides, Cutbeard, you have been pre-acquainted with her birth, education, and qualities, or else you would not prefer her to my acceptance, in the weighty consequence of marriage. [*Makes a leg.*]—This I conceive, Cutbeard. Answer me not but with your leg, unless it be otherwise. [*Bows again.*]—Very well done, Cutbeard. Give aside now a little, and leave me to examine her condition, and aptitude to my affection. [*Goes about her and views her.*]—She is exceeding fair, and of a special good favour; a sweet composition or harmony of limbs; her temper of beauty has the true height of my blood. The knave hath exceedingly well fitted me without: I will now try her within.—Come near, fair gentlewoman; let not my behaviour seem rude, though unto you, being rare, it may haply appear strange. [EPICŒNE *curtsies.*] Nay, lady, you may speak, though Cutbeard and my man might not; for of all sounds, only the sweet voice of a fair lady has the just length of mine ears. I beseech you, say, lady; out of the first fire of meeting eyes, they say, love is stricken: do you feel any such motion suddenly shot into you, from any part you see in me? ha, lady? [EPI. *curtsies.*]—Alas, lady, these answers by silent curtsies from you are too courtless and simple. I have ever had my breeding in court; and she that shall be my wife, must be accomplished with courtly and audacious ornaments. Can you speak, lady?

Epi. [*softly.*] Judge you, forsooth.
Mor. What say you, lady? Speak out, I beseech you.
Epi. Judge you, forsooth.
Mor. On my judgment, a divine softness! But can you naturally, lady, as I enjoin these by doctrine and industry, refer yourself to the search of my judgment, and, not taking pleasure in your tongue, which is a woman's chiefest pleasure, think it plausible to answer me by silent gestures, so long as my speeches jump right with what you conceive? [EPI. *curtsies.*]—Excellent! divine! if it were possible she should hold out thus!—Peace, Cutbeard, thou art made for ever, as thou hast made me, if this felicity have lasting: but I will try her further. Dear lady, I am courtly, I tell you, and I must have mine ears banquetted with pleasant and witty conferences, pretty girds, scoffs, and dalliance in her that I mean to choose for my bed-fere. The ladies in court think it a most desperate impair to their quickness of wit, and good carriage, if they cannot give occasion for a man to court 'em; and when an amorous discourse is set on foot, minister as good matter to continue it, as himself: And do you alone so much differ from all them, that what they, with so much circumstance, affect and toil for, to seem learned, to seem judicious, to seem sharp and conceited, you can bury in yourself with silence, and rather trust your graces to the fair conscience of virtue, than to the world's or your own proclamation?

Epi. [*softly.*] I should be sorry else.
Mor. What say you, lady? good lady, speak out.
Epi. I should be sorry else.
Mor. That sorrow doth fill me with gladness. O Morose,

thou art happy above mankind! pray that thou mayest contain thyself. I will only put her to it once more, and it shall be with the utmost touch and test of their sex. But hear me, fair lady; I do also love to see her whom I shall choose for my heifer, to be the first and principal in all fashions, precede all the dames at court by a fortnight, have council of tailors, lineners, lace-women, embroiderers; and sit with them sometimes twice a day upon French intelligences, and then come forth varied like nature, or oftener than she, and better by the help of art, her emulous servant. This do I affect: and how will you be able, lady, with this frugality of speech, to give the manifold but necessary instructions for that bodice, these sleeves, those skirts, this cut, that stitch, this embroidery, that lace, this wire, those knots, that ruff, those roses, this girdle, that fan, the t'other scarf, these gloves? Ha, what say you, lady?

Epi. [*softly.*] I'll leave it to you, sir,

Mor. How, lady? pray you rise a note.

Epi. I leave it to wisdom and you, sir.

Mor. Admirable creature! I will trouble you no more: I will not sin against so sweet a simplicity. Let me now be bold to print on those divine lips the seal of being mine.—Cutbeard, I give thee the lease of thy house free; thank me not but with thy leg. [CUTBEARD *shakes his head*]—I know what thou would'st say, she's poor, and her friends deceased. She has brought a wealthy dowry in her silence, Cutbeard; and in respect of her poverty, Cutbeard, I shall have her more loving and obedient, Cutbeard. Go thy ways, and get me a minister presently, with a soft low voice, to marry us: and pray him he will not be impertinent, but brief as he can; away: softly, Cutbeard. [*Exit* CUT.]—Sirrah, conduct your mistress into the dining-room—your now mistress. [*Exit* MUTE, *followed by* EPI.]—O my felicity! how shall I be revenged on mine insolent kinsman, and his plots to fright me from marrying! This night I will get an heir, and thrust him out of my blood, like a stranger. He would be knighted, forsooth, and thought by that means to reign over me; his title must do it. No, kinsman, I will now make you bring me the tenth lord's and the sixteenth lady's letter, kinsman; and it shall do you no good, kinsman. Your knighthood itself shall come on its knees, and it shall be rejected; it shall be sued for its fees to execution, and not be redeemed; it shall cheat at the twelve-penny ordinary, it knighthood, for its diet, all the term-time, and tell tales for it in the vacation to the hostess; or it knighthood shall do worse—take sanctuary in Cole-harbour, and fast. It shall fright all it friends with borrowing letters; and when one of the fourscore hath brought it knighthood ten shillings, it knighthood shall go to the Cranes, or the Bear at the Bridgefoot, and be drunk in fear; it shall not have money to discharge one tavern-reckoning, to invite the old creditors to forbear it knighthood, or the new, that should be, to trust it knighthood. It shall be the tenth name in the bond to take up the commodity of pipkins and stone-jugs; and the part thereof shall not furnish it knighthood forth for the attempting of a baker's widow—a brown baker's widow. It shall give it knighthood's name to all gamesome citizen's wives, and be refused, when the master of a dancing-school, or how do you call him, the worst reveller in the town is taken. It shall want clothes, and by reason of that, wit, to fool to lawyers. It shall not have hope to repair itself by Constantinople, Ireland, or Virginia; but the best and last fortune to it knighthood shall be to make Dol Tear-sheet or Kate Common a lady, and so it knighthood may eat. [*Exit.*

SCENE IV.—*A Lane, near* MOROSE'S *House.*

Enter TRUEWIT, DAUPHINE, *and* CLERIMONT.

True. Are you sure he is not gone by?
Daup. No, I staid in the shop ever since.
Cler. But he may take the other end of the lane.
Daup. No, I told him I would be here at this end: I appointed him hither.
True. What a barbarian it is to stay then!
Daup. Yonder he comes.
Cler. And his charge left behind him, which is a very good sign, Dauphine.

Enter CUTBEARD.

Daup. How now, Cutbeard! Succeeds it, or no?
Cut. Past imagination, sir, *omnia secunda;* you could not have prayed to have had it so well. *Saltat senex,* as it is in the proverb; he does triumph in his felicity, admires the party! He has given me the lease of my house too! and I am now going for a silent minister to marry them, and away.
True. 'Slight! get one of the silenced ministers; a zealous brother would torment him purely.
Cut. Cum privilegio, sir.
Daup. Oh, by no means; let's do nothing to hinder it now: when 'tis done and finished, I am for you, for any device of vexation.
Cut. And that shall be within this half hour, upon my dexterity, gentlemen. Contrive what you can in the meantime, *bonis avibus.* [*Exit.*
Cler. How the slave doth Latin it!
True. It would be made a jest to posterity, sirs, this day's mirth, if ye will.

Cler. Beshrew his heart that will not, I pronounce.

Daup. And for my part. What is it?

True. To translate all La-Foole's company, and his feast thither, to-day, to celebrate this bride-ale.

Daup. Ay, marry; but how will 't be done?

True. I'll undertake the directing of all the lady-guests thither, and then the meat must follow.

Cler. For Heaven's sake, let's affect it; it will be an excellent comedy of affliction, so many several noises.

Daup. But are they not at the other place, already, think you?

True. I'll warrant you for the college-honours: one of their faces has not the priming colour laid on yet, nor the other her smock sleeked.

Cler. Oh, but they'll rise earlier than ordinary to a feast.

True. Best go see, and assure ourselves.

Cler. Who knows the house?

True. I'll lead you: Were you never there yet?

Daup. Not I.

Cler. Nor I.

True. Where have you lived then? not know Tom Otter!

Cler. No: for Heaven's sake, what is he?

True. An excellent animal, equal with your Daw or La-Foole, if not transcendant; and does Latin it as much as your barber: He is his wife's subject; he calls her princess, and at such times as these follows her up and down the house like a page, with his hat off, partly for heat, partly for reverence. At this instant he is marshalling of his bull, bear, and horse.

Daup. What be those, in the name of Sphynx?

True. Why, sir, he has been a great man at the Bear-garden in his time; and from that subtle sport has ta'en the witty denomination of his chief carousing cups. One he calls his bull, another his bear, another his horse. And then he has his lesser glasses, that he calls his deer and his ape; and several degrees of them too; and never is well, nor thinks any entertainment perfect, till these be brought out, and set on the cupboard.

Cler. For God's love!—we should miss this, if we should not go.

True. Nay, he has a thousand things as good, that will speak him all day. He will rail on his wife, with certain commonplaces, behind her back; and to her face——

Daup. No more of him. Let's go see him, I petition you.

[*Exeunt.*

ACT III.

SCENE I.—*A Room in* OTTER's *House.*

Enter Captain OTTER *with his cups, and* Mistress OTTER.

Ott. Nay, good princess, hear me *pauca verba*.

Mrs. Ott. By that light, I'll have you chained up, with your bull-dogs and bear-dogs, if you be not civil the sooner. I'll send you to kennel, i'faith. You were best bait me with your bull, bear, and horse. Never a time that the courtiers or collegiates come to the house, but you make it a Shrove Tuesday! I would have you get your Whitsuntide velvet cap, and your staff in your hand, to entertain them: yes, in troth, do.

Ott. Not so, princess, neither; but under correction, sweet princess, give me leave.——These things I am known to the courtiers by: It is reported to them for my humour, and they receive it so, and do expect it. Tom Otter's bull, bear and horse is known all over England, *in rerum natura*.

Mrs. Ott. 'Fore me, I will *na-ture* them over to Paris-garden, and *na-ture* you thither too, if you pronounce them again. Is a bear a fit beast, or a bull, to mix in society with great ladies? Think in your discretion, in any good policy.

Ott. The horse, then, good princess.

Mrs. Ott. Well, I am contented for the horse; they love to be well horsed, I know. I love it myself.

Ott. And it is a delicate fine horse this: *Poetarum Pegasus*. Under correction, princess, Jupiter did turn himself into a—*taurus*, or bull, under correction, good princess.

Enter TRUEWIT, CLERMONT, *and* DAUPHINE, *behind.*

Mrs. Ott. By my integrity, I'll send you over to the Bankside; I'll commit you to the master of the Garden, if I hear but a syllable more. Must my house or my roof be polluted with the scent of bears and bulls, when it is perfumed for great ladies? Is this according to the instrument, when I married you? that I would be princess, and reign in mine own house; and you would be my subject, and obey me? What did you bring me, should make you thus peremptory? Do I allow you your half-crown a day, to spend where you will, among your gamesters, to vex and torment me at such times as these? Who gives you your maintenance, I pray you? who allows you your horse-meat and man's meat? your three suits of apparel a year? your four pair of stockings, one silk, three worsted? your clean linen, your bands and cuffs, when I can get you to wear them?—'tis marle you have them on now.—Who graces you with courtiers or great personages, to speak to you out of their coaches, and come home to your house? Were you ever so much as looked upon by a lord or a lady, before I married you, but on the Easter or Whitsun-holidays? and then out at the banqueting-house window, when Ned Whiting or George Stone were at the stake?

True. For God's sake, let's go stave her off him.

Mrs. Ott. Answer me to that. And did not I take you up from thence, in an old greasy buff-doublet, with points, and green velvet sleeves, out at the elbows? you forget this.

True. She'll worry him, if we help not in time.

[*They come forward.*

Mrs. Ott. Oh, here are some of the gallants! Go to, behave yourself distinctly, and with good morality; or, I protest, I'll take away your exhibition.

True. By your leave, fair Mistress Otter, I'll be bold to enter these gentlemen in your acquaintance.

Mrs. Ott. It shall not be obnoxious, or difficil, sir.

True. How does my noble captain? Is the bull, bear, and horse in *rerum natura* still?

Ott. Sir, *sic visum superis.*

Mrs. Ott. I would you would but intimate them, do. Go your ways in, and get toasts and butter made for the woodcocks: that's a fit province for you. [*Drives him off.*

Cler. Alas, what a tyranny is this poor fellow married to!

True. Oh, but the sport will be anon, when we get him loose.

Daup. Dares he ever speak?

True. No Anabaptist ever railed with the like license: but mark her language in the meantime, I beseech you.

Mrs. Ott. Gentlemen, you are very aptly come. My cousin, Sir Amorous, will be here briefly.

True. In good time, lady. Was not Sir John Daw here, to ask for him, and the company?

Mrs. Ott. I cannot assure you, Master Truewit. Here was a very melancholy knight in a ruff, that demanded my subject for somebody, a gentleman, I think.

Cler. Ay, that was he, lady.

Mrs. Ott. But he departed straight, I can resolve you.

Daup. What an excellent choice phrase this lady expresses in.

True. Oh, sir, she is the only authentical courtier, that is not naturally bred one, in the city.

Mrs. Ott. You have taken that report upon trust, gentlemen.

True. No, I assure you, the court governs it so, lady, in your behalf.

Mrs. Ott. I am the servant of the court and courtiers, sir.

True. They are rather your idolaters.

Mrs. Ott. Not so, sir.

Enter CUTBEARD.

Daup. How now, Cutbeard! any cross?

Cut. Oh no, sir, *omnia bene.* 'Twas never better on the hinges; all's sure. I have so pleased him with a curate, that he's gone to 't almost with the delight he hopes for soon.

Daup. What is he for a vicar?

Cut. One that has catched a cold, sir, and can scarce be heard six inches off; as if he spoke out of a bulrush that were not picked, or his throat were full of pith: a fine quick fellow, and an excellent barber of prayers. I came to tell you, sir, that you might *omnem movere lapidem,* as they say, be ready with your vexation.

Daup. Gramercy, honest Cutbeard! be thereabouts with thy key, to let us in.

Cut. I will not fail you, sir; *ad manum.* [*Exit.*

True. Well, I'll go watch my coaches.

Cler. Do; and we'll send Daw to you, if you meet him not.

[*Exit* TRUEWIT.

Mrs. Ott. Is Master Truewit gone?

Daup. Yes, lady, there is some unfortunate business fallen out.

Mrs. Ott. So I adjudged by the physiognomy of the fellow that came in; and I had a dream last night too of the new pageant, and my lady mayoress, which is always very ominous to me. I told it my Lady Haughty t' other day, when her honour came hither to see some China stuffs; and she expounded it out of Artemidorus, and I have found it since very true. It has done me many affronts.

Cler. Your dream, lady?

Mrs. Ott. Yes, sir, anything I do but dream of the city. It stained me a damask table-cloth, cost me eighteen pound at one time; and burnt me a black satin gown, as I stood by the fire at my lady Centaure's chamber in the college, another time. A third time, at the lords' masque, it dropt all my wire and my ruff with wax candle, that I could not go up to the banquet. A fourth time, as I was taking coach to go to Ware, to meet a friend, it dashed me a new suit all over (a crimson satin doublet, and black velvet skirts) with a brewer's horse, that I was fain to go in and shift me, and kept my chamber a leash of days for the anguish of it.

Daup. These were dire mischances, lady.

Cler. I would not dwell in the city, an 'twere so fatal to me.

Mrs. Ott. Yes, sir; but I do take advice of my doctor to dream of it as little as I can.

Daup. You do well, Mistress Otter.

Enter Sir JOHN DAW, *and is taken aside by* CLERIMONT.

Mrs. Ott. Will it please you to enter the house farther, gentlemen?

Daup. And your favour, lady: but we stay to speak with a knight, Sir John Daw, who is here come. We shall follow you, lady.

Mrs. Ott. At your own time, sir. It is my cousin Sir Amorous his feast——

Daup. I know it, lady.

Mrs. Ott. And mine together. But it is for his honour, and therefore I take no name of it, more than of the place.

Daup. You are a bounteous kinswoman.

Mrs. Ott. Your servant, sir. [*Exit.*

Cler. [*coming forward with* DAW.] Why, do not you know it, Sir John Daw?

Daw. No, I am a rook if I do.

Cler. I'll tell you, then; she's married by this time. And, whereas you were put in the head, that she was gone with Sir Dauphine, I assure you, Sir Dauphine has been the noblest, honestest friend to you, that ever gentleman of your quality could boast of. He has discovered the whole plot, and made your mistress so acknowledging, and indeed so ashamed of her injury to you, that she desires you to forgive her, and but grace her wedding with your presence to-day. She is to be married to a very good fortune, she says, his uncle, old Morose; and she willed me in private to tell you, that she shall be able to do you more favours, and with more security now than before.

Daw. Did she say so, i' faith?

Cler. Why, what do you think of me, Sir John! Ask Sir Dauphine.

Daw. Nay, I believe you. Good Sir Dauphine did she desire me to forgive her?

Daup. I assure you, Sir John, she did.

Daw. Nay, then, I do with all my heart, and I'll be jovial.

Cler. Yes, for look you, sir, this was the injury to you. La-Foole intended this feast to honour her bridal day, and make you the property to invite the college ladies, and promise to bring her; and then at the time she would have appeared, as his friend, to have given you the dor. Whereas now, Sir Dauphine has brought her to a feeling of it, with this kind of satisfaction, that you shall bring all the ladies to the place where she is, and be very jovial; and there, she will have a dinner, which shall be in your name: and so disappoint La-Foole, to make you good again, and, as it were, a saver in the main.

Daw. As I am a knight, I honour her; and forgive her heartily.

Cler. About it then presently. Truewit is gone before to

confront the coaches, and to acquaint you with so much, if he meet you. Join with him, and 'tis well.

Enter Sir AMOROUS LA-FOOLE.

See; here comes your antagonist; but take you no notice, but be very jovial.

La-F. Are the ladies come, Sir John Daw, and your mistress? [*Exit* DAW.]—Sir Dauphine! you are exceeding welcome, and honest Master Clerimont. Where's my cousin? did you see no collegiates, gentlemen?

Daup. Collegiates! do you not hear, Sir Amorous, how you are abused?

La-F. How, sir!

Cler. Will you speak so kindly to Sir John Daw, that has done you such an affront?

La-F. Wherein, gentlemen? let me be a suitor to you to know, I beseech you.

Cler. Why, sir, his mistress is married to-day to Sir Dauphine's uncle, your cousin's neighbour, and he has diverted all the ladies, and all your company thither, to frustrate your provision, and stick a disgrace upon you. He was here now to have enticed us away from you too: but we told him his own, I think.

La-F. Has Sir John Daw wronged me so inhumanly?

Daup. He has done it, Sir Amorous, most maliciously and treacherously: but, if you'll be ruled by us, you shall quit him, i'faith.

La-F. Good gentlemen, I'll make one, believe it. How, I pray?

Daup. Marry, Sir, get me your pheasants, and your godwits, and your best meat, and dish it in silver dishes of your cousin's presently; and say nothing, but clap me a clean towel about you, like a sewer; and, bare-headed, march afore it with a good confidence ('tis but over the way, hard by), and we'll second you, where you shall set it on the board, and bid them welcome to't, which shall show 'tis yours, and disgrace his preparation utterly: and for your cousin, whereas she should be troubled here at home with care of making and giving welcome, she shall transfer all that labour thither, and be a principal guest herself; sit ranked with the college-honours, and be honoured, and have her health drunk as often, as bare, and as loud as the best of them.

La-F. I'll go tell her presently. It shall be done, that's resolved. [*Exit.*

Cler. I thought he would not hear it out, but 'twould take him.

Daup. Well, there be guests and meat now; how shall we do for music?

Cler. The smell of the venison, going through the streets, will invite one noise of fiddlers or other.

Daup. I would it would call the trumpeters hither!

Cler. 'Faith, there is hope; they have intelligence of all feasts. There's a good correspondence betwixt them and the London cooks: 'tis twenty to one but we have them.

Daup. 'Twill be a most solemn day for my uncle, and an excellent fit of mirth for us.

Cler. Ay, if we can hold up the emulation between Foole and Daw, and never bring them to expostulate.

Daup. Tut, flatter them both, as Truewit says, and you may take their understandings in a pursenet. They'll believe themselves to be just such men as we make them, neither more nor less. They have nothing, not the use of their senses, but by tradition.

Re-enter LA-FOOLE, *like a Sewer.*

Cler. See! Sir Amorous has his towel on already. Have you persuaded your cousin?

La-F. Yes, 'tis very feasible: she'll do anything, she says, rather than the La-Fooles shall be disgraced.

Daup. She is a noble kinswoman. It will be such a pestling device, Sir Amorous; it will pound all your enemy's practices to powder, and blow him up with his own mine, his own train.

La-F. Nay, we'll give fire, I warrant you.

Cler. But you must carry it privately, without any noise, and take no notice by any means——

Re-enter Captain OTTER.

Ott. Gentlemen, my princess says you shall have all her silver dishes, *festinate;* and she's gone to alter her tire a little, and go with you——

Cler. And yourself too, Captain Otter?

Daup. By any means, sir.

Ott. Yes, sir, I do mean it: but I would entreat my cousin Sir Amorous, and you, gentlemen, to be suitors to my princess, that I may carry my bull and my bear, as well as my horse.

Cler. That you shall do, Captain Otter.

La-F. My cousin will never consent, gentlemen.

Daup. She must consent, Sir Amorous, to reason.

La-F. Why, she says they are no decorum among ladies.

Ott. But they are *decora*, and that's better, sir.

Cler. Ay, she must hear argument. Did not Pasiphaë, who was a queen, love a bull? and was not Calisto, the mother of Arcas, turned into a bear, and made a star, Mistress Ursula, in the heavens?

Ott. Oh lord! that I could have said as much! I will have these stories painted in the Bear-garden, *ex Ovidii metamorphosi.*

Daup. Where is your princess, captain? pray be our leader.
Ott. That I shall, sir.
Cler. Make haste, good Sir Amorous. [*Exeunt.*

SCENE II.—*A Room in* MOROSE'S *House.*

Enter MOROSE, EPICŒNE, PARSON, *and* CUTBEARD.

Mor. Sir, there's an angel for yourself, and a brace of angels for your cold. Muse not at this manage of my bounty. It is fit we should thank fortune, double to nature, for any benefit she confers upon us; besides, it is your imperfection, but my solace.
Par. [*speaks as having a cold.*] I thank your worship; so it is mine, now.
Mor. What says he, Cutbeard?
Cut. He says, *præsto*, sir, whensoever your worship needs him, he can be ready with the like. He got this cold with sitting up late, and singing catches with cloth-workers.
Mor. No more, I thank him.
Par. God keep your worship, and give you much joy with your fair spouse!—uh! uh! uh!
Mor. Oh, oh! stay, Cutbeard! let him give me five shillings of my money back. As it is bounty to reward benefits, so it is equity to mulct injuries. I will have it. What says he?
Cler. He cannot change it, sir.
Mor. It must be changed.
Cut. Cough again. [*Aside to* Parson.
Mor. What says he?
Cut. He will cough out the rest, sir.
Par. Uh, uh, uh!
Mor. Away, away with him! stop his mouth! away! I forgive it—— [*Exit* CUT, *thrusting out the* Par.
Epi. Fie, Master Morose! that you will use this violence to a man of the church.
Mor. How!
Epi. It does not become your gravity, or breeding, as you pretend in court, to have offered this outrage on a waterman, or any more boisterous creature, much less on a man of his civil coat.
Mor. You can speak, then!
Epi. Yes, sir.
Mor. Speak out, I mean.
Epi. Ay, sir. Why, did you think you had married a statue, or a motion, only? one of the French puppets, with the eyes turned with a wire? or some innocent out of the hospital, that would stand with her hands thus, and a plaise mouth, and look upon you.

Mor. Oh immodesty! a manifest woman! What, Cutbeard!

Epi. Nay, never quarrel with Cutbeard, sir; it is too late now. I confess it doth bate somewhat of the modesty I had, when I writ simply maid: but I hope I shall make it a stock still competent to the estate and dignity of your wife.

Mor. She can talk!

Epi. Yes, indeed, sir.

Enter MUTE.

Mor. What, sirrah! None of my knaves there? where is this impostor Cutbeard.   [MUTE *makes signs*.

Epi. Speak to him, fellow, speak to him! I'll have none of this coacted, unnatural dumbness in my house, in a family where I govern.   [*Exit* MUTE.

Mor. She is my regent already! I have married a Penthesilea, a Semiramis; sold my liberty to a distaff.

Enter TRUEWIT.

True. Where's Master Morose?

Mor. Is he come again! Lord have mercy upon me!

True. I wish you all joy, Mistress Epicœne, with your grave and honourable match.

Epi. I return you the thanks, Master Truewit, so friendly a wish deserves.

Mor. She has acquaintance, too!

True. God save you, sir, and give you all contentment in your fair choice, here! Before, I was the bird of night to you, the owl; but now I am the messenger of peace, a dove, and bring you the glad wishes of many friends to the celebration of this good hour.

Mor. What hour, sir?

True. Your marriage hour, sir. I commend your resolution, that, notwithstanding all the dangers I laid afore you, in the voice of a night-crow, would yet go on, and be yourself. It shows you are a man constant to your own ends, and upright to your purposes, that would not be put off with left-handed cries.

Mor. How should you arrive at the knowledge of so much?

True. Why, did you ever hope, sir, committing the secrecy of it to a barber, that less than the whole town should know it? you might as well have told it to the conduit, or the bake-house, or the infantry that follow the Court, and with more security. Could your gravity forget so old and noted a remnant, as, *lippis et tonsoribus notum?* Well, sir, forgive it yourself now, the fault, and be communicable with your friends. Here will be three or four fashionable ladies from the college to visit you presently, and their train of minions and followers.

Mor. Bar my doors! bar my doors! Where are all my eaters? my mouths, now?—

Enter Servants.

Bar up my doors, you varlets!

Epi. He is a varlet that stirs to such an office. Let them stand open. I would see him that dares move his eyes toward it. Shall I have a barricado made against my friends, to be barred of any pleasure they can bring in to me with their honourable visitation? [*Exeunt* Ser.

Mor. Oh Amazonian impudence!

True. Nay, faith, in this, sir, she speaks but reason; and, methinks, is more continent than you. Would you go to bed so presently, sir, afore noon? a man of your head and hair should owe more to that reverend ceremony, and not mount the marriage-bed till the due season; and ascend it then with religion and fear. Those delights are to be steeped in the humour and silence of the night; and give the day to other open pleasures, and jollities of feasting, of music, of revels, of discourse: we'll have all, sir, that may make your Hymen high and happy.

Mor. Oh my torment, my torment!

True. Nay, if you endure the first half hour, sir, so tediously, and with this irksomeness; what comfort or hope can this fair gentlewoman make to herself hereafter, in the consideration of so many years as are to come——

Mor. Of my affliction. Good sir, depart, and let her do it alone.

True. I have done, sir.

Mor. That cursed barber.

True. Yes, faith, a cursed wretch indeed, sir.

Mor. I have married his cittern, that's common to all men. Some plague above the plague——

True. All Egypt's ten plagues.

Mor. Revenge me on him!

True. 'Tis very well, sir. If you laid on a curse or two more, I'll assure you he'll bear them. As, that he may get the plague with seeking to cure it, sir; or, that while he is curling another man's hair, his own may drop off; or, for burning some malefool's lock, he may have his brain beat out with the curling iron.

Mor. No, let the wretch live wretched. May he get the itch, and his shop so lousy, as no man dare come at him, nor he come at no man!

True. Aye, and if he would swallow all his balls for pills, let them purge him.

Mor. Let his warming-pan be ever cold.

True. A perpetual frost underneath it, sir.

Mor. Let him never hope to see fire again.

True. But in hell, sir.

Mor. His chairs be always empty, his scissors rust, and his combs mould in their cases.

True. Very dreadful that! And may he lose the invention, sir, of carving lanterns in paper.

Mor. Let there be none carted that year, to employ a bason of his: but let him be glad to eat his sponge for bread.

True. And drink lotium to it, and much good do him.

Mor. Or, for want of bread——

True. Eat ear-wax, sir. I'll help you. Or, draw his own teeth, and add them to the lute-string.

Mor. No, beat the old ones to powder, and make bread of them.

True. Yes, make meal of the mill-stones.

Mor. May all the botches and burns that he has cured on others break out upon him.

True. And he now forget the cure of them in himself, sir; or, if he do remember it, let him have scraped all his linen into lint for 't, and have not a rag left him for to set up with.

Mor. Let him never set up again, but have the gout n his hands for ever!—Now, no more, sir.

True. Oh, that last was too high set; you might go less with him, i' faith, and be revenged enough: as, that he be never able to new-paint his pole——

Mor. Good sir, no more, I forgot myself.

True. Or, want credit to take up with a comb-maker——

Mor. No more, sir.

True. Or, having broken his glass in a former despair, fall now into a much greater, of ever getting another——

Mor. I beseech you, no more.

True. Or, that he never be trusted with trimming of any but chimney-sweepers——

Mor. Sir——

True. Or, may he cut a collier's throat with his razor, by chance-medley, and yet be hanged for 't.

Mor. I will forgive him, rather than hear any more. I beseech you, sir.

Enter DAW, *introducing* LADY HAUGHTY, CENTAURE, MAVIS, *and* TRUSTY.

Daw. This way, madam.

Mor. Oh, the sea breaks in upon me! another flood! an inundation! I shall be overwhelmed with noise. It beats already at my shores. I feel an earthquake in myself for 't.

Daw. Give you joy, mistress.

Mor. Has she servants too!

Daw. I have brought some ladies here to see and know you. My Lady Haughty [*as he presents them severally*, EPI. *kisses them.*] this my Lady Centaure—Mistress Dol Mavis—Mistress Trusty, my Lady Haughty's woman. Where's your husband? let's see him: can he endure no noise? let me come to him.

Mor. What nomenclator is this!

True. Sir John Daw, sir, your wife's servant, this.

Mor. A Daw, and her servant! Oh, 'tis decreed, 'tis decreed of me, an she have such servants. [*Going.*

True. Nay, sir, you must kiss the ladies; you must not go away, now: they come toward you to seek you out.

Hau. I' faith, Master Morose, would you steal a marriage thus, in the midst of so many friends, and not acquaint us? Well, I'll kiss you, notwithstanding the justice of my quarrel; you shall give me leave, mistress, to use a becoming familiarity with your husband.

Epi. Your ladyship does me an honour in it, to let me know he is so worthy your favour: as you have done both him and me grace to visit so unprepared a pair to entertain you.

Mor. Compliment! compliment!

Epi. But I must lay the burden of that upon my servant here.

Hau. It shall not need, Mistress Morose; we will all bear, rather than one shall be opprest.

Mor. I know it: and you will teach her the faculty, if she be to learn it. [*Walks aside while the rest talk apart.*

Hau. Is this the silent woman?

Cen. Nay, she has found her tongue since she was married, Master Truewit says.

Hau. Oh, Master Truewit! 'save you. What kind of creature is your bride here? She speaks, methinks!

True. Yes, madam, believe it, she is a gentlewoman of very absolute behaviour, and of a good race.

Hau. And Jack Daw told us she could not speak!

True. So it was carried in plot, madam, to put her upon this old fellow, by Sir Dauphine, his nephew, and one or two more of us: but she is a woman of an excellent assurance, and an extraordinary happy wit and tongue. You shall see her make rare sport with Daw ere night.

Hau. And he brought us to laugh at her!

True. That falls out often, madam, that he that thinks himself the master wit is the master-fool. I assure your ladyship, ye cannot laugh at her.

Hau. No, we'll have her to the college: an she have wit, she shall be one of us, shall she not, Centaure? We'll make her a collegiate.

Cen. Yes, faith, madam, and Mavis and she will set up a side.

True. Believe it, madam, and Mistress Mavis she will sustain her part.

Mav. I'll tell you that when I have talked with her and tried her.

Hau. Use her very civilly, Mavis.
Mav. So I will, madam. [*Whispers her.*
Mor. Blessed minute! that they would whisper thus ever!
[*Aside.*
True. In the mean time, madam, would but your ladyship help to vex him a little: you know his disease, talk to him about the wedding ceremonies, or call for your gloves, or——
Hau. Let me alone. Centaure, help me.—Master Bridegroom, where are you?
Mor. Oh, it was too miraculously good to last! [*Aside.*
Hau. We see no ensigns of a wedding here; no character of a bride-ale: where be our scarves and our gloves? I pray you, give them us. Let us know your bride's colours, and yours at least.
Cen. Alas, madam, he has provided none.
Mor. Had I known your ladyship's painter, I would.
Hau. He has given it you, Centaure, i' faith. But do you hear, Master Morose? a jest will not absolve you in this manner. You that have sucked the milk of the court, and from thence have been brought up to the very strong meats and wine of it—been a courtier from the biggen to the night-cap, as we may say—and you to offend in such a high point of ceremony as this, and let your nuptials want all marks of solemnity! How much plate have you lost to-day (if you had but regarded your profit) what gifts, what friends, through your mere rusticity!
Mor. Madam——
Hau. Pardon me, sir, I must insinuate your errors to you; no gloves? no garters? no scarves? no epithalamium? no masque?
Daw. Yes, madam, I'll make an epithalamium, I promise my mistress. I have begun it already; will your ladyship hear it?
Hau. Ay, good Jack Daw.
Mor. Will it please your ladyship command a chamber, and be private with your friend? You shall have your choice of rooms to retire to after: my whole house is yours. I know it hath been your ladyship's errand into the city at other times, however now you have been unhappily diverted upon me; but I shall be loth to break any honourable custom of your ladyship's. And therefore, good madam——
Epi. Come, you are a rude bridegroom, to entertain ladies of honour in this fashion.
Cen. He is a rude groom indeed.
True. By that light you deserve to be grafted, and have your horns reach from one side of the island to the other. Do not mistake me, sir; I but speak this to give the ladies some heart again, not for any malice to you.
Mor. Is this your bravo, ladies?
True. As Heaven help me, if you utter such another word, I'll take Mistress Bride in, and begin to you in a very sad

cup; do you see? Go to, know your friends, and such as love you.

Enter CLERIMONT, *followed by a number of* Musicians.

Cler. By your leave, ladies. Do you want any music? I have brought you variety of noises. Play, sirs, all of you.
  [*Aside to the* Musicians, *who strike up altogether.*
Mor. Oh, a plot, a plot, a plot, a plot upon me! This day I shall be their anvil to work on, they will grate me asunder. 'Tis worse than the noise of a saw.
Cler. No, they are hair, rosin, and guts: I can give you the receipt.
True. Peace, boys!
Cler. Play! I say.
True. Peace, rascals! You see who's your friend now, sir: take courage, put on a martyr's resolution. Mock down all their attemptings with patience: 'tis but a day, and I would suffer heroically. Should an ass exceed me in fortitude? no. You betray your infirmity with your hanging dull ears, and make them insult: bear up bravely, and constantly.—[LA-FOOLE *passes over the stage as a Sewer followed by Servants carrying dishes, and* Mistress OTTER.]—Look you here, sir, what honour is done you unexpected, by your nephew; a wedding-dinner come, and a knight-sewer before it, for the more reputation: and fine Mistress Otter, your neighbour, in the rump or tail of it.
Mor. Is that Gorgon, that Medusa, come! hide me, hide me.
True. I warrant you, sir, she will not transform you. Look upon her with a good courage. Pray you entertain her, and conduct your guests in. No!—Mistress Bride, will you entreat in the ladies? your bridegroom is so shame-faced, here.
Epi. Will it please your ladyship, madam?
Hau. With the benefit of your company, mistress.
Epi. Servant, pray you perform your duties.
Daw. And glad to be commanded, mistress.
Cen. How like you her wit, Mavis?
Mav. Very prettily, absolutely well.
Mrs. Ott. 'Tis my place.
Mav. You shall pardon me, Mistress Otter.
Mrs. Ott. Why, I am a collegiate.
Mav. But not in ordinary.
Mrs. Ott. But I am.
Mav. We'll dispute that within.   [*Exeunt* Ladies.
Cler. Would this had lasted a little longer.
True. And that they had sent for the heralds.

Enter CAPTAIN OTTER.

—Captain Otter! what news?

Ott. I have brought my bull, bear, and horse in private, and yonder are the trumpeters without, and the drum, gentlemen.

[*The drum and trumbets sound within.*

Mor. Oh, oh, oh!

Ott. And we will have a rouse in each of them, anon, for bold Britons, i' faith. [*They sound again.*

Mor. Oh, oh, oh! [*Exit hastily.*

Omnes. Follow, follow, follow!

ACT IV.

SCENE I.—*A Room in* MOROSE'S *House.*

Enter TRUEWIT *and* CLERIMONT.

True. Was there ever poor bridegroom so tormented? or man, indeed?

Cler. I have not read of the like in the chronicles of the land.

True. Sure, he cannot but go to a place of rest, after all this purgatory.

Cler. He may presume it, I think.

True. The spitting, the coughing, the laughter, the neezing, dancing, noise of the music, and her masculine and loud commanding, and urging the whole family, makes him think he has married a fury.

Cler. And she carries it up bravely.

True. Ay, she takes any occasion to speak: that's the height on 't.

Cler. And how soberly Dauphine labours to satisfy him, that it was none of his plot!

True. And has almost brought him to the faith, in the article. Here he comes.—

Enter SIR DAUPHINE.

Where is he now? what's become of him, Dauphine?

Daup. Oh, hold me up a little, I shall go away in the jest else. He has got on his whole nest of night-caps, and locked himself up in the top of the house, as high as ever he can climb from the noise. I peeped in at a cranny, and saw him sitting over a crossbeam of the roof, like him on the saddler's horse in Fleet Street, upright: and he will sleep there.

Cler. But where are your collegiates?

Daup. Withdrawn with the bride in private.

True. Oh, they are instructing her in the college grammar. If she have grace with them, she knows all their secrets instantly.

Cler. Methinks the Lady Haughty looks well to-day, for all my dispraise of her in the morning. I think, I shall come about to thee again, Truewit.

True. Believe it, I told you right. Women ought to repair the losses time and years have made in their features, with dressings. And an intelligent woman, if she know by herself the least defect, will be most curious to hide it : and it becomes her. If she be short, let her sit much, lest, when she stands, she be thought to sit. If she have an ill foot, let her wear her gown the longer and her shoe the thinner. If a fat hand and scald nails, let her carve the less, and act in gloves. If a sour breath, let her never discourse fasting, and always talk at her distance. If she have black and rugged teeth, let her offer the less at laughter, especially if she laugh wide and open.

Cler. Oh, you shall have some women, when they laugh, you would think they brayed, it is so rude and——

True. Ay, and others, that will stalk in their gait like an estrich, and take huge strides. I cannot endure such a sight. I love measure in the feet, and number in the voice : they are gentlenesses, that oftentimes draw no less than the face.

Daup. How camest thou to study these creatures so exactly? I would thou wouldst make me a proficient.

True. Yes, but you must leave to live in your chamber, then, a month together upon Amadis de Gaul or Don Quixote, as you are wont ; and come abroad where the matter is frequent, to court, to tiltings, public shows and feasts, to plays, and church sometimes : thither they come to show their new tires too, to see and to be seen. In these places a man shall find whom to love, whom to play with, whom to touch once, whom to hold ever. The variety arrests his judgment. A wife to please a man comes not downdropping from the ceiling, as he lies on his back droning a tobacco-pipe. He must go where she is.

Daup. Yes, and be never the nearer.

True. Out, heretic ! That diffidence makes thee worthy it should be so.

Cler. He says true to you, Dauphine.

Daup. Why.

True. A man should not doubt to overcome any woman. Think he can vanquish them, and he shall : for though they deny, their desire is to be tempted. Penelope herself cannot hold out long. Ostend, you saw, was taken at last. You must persever, and hold to your purpose. They would solicit us, but that they are afraid. Howsoever, they wish in their hearts we should solicit them. Praise them, flatter them, you shall never want eloquence or trust : even the best delight to feel themselves that way rubbed. With praises you must mix kisses too : if they take any, any 'll take more—though they strive, they would be overcome.

Cler. Oh, but a man must beware of force.

True. It is to them an acceptable rudeness, and has oft-times the place of the greatest courtesy. She that might have been kissed, and you let her go free without touching, though then she seem to thank you, will ever hate you after; and glad in the face, is assuredly sad at the heart.

Cler. But all women are not to be taken all ways.

True. 'Tis true; no more than all birds, or all fishes. If you appear learned to an ignorant girl, or jocund to a sad, or witty to a foolish, why she presently begins to mistrust herself. You must approach them in their own height, their own line; for the contrary makes many, that fear to commit themselves to noble and worthy fellows, run into the embraces of a rascal. If she love wit, give verses, though you borrow them of a friend, or buy them, to have good. If valour, talk of your sword, and be frequent in the mention of quarrels, though you be staunch in fighting. If activity, be seen on your barbary often, or leaping over stools, for the credit of your back. If she love good clothes or dressing, have your learned council about you every morning, your French tailor, barber, linener, &c. Let your powder, your glass, and your comb be your dearest acquaintance. Take more care for the ornament of your head, than the safety; and wish the commonwealth rather troubled, than a hair about you. That will take her. Then, if she be covetous and craving, do you promise anything, and perform sparingly; so shall you keep her in appetite still. Seem as you would give, but be like a barren field, that yields little; or unlucky dice to foolish and hoping gamesters. Let your gifts be slight and dainty, rather than precious. Let cunning be above cost. Give cherries at time of year, or apricots; and say, they were sent you out of the country, though you bought them in Cheapside. Admire her tires: like her in all fashions; compare her in every habit to some deity; invent excellent dreams to flatter her, and riddles; or, if she be a great one, perform always the second parts to her: like what she likes, praise whom she praises, and fail not to make the household and servants yours, yea the whole family, and salute them by their names, ('tis but light cost, if you can purchase them so,) and make her physician your pensioner, and her chief woman. Nor will it be out of your gain to make love to her too, so she follow, not usher her lady's pleasure. All blabbing is taken away, when she comes to be a part of the crime.

Daup. On what courtly lap hast thou late slept, to come forth so sudden and absolute a courtling?

True. Good faith, I should rather question you, that are so hearkening after these mysteries. I begin to suspect your diligence, Dauphine. Speak, art thou in love in earnest?

Daup. Yes, by my troth, am I; 'twere ill dissembling before thee.

True. With which of them, I prithee?

Daup. With all the collegiates.

Cler. Out on thee! We'll keep you at home, believe it, in the stable.

True. No; I like him well. Men should love wisely, and all women; some one for the face, and let her please the eye; another for the skin, and let her please the touch; a third for the voice, and let her please the ear; and where the objects mix, let the senses so too. Thou would'st think it strange, if I should make them all in love with thee afore night!

Daup. I would say, thou hast the best philtre in the world, and couldst do more than Madam Medea, or Doctor Foreman.

True. If I do not, let me play the mountebank for my meat, while I live.

Daup. So be it, I say.

Enter OTTER, *with his three Cups,* DAW *and* LA FOOLE.

Ott. O Lord, gentlemen, how my knights and I have mist you here!

Cler. Why, captain, what service, what service?

Ott. To see me bring up my bull, bear, and horse to fight.

Daw. Yes, faith, the captain says we shall be his dogs to bait them.

Daup. A good employment.

True. Come on, let's see your course, then.

La-F. I am afraid my cousin will be offended, if she come.

Ott. Be afraid of nothing. Gentlemen, I have placed the drum and the trumpets, and one to give them the sign when you are ready. Here's my bull for myself, and my bear for Sir John Daw, and my horse for Sir Amorous. Now set your foot to mine, and yours to his, and——

La-F. Pray God my cousin come not.

Ott. St. George and St. Andrew, fear no cousins. Come, sound, sound! [*Drum and trumpets sound.*] *Et rauco strepuerunt cornua cantu.* [*They drink.*

True. Well said, captain, i'faith; well fought at the bull.

Cler. Well held at the bear.

True. Low, low! captain.

Daup. Oh, the horse has kicked off his dog already.

La-F. I cannot drink it, as I am a knight.

True. Ods so! Off with his spurs, somebody.

La-F. It goes against my conscience. My cousin will be angry with it.

Daw. I have done mine.

True. You fought high and fair, Sir John.

Cler. At the head.

Daup. Like an excellent bear-dog.

Cler. You take no notice of the business, I hope?

Daw. Not a word, sir; you see we are jovial.

Ott. Sir Amorous, you must not equivocate. It must be pulled down, for all my cousin.

Cler. 'Sfoot, if you take not your drink, they'll think you are discontented with something; you'll betray all, if you take the least notice.

La-F. Not I; I'll both drink and talk then.

Ott. You must pull the horse on his knees, Sir Amorous; fear no cousins. *Jacta est alea.*

True. Oh, now he's in his vein, and bold. The least hint given him of his wife now, will make him rail desperately.

Cler. Speak to him of her.

True. Do you, and I'll fetch her to the hearing of it. [*Exit.*

Daup. Captain He-Otter, your She-Otter is coming, your wife.

Ott. Wife! buz? *titivilitium!* There's no such thing in nature. I confess, gentlemen, I have a cook, a laundress, a house-drudge, that serves my necessary turns, and goes under that title; but he's an ass that will be so uxorious to tie his affections to one circle. Come, the name dulls appetite. Here, replenish again; another bout. [*Fills the cups again.*] Wives are nasty, sluttish animals.

Daup. Oh, captain.

Ott. As ever the earth bare, *tribus verbis.*—Where's Master Truewit?

Daw. He's slipt aside, sir.

Cler. But you must drink and be jovial.

Daw. Yes, give it me.

La-F. And me too.

Daw. Let's be jovial.

La-F. As jovial as you will.

Ott. Agreed. Now you shall have the bear, cousin, and Sir John Daw the horse, and I'll have the bull still. Sound, Tritons of the Thames! [*Drum and trumpets sound again.*] *Nunc est bibendum, nunc pede libero*——

Mor. [*above.*] Villains, murderers, sons of the earth and traitors, what do you there?

Cler. Oh, now the trumpets have waked him, we shall have his company.

Ott. A wife is a scurvy clogdogdo, an unlucky thing, a very forsaid bear-whelp, without any good fashion or breeding, *mala bestia.*

Re-enter TRUEWIT *behind, with* Mistress OTTER.

Daup. Why did you marry one then, captain?

Ott. A plague!——I married with six thousand pound, I. I was in love with that. I have not kissed my Fury these forty weeks.

Cler. The more to blame you, captain.

True. Nay, Mistress Otter, hear him a little first.

Ott. She has a breath worse than my grandmother's, *profecto*.

Mrs. Ott. O treacherous liar! kiss me, sweet Master Truewit, and prove him a slandering knave.

True. I'll rather believe you, lady.

Ott. And she has a peruke that's like a pound of hemp, made up in shoe-threads.

Mrs. Ott. O viper, mandrake!

Ott. A most vile face! and yet she spends me forty pound a year in mercury and hogs-bones. All her teeth were made in the Blackfriars, both her eyebrows in the Strand, and her hair in Silver-street. Every part of the town owns a piece of her.

Mrs. Ott. [*comes forward.*] I cannot hold.

Ott. She takes herself asunder still when she goes to bed into some twenty boxes; and about next day noon is put together again, like a great German clock: and so comes forth, and rings a tedious alarum to the whole house, and then is quiet again for an hour, but for her quarters.—Have you done me right, gentlemen?

Mrs. Ott. [*falls upon him and beats him.*] No, sir, I'll do you right with my quarters, with my quarters.

Ott. Oh, hold, good princess.

True. Sound, sound! [*Drum and trumpets sound.*

Cler. A battle, a battle!

Mrs. Ott. You notorious stinkardly bearward, does my breath smell?

Ott. Under correction, dear princess.—Look to my bear and my horse, gentlemen.

Mrs. Ott. Do I want teeth, and eyebrows, thou bull-dog?

True. Sound, sound still. [*They sound again.*

Ott. No, I protest, under correction——

Mrs. Ott. Ay, now you are under correction, you protest: but you did not protest before correction, sir. Thou Judas, to offer to betray thy princess! I'll make thee an example.

[*Beats him.*

Enter MOROSE *with his long sword.*

Mor. I will have no such examples in my house, Lady Otter.

Mrs. Ott. Ah!——

[Mrs. OTTER, DAW, *and* LA-FOOLE *run off.*

Mor. Mistress Mary Ambree, your examples are dangerous.—Rogues, hell-hounds, Stentors! out of my doors, you sons of noise and tumult, begot on an ill May-day, or when the galley-foist is afloat to Westminster! [*Drives out the musicians.*] A trumpeter could not be conceived but then.

Daup. What ails you, sir?

Mor. They have rent my roof, walls, and all my windows asunder, with their brazen throats. 　　　　[*Exit.*
　True. Best follow him, Dauphine.
　Daup. So I will. 　　　　　　　　　　　　　[*Exit.*
　Cler. Where's Daw and La-Foole?
　Ott. They are both run away, sir. Good gentlemen, help to pacify my princess, and speak to the great ladies for me. Now must I go lie with the bears this fortnight, and keep out of the way, till my peace be made, for this scandal she has taken. Did you not see my bull-head, gentlemen?
　Cler. Is't not on, captain?
　True. No; but he may make a new one, by that is on.
　Ott. Oh, here it is. An you come over, gentlemen, and ask for Tom Otter, we'll go down to Ratcliff, and have a course i' faith, for all these disasters. There is *bona spes* left.
　True. Away, captain, get off while you are well.
　　　　　　　　　　　　　　　　　　　　　[*Exit* OTTER.
　Cler. I am glad we are rid of him.
　True. You had never been, unless we had put his wife upon him. His humour is as tedious at last, as it was ridiculous at first. 　　　　　　　　　　　　　　　　　　　[*Exeunt.*

SCENE II.—*A long open Gallery in the same.*

Enter Lady HAUGHTY, Mistress OTTER, MAVIS, DAW, LA-FOOLE, CENTAURE, *and* EPICŒNE.

　Hau. We wondered why you shrieked so, Mistress Otter.
　Mrs. Ott. O Lord, madam, he came down with a huge long naked weapon in both his hands, and looked so dreadfully! Sure he's beside himself.
　Mav. Why, what made you there, Mistress Otter?
　Mrs. Ott. Alas, Mistress Mavis, I was chastising my subject, and thought nothing of him.
　Daw. Faith, mistress, you must do so too: learn to chastise. Mistress Otter corrects her husband so, he dares not speak but under correction.
　La-F. And with his hat off to her: 'twould do you good to see.
　Hau. In sadness, 'tis good and mature counsel; practise it, Morose. I'll call you Morose still now, as I call Centaure and Mavis; we four will be all one.
　Cen. And you'll come to the college, and live with us?
　Hau. Make him give milk and honey.
　Mav. Look how you manage him at first, you shall have him ever after.
　Cen. Let him allow you your coach and four horses, your

woman, your chambermaid, your page, your gentleman-usher, your French cook, and four grooms.

Hau. And go with us to Bedlam, to the china-houses, and to the Exchange.

Cen. It will open the gate to your fame.

Hau. Here's Centaure has immortalized herself, with taming of her wild male.

Mav. Ay, she has done the miracle of the kingdom.

Enter CLERIMONT *and* TRUEWIT.

Epi. But, ladies, do you count it lawful to have such plurality of servants, and do them all graces?

Hau. Why not? why should women deny their favours to men? are they the poorer or the worse?

Daw. Is the Thames the less for the dyers' water, mistress?

La-F. Or a torch for lighting many torches?

True. Well said, La-Foole; what a new one he has got!

Cen. They are empty losses women fear in this kind.

Hau. Besides, ladies should be mindful of the approach of age, and let no time want his due use. The best of our days pass first.

Mav. We are rivers, that cannot be called back, madam: she that now excludes her lovers, may live to lie a forsaken beldame, in a frozen bed.

Cen. 'Tis true, Mavis: and who will wait on us to coach then? or write, or tell us the news then, make anagrams of our names, and invite us to the Cock-pit, and kiss our hands all the playtime, and draw their weapons for our honours?

Hau. Not one.

Daw. Nay, my mistress is not altogether unintelligent of these things; here be in presence have tasted of her favours.

Cler. What a neighing hobby-horse is this!

Epi. But not with intent to boast them again, servant.—And have you those excellent receipts, madam, to keep yourselves from bearing of children?

Hau. Oh yes, Morose: how should we maintain our youth and beauty else? many births of a woman make her old, as many crops make the earth barren.

Enter MOROSE *and* DAUPHINE.

Mor. Oh, my cursed angel, that instructed me to this fate!

Daup. Why, sir?

Mor. That I should be seduced by so foolish a devil as a barber will make!

Daup. I would I had been worthy, sir, to have partaken your counsel; you should never have trusted it to such a minister.

Mor. Would I could redeem it with the loss of an eye, nephew, a hand, or any other member.

Daup. Marry, God forbid, sir, that you should maim yourself, to anger your wife.

Mor. So it would rid me of her!—and that I did supererogatory penance in a belfry, at Westminster-hall, in the Cock-pit, at the fall of a stag, the Tower-wharf—what place is there else?—London-bridge, Paris-garden, Billingsgate, when the noises are at their height, and loudest. Nay, I would sit out a play, that were nothing but fights at sea, drum, trumpet, and target.

Daup. I hope there shall be no such need, sir. Take patience, good uncle. This is but a day, and 't is well worn too now.

Mor. Oh, 't will be so for ever, nephew; I foresee it, for ever. Strife and tumult are the dowry that comes with a wife.

True. I told you so, sir, and you would not believe me.

Mor. Alas, do not rub those wounds, Master Truewit, to blood again: 't was my negligence. Add not affliction to affliction. I have perceived the effect of it, too late, in Madam Otter.

Epi. How do you, sir?

Mor. Did you ever hear a more unnecessary question? as if she did not see! Why, I do as you see, empress, empress.

Epi. You are not well, sir; you look very ill: something has distempered you.

Mor. Oh horrible, monstrous impertinencies! would not one of these have served, do you think, sir? would not one of these have served?

True. Yes, sir; but these are but notes of female kindness, sir; certain tokens that she has a voice, sir.

Mor. Oh, is it so! Come, an 't be no otherwise—— What say you?

Epi. How do you feel yourself, sir?

Mor. Again that!

True. Nay, look you, sir, you would be friends with your wife upon unconscionable terms; her silence.

Epi. They say you are run mad, sir.

Mor. Not for love, I assure you, of you; do you see?

Epi. Oh Lord, gentlemen! lay hold on him, for God's sake. What shall I do? who's his physician, can you tell, that knows the state of his body best, that I might send for him? Good sir, speak; I'll send for one of my doctors, else.

Mor. What, to poison me, that I might die intestate, and leave you possest of all!

Epi. Lord, how idly he talks, and how his eyes sparkle! he looks green about the temples! do you see what blue spots he has!

Cler. Ay, 't is melancholy.

Epi. Gentlemen, for Heaven's sake, counsel me. Ladies:—servant, you have read Pliny and Paracelsus; ne'er a word now to comfort a poor gentlewoman? Ay me, what fortune had I, to marry a distracted man!

Daw. I'll tell you, mistress——

True. How rarely she holds it up! [*Aside to* CLER.

Mor. What mean you, gentlemen?

Epi. What will you tell me, servant?

Daw. The disease in Greek is called μανια, in Latin *insania, furor, vel ecstasis melancholica*, that is, *egressio*, when a man *ex melancholico evadit fanaticus*.

Mor. Shall I have a lecture read upon me alive?

Daw. But he may be but *phreneticus* yet, mistress; and *phrenetis* is only *delirium*, or so.

Epi. Ay, that is for the disease, servant; but what is this to the cure? We are sure enough of the disease.

Mor. Let me go.

True. Why, we'll entreat her to hold her peace, sir.

Mor. Oh no, labour not to stop her. She is like a conduit-pipe, that will gush out with more force when she opens again.

Hau. I'll tell you, Morose, you must talk divinity to him altogether, or moral philosophy.

La-F. Ay, and there's an excellent book of moral philosophy, madam, of Reynard the Fox, and all the beasts, called Doni's Philosophy.

Cen. There is indeed, Sir Amorous La-Foole.

Mor. Oh misery!

La-F. I have read it, my Lady Centaure, all over, to my cousin here.

Mrs. Ott. Ay, and 'tis a very good book as any is, of the moderns.

Daw. Tut, he must have Seneca read to him, and Plutarch, and the ancients; the moderns are not for this disease.

Cler. Why, you discommended them too, to-day, Sir John.

Daw. Ay, in some cases: but in these they are best, and Aristotle's ethics.

Mav. Say you so, Sir John? I think you are deceived; you took it upon trust.

Hau. Where's Trusty, my woman? I'll end this difference. I pr'thee, Otter, call her. Her father and mother were both mad, when they put her to me.

Mor. I think so.—Nay, gentlemen, I am tame. This is but an exercise, I know, a marriage ceremony, which I must endure.

Hau. And one of them, I know not which, was cured with the Sick Man's Salve, and the other with Green's Groat's-worth of Wit.

True. A very cheap cure, madam.

Enter TRUSTY

Hau. Ay, 'tis very feasible,

Mrs. Ott. My lady called for you, Mistress Trusty: you must decide a controversy.

Hau. Oh, Trusty, which was it you said, your father, or your mother, that was cured with the Sick Man's Salve?

Trus. My mother, madam, with the Salve.

True. Then it was the sick woman's salve?

Trus. And my father with the Groat's-worth of Wit. But there was other means used: we had a preacher that would preach folk asleep still; and so they were prescribed to go to church, by an old woman that was their physician, thrice a week——

Epi. To sleep?

Trus. Yes, forsooth: and every night they read themselves asleep on those books.

Epi. Good faith, it stands with great reason. I would I knew where to procure those books.

Mor. Oh!

La-F. I can help you with one of them, Mistress Morose, the Groat's-worth of Wit.

Epi. But I shall disfurnish you, Sir Amorous: can you spare it?

La-F. Oh yes, for a week, or so; I'll read it myself to him.

Epi. No, I must do that, sir; that must be my office.

Mor. Oh, oh!

Epi. Sure he would do well enough, if he could sleep.

Mor. No, I should do well enough, if you could sleep. Have I no friend that will make her drunk, or give her a little laudanum, or opium?

True. Why, sir, she talks ten times worse in her sleep.

Mor. How!

Cler. Do you not know that, sir? never ceases all night.

True. And snores like a porpoise.

Mor. Oh redeem me, fate; redeem me, fate! For how many causes may a man be divorced, nephew?

Daup. I know not, truly, sir.

True. Some divine must resolve you in that, sir, or canon-lawyer.

Mor. I will not rest, I will not think of any other hope or comfort, till I know.   [*Exit with* DAUPHINE.

Cler. Alas, poor man!

True. You'll make him mad indeed, ladies, if you pursue this.

Hau. No, we'll let him breathe now, a quarter of an hour or so.

Cler. By my faith, a large truce!

Hau. Is that his keeper, that is gone with him?

Daw. It is his nephew, madam.

La-F. Sir Dauphine Eugenie.

Cen. He looks like a very pitiful knight——

Daw. As can be. This marriage has put him out of all.

La-F. He has not a penny in his purse, madam.

Daw. He is ready to cry all this day.

La-F. A very shark; he set me in the nick t'other night at Primero.

True. How these swabbers talk!

Cler. Ay, Otter's wine has swelled their humours above a spring-tide.

Hau. Good Morose, let's go in again. I like your couches exceeding well; we'll go lie and talk there.

[*Exeunt* HAU., CEN., MAV., TRUS., LA-FOOLE, *and* DAW.

Epi. [*following them.*] I wait on you, madam.

True. [*stopping her.*] 'Slight, I will have them as silent as signs, and their post too, ere I have done. Do you hear, lady-bride? I pray thee now, as thou art a noble wench, continue this discourse of Dauphine within; but praise him exceedingly: magnify him with all the height of affection thou canst;—I have some purpose in't: and but beat off these two rooks, Jack Daw and his fellow, with any discontentment hither, and I'll honour thee for ever.

Epi. I was about it here. It angered me to the soul, to hear them begin to talk so malépert.

True. Pray thee perform it, and thou winn'st me an idolater to thee everlasting.

Epi. Will you go in and hear me do't?

True. No, I'll stay here. Drive them out of your company, 'tis all I ask; which cannot be any way better done, than by extolling Dauphine, whom they have so slighted.

Epi. I warrant you; you shall expect one of them presently.

Cler. What a cast of kestrils are these, to hawk after ladies, thus!

True. Ay, and strike at such an eagle as Dauphine.

Cler. He will be mad when we tell him. Here he comes.

Re-enter DAUPHINE.

Cler. Oh, sir, you are welcome.

True. Where's thine uncle?

Daup. Run out of doors in his night-caps, to talk with a casuist about his divorce. It works admirably.

True. Thou would'st have said so, an thou hadst been here! The ladies have laughed at thee most comically, since thou went'st, Dauphine.

Cler. And asked, if thou wert thine uncle's keeper.

True. And the brace of baboons answered, yes; and said thou wert a pitiful poor fellow, and didst live upon posts, and hadst nothing but three suits of apparel, and some few benevolences that the lords gave thee to fool to them, and swagger.

Daup. Let me not live, I'll beat them : I'll bind them both to grand-madam's bed-posts, and have them baited with monkeys.

True. Thou shalt not need, they shall be beaten to thy hand, Dauphine, I have an execution to serve upon them, I warrant thee, shall serve ; trust my plot.

Daup. Ay, you have many plots ! so you had one to make all the girls in love with me.

True. Why, if I do it not yet afore night, as near as 'tis, and that they do not every one invite thee, and be ready to scratch for thee, take the mortgage of my wit.

Cler. 'Fore God, I'll be his witness thou shalt have it, Dauphine : thou shalt be his fool for ever, if thou dost not.

True. Agreed. Perhaps 'twill be the better estate. Do you observe this gallery, or rather lobby, indeed? Here are a couple of studies, at each end one : here will I act such a tragi-comedy between the Guelphs and the Ghibellines, Daw and La-Foole ——which of them comes out first, will I seize on ;—you two shall be the chorus behind the arras, and whip out between the acts and speak—If I do not make them keep the peace for this remnant of the day, if not of the year, I have failed once——I hear Daw coming : hide, [*they withdraw*] and do not laugh, for Heaven's sake.

Re-enter DAW.

Daw. Which is the way into the garden, trow?

True. Oh, Jack Daw ! I am glad I have met with you. In good faith, I must have this matter go no further between you : I must have it taken up.

Daw. What matter, sir? between whom?

True. Come, you disguise it : Sir Amorous and you. If you love me, Jack, you shall make use of your philosophy now, for this once, and deliver me your sword. This is not the wedding the Centaurs were at, though there be a she one here. [*Takes his sword.*] The bride has entreated me I will see no blood shed at her bridal : you saw her whisper me erewhile.

Daw. As I hope to finish Tacitus, I intend no murder.

True. Do you not wait for Sir Amorous?

Daw. Not I, by my knighthood.

True. And your scholarship too?

Daw. And my scholarship too.

True. Go to, then I return you your sword, and ask you mercy ; but put it not up, for you will be assaulted. I understood that you had apprehended it, and walked here to brave him ; and that you had held your life contemptible, in regard of your honour.

Daw. No, no ; no such thing, I assure you. He and I parted now, as good friends as could be.

True. Trust not you to that visor. I saw him since dinner with another face : I have known many men in my time vexed with losses, with deaths, and with abuses; but so offended a wight as Sir Amorous, did I never see or read of. For taking away his guests, sir, to-day, that's the cause ; and he declares behind your back with such threatenings and contempts———He said to Dauphine, you were the arrant'st ass———

Daw. Ay, he may say his pleasure———

True. And swears you are so protested a coward, that he knows you will never do him any manly or single right ; and therefore he will take his course.

Daw. I'll give him any satisfaction, sir—but fighting.

True. Ay, sir : but who knows what satisfaction he'll take : blood he thirsts for, and blood he will have ; and whereabouts on you he will have it, who knows but himself?

Daw. I pray you, Master Truewit, be you a mediator.

True. Well, sir, conceal yourself then in this study till I return. [*Puts him into the study.*] Nay, you must be content to be locked in ; for, for mine own reputation, I would not have you seen to receive a public disgrace, while I have the matter in managing. 'Ods so, here he comes ; keep your breath close, that he do not hear you sigh.—In good faith, Sir Amorous, he is not this way ; I pray you be merciful, do not murder him ; he is a Christian, as good as you : you are armed as if you sought revenge on all his race. Good Dauphine, get him away from this place. I never knew a man's choler so high, but he would speak to his friends, he would hear reason.—Jack Daw, Jack ! asleep !

Daw. [*within.*] Is he gone, Master Truewit ?

True. Ay ; did you hear him ?

Daw. O Lord ! yes.

True. What a quick ear fear has !

Daw. [*comes out of the closet.*] But is he so armed as you say ?

True. Armed ! did you ever see a fellow set out to take possession ?

Daw. Ay, sir.

True. That may give you some light to conceive of him ; but 'tis nothing to the principal. Some false brother in the house has furnished him strangely ; or, if it were out of the house, it was Tom Otter.

Daw. Indeed he's a captain, and his wife is his kinswoman.

True. He has got somebody's old two-hand sword, to mow you off at the knees ; and that sword hath spawned such a dagger !...But then he is so hung with pikes, halberds, petronels, calivers and muskets, that he looks like a justice of peace's hall ; a man of two thousand a year is not cessed at so many weapons as he has on. There was never fencer challenged at so many several foils. You would think he meant to murder all St. Pulchre's parish. If he could but victual himself for half-a-year in his breeches, he is sufficiently armed to over-run a country.

Daw. Good Lord! what means he, sir? I pray you, Master Truewit, be you a mediator.

True. Well, I'll try if he will be appeased with a leg or an arm; if not you must die once.

Daw. I would be loth to lose my right arm, for writing madrigals.

True. Why, if he will be satisfied with a thumb or a little finger, all's one to me. You must think, I'll do my best.

[*Shuts him up again*

Daw. Good sir, do.

[CLERIMONT *and* DAUPHINE *come forward.*

Cler. What hast thou done

True. He will let me do nothing, he does all afore; he offers his left arm.

Cler. His left wing for a Jack Daw.

Daup. Take it by all means.

True. How! maim a man for ever, for a jest? What a conscience hast thou!

Daup. 'Tis no loss to him; he has no employment for his arms, but to eat spoon-meat. Beside, as good maim his body as his reputation.

True. He is a scholar and a wit, and yet he does not think so. But he loses no reputation with us; for we all resolved him an ass before. To your places again.

Cler. I pray thee, let be me in at the other a little.

True. Look, you'll spoil all; these be ever your tricks.

Cler. No, but I could hit of some things that thou wilt miss, and thou wilt say are good ones.

True. I warrant you. I pray forbear, I'll leave it off, else.

Daup. Come away, Clerimont.

[DAUP. *and* CLER. *withdraw as before.*

Enter LA-FOOLE.

True. Sir Amorous!

La-F. Master Truewit.

True. Whither were you going?

La-F. Down into the court.

True. By no means, sir.

La-F. Why, sir?

True. Enter here, if you love your life.

[*Opening the door of the other study.*

La-F. Why? why?

True. Question till your throat be cut, do: dally till the enraged soul find you.

La-F. Who is that?

True. Daw it is: will you in?

La-F. Ay, ay, I'll in: what's the matter?

True. Nay, if he had been cool enough to tell us that, there had been some hope to atone you; but he seems so implacably enraged!

La-F. 'Slight, let him rage! I'll hide myself.

True. Do, good sir. But what have you done to him within, that should provoke him thus? You have broke some jest upon him afore the ladies.

La-F. Not I, never in my life, broke jest upon any man. The bride was praising Sir Dauphine, and he went away in snuff, and I followed him; unless he took offence at me in his drink, erewhile, that I would not pledge all the horse full.

True. By my faith, and that may be; you remember well: but he walks the round up and down, through every room of the house, with a towel in his hand, crying, Where's La-Foole? Who saw La-Foole? And when Dauphine and I demanded the cause, we can force no answer from him, but—O revenge, how sweet art thou! I will strangle him in this towel!—which leads us to conjecture that the main cause of his fury is, for bringing your meat to-day, with a towel about you, to his discredit.

La-F. Like enough. Why, an he be angry for that, I'll stay here till his anger be blown over.

True. A good becoming resolution, sir; if you can put it on o' the sudden.

La-F. Yes, I can put it on: or, I'll away into the country presently.

True. How will you go out of the house, sir? he knows you are in the house, and he'll watch this se'ennight, but he'll have you; he'll outwait a serjeant for you.

La-F. Why, then I'll stay here.

True. You must think how to victual yourself in time then.

La-F. Why, sweet Master Truewit, will you entreat my cousin Otter to send me a cold venison pasty, a bottle or two of wine, and a chamber-pot?

True. A stool were better, sir, of Sir Ajax his invention.

La-F. Ay, that will be better, indeed; and a pallet to lie on.

True. Oh, I would not advise you to sleep by any means.

La-F. Would you not, sir? Why, then I will not,

True. Yet, there's another fear——

La-F. Is there! what is't?

True. No, he cannot break open this door with his foot, sure.

La-F. I'll set my back against it, sir. I have a good back.

True. But then if he should batter.

La-F. Batter! if he dare, I'll have an action of battery against him.

True. Cast you the worst. He has sent for powder already,

and what he will do with it, no man knows: perhaps blow up the corner of the house where he suspects you are. Here he comes; in quickly.—[*Thrusts in* LA-FOOLE *and shuts the door.*]—I protest, Sir John Daw, he is not this way: what will you do? Before God, you shall hang no petard here? I'll die rather. Will you not take my word? I never knew one but would be satisfied. Sir Amorous [*speaks through the keyhole*], there's no standing out: he has made a petard of an old brass pot, to force your door. Think upon some satisfaction, or terms to offer him.

La-F. [*within.*] Sir, I'll give him any satisfaction: I dare give any terms.

True. You'll leave it to me then?

La-F. Ay, sir: I'll stand to any conditions.

True. [*beckoning forward* CLER. *and* DAUPH.] How now, what think you, sirs? were 't not a difficult thing to determine which of these two fear'd most?

Cler. Yes, but this fears the bravest: the other a whiniling dastard, Jack Daw! But La-Foole, a brave heroic coward! and is afraid in a great look and a stout accent; I like him rarely.

True. Had it not been pity these two should have been concealed?

Cler. Shall I make a motion?

True. Briefly: for I must strike while 't is hot.

Cler. Shall I go fetch the ladies to the catastrophe?

True. Umph! ay, by my troth.

Daup. By no mortal means. Let them continue in the state of ignorance, and err still; think them wits and fine fellows, as they have done. 'Twere sin to reform them.

True. Well, I will have them fetch'd, now I think on 't, for a private purpose of mine: do, Clerimont, fetch them, and discourse to them all that's past, and bring them into the gallery here.

Daup. This is thy extreme vanity, now: thou think'st thou wert undone, if every jest thou mak'st were not published.

True. Thou shalt see how unjust thou art presently. Clerimont, say it was Dauphine's plot. [*Exit* CLERIMONT.] Trust me not, if the whole drift be not for thy good. There is a carpet in the next room, put it on, with this scarf over thy face, and a cushion on thy head, and be ready when I call Amorous. Away! [*Exit* DAUP.] John Daw!

[*Goes to* DAW'S *closet and brings him out.*]

Daup. What good news, sir?

True. Faith, I have followed and argued with him hard for you. I told him you were a knight and a scholar, and that you knew fortitude did consist *magis patiendo quam faciendo, magis ferendo quam feriendo.*

Daw. It doth so indeed, sir.

True. And that you would suffer, I told him. So at first he demanded by my troth, in my conceit, too much.

Daw. What was it, sir?

True. Your upper lip and six of your fore-teeth.

Daw. 'Twas unreasonable.

True. Nay, I told him plainly, you could not spare them all. So after long argument *pro et con,* as you know, I brought him down to your two butter-teeth, and them he would have.

Daw. Oh, did you so? Why, he shall have them.

True. But he shall not, sir, by your leave. The conclusion is this, sir : because you shall be very good friends hereafter, and this never to be remembered or upbraided ; besides, that he may not boast he has done any such thing to you in his own person, he is to come here in disguise, give you five kicks in private, sir, take your sword from you, and lock you up in that study during pleasure : which will be but a little while, we'll get it released presently.

Daw. Five kicks! He shall have six, sir, to be friends.

True. Believe me, you shall not over-shoot yourself, to send him that word by me.

Daw. Deliver it, sir ; he shall have it with all my heart, to be friends.

True. Friends! Nay, an he should not be so, and heartily too, upon these terms, he shall have me to enemy while I live. Come, sir, bear it bravely.

Daw. O, Lord, sir, 'tis nothing.

True. True: what's six kicks to a man that reads Seneca?

Daw. I have had a hundred, sir.

True. Sir Amorous!

Re-enter DAUPHINE *disguised.*

No speaking one to another, or rehearsing old matters.

Daw. [*as* DAUP. *kicks him.*] One, two, three, four, five. I protest, Sir Amorous, you shall have six.

True. Nay, I told you, you should not talk. Come give him six, an he will needs. [DAUPHINE *kicks him again.*]—Your sword. [*Takes his sword.*] Now return to your safe custody ; you shall presently meet afore the ladies, and be the dearest friends one to another. [*Puts* DAW *into the study.*] Give me the scarf now, thou shalt beat the other bare-faced. Stand by : [DAUPHINE *retires, and* TRUEWIT *goes to the other closet, and releases* LA-FOOLE.] Sir Amorous!

La-F. What's here! A sword?

True. I cannot help it; without I should take the quarrel upon myself. Here he has sent you his sword——

La-F. I'll receive none on 't.

True. And he wills you to fasten it against a wall, and break your head in some few several places against the hilts.

La-F. I will not: tell him roundly. I cannot endure to shed my own blood.

True. Will you not?

La-F. No. I'll beat it against a fair flat wall, if that will satisfy him: if not, he shall beat it himself, for Amorous.

True. Why, this is strange starting off, when a man undertakes for you! I offered him another condition; will you stand to that?

La-F. Ay, what is't?

True. That you will be beaten in private.

La-F. Yes, I am content, at the blunt.

Enter, above, HAUGHTY, CENTAURE, MAVIS, Mistress OTTER, EPICŒNE, *and* TRUSTY.

True. Then you must submit yourself to be hoodwinked in this scarf, and be led to him, where he will take your sword from you, and make you bear a blow over the mouth, gules, and tweaks by the nose *sans nombre*.

La-F. I am content. But why must I be blinded?

True. That's for your good, sir; because if he should grow insolent upon this, and publish it hereafter to your disgrace (which I hope he will not do), you might swear safely, and protest, he never beat you, to your knowledge.

La-F. Oh, I conceive.

True. I do not doubt but you'll be perfect good friends upon't, and not dare to utter an ill thought one of another in future.

La-F. Not I, as God help me, of him.

True. Nor he of you, sir. If he should, [*binds his eyes*]. Come, sir. [*Leads him forward.*]—All hid, Sir John!

Enter DAUPHINE, *and tweaks him by the nose.*

La-F. Oh, Sir John, Sir John! Oh, o-o-o-o-o-Oh——

True. Good Sir John, leave tweaking, you'll blow his nose off.—'Tis Sir John's pleasure, you should retire into the study. [*Puts him up again*]—Why, now you are friends. All bitterness between you, I hope, is buried: you shall come forth, by and by, Damon and Pythias upon't, and embrace with all the rankness of friendship that can be.—I trust, we shall have them tamer in their language hereafter. Dauphine, I worship thee. God's will, the ladies have surprised us!

Enter HAUGHTY, CENTAURE, MAVIS, Mistress OTTER, EPICŒNE, *and* TRUSTY *behind.*

Hau. Centaure, how our judgments were imposed on by these adulterate knights!

Cen. Nay, madam,' Mavis was more deceived than we; 'twas her commendation uttered them in the college.
Mav. I commended but their wits, madam, and their braveries. I never looked toward their valours.
Hau. Sir Dauphine is valiant, and a wit too, it seems.
Mav. And a bravery too.
Hau. Was this his project?
Mrs. Ott. So Master Clerimont intimates, madam.
Hau. Good Morose, when you come to the college, will you bring him with you? He seems a very perfect gentleman.
Epi. He is so, madam, believe it.
Cen. But when will you come, Morose?
Epi. Three or four days hence, madam, when I have got me a coach and horses.
Hau. No, to-morrow, good Morose; Centaure shall send you her coach.
Mav. Yes, faith, do, and bring Sir Dauphine with you.
Hau. She has promised that, Mavis.
Mav. He is a very worthy gentleman in his exteriors, madam.
Hau. Ay, he shows he is judicial in his clothes.
Cen. And yet not so superlatively neat as some, madam, that have their faces set in a brake.
Hau. Ay, and have every hair in form.
Mav. That wear purer linen than ourselves, and profess more neatness than the French hermaphrodite!
Epi. Ay, ladies, they, what they tell one of us, have told a thousand; and are the only thieves of our fame, that think to take us with that perfume, or with that lace, and laugh at us unconscionably when they have done.
Hau. But Sir Dauphine's carelessness becomes him.
Cen. I could love a man for such a nose.
Mav. Or such a leg.
Cen. He has an exceeding good eye, madam.
Mav. And a very good lock.
Cen. Good Morose, bring him to my chamber first.
Mrs. Ott. Please your honours to meet at my house, madam.
True. See how they eye thee, man! they are taken, I warrant thee. [HAUGHTY *comes forward.*
Hau. You have unbraced our brace of knights here, Master Truewit.
True. Not I, madam; it was Sir Dauphine's engine: who, if he have disfurnish'd your ladyship of any guard or service by it, is able to make the place good again in himself.
Hau. There is no suspicion of that, sir.
Cen. God so, Mavis, Haughty is kissing.
Mav. Let us go too, and take part. [*They come forward.*

Hau. But I am glad of the fortune (beside the discovery of two such empty caskets) to gain the knowledge of so rich a mine of virtue as Sir Dauphine.

Cen. We would be all glad to style him of our friendship, and see him at the college.

Mav. He cannot mix with a sweeter society, I'll prophesy; and I hope he himself will think so.

Daup. I should be rude to imagine otherwise, lady.

True. Did not I tell thee, Dauphine! Why, all their actions are governed by crude opinion, without reason or cause; they know not why they do anything; but, as they are inform'd, believe, judge, praise, condemn, love, hate, and in emulation one of another, do all these things alike. Only they have a natural inclination sways them generally to the worst, when they are left to themselves. But pursue it, now thou hast them.

Hau. Shall we go in again, Morose?

Epi. Yes, madam.

Cen. We'll entreat Sir Dauphine's company.

True. Stay, good madam, the interview of the two friends, Pylades and Orestes: I'll fetch them out to you straight.

Hau. Will you, Master Truewit?

Daup. Ay, but noble ladies, do not confess in your countenance, or outward bearing to them, any discovery of their follies, that we may see how they will bear up again, with what assurance and erection.

Hau. We will not, Sir Dauphine.

Cen., Mav. Upon our honours, Sir Dauphine.

True. [*goes to the first closet.*] Sir Amorous, Sir Amorous! The ladies are here.

La-F. [*within.*] Are they?

True. Yes; but slip out by-and-by, as their backs are turned, and meet Sir John here, as by chance, when I call you. [*Goes to the other.*] Jack Daw.

Daw. [*within.*] What say you, sir?

True. Whip out behind me suddenly, and no anger in your looks to your adversary. Now, now!

[LA-FOOLE *and* DAW *slip out of their respective closets and salute each other.*

La-F. Noble Sir John Daw, where have you been?

Daw. To seek you, Sir Amorous.

La-F. Me! I honour you.

Daw. I prevent you, sir.

Cler. They have forgot their rapiers.

True. Oh, they meet in peace, man.

Daup. Where's your sword, Sir John?

Cler. And yours, Sir Amorous?

Daw. Mine! My boy had it forth to mend the handle, e'en now.

La-F. And my gold handle was broke too, and my boy had it forth.

Daup. Indeed, sir!—How their excuses meet!

Cler. What a consent there is in the handles!

True. Nay, there is so in the points too, I warrant you.

Enter MOROSE, *with the two swords drawn in his hands.*

Mrs. Ott. Oh, me! madam, he comes again, the madman! Away! [Ladies, DAW *and* LA-FOOLE *run off.*

Mor. What make these naked weapons here, gentlemen?

True. Oh, sir! here hath like to have been murder since you went; a couple of knights fallen out about the bride's favours! We were fain to take away their weapons; your house had been begged by this time else.

Mor. For what?

Cler. For manslaughter, sir, as being accessory.

Mor. And for her favours?

True. Ay, sir, heretofore, not present—Clerimont, carry them their swords now. They have done all the hurt they will do.
[*Exit* CLER. *with the two swords.*

Daup. Have you spoke with the lawyer, sir?

Mor. Oh no! there is such a noise in the court, that they have frighted me home with more violence than I went! such speaking and counter speaking, with their several voices of citations, appellations, allegations, certificates, attachments, interrogatories, references, convictions, and afflictions indeed, among the doctors and proctors, that the noise here is silence to 't, a kind of calm midnight!

True. Why, sir, if you would be resolved indeed, I can bring you hither a very sufficient lawyer, and a learned divine, that shall enquire into every least scruple for you.

Mor. Can you, Master Truewit?

True. Yes, and are very sober, grave persons, that will dispatch it in a chamber, with a whisper or two.

Mor. Good, sir, shall I hope this benefit from you, and trust myself into your hands?

True. Alas, sir! your nephew and I have been ashamed and oft-times mad, since you went, to think how you are abused. Go in, good sir, and lock yourself up till we call you; we'll tell you more anon, sir.

Mor. Do your pleasure with me, gentlemen; I believe in you, and that deserves no delusion. [*Exit.*

True. You shall find none, sir;—but heap'd, heap'd plenty of vexation.

Daup. What wilt thou do now, Wit?

True. Recover me hither Otter and the Barber, if you can, by any means, presently.

Daup. Why? to what purpose?

True. Oh, I'll make the deepest divine, and gravest lawyer, out of them two for him——

Daup. Thou canst not, man; these are waking dreams.

True. Do not fear me. Clap but a civil gown with a welt on the one, and a canonical cloke with sleeves on the other, and give them a few terms in their mouths, if there come not forth as able a doctor and complete a parson, for this turn, as may be wish'd, trust not my election: and I hope, without wronging the dignity of either profession, since they are but persons put on, and for mirth's sake to torment him. The barber smatters Latin, I remember.

Daup. Yes, and Otter too.

True. Well, then, if I make them not wrangle out this case to his no comfort, let me be thought a Jack Daw or La-Foole, or anything worse. Go you to your ladies, but first send for them.

Daup. I will. [*Exeunt.*

———————————ACT V.———————————

SCENE I.—*A Room in* MOROSE'S *House.*

Enter LA-FOOLE, CLERIMONT, *and* DAW.

La-F. Where had you our swords, Master Clerimont?

Cler. Why, Dauphine took them from the madman.

La-F. And he took them from our boys, I warrant you.

Cler. Very like, sir.

La-F. Thank you, good Master Clerimont. Sir John Daw and I are both beholden to you.

Cler. Would I knew how to make you so, gentlemen!

Daw. Sir Amorous and I are your servants, sir.

Enter MAVIS.

Mav. Gentlemen, have any of you a pen and ink? I would fain write out a riddle in Italian, for Sir Dauphine to translate.

Cler. Not I, in troth, lady; I am no scrivener.

Daw. I can furnish you, I think, lady.
[*Exeunt* DAW *and* MAVIS.

Cler. He has it in the haft of a knife, I believe.

La-F. No, he has his box of instruments.

Cler. Like a surgeon!

La-F. For the mathematics: his square, his compasses, his brass pens, and black-lead, to draw maps of every place and person where he comes.

Cler. How, maps of persons!

La-F. Yes, sir, of Nomentack when he was here, and of the prince of Moldavia, and of his mistress, Mistress Epicœne.

Re-enter DAW.

Cler. Away! he hath not found out her latitude, I hope.

La-F. You are a pleasant gentleman, sir.

Cler. Faith, now we are in private, let's wanton it a little, and talk waggishly.—Sir John, I am telling Sir Amorous here, that you two govern the ladies wherever you come; you carry the feminine gender afore you.

Daw. They shall rather carry us afore them, if they will, sir.

Cler. Nay, I believe that they do, withal—but that you are the prime men in their affections, and direct all their actions——

Daw. Not I; Sir Amorous is.

La-F. I protest, Sir John is.

Daw. As I hope to rise in the state, Sir Amorous, you have the person.

La-F. Sir John, you have the person, and the discourse too.

Daw. Not I, sir, I have no discourse—and then you have activity, beside.

La-F. I protest, Sir John, you come as high from Tripoli as I do, every whit: and lift as many join'd stools, and leap over them, if you would use it.

Cler. Well, agree on't together, knights; for between you, you divide the kingdom or commonwealth of ladies' affections: I see it, and can perceive a little how they observe you, and fear you, indeed. You could tell strange stories, my masters, if you would, I know.

Daw. Faith, we have seen somewhat, sir.

La-F. That we have——velvet petticoats, and wrought smocks, or so.

Daw. Ay, and——

Cler. Nay, out with it, Sir John; do not envy your friend the pleasure of hearing, when you have had the delight of tasting.

Daw. Why—a—Do you speak, Sir Amorous.

La-F. No, do you, Sir John Daw.

Daw. I' faith, you shall.

La-F. I' faith, you shall.

Daw. Why, we have been——

La-F. In the great bed at Ware together in our time. On, Sir John.

Daw. Nay, do you, Sir Amorous.

Cler. And these ladies with you, knights?

La-F. No, excuse us, sir.

Daw. We must not wound reputation.

La-F. No matter—they were these, or others. Our bath cost us fifteen pound when we came home.

Cler. Do you hear, Sir John? You shall tell me but one thing truly, as you love me.

Daw. If I can, I will, sir.

Cler. You lay in the same house with the bride, here?

Daw. Yes, and conversed with her hourly, sir.

Cler. And what humour is she of? Is she coming and open, free?

Daw. Oh, exceeding open, sir, I was her servant, and Sir Amorous was to be.

Cler. Come, you have both had favours from her: I know, and have heard so much.

Daw. Oh, no, sir.

La-F. You shall excuse us, sir; we must not wound reputation.

Cler. Tut, she is married now, and you cannot hurt her with any report; and therefore speak plainly: how many times, i'faith? Which of you led first? Ha!

La-F. Sir John, indeed.

Daw. Oh, it pleases him to say so, sir; but Sir Amorous knows what's what, as well.

Cler. Dost thou, i' faith, Amorous?

La-F. In a manner, sir.

Cler. Why, I commend you, lads. Little knows Don Bridegroom of this; nor shall he, for me.

Daw. Hang him, mad ox!

Cler. Speak softly; here comes his nephew, with the Lady Haughty: he'll get the ladies from you, sirs, if you look not to him in time.

La-F. Why, if he do, we'll fetch them home again, I warrant you.   [*Exit with* DAW. CLER. *walks aside.*

Enter DAUPHINE *and* HAUGHTY.

Hau. I assure you, Sir Dauphine, it is the price and estimation of your virtue only, that hath embarked me to this adventure; and I could not but make out to tell you so: nor can I repent me of the act, since it is always an argument of some virtue in ourselves, that we love and affect it so in others.

Daup. Your ladyship sets too high a price on my weakness.

Hau. Sir, I can distinguish gems from pebbles——

Daup. Are you so skilful in stones?   [*Aside.*

Hau. And howsoever I may suffer in such a judgment as yours, by admitting equality of rank or society with Centaure or Mavis——

Daup. You do not, madam; I perceive they are your mere foils.

Hau. Then, are you a friend to truth, sir; it makes me love you the more. It is not the outward, but the inward man that I affect. They are not apprehensive of an eminent perfection, but love flat and dully.

Cen. [*within.*] Where are you, my Lady Haughty?

Hau. I come presently, Centaure. My chamber, sir, my page shall show you; and Trusty, my woman, shall be ever awake for you: you need not fear to communicate anything with her, for she is a Fidelia. I pray you wear this jewel for my sake, Sir Dauphine—

Enter CENTAURE.

Where's Mavis, Centaure?

Cen. Within, madam, a-writing. I'll follow you presently: [*Exit* HAU.] I'll but speak a word with Sir Dauphine.

Daup. With me, madam?

Cen. Good Sir Dauphine, do not trust Haughty, nor make any credit to her, whatever you do besides. Sir Dauphine, I give you this caution, she is a perfect courtier, and loves nobody but for her uses; and for her uses she loves all. Besides, her physicians give her out to be none o' the clearest, whether she pay them or no, Heaven knows; and she's above fifty too, and pargets! See her in a forenoon. Here comes Mavis, a worse face than she! You would not like this by candle-light.

Re-enter MAVIS.

If you'll come to my chamber one o' these mornings early, or late in an evening, I'll tell you more. Where's Haughty, Mavis?

Mav. Within, Centaure.

Cen. What have you there?

Mav. An Italian riddle for Sir Dauphine,—you shall not see it, i'faith, Centaure.—[*Exit* CEN.]—Good Sir Dauphine, solve it for me: I'll call for it anon. [*Exit.*

Cler. [*coming forward.*] How now, Dauphine! how dost thou quit thyself of these females?

Daup. 'Slight, they haunt me like fairies, and give me jewels here; I cannot be rid of them.

Cler. Oh, you must not tell though.

Daup. Mass, I forgot that: I was never so assaulted. One loves for virtue, and bribes me with this;—[*shews the jewel.*]— another loves me with caution, and so would possess me; a third brings me a riddle here: and all are jealous, and rail each at other.

Cler. A riddle! pray let me see it. [*Reads.*

Sir Dauphine, I chose this way of intimation for privacy. The ladies here, I know, have both hope and purpose to make a collegiate and servant of you. If I might be so honoured, as to appear at any end of so noble a work, I would enter into a fame of taking physic to-morrow, and continue it four or five days, or longer, for your visitation. MAVIS.

By my faith, a subtle one! Call you this a riddle? what's their plain-dealing, trow?

Daup. We lack Truewit to tell us that.

Cler. We lack him for somewhat else too: his knights reforma-does are wound up as high and insolent as ever they were.

Daup. You jest.

Cler. No drunkards, either with wine or vanity, ever confessed such stories of themselves. I would not give a fly's leg in balance against all the women's reputations here, if they could be but thought to speak truth: and for the bride, they have made their affidavit against her directly——

Daup. What, that they have lain with her?

Cler. Yes; and tell times and circumstances, with the cause why, and the place where. I had almost brought them to affirm that they had done it to-day.

Daup. Not both of them?

Cler. Yes, faith; with a sooth or two more I had effected it. They would have set it down under their hands.

Daup. Why, they will be our sport, I see, still, whether we will or no.

Enter TRUEWIT.

True. Oh, are you here? Come, Dauphine; go call your uncle presently: I have fitted my divine and my canonist, dyed their beards and all. The knaves do not know themselves, they are so exalted and altered. Preferment changes any man. Thou shalt keep one door and I another, and then Clerimont in the midst, that he may have no means of escape from their cavilling, when they grow hot once again. And then the women, as I have given the bride her instructions, to break in upon him in the l'envoy. Oh, 'twill be full and twanging! Away! fetch him.
[*Exit* DAUPHINE.

Enter OTTER *disguised as a divine, and* CUTBEARD *as a canon lawyer.*

Come, master doctor, and master parson, look to your parts now, and discharge them bravely; you are well set forth, perform it as well. If you chance to be out, do not confess it with standing still, or humming, or gaping one at another; but go on, and talk aloud and eagerly; use vehement action, and only remember your terms, and you are safe. Let the matter go where it will: you have many will do so. But at first be very solemn and grave, like your garments, though you lose yourselves after, and skip out like a brace of jugglers on a table. Here he comes: set your faces, and look superciliously, while I present you.

Re-enter DAUPHINE *with* MOROSE.

Mor. Are these the two learned men?
True. Yes, sir; please you salute them.
Mor. Salute them? I had rather do anything than wear out time so unfruitfully, sir. I wonder how these common forms, as *God save you*, and *You are welcome*, are come to be a habit in our lives: or, *I am glad to see you!* when I cannot see what the profit can be of these words, so long as it is no whit better with him whose affairs are sad and grievous, that he hears this salutation.
True. 'Tis true, sir; we'll go to the matter then.—Gentlemen, master doctor, and master parson, I have acquainted you sufficiently with the business for which you are come hither; and you are not now to inform yourselves in the state of the question, I know. This is the gentleman who expects your resolution, and therefore, when you please, begin.
Ott. Please you, master doctor.
Cut. Please you, good master parson.
Ott. I would hear the canon-law speak first.
Cut. It must give place to positive divinity, sir.
Mor. Nay, good gentlemen, do not throw me into circumstances. Let your comforts arrive quickly at me, those that are. Be swift in affording me my peace, if so I shall hope any. I love not your disputations, or your court-tumults. And that it be not strange to you, I will tell you: My father, in my education, was wont to advise me that I should always collect and contain my mind, not suffering it to flow loosely; that I should look to what things were necessary to the carriage of my life, and what not; embracing the one and eschewing the other: in short, that I should endear myself to rest, and avoid turmoil; which now is grown to be another nature to me. So that I come not to your public pleadings, or your places of noise; not that I neglect those things that make for the dignity of the commonwealth: but for the mere avoiding of clamours and impertinences of orators, that know not how to be silent. And for the cause of noise, am I now a suitor to you. You do not know in what a misery I have been exercised this day, what a torrent of evil! my very house turns round with the tumult! I dwell in a windmill: the perpetual motion is here, and not at Eltham.
True. Well, good master doctor, will you break the ice? master parson will wade after.
Cut. Sir, though unworthy, and the weaker, I will presume.
Ott. 'Tis no presumption, *domine* doctor.

I

Mor. Yet again!

Cut. Your question is, For how many causes a man may have *divortium legitimum*, a lawful divorce? First, you must understand the nature of the word, divorce, *à divertendo*——

Mor. No excursions upon words, good doctor; to the question briefly.

Cut. I answer then, the canon law affords divorce but in few cases; and the principal is in the common case, the adulterous case: But there are *duodecim impedimenta*, twelve impediments, as we call them, all which do not *dirimere contractum*, but *irritum reddere matrimonium*, as we say in the canon law, *not take away the bond, but cause a nullity therein*.

Mor. I understood you before; good sir, avoid your impertinency of translation.

Ott. He cannot open this too much, sir, by your favour.

Mor. Yet more!

True. Oh, you must give the learned men leave, sir.—To your impediments, master doctor.

Cut. The first is *impedimentum erroris*.

Ott. Of which there are several species.

Cut. Ay, as *error personæ*.

Ott. If you contract yourself to one person, thinking her another.

Cut. Then, *error fortunæ*.

Ott. If she be a beggar, and you thought her rich.

Cut. Then, *error qualitatis*.

Ott. If she prove stubborn or head-strong, that you thought obedient.

Mor. How! is that, sir, a lawful impediment? One at once, I pray you, gentlemen.

Ott. Ay, *ante copulam*, but not *post copulam*, sir.

Cut. Master parson says right. *Nec post nuptiarum benedictionem*. It doth indeed but *irrita reddere sponsalia*, annul the contract; after marriage it is of no obstancy.

True. Alas, sir, what a hope are we fallen from by this time!

Cut. The next is *conditio*: if you thought her free born, and she prove a bond-woman, there is impediment of estate and condition.

Ott. Ay, but, master doctor, those servitudes are *sublatæ* now, among us Christians.

Cut. By your favour, master parson——

Ott. You shalt give me leave, master doctor.

Mor. Nay, gentlemen, quarrel not in that question; it concerns not my case: pass to the third.

Cut. Well, then, the third is *votum*: if either party have made a vow of chastity. But that practice, as master parson said of the other, is taken away among us, thanks be to discipline.

The fourth is *cognatio* : if the persons be of kin within the degrees.

Ott. Ay: do you know what the degrees are, sir?

Mor. No, nor I care not, sir; they offer me no comfort in the question, I am sure.

Cut. But there is a branch of this impediment may, which is *cognatio spiritualis*; if you were her godfather, sir, then the marriage is incestuous.

Ott. That comment is absurd and superstitious, master doctor: I cannot endure it. Are we not all brothers and sisters and as much akin in that as godfathers and goddaughters?

Mor. Oh me! to end the controversy, I never was a godfather, I never was a godfather in my life, sir. Pass to the next.

Cut. The fifth is *crimen adulterii*; the known case. The sixth, *cultus disparitas*, difference of religion: have you ever examined her, what religion she is of?

Mor. No, I would rather she were of none, than be put to the trouble of it.

Ott. You may have it done for you, sir.

Mor. By no means, good sir; on to the rest: shall you ever come to an end, think you?

True. Yes, he has done half, sir.—Be patient, and expect, sir.

Cut. The seventh is, *vis*: if it were upon compulsion or force.

Mor. Oh, no, it was too voluntary, mine; too voluntary.

Cut. The eighth is, *ordo*; if ever she have taken holy orders.

Ott. That's superstitious too.

Mor. No matter, master parson; would she would go into a nunnery yet.

Cut. The ninth is, *ligamen*; if you were bound, sir, to any other before.

Mor. I thrust myself too soon into these fetters.

Cut. The tenth is, *publica honestas*; which is *inchoata quædam affinitas.*

Ott. Ay, or *affinitas orta ex sponsalibus*; and is but *leve impedimentum.*

Mor. I feel no air of comfort blowing to me, in all this.

Cut. The eleventh is, *affinitas ex fornicatione.*

Ott. Which is no less *vera affinitas*, than the other, master doctor.

Cut. True, *quæ oritur ex legitimo matrimonio.*

Cut. You say right, venerable doctor: and, *nascitur ex eo, quod per conjugium duæ personæ efficiuntur una caro*——

True. Hey-day, now they begin!

Cut. I conceive you, master parson: *ita per fornicationem æque est verus pater, qui sic generat*——

Ott. Et vere filius qui sic generatur*——

Mor. What's all this to me?

Cler. Now it grows warm.

Cut. The twelfth and last is, *si forte coire nequibis.*

Ott. Ay, that is *impedimentum gravissimum:* it doth utterly annul, and annihilate, that. If you have *manifestam frigiditatem*, you are well, sir.

True. Why, there is comfort come at length, sir. Confess yourself but a man unable, and she will sue to be divorced first.

Ott. Ay, or if there be *morbus perpetuus, et insanabilis;* as *paralysis, elephantiasis,* or so——

Daup. Oh, but *frigiditas* is the fairer way, gentlemen.

Ott. You say troth, sir, and as it is in the canon, master doctor——

Cut. I conceive you, sir.

Cler. Before he speaks!

Ott. That a boy, or child, under years, is not fit for marriage, because he cannot *reddere debitum.* So your *omnipotentes*——

True. Your *impotentes*, you lobster! [*Aside to* OTT.

Ott. Your *impotentes*, I should say, are *minime apti ad contrahenda matrimonium.*

True. Matrimonium! we shall have most unmatrimonial Latin with you: *matrimonia,* and be hanged.

Daup. You put them out, man.

Cut. But then there will arise a doubt, master parson, in our case, *post matrimonium:* that *frigiditate præditus*—do you conceive me, sir?

Ott. Very well, sir.

Cut. Who cannot *uti uxore pro uxore,* may *habere eam pro sorore.*

Ott. Absurd, absurd, absurd, and merely apostatical!

Cut. You shall pardon me, master parson, I can prove it.

Ott. You can prove a will, master doctor; you can prove nothing else. Does not the verse of your own canon say,

> Hæc socianda vetant connubia, facta retractant?

Cut. I grant you; but how do they *retractare*, master parson?

Mor. Oh, this was it I feared.

Ott. In æternum, sir.

Cut. That's false in divinity, by your favour.

Ott. 'Tis false in humanity to say so. Is he not *prorsus inutilis ad thorum?* Can he *præstare fidem datam?* I would fain know.

Cut. Yes; how if he do *convalere?*

Ott. He cannot *convalere,* it is impossible.

True. Nay, good sir, attend the learned men: they'll think you neglect them else.

Cut. Or, if he do *simulare* himself *frigidum, odio uxoris,* or so?

Ott. I say, he is *adulter manifestus* then.
Daup. They dispute it very learnedly, i' faith.
Ott. And *prostitutor uxoris;* and this is positive.
Mor. Good sir, let me escape.
True. You will not do me that wrong, sir?
Ott. And, therefore, if he be *manifeste frigidus*, sir——
Cut. Ay, if he be *manifeste frigidus*, I grant you——
Ott. Why, that was my conclusion.
Cut. And mine too.
True. Nay, hear the conclusion, sir.
Ott. Then *frigiditatis causa*——
Cut. Yes, *causa frigiditatis*——
Mor. Oh, mine ears!
Ott. She may have *libellum divortii* against you.
Cut. Ay, *divortii libellum* she will sure have.
Mor. Good echoes, forbear.
Ott. If you confess it——
Cut. Which I would do, sir——
Mor. I will do anything.
Ott. And clear myself *in foro conscientiæ*——
Cut. Because you want indeed——
Mor. Yet more!
Ott. *Exercendi potestate.*

EPICŒNE *rushes in, followed by* HAUGHTY, CENTAURE, MAVIS, Mistress OTTER, DAW, *and* LA-FOOLE.

Epi. I will not endure it any longer. Ladies, I beseech you, help me. This is such a wrong as never was offered to poor bride before: upon her marriage-day to have her husband conspire against her, and a couple of mercenary companions to be brought in for form's sake, to persuade a separation! If you had blood or virtue in you, gentlemen, you would not suffer such earwigs about a husband, or scorpions to creep between man and wife.
Mor. Oh the variety and changes of my torment!
Hau. Let them be cudgelled out of doors by our grooms.
Cen. I'll lend you my footman.
Mav. We'll have our men blanket them in the hall.
Mrs. Ott. As there was one at our house, madam, for peeping in at the door.
Daw. Content, i' faith.
True. Stay, ladies and gentlemen; you'll hear before you proceed?
Mav. I'd have the bridegroom blanketted too.
Cen. Begin with him first.
Hau. Yes, by my troth.
Mor. O mankind generation!

Daup. Ladies, for my sake forbear.

Hau. Yes, for Sir Dauphine's sake.

Cen. He shall command us.

La-F. He is as fine a gentleman of his inches, madam, as any is about the town, and wears as good colours when he lists.

True. Be brief, sir, and confess your infirmity: she'll be a-fire to be quit of you, if she but hear that named once, you shall not intreat her to stay: she'll fly you like one that had the marks upon him.

Mor. Ladies, I must crave all your pardons——

True. Silence, ladies.

Mor. For a wrong I have done to your whole sex, in marrying this fair and virtuous gentlewoman——

Cler. Hear him, good ladies.

Mor. Being guilty of an infirmity, which, before I conferred with these learned men, I thought I might have concealed——

True. But now being better informed in his conscience by them, he is to declare it, and give satisfaction, by asking your public forgiveness.

Mor. I am no man, ladies.

All. How!

Mor. Utterly unable in nature, by reason of frigidity, to perform the duties, or any the least office of a husband.

Mav. Now out upon him, prodigious creature!

Cen. Bridegroom uncarnate!

Hau. And would you offer it to a young gentlewoman?

Mrs. Ott. A lady of her longings?

Epi. Tut, a device, a device, this! It smells rankly, ladies. A mere comment of his own.

True. Why, if you suspect that, ladies, you may have him searched——

Daw. As the custom is, by a jury of physicians.

La-F. Yes, faith, 'twill be brave.

Mor. Oh, me, must I undergo that?

Mrs. Ott. No, let women search him, madam; we can do it ourselves.

Mor. Out on me! worse.

Epi. No, ladies, you shall not need, I'll take him with all his faults.

Mor. Worst of all!

Cler. Why then, 'tis no divorce, doctor, if she consent not?

Cut. No, if the man be *frigidus*, it is *de parte uxoris*, that we grant *libellum divortii*, in the law.

Ott. Ay, it is the same in theology.

Mor. Worse, worse than worst!

True. Nay, sir, be not utterly disheartened; we have yet a small relic of hope left, as near as our comfort is blown out. Clerimont, produce your brace of knights. What was that, master parson, you told me *in errore qualitatis*, e'en now?—Dauphine, whisper the bride, that she carry it as if she were guilty, and ashamed. [*Aside.*

Ott. Marry, sir, *in errore qualitatis*, (which master doctor did forbear to urge,) if she be found *corrupta*, that is, vitiated or broken up, that was *pro virgine desponsa*, espoused for a maid——

Mor. What then, sir?

Ott. It doth *dirimere contractum*, and *irritum reddere* too.

True. If this be true we are happy again, sir, once more. Here are an honourable brace of knights, that shall affirm so much.

Daw. Pardon us, good Master Clerimont.

La-F. You shall excuse us, Master Clerimont.

Cler. Nay, you must make it good now, knights, there is no remedy: I'll eat no words for you, nor no men: you know you spoke it to me.

Daw. Is this gentleman-like, sir?

True. Jack Daw, he's worse than Sir Amorous; fiercer a great deal. [*Aside to* DAW.] Sir Amorous, beware, there be ten Daws in this Clerimont. [*Aside to* LA-FOOLE.

La-F. I'll confess it, sir.

Daw. Will you, Sir Amorous, will you wound reputation?

La-F. I am resolved.

True. So should you be too, Jack Daw: what should keep you off? she's but a woman, and in disgrace: he'll be glad on 't.

Daw. Will he? I thought he would have been angry.

Cler. You will dispatch, knights; it must be done, i'faith.

True. Why, an it must, it shall, sir, they say: they'll ne'er go back. Do not tempt his patience. [*Aside to them.*

Daw. Is it true indeed, sir?

La-F. Yes, I assure you, sir.

Mor. What is true, gentlemen? what do you assure me?

Daw. That we have known your bride, sir——

La-F. In good fashion. She was our mistress or so——

Cler. Nay, you must be plain, knights, as you were to me.

Ott. Ay, the question is, if you have *carnaliter*, or no?

La-F. Carnaliter! what else, sir?

Ott. It is enough: a plain nullity.

Epi. I am undone, I am undone!

Mor. Oh, let me worship and adore you, gentlemen!

Epi. I am undone. [*Weeps.*

Mor. Yes, to my hand, I thank these knights. Master parson, let me thank you otherwise. [*Gives him money.*

Cen. And have they confest?

Mav. Now out upon them, informers!

True. You see what creatures you may bestow your favours on, madams.

Hau. I would except against them as beaten knights, wench, and not good witnesses in law.

Mrs. Ott. Poor gentlewoman, how she takes it!

Hau. Be comforted, Morose, I love you the better for't.

Cen. So do I, I protest.

Cut. But, gentlemen, you have not known her since *matrimonium?*

Daw. Not to-day, master doctor.

La-F. No, sir, not to-day.

Cut. Why, then I say, for any act before, the *matrimonium* is good and perfect; unless the worshipful bridegroom did precisely, before witness, demand if she were *virgo ante nuptias.*

Epi. No, that he did not, I assure you, master doctor.

Cut. If he cannot prove that, it is *ratum conjugium*, notwithstanding the premises; and they do no way *impedire.* And this is my sentence, this I pronounce.

Ott. I am of master doctor's resolution too, sir; if you made not that demand *ante nuptias.*

Mor. O my heart! wilt thou break? wilt thou break? This is worst of all worst worsts that hell could have devised! Marry her so, and so much noise!

Daup. Come, I see now plain confederacy in this doctor and this parson, to abuse a gentleman. You study his affliction. I pray be gone, companions.—And, gentlemen, I begin to suspect you for having parts with them.—Sir, will it please you hear me?

Mor. Oh, do not talk to me; take not from me the pleasure of dying in silence, nephew.

Daup. Sir, I must speak to you. I have been long your poor despised kinsman, and many a hard thought has strengthened you against me: but now it shall appear if either I love you or your peace, and prefer them to all the world beside. I will not be long or grievous to you, sir. If I free you of this unhappy match absolutely, and instantly, after all this trouble, and almost in your despair, now——

Mor. It cannot be.

Daup. Sir, that you be never troubled with a murmur of it more, what shall I hope for, or deserve of you?

Mor. Oh, what thou wilt, nephew! Thou shalt deserve me, and have me.

Daup. Shall I have your favour perfect to me, and love hereafter?

Mor. That, and any thing beside. Make thine own conditions. My whole estate is thine: manage it, I will become thy ward.

Daup. Nay, sir, I will not be so unreasonable.

Epi. Will Sir Dauphine be mine enemy too?

Daup. You know I have been long a suitor to you, uncle, that out of your estate, which is fifteen hundred a-year, you would allow me but five hundred during life, and assure the rest upon me after; to which I have often, by myself and friends, tendered you a writing to sign, which you would never consent or incline to. If you please but to effect it now——

Mor. Thou shalt have it, nephew: I will do it, and more.

Daup. If I quit you not presently, and for ever, of this cumber, you shall have power instantly, afore all these, to revoke your act, and I will become whose slave you will give me to, for ever.

Mor. Where is the writing? I will seal to it, that, or to a blank, and write thine own conditions.

Epi. Oh me, most unfortunate, wretched gentlewoman!

Hau. Will Sir Dauphine do this?

Epi. Good sir, have some compassion on me.

Mor. Oh, my nephew knows you, belike; away, crocodile!

Cen. He does it not sure without good ground.

Daup. Here, sir.   [*Gives him the parchments.*

Mor. Come, nephew, give me the pen; I will subscribe to anything, and seal to what thou wilt, for my deliverance. Thou art my restorer. Here, I deliver it thee as my deed. If there be a word in it lacking, or writ with false orthography, I protest before [Heaven] I will not take the advantage.

                            [*Returns the writings.*

Daup. Then here is your release, sir [*takes off* EPICŒNE'S *peruke and other disguises.*] You have married a boy, a gentleman's son, that I have brought up this half year at my great charges, and for this composition, which I have now made with you.—What say you, master doctor? This is *justum impedimentum*, I hope, *error personæ?*

Ott. Yes, sir, *in primo gradu.*

Cut. In primo gradu.

Daup. I thank you, good Doctor Cutbeard, and Parson Otter. [*Pulls their false beards and gowns off.*] You are beholden to them, sir, that have taken this pains for you; and my friend, Master Truewit, who enabled them for the business. Now you may go in and rest; be as private as you will, sir.—[*Exit* MOROSE.]—I'll not trouble you, till you trouble me with your funeral, which I care not how soon it come.—Cutbeard, I'll make your lease good. Thank me not, but with your leg, Cutbeard. And Tom Otter, your princess shall be reconciled to you.—How now, gentlemen, do you look at me?

Cler. A boy!

Daup. Yes, Mistress Epicœne.

True. Well, Dauphine, you have lurched your friends of the better half of the garland, by concealing this part of the plot: but much good do it thee, thou deserv'st it, lad. And, Clerimont, for thy unexpected bringing these two to confession, wear my part of it freely. Nay, Sir Daw and Sir La-Foole, you see the gentlewoman that has done you the favours! we are all thankful to you, and so should the woman-kind here, specially for lying on her, though not with her! you meant so, I am sure. But that we have stuck it upon you to-day, in your imagined persons, and so lately, this Amazon, the champion of the sex, should beat you now thriftily, for the common slanders which ladies receive from such cuckoos as you are. You are they that, when no merit or fortune can make you hope to enjoy their bodies, will yet lie with their reputations, and make their fame suffer. Away, you common moths of these, and all ladies' honours. Go, travel to make legs and faces, and come home with some new matter to be laughed at; you deserve to live in an air as corrupted as that wherewith you feed rumour.—[*Exeunt* DAW *and* LA-FOOLE.]—Madams, you are mute, upon this new metamorphosis! But here stands she that has vindicated your fames. Take heed of such insectæ hereafter. And let it not trouble you, that you have discovered any mysteries to this young gentleman: he is almost of years, and will make a good visitant within this twelvemonth. In the meantime, we'll all undertake for his secrecy, that can speak so well of his silence. [*Coming forward.*]—Spectators, if you like this comedy, rise cheerfully, and now Morose is gone in, clap your hands. It may be, that noise will cure him, at least please him. [*Exeunt.*

THE SAD SHEPHERD;

OR,

A TALE OF ROBIN HOOD.

ARGUMENT.

ACT I.

ROBIN HOOD, having invited all the shepherds and shepherdesses of the vale of Belvoir to a feast in the forest of Sherwood, and trusting to his mistress, Maid Marian, with her woodmen, to kill him venison against the day: having left the like charge with Friar Tuck, his chaplain and steward, to command the rest of his merry men to see the bower made ready, and all things in order for the entertainment: meeting with his guests at their entrance into the wood, welcomes them and conducts them to his bower. Where, by the way, he receives the relation of the SAD SHEPHERD, Æglamour, who is fallen into a deep melancholy for the loss of his beloved Earine, reported to have been drowned in passing over the Trent, some few days before. They endeavour in what they can to comfort him: but his disease having taken such strong root, all is in vain, and they are forced to leave him. In the mean time, Marian is come from hunting with the huntsmen, where the lovers interchangeably express their loves. Robin Hood enquires if she hunted the deer at force, and what sport he made? how long he stood, and what head he bore? All which is briefly answered, with a relation of breaking him up, and the raven and her bone. The suspect had of that raven to be Maudlin, the witch of Paplewick, whom one of the huntsmen met in the morning at the rousing of the deer, and is confirmed, by her being then in Robin Hood's kitchen, in the chimney corner, broiling the same bit which was thrown to the raven at the quarry or fall of the deer. Marian being gone in to show the deer to some of the shepherdesses, returns instantly to the scene, discontented; sends away the venison she had killed, to her they call the witch; quarrels with her love, Robin Hood, abuseth him, and his guests the shepherds; and so departs, leaving them all in wonder and perplexity.

ACT II.

The witch Maudlin having taken the shape of Marian to abuse Robin Hood, and perplex his guests, cometh forth with her daughter Douce, reporting in what confusion she had left them; defrauded them of their venison, made them suspicious each of the other; but most of all, Robin Hood so jealous of his Marian, as she hopes no effect of love would ever reconcile them; glorying so far in the extent of her mischief, as she confesseth to have surprised Earine, stripped her of her garments, to make her daughter appear fine at this feast in them ; and to have shut the maiden up in a tree, as her son's prize, if he could win her ; or his prey if he would force her. Her son, a rude, bragging swineherd, comes to the tree to woo her, (his mother and sister stepping aside to overhear him) and first boasts his wealth to her, and his possessions ; which move not. Then he presents her gifts, such as himself is taken with, but she utterly shows a scorn and loathing both of him and them. His mother is angry, rates him, instructs him what to do the next time, and persuades her daughter to show herself about the bower : tells how she shall know her mother, when she is transform'd, by her broidered belt. Meanwhile the young shepherdess Amie, being kist by Karolin, Earine's brother, falls in love ; but knows not what love is: but describes her disease so innocently, that Marian pities her. When Robin Hood and the rest of his guests invited, enter to Marian, upbraiding her with sending away their venison to Mother Maudlin by Scathlock, which she denies ; Scathlock affirms it ; but seeing his mistress weep and to forswear it, begins to doubt his own understanding, rather than affront her farther ; which makes Robin Hood and the rest to examine themselves better. But Maudlin, the witch, entering like herself, comes to thank her for her bounty; at which Marian is more angry, and more denies the deed. Scathlock enters, tells he has brought it again, and delivered it to the cook. The witch is inwardly vext the venison is so recovered from her by the rude huntsman, and murmurs and curses ; bewitches the cook, mocks poor Amie and the rest ; discovereth her ill nature, and is a means of reconciling them all. For the sage shepherd suspecteth her mischief, if she be not prevented : and so persuadeth to seize on her. Whereupon Robin Hood dispatcheth out his woodmen to hunt and take her.

ACT III.

Puck-Hairy discovereth himself in the forest and discourseth his offices, with their necessities, briefly ; after which, Douce entering in the habit of Earine, is pursued by Karol ; who (mistaking her at first to be his sister) questions her how she came by those garments. She answers, by her mother's gift. The Sad Shepherd coming in the while, she runs away affrighted, and leaves Karol suddenly; Æglamour, thinking it to be Earine's ghost he saw, falls into a melancholic expression of his phant'sie to Karol, and questions him sadly about that point, which moves compassion in Karol of his mistake still. When Clarion and Lionel enter to call Karol to Amie, Karol reports to them Æglamour's passion, with much regret. Clarion resolves to seek him. Karol to return with Lionel. By the way, Douce and her mother (in the shape of Marian) meet them, and would divert them, affirming Amie to be recovered, which Lionel wondered at to be so soon. Robin Hood enters, they tell him the relation of the witch, thinking her to be Marian ; Robin suspecting her to be Maudlin, lays hold of her girdle suddenly, but she, striving to get free, they both run out, and he returns with the belt broken. She following in her own shape, demanding it, but at a distance, as fearing to be seized upon again ; and seeing she cannot recover it, falls into a rage, and cursing, resolving to trust to her old arts, which she calls her daughter to assist in. The shepherds, content with this discovery, go home triumphing, make the relation to Marian. Amie is gladded with the sight of Karol, &c. In the mean time, enters Lorel, with purpose to ravish Earine, and calling her forth to that lewd end, he by the hearing of Clarion's footing is staid, and forced to commit her hastily to the tree again ; where Clarion coming by, and hearing a voice singing, draws near unto it ; but Æglamour hearing it also, and knowing it to be Earine's, falls into a superstitious commendation of it ; as being an angel's, and in the air ; when Clarion espies a hand put forth from the tree, and makes towards it, leaving Æglamour to his wild phant'sie, who quitteth the place: and Clarion beginning to court the hand, and make love to it, there ariseth a mist suddenly, which darkening all the place, Clarion loseth himself and the tree where Earine is enclosed, lamenting his misfortune, with the unknown nymph's misery. The air clearing, enters the witch, with her son and daughter, tells them how she had caused that late darkness, to free Lorel from surprisal, and his prey from being rescued from him: bids him look to her, and lock her up more carefully, and follow her, to assist a work she hath in hand, of recovering her lost girdle; which she laments the loss of with cursings, execrations, wishing confusion to their feast and meeting, sends her son and daughter to gather certain simples for the purpose, and bring them to her dell. This Puck hearing, prevents, and shows her error still. The huntsmen having found her footing, follow the track, and prick after her. She gets to her dell, and takes her form. Enter [the huntsmen,] Alken has spied her sitting with her spindle, threads, and images. They are eager to seize her presently, but Alken persuades them to let her begin her charms, which they do. Her son and daughter come to her; the huntsmen are affrighted as they see her work go forward. And over-hasty to apprehend her, she escapeth them all, by the help and delusions of Puck.

PERSONS OF THE PLAY.

ROBIN HOOD, *the Chief Woodman, Master of the Feast.*
FRIAR TUCK, *his Chaplain and Steward.*
LITTLE JOHN, *Bow-bearer.*
SCARLET, } *two Brothers,*
SCATHLOCK, } *Huntsmen.*
GEORGE-A-GREEN, *Huisher of the Bower.*
MUCH, *Bailiff, or Acator.*

THE GUESTS INVITED.

ÆGLAMOUR, *the* SAD,
CLARION, *the Rich,*
LIONEL, *the Courteous,* } *Shepherds.*
ALKEN, *the Sage,*
KAROLIN, *the Kind,*

LOREL, *the Rude, a Swineherd, the Witch's Son.*
PUCK-HAIRY, *or* ROBIN GOODFELLOW, *their Hind.*
REUBEN, *the Reconciler, a devout Hermit.*

MARIAN, ROBIN HOOD'S *Lady.*
EARINE, *the Beautiful,* }
MELLIFLEUR, *the Sweet,* } *Shepherdesses.*
AMIE, *the Gentle,* }
MAUDLIN, *the Envious, the Witch of Paplewick.*
DOUCE, *the Proud, her daughter.*

Musicians, Foresters, &c.

SCENE.—SHERWOOD.

PROLOGUE.

Enter The PROLOGUE.

He that hath feasted you these forty years,
And fitted fables for your finer ears,
 Although at first he scarce could hit the bore ;
Yet you, with patience, hearkening more and more,
At length have grown up to him, and made known
 The working of his pen is now your own :
He prays you would vouchsafe, for your own sake,
To hear him this once more, but sit awake.
 And though he now present you with such wool
As from mere English flocks his muse can pull,
 He hopes when it is made up into cloth,
Not the most curious head here will be loth

To wear a hood of it, it being a fleece,
To match or those of Sicily or Greece.
His scene is Sherwood, and his play a Tale
Of Robin Hood's inviting from the vale
Of Belvoir, all the Shepherds to a feast ;
Where, by the casual absence of one guest,
The mirth is troubled much, and in one man
As much of sadness shown as passion can :
The sad young shepherd, whom we here present,
Like his woes figure, dark and discontent,
      [*The Sad Shepherd passeth silently over the stage.*
For if his lost love, who in the Trent is said
To have miscarried ; 'las ! what knows the head
Of a calm river, whom the feet have drown'd ?—
Hear what his sorrows are ; and if they wound
Your gentle breasts, so that the end crown all,
Which in the scope of one day's chance may fall ;
Old Trent will send you more such tales as these,
And shall grow young again as one doth please.
      [*Exit, but instantly re-enters.*
  But here's an heresy of late let fall,
That mirth by no means fits a pastoral ;
Such say so, who can make none, he presumes :
Else there's no scene more properly assumes
The sock. For whence can sport in kind arise,
But from the rural routs and families ?
Safe on this ground, then, we not fear to-day,
To tempt your laughter by our rustic play ;
Wherein if we distaste, or be cried down,
We think we therefore shall not leave the town ;
Nor that the fore-wits that would draw the rest
Unto their liking, always like the best.
The wise and knowing critic will not say,
This worst, or better is, before he weigh
Whe'er every piece be perfect in the kind :
And then, though in themselves he difference find,
Yet if the place require it where they stood,
The equal fitting makes them equal good.
You shall have love and hate, and jealousy,
As well as mirth, and rage, and melancholy :
Or whatsoever else may either move,
Or stir affections, and your likings prove.
But that no style for pastoral should go
Current, but what is stamped with *Ah !* and *Oh !*
Who judgeth so, may singularly err ;
As if all Poesie had one character
In which what were not written, were not right ;
Or that the man who made such one poor flight,
In his whole life, had with his winged skill
Advanced him upmost on the muses' hill.
When he like poet yet remains, as those
Are painters who can only make a rose.
From such your wits redeem you, or your chance,
Lest to a greater height you do advance
Of folly, to contemn those that are known
Artificers, and trust such as are none !

ACT I.

SCENE I.—SHERWOOD FOREST.—*A distant prospect of hills, valleys, cottages, a castle, river, pastures, herds, flocks, &c.* ROBIN HOOD'S *bower in the foreground.*

Enter ÆGLAMOUR.

Æg. Here she was wont to go! and here! and here!
Just where those daisies, pinks, and violets grow:
The world may find the spring by following her,
For other print her airy steps ne'er left.
Her treading would not bend a blade of grass,
Or shake the downy blow-ball from his stalk!
But like the soft west wind she shot along,
And where she went, the flowers took thickest root,
As she had sowed them with her odorous foot. [*Exit.*

SCENE II.—*Another Part of the same.*

Enter MARIAN, Friar TUCK, JOHN, GEORGE-A-GREEN, MUCH, Woodmen, &c.

Mar. Know you, or can you guess, my merry men,
What 'tis that keeps your master, Robin Hood,
So long, both from his Marian and the wood?
 Tuck. Forsooth, madam, he will be here by noon,
And prays it of your bounty, as a boon,
That you by then have killed him venison some,
To feast his jolly friends, who hither come
In threaves to frolic with him, and make cheer:
Here's Little John hath harboured you a deer,
I see by his tackling.
 John. And a hart of ten,
I trow he be, madam, or blame your men:
For by his slot, his entries, and his port,
His frayings, fewmets, he doth promise sport,
And standing 'fore the dogs; he bears a head
Large and well-beamed, with all rights summed and spread.
 Mar. Let's rouse him quickly, and lay on the hounds.
 John. Scathlock is ready with them on the grounds;
So is his brother Scarlet: now they have found
His lair, they have him sure within the pound.
 Mar. Away then, when my Robin bids a feast,
'Twere sin in Marian to defraud a guest.
  [*Exeunt* MARIAN *and* JOHN *with the* Woodmen.
 Tuck. And I, the chaplain, here am left to be
Steward to-day, and charge you all in fee,

To d'on your liveries, see the bower drest,
And fit the fine devices for the feast:
  You, George, must care to make the baldrick trim,
And garland that must crown, or her, or him,
Whose flock this year hath brought the earliest lamb.
  George. Good Father Tuck, at your commands I am
To cut the table out o' the green sword,
Or any other service for my lord;
To carve the guests large seats; and these lain in
With turf, as soft and smooth as the mole's skin:
And hang the bulled nosegays 'bove their heads.
     *   *   *   *   *
The piper's bank, whereon to sit and play:
And a fair dial to mete out the day.
Our master's feast shall want no just delights,
His entertainments must have all the rites.
  Much. Ay, and all choice that plenty can send in;
Bread, wine, acates, fowl, feather, fish, or fin,
For which my father's nets have swept the Trent——

Enter ÆGLAMOUR.

  Æg. And have you found her?
  Much. Whom?
  Æg. My drowned love,
Earine! the sweet Earine!
The bright and beautiful Earine:
Have you not heard of my Earine?
Just by your father's mill—I think I am right—
Are not you Much the Miller's son?
  Much. I am.
  Æg. And bailiff to brave Robin Hood?
  Much. The same.
  Æg. Close by your father's mills, Earine,
Earine was drowned! Oh, my Earine!
Old Maudlin tells me so, and Douce her daughter—
Have you swept the river, say you, and not found her?
  Much. For fowl and fish, we have.
  Æg. Oh, not for her!
You are goodly friends! right charitable men!
Nay, keep your way and leave me; make your toys,
Your tales, your posies, that you talked of; all
Your entertainments: you not injure me.
Only if I may enjoy my cypress wreath,
And you will let me weep, 'tis all I ask,
Till I be turned to water, as was she?
And troth, what less suit can you grant a man?
  Tuck. His phantasie is hurt, let us now leave him;
The wound is yet too fresh to admit searching.   [*Exit.*

SCENE II.]   *THE SAD SHEPHERD.*   273

   Æg. Searching ! where should I search, or on what track ?
Can my slow drop of tears, or this dark shade
About my brows, enough describe her loss !
Earine ! oh my Earine's loss !
No, no, no, no ; this heart will break first.
   George. How will this sad disaster strike the ears
Of bounteous Robin Hood, our gentle master !
   Much. How will it mar his mirth, abate his feast ;
And strike a horror into every guest !
                                     [*Exeunt* GEORGE *and* MUCH.
   Æg. If I could knit whole clouds about my brows,
And weep like Swithin, or those watery signs,
The Kids, that rise then, and drown all the flocks
Of those rich shepherds, dwelling in this vale ;
Those careless shepherds that did let her drown !
Then I did something : or could make old Trent
Drunk with my sorrow, to start out in breaches,
To drown their herds, their cattle, and their corn ;
Break down their mills, their dams, o'erturn their weirs,
And see their houses and whole livelihood
Wrought into water with her, all were good :
I'd kiss the torrent, and those whirls of Trent,
That sucked her in, my sweet Earine !
When they have cast her body on the shore,
And it comes up as tainted as themselves,
All pale and bloodless, I will love it still,
For all that they can do, and make them mad,
To see how I will hug it in mine arms !
And hang upon her looks, dwell on her eyes,
Feed round about her lips, and eat her kisses,
Suck off her drowned flesh !—and where's their malice !
Not all their envious sousing can change that.
But I will still study some revenge past this—
                                   [*Music of all sorts is heard.*
I pray you give me leave, for I will study,
Though all the bells, pipes, tabors, timburines ring,
That you can plant about me ; I will study.

   Enter ROBIN HOOD, CLARION, MELLIFLEUR, LIONEL, AMIE,
          ALKEN, TUCK, Musicians, &c.

   Rob. Welcome, bright Clarion, and sweet Mellifleur,
The courteous Lionel, fair Amie ; all
My friends and neighbours, to the jolly bower
Of Robin Hood, and to the green-wood walks !
Now that the shearing of your sheep is done,
And the washed flocks are lighted of their wool,
The smoother ewes are ready to receive

The mounting rams again ; and both do feed,
As either promised to increase your breed
At eaning-time, and bring you lusty twins :
Why should or you or we so much forget
The season in ourselves, as not to make
Use of our youth and spirits, to awake
The nimble horn-pipe, and the timburine,
And mix our songs and dances in the wood,
And each of us cut down a triumph-bough ?—
Such are the rites the youthful June allow.

   Cla. They were, gay Robin ; but the sourer sort
Of shepherds now disclaim in all such sport :
And say, our flock the while are poorly fed,
When with such vanities the swains are led.

   Tuck. Would they, wise Clarion, were not hurried more
With covetise and rage, when to their store
They add the poor man's yeanling, and dare sell
Both fleece and carcass, not gi'ing him the fell!
When to one goat they reach that prickly weed,
Which maketh all the rest forbear to feed ;
Or strew tods' hairs, or with their tails do sweep
The dewy grass, to d'off the simpler sheep ;
Or dig deep pits their neighbour's neat to vex,
To drown the calves, and crack the heifers' necks;
Or with pretence of chasing thence the brock,
Send in a cur to worry the whole flock!

   Lio. O friar, those are faults that are not seen,
Ours open, and of worst example been.
They call ours Pagan pastimes, that infect
Our blood with ease, our youth with all neglect ;
Our tongues with wantonness, our thoughts with lust ;
And what they censure ill, all others must.

   Rob. I do not know what their sharp sight may see,
Of late, but I should think it still might be
As 'twas, an happy age, when on the plains
The woodmen met the damsels, and the swains
The neat-herds, ploughmen, and the pipers loud,
And each did dance, some to the kit or crowd,
Some to the bag-pipe ; some the tabret moved,
And all did either love, or were beloved.

   Lio. The dextrous shepherd then would try his sling,
Then dart his hook at daisies, then would sing ;
Sometimes would wrestle.

   Cla. Ay, and with a lass :
And give her a new garment on the grass :
After a course at barley-break or base.

   Lio. And all these deeds were seen without offence,
Or the least hazard of their innocence.

SCENE II.]   *THE SAD SHEPHERD.*   275

 Rob. Those charitable times had no mistrust :
Shepherds knew how to love, and not to lust.
 Cla. Each minute that we lose thus, I confess,
Deserves a censure on us, more or less ;
But that a sadder chance hath given allay
Both to the mirth and music of this day.
Our fairest shepherdess we had of late,
Here upon Trent, is drowned ; for whom her mate,
Young Æglamour, a swain who best could tread
Our country dances, and our games did lead,
Lives like the melancholy turtle, drowned
Deeper in woe than she in water : crowned
With yew and cypress, and will scarce admit
The physic of our presence to his fit.
 Lio. Sometimes he sits, and thinks all day, then walks,
Then thinks again, and sighs, weeps, laughs and talks;
And 'twixt his pleasing frenzy and sad grief,
Is so distracted, as no sought relief
By all our studies can procure his peace.
 Cla. The passion finds in him that large increase,
As we doubt hourly we shall lose him too.
 Rob. You should not cross him then, whate'er you do.
For phant'sie stopped, will soon take fire, and burn
Into an anger, or to a phrensie turn.
 Cla. Nay, so we are advised by Alken here,
A good sage shepherd, who, although he wear
An old worn hat and cloke, can tell us more
Than all the forward fry, that boast their lore.
 Lio. See, yonder comes the brother of the maid,
Young Karolin : how curious and afraid
He is at once ! willing to find him out,
And loth to offend him.

Enter KAROLIN.

 Kar. Sure he's here about.
 Cla. See where he sits.
    [*Points to* ÆGLAMOUR, *sitting upon a bank hard by.*
 Æg. It will be rare, rare, rare !
An exquisite revenge ! but peace, no words !
Not for the fairest fleece of all the flock :
If it be known afore, 'tis all worth nothing !
I'll carve it on the trees, and in the turf,
On every green sword, and in every path,
Just to the margin of the cruel Trent.
There will I knock the story in the ground,
In smooth great pebble, and moss fill it round,
Till the whole country read how she was drowned :

And with the plenty of salt tears there shed,
Quite alter the complexion of the spring.
Or I will get some old, old grandam thither,
Whose rigid foot but dipped into the water,
Shall strike that sharp and sudden cold throughout,
As it shall lose all virtue ; and those nymphs,
Those treacherous nymphs pulled in Earine,
Shall stand curled up like images of ice,
And never thaw ! mark, never ! a sharp justice !
Or stay, a better ! when the year's at hottest,
And that the dog-star foams, and the stream boils,
And curls, and works, and swells ready to sparkle,
To fling a fellow with a fever in,
To set it all on fire till it burn
Blue as Scamander, 'fore the walls of Troy,
When Vulcan leaped into him to consume him.
    Rob. A deep hurt phant'sie !   [*They approach him.*
    Æg. Do you not approve it ?
    Rob. Yes, gentle Æglamour, we all approve,
And come to gratulate your just revenge :
Which, since it is so perfect, we now hope
You'll leave all care thereof, and mix with us,
In all the proffered solace of the spring.
    Æg. A spring, now she is dead ! of what ? of thorns,
Briars and brambles ? thistles, burs and docks ?
Cold hemlock, yew ? the mandrake or the box ?
These may grow still ; but what can spring beside ?
Did not the whole earth sicken when she died ?
As if there since did fall one drop of dew,
But what was wept for her ! or any stalk
Did bear a flower, or any branch a bloom,
After her wreath was made ! In faith, in faith,
You do not fair to put these things upon me,
Which can in no sort be : Earine,
Who had her very being and her name,
With the first knots or buddings of the spring,
Born with the primrose, or the violet,
Or earliest roses blown ; when Cupid smiled ;
And Venice led the Graces out to dance,
And all the flowers and sweets in Nature's lap
Leaped out and made their solemn conjuration,
To last but while she lived ! Do not I know
How the vale withered the same day ? how Dove,
Dean, Eye, and Erwash, Idel, Snite and Soare,
Each broke his urn and twenty waters more,
That swelled proud Trent, shrunk themselves dry ? that since
No sun or moon or other cheerful star,
Looked out of heaven, but all the cope was dark,

As it were hung so for her exequies !
And not a voice or sound to ring her knell ;
But of that dismal pair, the screeching-owl,
And buzzing hornet ! Hark ! hark ! hark ! the foul
Bird ! how she flutters with her wicker wings !
Peace ! you shall hear her screech.
  Cla. Good Karolin, sing,
Help to divert this phant'sie.
    Kar. All I can.   [*Sings while* ÆG. *reads the song.*

      Though I am young and cannot tell
      Either what Death or Love is well,
      Yet, I have heard they both bear darts,
      And both do aim at human hearts :
      And then again, I have been told,
      Love wounds with heat, as Death with cold ;
      So that I fear they do but bring
      Extremes to touch, and mean one thing.

      As in a ruin we it call
      One thing to be blown up or fall ;
      Or to our end, like way may have
      By flash of lightning, or a wave :
      So Love's inflamed shaft or brand
      May-kill as soon as Death's cold hand,
      Except Love's fires the virtue have
      To fright the frost out of the grave.

  Æg. Do you think so ? are you in that good heresy,
I mean, opinion ? if you be, say nothing :
I'll study it as a new philosophy,
But by myself alone : now you shall leave me
Some of these nymphs here will reward you ; this,
This pretty maid, although but with a kiss.
            [*He forces* AMIE *to kiss* KAROLIN.
Lived my Earine, you should have twenty :
For every line here, one ; I would allow them
From mine own store, the treasure I had in her :
Now I am poor as you.   [*Exit.*
  Kar. And I a wretch !
  Cla. Yet keep an eye upon him, Karolin.   [*Exit* KAROLIN.
  Mel. Alas, that ever such a generous spirit
As Æglamour's, should sink by such a loss !
  Cla. The truest lovers are least fortunate :
Look all their lives and legends, what they call
The lovers' scriptures, Heliodores or Tatii,
Longi, Eustathii, Prodomi, you'll find it !
What think you father ?
  Alken. I have known some few,
And read of more who have had their dose, and deep,
Of these sharp bitter-sweets.
  Lio. But what is this

To jolly Robin, who the story is
Of all beatitude in love?
   Cla. And told
Here every day with wonder on the wold.
   Lio. And with fame's voice.
   Alken. Save that some folk delight
To blend all good of others with some spight.
   Cla. He and his Marian are the sum and talk
Of all that breathe here in the green-wood walk.
   Mel. Or Belvoir vale.
   Lio. The turtles of the wood.
   Cla. The billing pair.
   Alken. And so are understood
For simple loves, and sampled lives beside.
   Mel. Faith, so much virtue should not be envied.
   Alken. Better be so than pitied, Mellifleur:
For 'gainst all envy virtue is a cure;
But wretched pity ever calls on scorns.—   [*Horns within.*
The deer's brought home; I hear it by their horns.

       Enter MARIAN, JOHN *and* SCARLET.

   Rob. My Marian, and my mistress!
   Mar. My loved Robin!   [*They embrace.*
   Mel. The moon's at full, the happy pair are met.
   Mar. How hath this morning paid me for my rising!
First, with my sports; but most with meeting you.
I did not half so well reward my hounds,
As she hath me to-day; although I gave them
All the sweet morsels called tongue, ears, and dowcets!
   Rob. What, and the inch-pin!
   Mar. Yes.
   Rob. Your sports then pleased you?
   Mar. You are a wanton.
   Rob. One, I do confess,
I *want*-ed till you came: but now I have you,
I'll grow to your embraces, till two souls
Distilled into kisses through our lips,
Do make one spirit of love.   [*Kisses her.*
   Mar. O Robin, Robin!
   Rob. Breathe, breathe a while; what says my gentle Marian?
   Mar. Could you so long be absent?
   Rob. What, a week!
Was that so long?
   Mar. How long are lovers' weeks,
Do you think, Robin, when they are asunder?
Are they not prisoners' years?

Rob. To some they seem so ;
But being met again, they are schoolboys' hours.
  Mar. That have got leave to play, and so we use them.
  Rob. Had you good sport in your chase to-day ?
  John. Oh prime !
  Mar. A lusty stag.
  Rob. And hunted ye at force ?
  Mar. In a full cry.
  John. And never hunted change !
  Rob. You had stanch hounds then ?
  Mar. Old and sure ; I love
No young rash dogs, no more than changing friends.
  Rob. What relays set you ?
  John. None at all : we laid not
In one fresh dog.
  Rob. He stood not long then ?
  Scar. Yes,
Five hours and more. A great, large deer !
  Rob. What head ?
  John. Forked: a hart of ten.
  Mar. He is good venison,
According to the season in the blood,
I'll promise all your friends, for whom he fell.
  John. But at his fall there hapt a chance.
  Mar. Worth mark.
  Rob. Ay, what was that, sweet Marian ? [*Kisses her.*
  Mar. You'll not hear ?
  Rob. I love these interruptions in a story ;
                                           [*Kisses her again.*
They make it sweeter.
  Mar. You do know as soon
As the assay is taken—   [*Kisses her again.*
  Rob. On, my Marian :
I did but take the assay.
  Mar. You stop one's mouth,
And yet you bid one speak—when the arbor's made—
  Rob. Pulled down, and paunch turned out.
  Mar. He that undoes him,
Doth cleave the brisket bone, upon the spoon
Of which a little gristle grows ; you call it——
  Rob. The raven's bone.
  Mar. Now o'er head sat a raven,
On a sere bough, a grown great bird, and hoarse !
Who, all the while the deer was breaking up,
So croaked and cried for it, as all the huntsmen,
Especially old Scathlock, thought it ominous ;
Swore it was Mother Maudlin, whom he met
At the day-dawn, just as he roused the deer

Out of his lair: but we made shift to run him
Off his four legs, and sunk him ere we left.

Enter SCATHLOCK.

Is the deer come?
  Scath. He lies within on the dresser.
  Mar. Will you go see him, Mellifleur?
  Mel. I attend you.
  Mar. Come, Amie, you'll go with us?
  Amie. I am not well.
  Lio. She's sick of the young shepherd that bekissed her.
  Mar. Friend, cheer your friends up, we will eat him merrily.
                        [*Exeunt* MAR., MEL., *and* AMIE.
  Alken. Saw you the raven, friend?
  Scath. Ay, quha suld let me?
I suld be afraid o' you, sir, suld I?
  Clar. Huntsman,
A dram more of civility would not hurt you.
  Rob. Nay, you must give them all their rudenesses;
They are not else themselves without their language.
  Alken. And what do you think of her?
  Scath. As of a witch.
They call her a wise woman, but I think her
An arrant witch.
  Clar. And wherefore think you so?
  Scath. Because I saw her since broiling the bone
Was cast her at the quarry.
  Alken. Where saw you her?
  Scath. In the chimley-nuik within: she's there now.

Re-enter MARIAN.

  Rob. Marian!
Your hunt holds in his tale still; and tells more
  Mar. My hunt! what tale?
  Rob. How! cloudy, Marian!
What look is this?
  Mar. A fit one, sir, for you.
Hand off, rude ranger!—Sirrah, get you in.   [*To* SCATHLOCK.
And bear the venison hence: It is too good
For these coarse rustic mouths, that cannot open,
Or spend a thank for't. A starved mutton's carcase
Would better fit their palates. See it carried
To Mother Maudlin's, whom you call the witch, sir.
Tell her I sent it to make merry with.
She'll turn us thanks at least! why stand'st thou, groom?
  Rob. I wonder he can move, that he's not fixed,
If that his feeling be the same with mine!

I dare not trust the faith of mine own senses,
I fear mine eyes and ears : this is not Marian !
Nor am I Robin Hood ! I pray you ask her,
Ask her, good shepherds, ask her all for me :
Or rather ask yourselves, if she be she ;
Or I be I.
   Mar. Yes, and you are the spy ;
And the spied spy that watch upon my walks,
To inform what deer I kill or give away !
Where ! when ! to whom ! but spy your worst, good spy,
I will dispose of this where least you like !
Fall to your cheese-cakes, curds, and clouted cream,
Your fools, your flawns ; and [swill] of ale a stream
To wash it from your livers : strain ewe's milk
Into your cyder syllabubs, and be drunk
To him whose fleece hath brought the earliest lamb
This year; and wears the baudric at your board !
Where you may all go whistle and record
This in your dance ; and foot it lustily.   [*Exit.*
   Rob. I pray you, friends, do you hear and see as I do ?
Did the same accents strike your ears ? and objects
Your eyes, as mine ?
   Alken. We taste the same reproaches.
   Lio. Have seen the changes.
   Rob. Are not we all changed,
Transformed from ourselves ?
   Lio. I do not know.
The best is silence.
   Alken. And to wait the issue.
   Rob. The dead or lazy wait for 't ! I will find it.   [*Exeunt.*

———————————— ACT II. ————————————

SCENE I.—*The Forest as before.*—*The Witch's dimble, cottage,
oak, well, &c.*

Enter MAUDLIN *in her proper shape, and* DOUCE *in the
dress of* EARINE.

   Maud. Have I not left them in a brave confusion ?
Amazed their expectation, got their venison,
Troubled their mirth and meeting, made them doubtful
And jealous of each other, all distracted,
And, in the close, uncertain of themselves ?
This can your mother do, my dainty Douce !
Take any shape upon her, and delude

The senses best acquainted with their owners!—
The jolly Robin, who hath bid this feast,
And made this solemn invitation,
I have possessed so with syke dislikes
Of his own Marian, that allbe he know her,
As doth the vauting hart his venting hind,
He ne'er fra' hence sall neis her in the wind,
To his first liking.
    Douce. Did you so distaste him?
    Maud. As far as her proud scorning him could bate,
Or blunt the edge of any lover's temper.
    Douce. But were ye like her, mother?
    Maud. So like, Douce,
As had she seen me her sel', her sel' had doubted
Whether had been the liker of the twa—
This can your mother do, I tell you, daughter!—
I ha' but dight ye yet in the out-dress,
And 'parel of Earine; but this raiment,
These very weeds sall make ye, as but coming
In view or ken of Æglamour, your form
Shall show too slippery to be looked upon,
And all the forests swear you to be she!
They shall rin after ye, and wage the odds,
Upon their own deceived sights, ye are her;
Whilst she, poor lass, is stocked up in a tree:
Your brother Lorel's prize! for so my largess
Hath lotted her to be,—your brother's mistress,
Gif she can be reclaimed; gif not, his prey!
And here he comes new claithed, like a prince
Of swineherds! syke he seems, dight in the spoils
Of those he feeds, a mighty lord of swine!
He's command now to woo. Let's step aside,
And hear his love-craft.   [*They stand aside.*

Enter LOREL *gaily dressed, and releases* EARINE *from the oak.*

                    See he opes the door,
And takes her by the hand, and helps her forth:
This is true courtship, and becomes his ray.
    Lor. [*leading* EARINE *forward.*] Ye kind to others, but ye
        coy to me,
Deft mistress! whiter than the cheese new prest,
Smoother than cream, and softer than the curds!
Why start ye from me ere ye hear me tell
My wooing errand, and what rents I have?
Large herds and pastures! swine and kie mine own!
And though my nase be camused, my lips thick,
And my chin bristled, Pan, great Pan, was such,

Who was the chief of herdsmen, and our sire !
I am na fay, na incubus, na changlin,
But a good man, that lives o' my awn geer :
This house, these grounds, this stock is all my awn.
    Ear. How better 'twere to me, this were not known!
    Maud. She likes it not ; but it is boasted well.
    Lor. An hundred udders for the pail I have,
That give me milk and curds, that make me cheese
To cloy the markets ! twenty swarm of bees,
Whilk all the summer hum about the hive,
And bring me wax and honey in bilive.
An aged oak, the king of all the field,
With a broad beech there grows before my dur,
That mickle mast unto the ferm doth yield.
A chesnut, whilk hath larded mony a swine,
Whose skins I wear to fend me fra the cold ;
A poplar green, and with a kerved seat,
Under whose shade I solace in the heat ;
And thence can see gang out and in my neat.
Two trilland brooks, each, from his spring, doth meet,
And make a river to refresh my feet ;
In which each morning, ere the sun doth rise,
I look myself, and clear my pleasant eyes,
Before I pipe ; for therein I have skill
'Bove other swineherds. Bid me, and I will
Straight play to you, and make you melody.
    Ear. By no means. Ah ! to me all minstrelsy
Is irksome, as are you.
    Lor. Why scorn you me ?
Because I am an herdsman, and feed swine !
I am a lord of other geer :—This fine
Smooth bawson cub, the young grice of a gray,
Twa tiny urchins, and this ferret gay.
    Ear. Out on 'em ! what are these ?
    Lor. I give 'em ye,
As presents, mistress.
    Ear. Oh the fiend on thee !
Gae, take them hence ; they fewmand all the claithes,
And prick my coats : hence with 'em, limmer lown,
Thy vermin and thyself, thyself art one !
Ay, lock me up—all 's well when thou art gone.
                  [LOREL *leads her to the tree and shuts her in.*
                    [MAUDLIN *and* DOUCE *come forward.*
    Lor. Did you hear this ? she wished me at the fiend,
With all my presents !
    Maud. A tu lucky end
She wishand thee, foul limmer, dritty lown !
Gud faith, it duills me that I am thy mother :

And see, thy sister scorns thee for her brother.
Thou woo thy love, thy mistress, with twa hedgehogs :
A stinkand brock, a polecat? out, thou houlet !
Thou shouldst have given her a madge-owl, and then
Thou'dst made a present o' thyself, owl-spiegle !
   Douce. Why, mother, I have heard ye bid to give ;
And often as the cause calls.
   Maud. I know well,
It is a witty part sometimes to give ;
But what? to wham? no monsters, nor to maidens,
He suld present them with mare pleasand things,
With which his sire gat him, he's get another,
And so beget posterity upon her ;
This he should do !—False gelden, gang thy gait,
And do thy turns betimes ; or I 'se gar take
Thy new breikes fra' thee, and thy dublet tu :—
The tailleur and the sowter sall undu
All they have made, except thou manlier woo !   [*Exit* LOREL.
   Douce. Gud mother, gif you chide him, he'll do wairs.
   Maud. Hang him ! I geif him to the devil's eirs.
But ye, my Douce, I charge ye, shew your sel'
Tu all the shepherds bauldly ; gaing amang 'em,
Be mickel in their eye, frequent and fugeand :
And gif they ask ye of Earine,
Or of these claithes, say, that I gave 'em ye,
And say no more. I have that wark in hand,
That web upon the luime, shall gar 'em think
By then, they feeling their own frights and fears,
I'se pu' the world or nature 'bout their ears.—
But, hear ye, Douce, because ye may meet me
In mony shapes to-day, where'er you spy
This browdered belt with characters, 'tis I.
A Gypsan lady, and a right beldame,
Wrought it by moonshine for me, and star-light,
Upon your grannam's grave, that very night
We earthed her in the shades ; when our dame Hecate
Made it her gaing night over the kirk-yard,
With all the barkand parish-tikes set at her,
While I sat whyrland of my brazen spindle :
At every twisted thrid my rock let fly
Unto the sewster, who did sit me nigh,
Under the town turnpike ; which ran each spell
She stitched in the work, and knit it well.
See ye take tent to this, and ken your mother.   [*Exeunt.*

SCENE II.—*Another part of the Forest—The Entrance to* ROBIN HOOD'S *Bower.*

AMIE *discovered lying on a bank*, MARIAN *and* MELLIFLEUR *sitting by her.*

Mar. How do you, sweet Amie, yet?
Mel. She cannot tell;
If she could sleep, she says, she should do well.
She feels a hurt, but where, she cannot show
Any least sign, that she is hurt or no:
Her pain's not doubtful to her, but the seat
Of her pain is: her thoughts too work and beat,
Opprest with cares; but why she cannot say:
All matter of her care is quite away.
   Mar. Hath any vermin broke into your fold?
Or any rot seized on your flock, or cold?
Or hath your feighting ram burst his hard horn,
Or any ewe her fleece, or bag hath torn,
My gentle Amie?
   Amie. Marian, none of these.
   Mar. Have you been stung by wasps, or angry bees,
Or rased with some rude bramble or rough briar?
   Amie. No, Marian, my disease is somewhat nigher.
I weep, and boil away myself in tears;
And then my panting heart would dry those fears:
I burn, though all the forest lend a shade;
And freeze, though the whole wood one fire were made.
   Mar. Alas!
   Amie. I often have been torn with thorn and briar,
Both in the leg and foot, and somewhat higher;
Yet gave not then such fearful shrieks as these.   [*Sighs.*
I often have been stung too with curst bees,
Yet not remember that I then did quit
Either my company or mirth for it.   [*Sighs again.*
And therefore what it is that I feel now,
And know no cause of it, nor where, nor how
It entered in me, nor least print can see,
I feel, afflicts me more than briar or bee.   [*Again.*
How often when the sun, heaven's brightest birth,
Hath with his burning fervour cleft the earth,
Under a spreading elm or oak, hard by
A cool, clear fountain, could I sleeping lie,
Safe from the heat! but now no shady tree,
Nor purling brook, can my refreshing be.
Oft when the meadow were grown rough with frost,
The rivers ice-bound, and their currents lost,

My thick warm fleece I wore, was my defence;
Or large good fires I made, drave winter thence:
But now my whole flock's fells, nor this thick grove,
Enflamed to ashes, can my cold remove.
It is a cold and heat that does outgo
All sense of winters, and of summers so.

Enter ROBIN HOOD, CLARION, LIONEL *and* ALKEN.

 Rob. Oh, are you here, my mistress?
 Mar. I, my love!   [*Runs to embrace him.*
Where should I be but in my Robin's arms,
The sphere which I delight in so to move?
 Rob. [*he puts her back.*] What, *the rude ranger, and spied spy!*
   hand off;
You are for no such rustics.
 Mar. What means this,
Thrice worthy Clarion, or wise Alken? know ye?
 Rob. 'Las, no, not they: *a poor starved mutton's carcase*
Would better fit their palates than your venison.
 Mar. What riddle's this? Unfold yourself, dear Robin.
 Rob. You have not sent your venison hence by Scathlock,
To Mother Maudlin.
 Mar. I, to Mother Maudlin!
Will Scathlock say so?
 Rob. Nay, we will all swear so.
For all did hear it when you gave the charge so,
Both Clarion, Alken, Lionel and myself.
 Mar. Good honest shepherds, masters of your flocks,
Simple and virtuous men, no others' hirelings;
Be not you made to speak against your conscience,
That which may soil the truth. I send the venison
Away by Scathlock, and to Mother Maudlin!
I came to show it here to Mellifleur,
I do confess; but Amie's falling ill
Did put us off it: since, we employed ourselves
In comforting of her.

Enter SCATHLOCK.

Oh, here he is!
Did I, sir, bid you bear away the venison
To Mother Maudlin?
 Scath. Ay, gud faith, madam,
Did you, and I ha' done it.
 Mar. What have you done?
 Scath. Obeyed your hests, madam; done your commands.
 Mar. Done my commands, dull groom! fetch it again,
Or kennel with the hounds. Are these the arts,   [*Weeps.*

Robin, you rede your rude ones of the wood,
To countenance your quarrels and mistakings?
Or are the sports to entertain your friends
Those formed jealousies? Ask of Mellifleur
If I were ever from her, here, or Amie,
Since I came in with them; or saw this Scathlock
Since I related to you his tale of the raven.
  Scath. Ay, say you so! |*Exit.*
  Mel. She never left my side
Since I came here, nor I hers.
  Cla. This is strange:
Our best of senses were deceived, our eyes, then.
  Lio. And ears too.
  Mar. What you have concluded on,
Make good, I pray you.
  Amie. Oh, my heart, my heart!
  Mar. My heart it is wounded, pretty Amie;
Report not you your griefs: I'll tell for all.
  Mel. Somebody is to blame, there is a fault.
  Mar. Try if you can take rest: a little slumber
Will refresh you, Amie.   [AMIE *sleeps.*
  Alken. What's her grief?
  Mar. She does not know: and therein she is happy.

                Enter JOHN *and* MAUDLIN.

  John. Here's Mother Maudlin come to give you thanks,
Madam, for some late gift she hath received—
Which she s not worthy of, she says, but cracks
And wonders of it; hops about the house,
Transported with the joy.
  Maud. Send me a stag,
A whole stag, madam, and so fat a deer!
So fairly hunted, and at such a time too,
When all your friends were here!   [*Skips and dances.*
  Rob. Do you mark this, Clarion?
Her own acknowledgment!
  Maud. 'Twas such a bounty
And honour done to your poor beadswoman,
I know not how to owe it, but to thank you;
And that I come to do: I shall go round,
And giddy with the joy of the good turn.

            Look out, look out, gay folk about,
            And see me spin the ring I am in
            Of mirth and glee, with thanks for fee
            The heart puts on, for th' venison
            My lady sent, which shall be spent
            In draughts of wine, to fume up fine

Into the brain, and down again
Fall in a swoun, upon the groun'.
[Turns rapidly 'round as she speaks, till she falls.

Rob. Look to her, she is mad.
Maud. [rising.] My son hath sent you
A pot of strawberries gathered in the wood,
His hogs would else have rooted up, or trod;
With a choice dish of wildlings here to scald
And mingle with your cream.
Mar. Thank you, good Maudlin,
And then your son. Go, bear them in to Much,
The acater, let him thank her. Surely, mother,
You were mistaken, or my woodmen more,
Or most myself, to send you all our store
Of venison, hunted for ourselves this day:
You will not take it, mother, I dare say,
If we entreat you, when you know our guests;
Red deer is head still of the forest feasts.
Maud. But I knaw ye, a right free-hearted lady,
Can spare it out of superfluity:
I have departit it 'mong my poor neighbours,
To speak your largess.
Mar. I not gave it, mother;
You have done wrong then: I know how to place
My gifts, and where; and when to find my seasons
To give, not throw away my courtesies.
Maud. Count you this thrown away?
Mar. What's ravished from me
I count it worse, as stolen; I lose my thanks
But leave this quest: they fit not you nor me,
Maudlin, contentions of this quality.—

Re-enter SCATHLOCK.

How now!
Scath. Your stag's returned upon my shoulders,
He has found his way into the kitchen again
With his two legs; if now your cook can dress him.—
'Slid, I thought the swineherd would have beat me,
He looked so big! the sturdy karl, lewd Lorel!
Mar. There, Scathlock, for thy pains;—*[Gives him money.]*--
thou hast deserved it. *[Exit* SCATH
Maud. Do you give a thing, and take a thing, madam?
Mar. No, Maudlin, you had imparted to your neighbours;
And much good do it them! I have done no wrong.
Maud. The spit stand still, no broches turn
Before the fire, but let it burn
Both sides and hanches, till the whole
Converted be into one coal!

Cla. What devil's pater noster mumbles she?
Alken. Stay, you will hear more of her witchery.
Maud. The swilland dropsy enter in
    The lazy cuke, and swell his skin;
    And the old mortmal on his shin
    Now prick, and itch, withouten blin.
Cla. Speak out, hag, we may hear your devil's mattins.
Maud. The pain we call St. Anton's fire,
    The gout, or what we can desire,
    To cramp a cuke, in every limb,
    Before they dine, yet, seize on him.
Alken. A foul ill spirit hath possessed her.
Amie. [*starting.*] O Karol, Karol! call him back again.
Lio. Her thoughts do work upon her in her slumber,
And may express some part of her disease.
Rob. Observe, and mark, but trouble not her ease.
Amie. Oh, oh!
Mar. How is it, Amie?
Mel. Wherefore start you?
Amie. O Karol! he is fair and sweet.
Maud. What then?
Are there not flowers as sweet and fair as men?
The lily is fair, and rose is sweet.
Amie. Ay, so!
Let all the roses and the lilies go:
Karol is only fair to me.
Mar. And why?
Amie. Alas, for Karol, Marian, I could die!
Karol, he singeth sweetly too.
Maud. What then?
Are there not birds sing sweeter far than men?
Amie. I grant the linnet, lark, and bull-finch sing,
But best the dear good angel of the spring,
The nightingale.
Maud. Then why, then why, alone,
Should his notes please you?
Amie. I not long agone
Took a delight with wanton kids to play,
And sport with little lambs a summer's-day,
And view their frisks: methought it was a sight
Of joy to see my two brave rams to fight!
Now Karol only all delight doth move,
All that is Karol, Karol I approve!
This very morning but—I did bestow
(It was a little 'gainst my will I know)
A single kiss upon the silly swain,
And now I wish that very kiss again.
His lip is softer, sweeter than the rose,

K

His mouth and tongue with dropping honey flows;
The relish of it was a pleasing thing.
   Maud. Yet, like the bees, it had a little sting.
   Amie. And sunk and sticks yet in my marrow deep;
And what doth hurt me, I now wish to keep.
   Mar. Alas, how innocent her story is!
   Amie. I do remember, Marian, I have oft
With pleasure kist my lambs and puppies soft;
And once a dainty fine roe-fawn I had,
Of whose outskipping bounds I was as glad
As of my health; and him I oft would kiss;
Yet had his no such sting or pain as this:
They never pricked or hurt my heart; and, for
They were so blunt and dull, I wish no more.
But this, that hurts and pricks, doth please; this sweet
Mingled with sour I wish again to meet:
And that delay, methinks, most tedious is,
That keeps or hinders me of Karol's kiss.
   Mar. We'll send for him, sweet Amie, to come to you.
   Maud. But I will keep him off, if charms will do it.
                                                [*Exit muttering.*
   Cla. Do you mark the murmuring hag, how she doth mutter?
   Rob. I like her not; and less her manners now.
   Alken. She is a shrewd, deformed piece, I vow.
   Lio. As crooked as her body.
   Rob. I believe
She can take any shape, as Scathlock says.
   Alken. She may deceive the sense, but really
She cannot change herself.
   Rob. Would I could see her
Once more in Marian's form! for I am certain
Now, it was she abused us; as I think
My Marian and my love now innocent:
Which faith I seal unto her with this kiss,
And call you all to witness of my pennance.   [*Kisses* MARIAN.
   Alken. It was believed before, but now confirmed,
That we have seen the monster.

        Enter Friar TUCK, JOHN, MUCH, *and* SCARLET.

   Tuck. Hear you how
Poor Tom the cook is taken! all his joints
Do crack, as if his limbs were tied with points
His whole frame slackens; and a kind of rack
Runs down along the spondils of his back;
A gout or cramp now seizeth on his head,
Then falls into his feet; his knees are lead;
And he can stir his either hand no more
Than a dead stump, to his office, as before.

Alken. He is bewitched.
Cla. This is an argument
Both of her malice and her power, we see.
Alken. She must by some device restrained be,
Or she'll go far in mischief.
Rob. Advise how,
Sage shepherd; we shall put it straight in practice.
Alken. Send forth your woodmen then into the walks,
Or let them prick her footing hence; a witch
Is sure a creature of melancholy,
And will be found or sitting in her fourm,
Or else, at relief, like a hare.
Cla. You speak,
Alken, as if you knew the sport of witch-hunting,
Or starting of a hag.

Enter GEORGE

Rob. Go, sirs, about it,
Take George, here, with you, he can help to find her;
Leave Tuck and Much behind to dress the dinner,
In the cook's stead.
Much. We'll care to get that done.
Rob. Come, Marian, let's withdraw into the bower.

Exeunt all but JOHN, SCARLET, SCATHLOCK, *and* GEORGE

John. Rare sport, I swear, this hunting of the witch
Will make us.
Scar. Let's advise upon 't like huntsmen.
George. An we can spy her once, she is our own.
Scath. First, think which way she fourmeth, on what wind;
Or north, or south.
George. For as the shepherd said,
A witch is a kind of hare.
Scath. And marks the weather,
As the hare does.
John. Where shall we hope to find her?

Re-enter ALKEN.

Alken. I have ask'd leave to assist you, jolly huntsmen,
If an old shepherd may be heard among you;
Not jeer'd or laugh'd at.
John. Father, you will see
Robin Hood's household know more courtesy.
Scath. Who scorns at eld, peels off his own young hairs.
Alken. Ye say right well: know ye the witch's dell?
Scath. No more than I do know the walks of hell.

Alken. Within a gloomy dimble she doth dwell,
Down in a pit, o'ergrown with brakes and briars,
Close by the ruins of a shaken abbey,
Torn with an earthquake down unto the ground,
'Mongst graves and grots, near an old charnel-house,
Where you shall find her sitting in her fourm,
As fearful and melancholic as that
She is about; with caterpillar's kells,
And knotty cob-webs, rounded in with spells.
Thence she steals forth to relief in the fogs,
And rotten mists, upon the fens and bogs,
Down to the drowned lands of Lincolnshire;
To make ewes cast their lambs, swine eat their farrow,
The housewives' tun not work, nor the milk churn!
Writhe children's wrists, and suck their breath in sleep,
Get vials of their blood! and where the sea
Casts up his slimy ooze, search for a weed
To open locks with, and to rivet charms,
Planted about her in the wicked feat
Of all her mischiefs, which are manifold.
  John. I wonder such a story could be told
Of her dire deeds.
  George. I thought a witch's banks
Had inclosed nothing but the merry pranks
Of some old woman.
  Scar. Yes, her malice more.
  Scath. As it would quickly appear had we the store
Of his collects.
  George. Ay, this gud learned man
Can speak her right.
  Scar. He knows her shifts and haunts.
  Alken. And all her wiles and turns. The venom'd plants
Wherewith she kills! where the sad mandrake grows,
Whose groans are dreadful; the dead-numbing night-shade,
The stupifying hemlock, adder's tongue,
And martagan: the shrieks of luckless owls
We hear, and croaking night-crows in the air!
Green-bellied snakes, blue fire-drakes in the sky,
And giddy flitter-mice, with leather wings!
The scaly beetles, with their habergeons,
That make a humming murmur as they fly!
There in the stocks of trees, white faies do dwell,
And span-long elves that dance about a pool,
With each a little changeling in their arms!
The airy spirits play with falling stars,
And mount the sphere of fire to kiss the moon!
While she sits reading by the glow-worm's light,
Or rotten wood, o'er which the worm hath crept,

The baneful schedule of her nocent charms,
And binding characters, through which she wounds
Her puppets, the sigilla of her witchcraft.
All this I know, and I will find her for you;
And show you her sitting in her fourm; I'll lay
My hand upon her, make her throw her skut
Along her back, when she doth start before us.
But you must give her law: and you shall see her
Make twenty leaps and doubles; cross the paths,
And then squat down beside us.

John. Crafty croan!
I long to be at the sport, and to report it.

Scar. We'll make this hunting of the witch as famous
As any other blast of venery.

Scath. Hang her, foul hag! she'll be a stinking chase.
I had rather ha' the hunting of her heir.

George. If we should come to see her cry, "So ho!" once.

Alken. That I do promise, or I am no good hag-finder.

[*Exeunt.*

ACT III.

SCENE I.—*The Forest.*

Enter PUCK-HAIRY.

Puck. The fiend hath much to do, that keeps a school,
Or is the father of a family;
Or governs but a country academy:
His labours must be great, as are his cares,
To watch all turns, and cast how to prevent them.
This dame of mine here, Maud, grows high in evil,
And thinks she does all, when 't is I, her devil,
That both delude her, and must yet protect her.
She's confident in mischief, and presumes
The changing of her shape will still secure her;
But that may fail, and divers hazards meet
Of other consequence, which I must look to,
Not let her be surprised on the first catch.
I must go dance about the forest now,
And firk it like a goblin, till I find her.
Then will my service come worth acceptation,
When not expected of her; when the help
Meets the necessity, and both do kiss,
'Tis call'd the timing of a duty, this.

[*Exit.*

SCENE II.—*Another Part of the same.*

Enter KAROL., *and* DOUCE *in the dress of* EARINE.

Kar. Sure, you are very like her! I conceived
You had been she, seeing you run afore me:
For such a suit she made her 'gainst this feast,
In all resemblance, or the very same;
I saw her in it; had she lived to enjoy it,
She had been there an acceptable guest
To Marian, and the gentle Robin Hood,
Who are the crown and ghirland of the wood.
   Douce. I cannot tell, my mother gave it me,
And bade me wear it.
   Kar. Who, the wise good woman,
Old Maud of Paplewick?

Enter ÆGLAMOUR.

   Douce. Yes;—this sullen man
I cannot like him. I must take my leave.   [*Exit.*
   Æg. What said she to you?
   Kar. Who?
   Æg. Earine.
I saw her talking with you, or her ghost;
For she indeed is drowned in old Trent's bottom
Did she not tell who would have pulled her in,
And had her maidenhead upon the place,
The river's brim, the margin of the flood?
No ground is holy enough (you know my meaning),
Lust is committed in king's palaces,
And yet their majesties not violated!   [*Exit.*
No words!
   Kar. How sad and wild his thoughts are!—gone?

Re-enter ÆGLAMOUR.

   Æg. But she, as chaste as was her name, Earine,
Died undeflowered: and now her sweet soul hovers
Here in the air above us, and doth haste
To get up to the moon and Mercury;
And whisper Venus in her orb; then spring
Up to old Saturn, and come down by Mars,
Consulting Jupiter, and seat herself
Just in the midst with Phœbus, tempering all
The jarring spheres, and giving to the world
Again his first and tuneful planetting.
Oh what an age will here be of new concords!

Delightful harmony! to rock old sages,
Twice infants, in the cradle of speculation,
And throw a silence upon all the creatures! [*Exit*.
   Kar. A cogitation of the highest rapture!

Re-enter ÆGLAMOUR.

   Æg. The loudest seas and most enraged winds
Shall lose their clangor; tempest shall grow hoarse,
Loud thunder dumb, and every speece of storm
Laid in the lap of listening Nature, hushed
To hear the changed chime of this eighth sphere.
Take tent, and hearken for it, lose it not. [*Exit*.

Enter CLARION *and* LIONEL.

   Cla. Oh, here is Karol! Was not that the Sad
Shepherd slipped from him?
   Lio. Yes, I guess it was.
Who was that left you, Karol?
   Kar. The lost man;
Whom we shall never see himself again,
Or ours, I fear; he starts away from hand so,
And all the touches or soft strokes of reason
You can apply! no colt is so unbroken,
Or hawk yet half so haggard or unmanned!
He takes all toys that his wild phant'sie proffers,
And flies away with them: he now conceives
That my lost sister, his Earine,
Is lately turned a sphere amid the seven;
And reads a music-lecture to the planets!
And with this thought he's run to call 'em hearers.
   Cla. Alas, this is a strained but innocent phant'sie!
I'll follow him, and find him if I can:
Meantime, go you with Lionel, sweet Karol;
He will acquaint you with an accident,
Which much desires your presence on the place. [*Exit*.
   Kar. What is it, Lionel, wherein I may serve you?
Why do you so survey and circumscribe me,
As if you struck one eye into my breast,
And with the other took my whole dimensions?
   Lio. I wish you had a window in your bosom,
Or in your back, I might look thorough you,
And see your in-parts, Karol, liver, heart;
For there the seat of Love is: whence the boy,
The winged archer, hath shot home a shaft
Into my sister's breast, the innocent Amie,
Who now cries out, upon her bed, on Karol.

Sweet-singing Karol, the delicious Karol,
That kissed her like a Cupid! In your eyes,
She says, his stand is, and between your lips
He runs forth his divisions to her ears,
But will not 'bide there, 'less yourself do bring him.
Go with me, Karol, and bestow a visit
In charity upon the afflicted maid,
Who pineth with the languor of your love.
    [*As they are going out, enter* MAUDLIN (*in the shape of* MARIAN) *and* DOUCE.

Maud. Whither intend you? Amie is recovered,
Feels no such grief as she complained of lately.
This maiden hath been with her from her mother
Maudlin, the cunning woman, who hath sent her
Herbs for her head, and simples of that nature,
Have wrought upon her a miraculous cure;
Settled her brain to all our wish and wonder.

Lio. So instantly! you know I now but left her,
Possess'd with such a fit almost to a phrensie:
Yourself too feared her, Marian, and did urge
My haste to seek out Karol, and to bring him.

Maud. I did so: but the skill of that wise woman,
And her great charity of doing good,
Hath by the ready hand of this deft lass,
Her daughter, wrought effects beyond belief,
And to astonishment; we can but thank,
And praise, and be amazed, while we tell it. [*Exit with* DOUCE.

Lio. 'Tis strange, that any art should so help nature
In her extremes.

Kar. Then it appears most real,
When the other is deficient.

    Enter ROBIN HOOD.

Rob. Wherefore stay you
Discoursing here, and haste not with your succours
To poor afflicted Amie, that so needs them?

Lio. She is recovered well, your Marian told us
But now here:
    Re-enter MAUDLIN *as before.*
    See, she is returned to affirm it

Rob. My Marian!

Maud. Robin Hood! is he here?   [*Attempts to run out.*

Rob. Stay;
What was't you told my friend?
    [*He seizes* MAUD. *by the girdle, and runs out with her, but returns immediately with the broken girdle in his hand, followed at a distance by the witch, in her own shape.*

Maud. Help, murder, help!
You will not rob me, outlaw? thief, restore
My belt that ye have broken!
    Rob. Yes, come near.
    Maud. Not in your gripe.
    Rob. Was this the charmed circle,
The copy that so cozened and deceived us?
I'll carry hence the trophy of your spoils:
My men shall hunt you too upon the start,
And course you soundly.
    Maud. I shall make them sport,
And send some home without their legs or arms.
I'll teach them to climb stiles, leap ditches, ponds,
And lie in the waters, if they follow me.
    Rob. Out, murmuring hag.   [*Exeunt all but* MAUD.
    Maud. I must use all my powers,
Lay all my wits to piecing of this loss.
Things run unluckily: where's my Puck-Hairy?
Hath he forsook me?

              Enter PUCK-HAIRY.

    Puck. At your beck, madam.
    Maud. O Puck, my goblin! I have lost my belt,
The strong thief, Robin Outlaw, forced it from me.
    Puck. They are other clouds and blacker threat you, dame;
You must be wary, and pull in your sails,
And yield unto the weather of the tempest.
You think your power's infinite as your malice,
And would do all your anger prompts you to;
But you must wait occasions, and obey them:
Sail in an egg-shell, make a straw your mast,
A cobweb all your cloth, and pass unseen,
Till you have 'scaped the rocks that are about you.
    Maud. What rocks about me?
    Puck. I do love, madam,
To show you all your dangers,—when you're past them!
Come, follow me, I'll once more be your pilot,
And you shall thank me.   [*Exit.*
    Maud. Lucky, my loved goblin!
              [*As she is going out,* LOREL *meets her.*
Where are you going now?
    Lor. Unto my tree,
To see my mistress.
    Maud. Gang thy gait, and try
Thy turns with better luck, or hang thyself.—

POEMS.

CONTENTS.

	PAGE
SONG TO CELIA	301
THE TRIUMPH OF CHARIS	301
IN THE PERSON OF WOMANKIND	302
MY PICTURE, LEFT IN SCOTLAND	303
TO THE MEMORY OF MY BELOVED MASTER, WILLIAM SHAKESPEARE	303
EPITAPH ON THE COUNTESS OF PEMBROKE	305
AN ELEGY	305
A PINDARIC ODE	306
AN EPITAPH ON SALATHIEL PAVY	310
EPITAPH ON ELIZABETH, L.H.	310
SONG	311
ODE TO SIR WILLIAM SIDNEY ON HIS BIRTHDAY	311
BEN JONSON'S ODE TO HIMSELF UPON THE CENSURE OF HIS "NEW INN"	313
ON SOMETHING, THAT WALKS SOMEWHERE	314
TO WILLIAM CAMDEN	314
ON MY FIRST DAUGHTER	315
ON MY FIRST SON	315
TO THOMAS LORD CHANCELLOR EGERTON	316
OF LIFE AND DEATH	316
INVITING A FRIEND TO SUPPER	316
A HYMN TO GOD THE FATHER	317
LEGES CONVIVIALES	318

POEMS.

SONG TO CELIA.

DRINK to me only with thine eyes,
   And I will pledge with mine;
Or leave a kiss but in the cup,
   And I'll not look for wine.
The thirst, that from the soul doth rise,
   Doth ask a drink divine:
But might I of Jove's nectar sup,
   I would not change for thine.

I sent thee late a rosy wreath,
   Not so much honouring thee
As giving it a hope, that there
   It could not wither'd be.
But thou thereon didst only breathe,
   And sent'st it back to me:
Since when it grows, and smells, I swear,
   Not of itself, but thee.

THE TRIUMPH OF CHARIS.

SEE the chariot at hand here of Love,
   Wherein my Lady rideth!
Each that draws is a swan or a dove,
   And well the car Love guideth.
As she goes, all hearts do duty
            Unto her beauty;
And enamour'd, do wish, so they might
            But enjoy such a sight,
That they still were to run by her side,
Through swords, through seas, whither she would ride.

Do but look on her eyes, they do light
   All that Love's world compriseth !
Do but look on her hair, it is bright
   As Love's star when it riseth !
Do but mark, her forehead's smoother
          Than words that soothe her :
And from her arched brows, such a grace
          Sheds itself through the face,
As alone there triumphs to the life
All the gain, all the good of the elements' strife.

Have you seen but a bright lily grow,
   Before rude hands have touched it ?
Have you marked but the fall of the snow
   Before the soil hath smutched it ?
Have you felt the wool of the beaver ?
          Or swan's down ever ?
Or have smelt o' the bud of the briar ?
          Or the nard in the fire ?
Or have tasted the bag of the bee ?
Oh so white ! Oh so soft ! Oh so sweet is she !

IN THE PERSON OF WOMANKIND.

A SONG APOLOGETIC.

MEN, if you love us, play no more
   The fools or tyrants with your friends,
To make us still sing o'er and o'er
   Our own false praises, for your ends :
     We have both wits and fancies too,
     And if we must, let's sing of you.

Nor do we doubt, but that we can,
   If we would search with care and pain,
Find some one good, in some one man ;
   So going thorough all your strain,
     We shall at last, of parcels make
     One good enough for a song's sake.

And as a cunning painter takes
   In any curious piece you see,
More pleasure while the thing he makes,
   Than when 'tis made ; why, so will we.
     And having pleased our art, we'll try
     To make a new, and hang that by.

MY PICTURE, LEFT IN SCOTLAND.

I NOW think, Love is rather deaf than blind,
   For else it could not be,
            That she,
Whom I adore so much, should so slight me,
And cast my suit behind :
I'm sure my language to her was as sweet,
    And every close did meet
      In sentence of as subtle feet,
    As hath the youngest he,
      That sits in shadow of Apollo's tree.
Oh ! but my conscious fears,
    That fly my thoughts between,
Tell me that she hath seen
    My hundreds of gray hairs,
      Told seven and forty years,
Read so much waste, as she cannot embrace
My mountain belly, and my rocky face,
And all these, through her eyes, have stopt her ears.

TO THE MEMORY OF MY BELOVED MASTER,
WILLIAM SHAKESPEARE.

To draw no envy, SHAKESPEARE, on thy name,
Am I thus ample to thy book and fame ;
While I confess thy writings to be such,
As neither man, nor Muse, can praise too much.
'Tis true, and all men's suffrage. But these ways
Were not the paths I meant unto thy praise ;
For silliest ignorance on these may light,
Which, when it sounds at best, but echoes right ;
Or blind affection, which doth ne'er advance
The truth, but gropes, and urgeth all by chance ;
Or crafty malice might pretend this praise,
And think to ruin, where it seemed to raise.
These are, as some infamous bawd or whore,
Should praise a matron ; what could hurt her more ?
But thou art proof against them, and, indeed,
Above the ill fortune of them, or the need.
I therefore will begin : Soul of the age !
The applause ! delight ! the wonder of our stage !
My SHAKESPEARE rise ! I will not lodge thee by
Chaucer, or Spenser, or bid Beaumont lie

A little further off, to make thee room :
Thou art a monument without a tomb,
And art alive still, while thy book doth live,
And we have wits to read and praise to give.
That I not mix thee so, my brain excuses,
I mean with great, but disproportioned Muses :
For if I thought my judgment were of years,
I should commit thee surely with thy peers,
And tell how far thou didst our Lily outshine,
Or sporting Kyd, or Marlow's mighty line.
And though thou hadst small Latin and less Greek,
From thence to honour thee, I will not seek
For names : but call forth thundering Æschylus,
Euripides, and Sophocles to us.
Pacuvius, Accius, him of Cordoua dead,
To live again, to hear thy buskin tread,
And shake a stage : or when thy socks were on,
Leave thee alone for the comparison
Of all, that insolent Greece, or haughty Rome
Sent forth, or since did from their ashes come.
Triumph, my Britain, thou hast one to show,
To whom all scenes of Europe homage owe.
He was not of an age, but for all time !
And all the Muses still were in their prime,
When, like Apollo, he came forth to warm
Our ears, or like a Mercury to charm !
Nature herself was proud of his designs,
And joyed to wear the dressing of his lines !
Which were so richly spun, and woven so fit,
As, since, she will vouchsafe no other wit.
The merry Greek, tart Aristophanes,
Neat Terence, witty Plautus, now not please ;
But antiquated and deserted lie,
As they were not of nature's family.
Yet must I not give nature all ; thy art,
My gentle Shakespeare, must enjoy a part.
For though the poet's matter nature be,
His art doth give the fashion : and, that he
Who casts to write a living line, must sweat,
(Such as thine are) and strike the second heat
Upon the Muses' anvil ; turn the same,
And himself with it, that he thinks to fame ;
Or for the laurel, he may gain a scorn ;
For a good poet's made, as well as born.
And such wert thou ! Look how the father's face
Lives in his issue, even so the race
Of Shakespeare's mind and manners brightly shines
In his well turnéd, and true filéd lines ;

In each of which he seems to shake a lance,
As brandished at the eyes of ignorance.
Sweet Swan of Avon! what a sight it were
To see thee in our water yet appear,
And make those flights upon the banks of Thames,
That so did take Eliza, and our James!
But stay, I see thee in the hemisphere
Advanced, and made a constellation there!
Shine forth, thou Star of poets, and with rage,
Or influence, chide, or cheer the drooping stage,
Which, since thy flight from hence, hath mourned like night,
And despairs day, but for thy volume's light.

EPITAPH ON THE COUNTESS OF PEMBROKE.

UNDERNEATH this sable herse
Lies the subject of all verse,
SIDNEY'S sister, PEMBROKE'S mother;
Death! ere thou hast slain another,
Learned and fair, and good as she,
Time shall throw a dart at thee.

AN ELEGY.

THOUGH beauty be the mark of praise,
  And yours of whom I sing, be such,
  As not the world can praise too much,
Yet 'tis your virtue now I raise.

A virtue, like allay, so gone
  Throughout your form; as though that move,
  And draw, and conquer all men's love,
This subjects you to love of one,

Wherein you triumph yet; because
  'Tis of yourself, and that you use
  The noblest freedom, not to choose
Against or faith, or honour's laws.

But who could less expect from you,
  In whom alone Love lives agen?
  By whom he is restored to men;
And kept, and bred, and brought up true?

His falling temples you have reared,
   The withered garlands ta'en away;
   His altars kept from the decay
That envy wished and nature feared:

And on them burn so chaste a flame,
   With so much loyalty's expense,
   As Love t' acquit such excellence,
Is gone himself into your name.

And you are he; the deity
   To whom all lovers are designed,
   That would their better objects find;
Among which faithful troop am I.

Who, as an offering at your shrine,
   Have sung this hymn, and here entreat
   One spark of your diviner heat
To light upon a love of mine.

Which, if it kindle not, but scant
   Appear, and that to shortest view,
   Yet give me leave t' adore in you
What I, in her, am grieved to want.

A PINDARIC ODE

*To the immortal memory and friendship of that noble pair,
Sir Lucius Cary and Sir H. Morison.*

I.

THE STROPHE, OR TURN.

BRAVE infant of Saguntum, clear
   Thy coming forth in that great year,
When the prodigious Hannibal did crown
His rage, with razing your immortal town.
      Thou looking then about,
      Ere thou wert half got out,
   Wise child, didst hastily return,
   And mad'st thy mother's womb thine urn.
How summ'd a circle didst thou leave mankind
Of deepest lore, could we the centre find!

THE ANTISTROPHE, OR COUNTER-TURN.

Did wiser nature draw thee back,
   From out the horror of that sack;
Where shame, faith, honour, and regard of right,
Lay trampled on? the deeds of death and night

　　　　Urged, hurried forth, and hurl'd
　　　　　Upon the affrighted world;
　　　Fire, famine, and fell fury met,
　　　　And all on utmost ruin set:
　　As, could they but life's miseries foresee,
　　No doubt all infants would return like thee.

　　　　　　THE EPODE, OR STAND.

For what is life, if measured by the space,
　　　　　　Not by the act?
Or maskéd man, if valued by his face,
　　　　　　Above his fact?
　　　　Here's one outlived his peers,
　　　　And told forth fourscore years:
　　He vexéd time, and busied the whole state;
　　　　Troubled both foes and friends;
　　　　But ever to no ends:
What did this stirrer but die late?
How well at twenty had he fallen or stood!
For three of his fourscore he did no good.

　　　　　　　　II.

　　　　　　THE STROPHE, OR TURN.

　　He entered well by virtuous parts,
　　　Got up, and thrived with honest arts,
He purchased friends, and fame, and honours then
And had his noble name advanced with men:
　　　　But weary of that flight,
　　　　He stooped in all men's sight
　　To sordid flatteries, acts of strife,
　　And sunk in that dead sea of life,
So deep, as he did then death's waters sup,
But that the cork of title buoyed him up.

　　　　　THE ANTISTROPHE, OR COUNTER-TURN

　　Alas! but MORISON fell young:
　　　He never fell,—thou fall'st, my tongue.
He stood a soldier to the last right end,
A perfect patriot and a noble friend;
　　　　But most, a virtuous son.
　　　　All offices were done
　　By him, so ample, full, and round,
　　　In weight, in measure, number, sound,
As, though his age imperfect might appear,
His life was of humanity the sphere.

THE EPODE, OR STAND.

  Go now, and tell our days summed up with fears,
    And make them years;
  Produce thy mass of miseries on the stage,
    To swell thine age:
    Repeat of things a throng,
    To show thou hast been long,
  Not lived; for life doth her great actions spell,
    By what was done and wrought
    In season, and so brought
  To light: her measures are, how well
Each syllabe answered, and was formed, how fair;
These make the lines of life, and that's her air!

III.

THE STROPHE, OR TURN.

   It is not growing like a tree
   In bulk, doth make men better be;
  Or standing long an oak, three hundred year,
  To fall a log at last, dry, bald, and sear:
    A lily of a day,
    Is fairer far, in May,
  Although it fall and die that night;
  It was the plant and flower of light.
In small proportions we just beauties see;
And in short measures, life may perfect be.

THE ANTISTROPHE, OR COUNTER-TURN.

  Call, noble LUCIUS, then, for wine,
  And let thy locks with gladness shine:
  Accept this Garland, plant it on thy head,
  And think, nay know, thy MORISON's not dead.
    He leaped the present age,
    Possest with holy rage,
  To see that bright eternal day;
  Of which we priests and poets say
Such truths, as we expect for happy men:
And there, he lives with memory, and BEN.

THE EPODE, OR STAND.

  JONSON, who sung this of him, ere he went,
    Himself, to rest,
  Or taste a part of that full joy he meant
    To have exprest,

In this bright asterism!—
Where it were friendship's schism,
Were not his Lucius long with us to tarry,
    To separate these twi-
    Lights, the Dioscuri;
And keep the one half from his Harry.
But fate doth so alternate the design,
Whilst that in heaven, this light on earth must shine,—

IV.

THE STROPHE, OR TURN.

And shine as you exalted are;
Two names of friendship, but one star:
Of hearts the union, and those not by chance
Made, or indenture, or leased out t' advance
    The profits for a time.
    No pleasures vain did chime,
Of rhymes, or riots, at your feasts,
Orgies of drink, or feigned protests:
But simple love of greatness and of good:
That knits brave minds and manners more than blood.

THE ANTISTROPHE, OR COUNTER-TURN.

This made you first to know the why
You liked, then after, to apply
That liking; and approach so one the t' other,
Till either grew a portion of the other;
    Each styled by his end,
    The copy of his friend.
You lived to be the great sir-names,
And titles, by which all made claims
Unto the Virtue: nothing perfect done,
But as a CARY or a MORISON.

THE EPODE, OR STAND.

And such a force the fair example had,
    As they that saw
The good, and durst not practise it, were glad
    That such a law
    Was left yet to mankind;
    Where they might read and find
Friendship, indeed, was written not in words;
    And with the heart, not pen,
    Of two so early men
Whose lines her rolls were, and records:
Who, ere the first down bloomèd on the chin,
Had sowed these fruits, and got the harvest in.

AN EPITAPH ON SALATHIEL PAVY.

WEEP with me, all you that read
    This little story:
And know, for whom a tear you shed
    Death's self is sorry.
'Twas a child that so did thrive
    In grace and feature,
As heaven and nature seem'd to strive
    Which owned the creature.
Years he numbered scarce thirteen
    When fates turned cruel,
Yet three filled zodiacs had he been
    The stage's jewel;
And did act, what now we moan,
    Old men so duly,
As, sooth, the Parcæ thought him one,
    He played so truly.
So, by error to his fate,
    They all consented;
But viewing him since, alas, too late!
    They have repented;
And have sought, to give new birth,
    In baths to steep him;
But being so much too good for earth,
    Heaven vows to keep him.

EPITAPH ON ELIZABETH, L. H.

WOULD'ST thou hear what man can say
In a little? reader, stay.

    Underneath this stone doth lie
As much beauty as could die:
Which in life did harbour give
To more virtue than doth live.

    If at all she had a fault,
Leave it buried in this vault.
One name was ELIZABETH,
The other let it sleep with death:
Fitter, where it died, to tell,
Than that it lived at all. Farewell!

SONG.

THAT WOMEN ARE BUT MEN'S SHADOWS.

FOLLOW a shadow, it still flies you,
   Seem to fly it, it will pursue :
So court a mistress, she denies you ;
   Let her alone, she will court you.
Say are not women truly, then,
Styled but the shadows of us men?

At morn and even shades are longest ;
   At noon they are or short or none :
So men at weakest, they are strongest,
   But grant us perfect, they 're not known.
Say are not women truly, then,
Styled but the shadows of us men?

ODE TO SIR WILLIAM SIDNEY ON HIS BIRTH-DAY.

NOW that the hearth is crowned with smiling fire,
   And some do drink, and some do dance,
         Some ring,
         Some sing,
   And all do strive to advance
The gladness higher ;
         Wherefore should I
         Stand silent by,
         Who not the least,
Both love the cause, and authors of the feast?

Give me my cup, but from the Thespian well,
   That I may tell to SIDNEY what
         This day
         Doth say,
   And he may think on that
Which I do tell ;
         When all the noise
         Of these forced joys,
         Are fled and gone,
And he with his best Genius left alone.

This day says, then, the number of glad years
  Are justly summed, that make you man ;
        Your vow
        Must now
  Strive all right ways it can,
T' outstrip your peers :
        Since he doth lack
        Of going back
        Little, whose will
Doth urge him to run wrong, or to stand still.

Nor can a little of the common store
  Of nobles' virtue, show in you ;
        Your blood
        So good
  And great, must seek for new,
And study more :
        Nor weary, rest
        On what 's deceas't.
        For they, that swell
With dust of ancestors, in graves but dwell.

'Twill be exacted of your name, whose son,
  Whose nephew, whose grandchild you are ;
        And men
        Will then
  Say you have followed far,
When well begun :
        Which must be now,
        They teach you how,
        And he that stays
To live until to morrow, hath lost two days.

So may you live in honour, as in name,
  If with this truth you be inspired ;
        So may
        This day
  Be more and long desired ;
And with the flame
        Of love be bright,
        As with the light
        Of bonfires ! then
The birth-day shines, when logs not burn, but men.

BEN JONSON'S ODE TO HIMSELF UPON THE CENSURE OF HIS "NEW INN."

JANUARY, 1630.

Come, leave the loathéd stage,
And the more loathsome age;
Where pride and impudence, in faction knit,
Usurp the chair of wit!
Indicting and arraigning every day
Something they call a play.
Let their fastidious, vain
Commission of the brain
Run on and rage, sweat, censure and condemn;
They were not made for thee, less thou for them.

Say that thou pour'st them wheat,
And they will acorns eat;
'Twere simple fury still thyself to waste
On such as have no taste!
To offer them a surfeit of pure bread,
Whose appetites are dead!
No, give them grains their fill,
Husks, draff to drink and swill:
If they love lees, and leave the lusty wine,
Envy them not, their palate's with the swine.

No doubt some mouldy tale,
Like Pericles and stale
As the shrieve's crusts, and nasty as his fish—
Scraps, out of every dish
Thrown forth, and raked into the common tub,
May keep up the Play-club:
There, sweepings do as well
As the best-ordered meal;
For who the relish of these guests will fit,
Needs set them but the alms-basket of wit.

And much good do't to you then:
Brave plush and velvet-men,
Can feed on orts; and, safe in your stage-clothes,
Dare quit, upon your oaths,
The stagers and the stage-wrights too, your peers,
Of larding your large ears

       With their foul comic socks,
       Wrought upon twenty blocks;
Which if they are torn, and turned, and patched enough,
The gamesters share your gilt, and you their stuff.

       Leave things so prostitute,
       And take the Alcaic lute,
Or thine own Horace, or Anacreon's lyre;
       Warm thee by Pindar's fire:
And though thy nerves be shrunk, and blood be cold
       Ere years have made thee old,
       Strike that disdainful heat
       Throughout, to their defeat,
As curious fools, and envious of thy strain,
May, blushing, swear no palsy's in thy brain.

       But when they hear thee sing.
       The glories of thy king,
His zeal to God, and his just awe o'er men,
       They may, blood-shaken then,
Feel such a flesh-quake to possess their powers
       As they shall cry, "Like ours,
       In sound of peace or wars,
       No harp e'er hit the stars,
In tuning forth the acts of his sweet reign;
And raising Charles his chariot 'bove his wain."

ON SOMETHING, THAT WALKS SOMEWHERE.

At Court I met it, in clothes brave enough,
To be a courtier; and looks grave enough,
To seem a statesman: as I near it came,
It made me a great face; I asked the name
A Lord, it cried, buried in flesh and blood,
And such from whom let no man hope least good,
For I will do none; and as little ill,
For I will dare none: Good Lord, walk dead still.

TO WILLIAM CAMDEN.

Camden! most reverend head, to whom I owe
All that I am in arts, all that I know;
(How nothing's that?) to whom my country owes
The great renown, and name wherewith she goes!

Than thee the age sees not that thing more grave,
More high, more holy, that she more would crave.
What name, what skill, what faith hast thou in things!
What sight in searching the most antique springs!
What weight, and what authority in thy speech!
Men scarce can make that doubt, but thou canst teach.
Pardon free truth, and let thy modesty,
Which conquers all, be once o'ercome by thee.
Many of thine, this better could, than I;
But for their powers, accept my piety.

ON MY FIRST DAUGHTER.

HERE lies, to each her parents ruth,
Mary, the daughter of their youth;
Yet all heaven's gifts being heaven's due,
It makes the father less to rue.
At six months end she parted hence
With safety of her innocence;
Whose soul heaven's Queen, whose name she bears,
In comfort of her mother's tears,
Hath placed amongst her virgin-train:
Where while that, severed, doth remain,
This grave partakes the fleshly birth;
Which cover lightly, gentle earth!

ON MY FIRST SON.

FAREWELL, thou child of my right hand, and joy;
My sin was too much hope of thee, lov'd boy:
Seven years thou wert lent to me, and I thee pay,
Exacted by thy fate, on the just day.
Oh, could I lose all father, now! for why,
Will man lament the state he should envy?
To have so soon 'scaped world's, and flesh's rage,
And, if no other misery, yet age!
Rest in soft peace, and ask'd, say here doth lie
BEN JONSON his best piece of poetry:
For whose sake henceforth all his vows be such,
As what he loves may never like too much.

TO THOMAS LORD CHANCELLOR EGERTON.

WHILST thy weighed judgments, EGERTON, I hear,
And know thee then a judge, not of one year;
Whilst I behold thee live with purest hands;
That no affection in thy voice commands;
That still thou 'rt present to the better cause;
And no less wise than skilful in the laws;
Whilst thou art certain to thy words, once gone,
As is thy conscience, which is always one :
The Virgin, long since fled from earth, I see,
To our times returned, hath made her heaven in thee.

OF LIFE AND DEATH.

THE ports of death are sins ; of life, good deeds;
Through which our merit leads us to our meeds.
How wilful blind is he, then, that would stray,
And hath it in his powers to make his way !
This world death's region is, the other life's;
And here, it should be one of our first strifes,
So to front death, as men might judge us past it :
For good men but see death, the wicked taste it.

INVITING A FRIEND TO SUPPER.

TO-NIGHT, grave sir, both my poor house and I
Do equally desire your company :
Not that we think us worthy such a guest,
But that your worth will dignify our feast,
With those that come ; whose grace may make that seem
Something, which else would hope for no esteem.
It is the fair acceptance, sir, creates
The entertainment perfect, not the cates.
Yet shall you have, to rectify your palate,
An olive, capers, or some better sallet
Ushering the mutton : with a short-legged hen,
If we can get her full of eggs, and then
Lemons and wine for sauce : to these, a coney
Is not to be despaired of for our money ;
And though fowl now be scarce, yet there are clerks,
The sky not falling, think we may have larks.

I'll tell you of more, and lie, so you will come:
Of partridge, pheasant, woodcock, of which some
May yet be there; and god-wit if we can;
Knat, rail, and ruff too. Howsoe'er, my man
Shall read a piece of Virgil, Tacitus,
Livy, or of some better book to us,
Of which we'll speak our minds, amidst our meat;
And I'll profess no verses to repeat:
To this if aught appear, which I not know of,
That will the pastry, not my paper, show of.
Digestive cheese, and fruit there sure will be;
But that which most doth take my muse and me
Is a pure cup of rich Canary wine,
Which is the Mermaid's now, but shall be mine:
Of which had Horace or Anacreon tasted,
Their lives, as do their lines, till now had lasted.
Tobacco, nectar, or the Thespian spring,
Are all but Luther's beer, to this I sing.
Of this we will sup free, but moderately,
And we will have no Pooly, or Parrot by;
Nor shall our cups make any guilty men:
But at our parting, we will be, as when
We innocently met. No simple word,
That shall be uttered at our mirthful board,
Shall make us sad next morning; or affright
The liberty, that we'll enjoy to-night.

A HYMN TO GOD THE FATHER.

HEAR me, O God!
   A broken heart
   Is my best part:
Use still thy rod,
   That I may prove
   Therein, thy love.

If thou hadst not
   Been stern to me,
   But left me free,
I had forgot
   Myself and thee.

For, sin's so sweet,
   As minds ill bent
   Rarely repent,
Until they meet
   Their punishment.

Who more can crave
  Than thou hast done?
   That gav'st a Son
To free a slave:
  First made of nought;
  With all since bought.

Sin, death, and hell
  His glorious name
  Quite overcame;
Yet I rebel,
  And slight the same.

But, I'll come in,
  Before my loss,
  Me farther toss,
As sure to win
  Under His cross.

LEGES CONVIVIALES.

QUOD FŒLIX FAUSTUMQUE CONVIVIS IN APOLLINE SIT.

1. NEMO ASYMBOLUS, NISI UMBRA, HUC VENITO.
2. IDIOTA, INSULSUS, TRISTIS, TURPIS, ABESTO.
3. ERUDITI, URBANI, HILARES, HONESTI, ADSCISCUNTOR.
4. NEC LECTÆ FŒMINÆ REPUDIANTOR.
5. IN APPARATU QUOD CONVIVIS CORRUGET NARES NIL ESTO.
6. EPULÆ DELECTU POTIUS QUAM SUMPTU PARANTOR.
7. OBSONATOR ET COQUUS CONVIVARUM GULÆ PERITI SUNTO.
8. DE DISCUBITU NON CONTENDITOR.
9. MINISTRI A DAPIBUS, OCULATI ET MUTI.
   A POCULIS, AURITI ET CELERES SUNTO.
10. VINA PURIS FONTIBUS MINISTRENTOR AUT VAPULET HOSPES.
11. MODERATIS POCULIS PROVOCARE SODALES FAS ESTO
12. AT FABULIS MAGIS QUAM VINO VELITATIO FIAT.
13. CONVIVÆ NEC MUTI NEC LOQUACES SUNTO.
14. DE SERIIS AC SACRIS POTI ET SATURI NE DISSERUNTO.
15. FIDICEN, NISI ACCERSITUS, NON VENITO.
16. ADMISSO RISU, TRIPUDIIS, CHOREIS, CANTU, SALIBUS,
   OMNI GRATIARUM FESTIVITATE SACRA CELEBRANTOR.
17. JOCI SINE FELLE SUNTO.
18. INSIPIDA POEMATA NULLA RECITANTOR.
19. VERSUS SCRIBERE NULLUS COGITOR.
20. ARGUMENTATIONIS TOTIUS STREPITUS ABESTO.

21 AMATORIIS QUERELIS, AC SUSPIRIIS LIBER ANGULUS ESTO.
22 LAPITHARUM MORE SCYPHIS PUGNARE, VITREA COL-
    LIDERE,
    FENESTRAS EXCUTERE, SUPELLECTILEM DILACERARE
    NEFAS ESTO.
23 QUI FORAS VEL DICTA, VEL FACTA ELIMINET, ELIMINATOR.
24 NEMINEM REUM POCULA FACIUNTO.
    FOCUS PERENNIS ESTO.

RULES FOR THE TAVERN ACADEMY;

*From the Latin of Ben Jonson, engraven in Marble over
the Chimney, in the Apollo of the
Old Devil Tavern, at Temple Bar; that being his Club-Room.*

NON VERBUM REDDERE VERBO.

I.

1 As the fund of our pleasure, let each pay his shot,
  Except some chance friend, whom a member brings in.
2 Far hence be the sad, the lewd fop, and the sot:
  For such have the plagues of good company been.

II.

3 Let the learned and witty, the jovial and gay,
  The generous and honest, compose our free state;
4 And the more to exalt our delight whilst we stay,
  Let none be debarred from his choice female mate.

III.

5 Let no scent offensive the chamber infest.
6 Let fancy, not cost, prepare all our dishes.
7 Let the caterer mind the taste of each guest;
  And the cook, in his dressing, comply with their wishes.

IV.

8 Let's have no disturbance about taking places,
  To shew your nice breeding, or out of vain pride.
9 Let the drawers be ready with wine and fresh glasses,
  Let the waiters have eyes, though their tongues must be
    ty'd.

V.

10 Let our wines without mixture or stum, be all fine,
   Or call up the master, and break his dull noddle.
11 Let no sober bigot here think it a sin,
   To push on the chirping and moderate bottle.

VI.

12 Let the contests be rather of books than of wine.
13 Let the company be neither noisy nor mute.
14 Let none of things serious, much less of divine,
   When belly and head's full, profanely dispute.

VII.

15 Let no saucy fiddler presume to intrude,
   Unless he is sent for to vary our bliss.
16 With mirth, wit, and dancing, and singing conclude.
   To regale every sense, with delight in excess.

VIII.

17 Let raillery be without malice or heat.
18 Dull poems to read let none privilege take.
19 Let no poetaster command or intreat
   Another extempore verses to make.

IX.

20 Let argument bear no unmusical sound,
   Nor jars interpose, sacred friendship to grieve.
21 For generous lovers let a corner be found,
   Where they in soft sighs may their passions relieve.

X.

22 Like the old Lapithites, with the goblets to fight,
   Our own 'mongst offences unpardoned will rank,
   Or breaking of windows, or glasses, for spight,
   And spoiling the goods for a rakehelly prank.

XI.

23 Whoever shall publish what's said, or what's done,
   Be he banished for ever our assembly divine.
24 Let the freedom we take be perverted by none,
   To make any guilty by drinking good wine.

BALLANTYNE PRESS : LONDON AND EDINBURGH

www.ingramcontent.com/pod-product-compliance
Lightning Source LLC
Chambersburg PA
CBHW022022240426
43667CB00042B/1051